Buddhist Ecumenism

Edited By
Prof. S R Bhatt

Originals
Delhi

Published in India 2016

ISBN 10: 81-8454-104-X
ISBN 13: 978-81-8454-104-5

Published by
ORIGINALS
(an imprint of Low Price Publications)
A-6, Nimri Commercial Centre,
Ashok Vihar Phase 4, Delhi-110052
Phone: +91-11-27302453 Fax: +91-11-47061936
e-mail: info@LPPindia.com
website: www.LPPindia.com

Marketed by
Low Price Publications
Delhi

Printed at
D K Fine Art Press P Ltd.
Delhi-110052

PRINTED IN INDIA

Contents

भारतीय सांस्कृतिक सम्बंध परिषद् | INDIAN COUNCIL FOR CULTURAL RELATIONS

प्रो. लोकेश चन्द्र
Prof. Lokesh Chandra
अध्यक्ष / President

Foreword

Prof. Lokesh Chandra, New Delhi

A volume that evokes our wonder in its sway and sweep of aspects covered and that too across the vast cosmopolis of Buddhism. It sanctifies our sense of humanity in the consciousness of the profound. To seek a life greater than our own, like a migrant bird we home down to earth as we advance together into unchartered frontiers. It renews to me the noble eight-fold path in its intrinsic enlightenment spanning the many lands where monks have trod across centuries. In the words of philosopher-poet of Kashmir, Abhinavagupta:

Though I had often seen the mountain,
I was filled with surprise as if it were for the first time
That it becomes new at every moment,
Is just the nature of the beautiful.

Kṣaṇe-kṣaṇe yannavatāmupaiti tadeva rūpaṁ ramaṇīyatāyāḥ

Ecumenism, in the title of the book, is in itself an indication of the universalism of the Buddha's 'Way of Values' to create greater wholes and to share the holism (not doctrine) of the mind with every human being, along with their diversities. The alterity of values were to own all humans of the world in theodiversity. The Greek word *oikouménē* means 'the inhabited world', its adjective means 'open to the whole world'. The Greek *oikos* is Sanskrit *okas* 'home' and *ménē* is the passive participle *-māna*, as in Sanskrit *jāyamāna*. It was a descriptive term used by the Greeks to describe the world they knew and later by the Romans to describe the Roman empire. In Sanskrit the participle-*māna* denotes a continuing process. Professor S.R. Bhatt has chosen a scintillating term that enshrines the depths of the Indo-European family of languages and echoes the psychosphere of Zeus of Homer and the *saṃ vo manāṃsi* of the Ṛgveda. So here is a chariot to roam the heavens, the mind, the thought of the time and space of the *Buddhakṣetras*, to me personally a quest of the beauty of life. When Lord Buddha left Vaiśālī for his last journey, he looked back and said "Oh, how beautiful is life" (Daisaku Ikeda, *The Living Buddhism*, 1976: 135). How inspiring is this book!

The first chapter begins with the Buddhist doctrine of *anattā* as opposed to the *ātman* of the Upaniṣads. Buddhist *anātman* is that no self exists as a permanent, eternal, independent within an individual existent. It was the disowning of the eternal (*śāśvata*) and the transcendent. Buddhism is homocentric and not theocentric; so no eternity. We are led to impermanence (*anityatā*) in the second chapter and its relationship to the scientific theory on substance where other structures on reality will survive in the ever-validating pluralism. The third chapter by Dragonetti on the two-fold reality of *saṁvṛti-satya* and *paramārtha-satya* and the nihilisation by *śūnyatā* have exercised the minds of thinkers for centuries. *Śūnyatā* to me is the "Creative Void". Professor G.G. Joseph in his non-European roots of mathematics points out that *śūnyatā* may have given rise to the concept of the zero digit, and zero may be said to act as a tangible reference to the intangible or the non-dual realm. The quantum theory indicates that sub-atomic phenomena arise and decay within a vacuum presumed to be empty. Various papers on *śūnyatā* are crucial in providing linguistic and philosophical models for physics and related disciplines as zero-based philosophical models are missing in the West.

Men have been drawn by the deep, oneriric, unfathomable silence of meditation where time falls into timeless. The caves of the human psyche are the wombs of transcendence: *dharmasya tattvaṁ nihitaṁ guhāyām*. Wayman's mindfulness and meditation (p. 69) is followed by Professor Bhatt's message of universal compassion which is the dire need of our violent times when altruism is a casualty. Kim elucidates Buddhist *karuṇā* 'compassion' as reconciliation to save us from the brink of atomic suicide. Professor Bhatt points out the ecological significance of the dhammacakka-ppavattana-sutta, and Mantatov speaks of ecological ethics as a *sine qua non* for global survival. Several chapters of this volume have an immediate relevance to global problems as providing philosophical, ethical and meditational moorings to the emergence of new modes of thinking leading to new social, political and technological intuitions and their implementation.

The second half of the book reflects on the journey of Buddhism beyond the bounds of India. Emperor Aśoka commenced this tread of Dharma by sending his son and daughter to Srilanka, another son to Khotan with ministers to found a kingdom, and his missionaries to the West, Africa and other continents.

Asian nations sought their identity, their scripts, literature, palaces, sanctuaries, political institutions, in fact all their panoply of culture and material civilization in the noble path of Buddhism. Buddhism became the way of the wonders of life and the rapture of faith. Chapters 15 onwards narrate the efflorescence of Buddhism in the multiple Asian lands as their civilizational development and spiritual sublimation. Sioris discusses the western view of tolerance and syncretism in Buddhism (p. 179) and cites professor Hajime Nakamura "heretics are nothing but an offshoot manifestation of the ultimate truth" (p. 187). Venerble Nandapaṇṇo dwells on the Thai practice of charity (*dāna*) as merit. Prince Diskul (p. 199) surveys Buddhist art in Thailand, which has illumined monasteries and palaces. Jiyu (p. 203) traces the fortunes of Buddhism from the period when the Chinese were forbidden to be Buddhist by law to its total integration in Chinese social and economic life, art and thought. Yu Xiantian (p. 209) elaborates cultural values of Buddhism in modern China, which believes that culture is power. Yu concludes: Buddhism "shall be the focus of the whole society in the future". We come to Japan with Chaudhuri who writes about Japanese perceptions of India from the earliest period of Prince Shotoku (574-622 A.D.). Thence to Buddhism and national culture in Korea by Rhi Ki-Yong, who points out that the name Seoul comes from 'Śrāvastī', and the role played by the Hwarang nobles of the Maitreya denomination to unite the kingdoms of Korea into a state. Thich Minh Chau traces the history of Vietnamese Buddhism, followed by Nguyen Xuan Vinh's detailed history of the introduction of Buddhism. Four long chapters on Vietnamese Buddhism are the crowning glory of this volume. History of Vietnamese Buddhism has been dealt with here extensively in English for the first time.

The final chapter is a birds-eyeview of Buddhism in the literatures of Indian languages. It ends with G.C. Nayak's observations on Wayman's appraisal of "not this, not this", and Upaniṣadic *neti neti* and *śūnyatā*, which are the continuity of Indic thought.

Professor S.R. Bhatt has done a yoeman's job to resurrect the learned papers that have been lying in disdain for thirty years ever since they were presented to an international conference on "Buddhism and National Cultures" organized by Indian Council for Cultural

Relations of the Ministry of External Affairs under the enlightened vision of Late Prime Minister Smt. Indira Gandhi, as a sequel to the Asian Relations Conference. All the distinguished scholars, some no more alive, had the depth of Dharma and the profundity of learning both traditional and modern. Professor Bhatt deserves the gratitude of enlightened minds to rescue these discourses from the darkness of amnesia. The learned presentations open our minds to new perceptions, to new "eyes of life". When humans shall speak a spiritual language, science and technology will be its dialects. Professor Bhatt you bloom the lotus in the calyx of the heart.

Professor Lokesh Chandra

27.08.2015

Preface

The present volume contains some of the papers presented in the First International Conference on "Buddhism and National Cultures" sponsored by Indian Council for Cultural Relations, Indian Council of Historical Research, Indian National Advisory Committee on Buddhist Studies and Indian Council of Philosophical Research in collaboration with Indian Council of Social Science Research, Sahitya Academy, Sangeet Natak Academy, Lalit Kala Academy and University Grants Commission in 1984. Prominent Buddhist scholars from different parts of the world participated.

I was the Convener of Philosophy Section. Some of the papers were with me and I thought to publish them as they are very valuable contributions to Buddhist thought and culture. I have added a few more papers to make this volume more representative. Our gratefulness is to all the scholars who made their rich contributions to this volume. Some of the scholars are no longer alive and we remember them with deep gratitude.

Buddhism is multifaceted and it is at once ancient and modern. It has large number of following almost all over the world. There is an underlying unity in all its multiple manifestations. Whatever be its form and in whichever country it exists the basic ideas and seminal concepts remain the same. In this sense it is ecumenical. It is both a view of reality and a way of life. Lord Buddha's message of truth, peace, compassion, tolerance and co-existence are as relevant to day as it was in the past. It is hoped that this volume will be informative as well as instructive to the readers.

Professor S.R. Bhatt

MP-23, Maurya Enclave,

Delhi-110034

srbhatt39@gmail.com

Chapter 1
The Teaching Peculiar to Buddhism
Phramaha Prayoon Mererk

What is essentially new in Buddhism as distinguished from previous and contemporaneous philosophies and religions? To answer this question, I write this paper, confining myself to metaphysical and epistemological theories. Taking evidence from the Pāli Nikāyas, I shall try to show that the *Anattā* doctrine and the *Vipassanā* meditation represent the theory and the method peculiar to Buddhism in the fields of metaphysics and epistemology respectively.

The Buddha preached his doctrine of anattā or not-self in contrast to the ātman or self theories whose chief proponents were the Vedic-Upaniṣadic thinkers. What, then, is ātman? According to Radhakrishṇan, "Ātman is the principle of man's life, the soul that pervades his being, his breath, *prāṇa*, his intellect, prajñā, and transcends them. Ātman is what remains when every thing that is not the self is eliminated"[1]. In the Chāndogya Upaniṣad it is stated that the self or ātman transcends the bodily self and also the self which experiences the dreaming and dreamless sleep.[2] The self is regarded as the subject of all experiences; it is the thinker of thoughts, the feeler of sensations and the doer of deeds. The self is said to be immortal.[3] As the substance of the person, the self is identified with God or Brahman, the substance of the universe. This identity is briefly expressed by the famous saying, "That art thou *(Tat tvam asi)*".[4] The self can be known, not by senses, reason or much learning, but by Yoga.[5]

In opposition to such a self theory stands the Buddhist doctrine of anattā. In the *Anattālakkhana-Sutta*,the Buddha analyzes the person into five aggregates, namely, corporeality, feeling, perception, mental formations and consciousness, and states that none of them is the self. Every body, feeling, perception, mental formations and consciousness should be thus regarded, as it really is, by right insight, – "this is not mine: this I am not: this is not my self."[6]

Some scholars, however, contend that the Buddha does not reject the self because his statement that the five aggregates are not-self implies that there is the self outside or beyond the aggregates. Mrs. Rhys Davids thought that it was "clear that the object of the utterance (i.e., one of the forms of the denial of self) was clearly to warn the new fellow-teachers never to identify the self, very man with his parts or instruments, namely, body or ways of mind. They were to see that this (body, mind) 'is not of me, that I am not it, that for me it is not the self'. But the Buddhist inference from it has for centuries been the adding : this self being neither body nor mind, there is no self. Logically this is quite unwarranted".[7] A similar approach to Mrs. Rhys Davids is followed by Radhakrishnan who says that "Buddha clearly tells us what the self is not, though he does not give any clear account of what it is. It is, however, wrong to think there is no self at all according to the Buddha".[8] Comparing the views of the Buddha with those of the Upaniṣads, he concludes: "Buddha holds the same view, though he does not state it definitely".[9] The position adopted by these eminent scholars is not tenable for the following reasons:

First, when the Buddha says that the five aggregates are not-self, he does not mean to imply that there is the self which transcends them. According to him, the transcendental self must be rejected because its existence cannot be proved. Thus he regards the self theory as a foolish doctrine (bāladhamma). He remarks : "The self, oh monks! and what belongs to self are not truly and really found, is it not, oh monks! a perfectly foolish doctrine to hold the point of view, 'This is the world, this is the self; after death I will become permanent, lasting, eternal, not liable to change, I will stand fast like unto the eternal'?"[10]

Second, the self theory, for the Buddha, is a wrong view (micchāditthi) because it has no corresponding reality. What is worse is the fact that the idea of the self generates suffering. Thus the Buddha says: "I do not see, monks, that grasping of the theory of self, from the grasping of which there would not arise grief, suffering, anguish, lamentation, despair,"[11] That is the crux of the Buddhist attitude towards the self theory. The self is considered as the manifestation of the strongest and subtlest form of grasping called *attavādupādāna*. The grasping of the self is the main cause of suffering. That is why the Buddha says :"In brief, the five aggregates of grasping are suffering".[12] Hence the main purpose of the Buddha's denial of the self is to enable his disciples to shed the grasping of the self theory. In order to attain

Nirvāṇa, one has to get rid of the personality belief (*sakkāyadiṭṭhi*) and the conceit of 'I am' (*asmimāna*). So long as grasping of the self in any forms persists, there can be no real emancipation.[13]

Lastly, the Buddha's doctrine of *anattā* is a necessary corollary to the teaching of *aniccā* (impermanance). The five aggregates are not-self because they are found to be impermanent. "Whatever is impermanent, that is subject to suffering; whatever is subject to suffering, that is not-self".[14] This is an interpretation of the three characteristics expressed in these words:

"All component things are impermanent.

All component things are subject to suffering.

All dhammas are not-self".[15]

Here it should be noted that in the third sentence the word 'dhammas' is used. Dhamma here means not only the conditioned things but also the non-conditioned, i.e., *Nirvāṇa*. Thus the statement, "All dhammas are not-self", indicates that everything is without the self. It is opposed to the Upaniṣadic view that ātman is the substance of the person and Brahman the substance of the universe. For the Buddha, the person and the universe are non-substantial. The phenomenal world is in the state of continuous flux or flow. All things are nothing but chains of momentary events unified by the law of Dependent Origination (*Paṭiccasamuppāda*).

Various reasons described above enable us to emphasize that the Buddha really rejects the self. The self theory finds no place in the Buddhist framework. If the self existed, then the Buddha's teachings would become redundant, for the cessation of suffering. The Buddha once took up a little pellet of cowdung in his hands and said to a monk: "If the getting of a selfhood so small as this, monk, were permanent, stable, eternal and unchanging by nature then the living of the holy life for the best destruction of suffering would not be set forth".[16]

As is mentioned earlier, the Buddha rejects the self for the reason that it cannot be found. The Buddha's position is similar to that of the empiricists. In the *Saṅgārava Sutta*, the Buddha classified his predecessors and contemporaries into three groups, viz., (1) the traditionalists (*anusāvikā*), (2) the rationalists and metaphyscians (*takkī, vimaṁsī*), and (3) the experientialists. The Buddha then says that he belongs to the third group.[17] According to him, an appeal to experience is necessary for judging the truth of a theory. The teaching of the Buddha is qualified as *ehi-passika*, inviting one to 'come and see', because it can be tested by experience. And experience here is not a mere sense experience but also intuition and insight.

The characteristic of not-self can be seen by intuitive "insight". "What is not-self, that is not mine, that I am not, that is not my self. Thus should it be *seen* by perfect wisdom as it really is".[18] In order to develop insight which sees thing as it is, one has to practise the Buddhist meditation. The word meditation is a poor substitute for the original term '*bhāvanā*' which means 'mental development'. It aims at knowing and seeing things as they are. There are two forms of *bhāvanā*: development of concentration (*samatha* or *samādhi*) and development of insight (*vipassanā*).

Concentration is the unwavering state of mind which is continuously engaged in a single object. In the state of concentration, the mind is freed from all kinds of hindrances, be they pre-judices, beliefs, desires, or doubts. The elimination of hindrances sets the mind in concentration and this in turn makes it possible for gaining knowledge and insight. Hence it is said that "concentration is the cause of knowing and seeing things as they are".[19] In this sense, concentration is not the ultimate goal of meditation. It is a path leading to *vipassanā*. Concentration is not purely Buddhist method for it forms part of almost all Indian religious practice. In the Upaniṣadic literature, concentration is known as Yoga. For the Upaniṣadic thinkers, Yoga is a method which renders ātman accessible to us. Concentration consists of different degrees, the highest of which is a mystic state. And it is in this state that an intuition of ātman arises.

The Buddha, before his Enlightenment, studied Yoga under different teachers and attained the highest mystic state; but he was not satisfied with it, because it did not give complete emancipation. In the mystic states such as 'the Sphere of Nothingness' or 'the Sphere of Neither-Perception-nor-Non-Perception', there is only emptiness: no ātman is found there. Here is the point where the Buddha departs from the Upaniṣadic thinkers: whereas the latter consider Yoga as the method for developing insight which sees ātman, the former considers it as the method that leads one to find only nothingness.

The Buddha later discovered a new method which helped him to attain the complete cessation of suffering. The method is called *Vipassanā Bhavanā* or Insight Meditation. It is the method unique to Buddhism. *Vipassanā* is a phenomenological analysis of physical and mental phenomena; it is a reflection (*anupassanā*) upon body, feelings, consciousness, and other mental properties.[20] By means of *Vipassanā*, one sees the three characteristics of things, namely, impermanence, suffering and not-self. As a result one attains *Nirvāṇa* or liberation. "Who sees by perfect wisdom as it really is, his mind, not grospring, is detached from taints, he is liberated".[21]

The conclusion which we can draw from the foregoing discussion is that the Buddha did preach the *anattā* doctrine, denying the self theory held by the Vedic-Upaniṣadic thinkers. The doctrine of *anattā* is "the teaching peculiar to Buddhas".[22] Buddhism, therefore, stands unique in the history of Indian philosophy and religion in rejecting the existence of the self. Apart from this, *Vipassanā* meditation is essentially Buddhist method invented for developing insight into the true nature of things. These two teachings, i.e., the *anattā* doctrine and the *Vipassanā* method, are original with the Buddha. They are teachings which are essentially new in Buddhism. Suffice it to say that the Buddha was born and brought up a Hindu, but died a Buddhist.

References

1. *The Principal Upaniṣads,* 1974, p. 73.
2. *Chāndogya Upaniṣad,* VIII 8.1 ff.
3. *Bṛhadāraṇyaka Upaniṣad,* III. 7. 20.
4. *Chāndogya Upaniṣad,* VI. 8. 7.
5. *Kaṭha Upaniṣad,* I. 3. 12.
6. *Saṁyutta Nikāya,* XXII. 59.
7. *What was the Original Gospel in Buddhism,* 1938, pp. 34-5.
8. *Indian Philosophy,* Vol. I, 1983, p. 386.
9. *Ibid.*, p. 388.
10. *Majjhima Nikāya*, I. 136.
11. *Majjhima Nikāya*, I. 137.
12. *Dīgha Nikāya*, II. 305.
13. *Saṁyutta Nikāya*, XXII. 89.
14. *Saṁyutta Nikāya,* XXII. 45.
15. *Dhammapada*, XX, 277-279.
16. *Saṁyutta Nikāya*, XXII. 96.
17. *Majjhima Nikāya,* II. 211.
18. *Saṁyutta Nikāya*, XXII 45.
19. *Saṁyutta Nikāya*, II. 30.
20. *Dīgha Nikāya sutta*, no. 22.
21. *Saṁyutta Nikāya*, XXII. 45.
22. *Majjhima Nikāya,* I. 380.

Chapter 2

Towards a Non-Substantialist Science; Buddhism, its doctrine of Impermanence *(Aniccā)* as Epistemology

Arjuna De Zoysa

Form is Emptiness and Emptiness is Form – The Heart Sutta

Buddhist investigations on the nature of reality begin with a simple observation; that of continuing change. The Buddha states as a foundational principle that change, or not remaining the same, is an observational invariant for all observers, independent of their means or positions in time and space. Thus, whether one observes one's self or a distant galaxy, change is an invariant observation. Buddhist cosmology describes the existence of many 'heavenly' type beings *(devas)* whose life spans in earthly terms are lengthy, but unlike in other religions, they are also subject to decay and death. That is change, not a creator God, rules over even the most pleasing of these extra-terrestrial states. Over a long enough time span no one except a religious minded metaphysician would deny this principle of change. The basis of metaphysics lies in the belief that conceptual thinking could know of 'truths' a-priori to observation. The Kantian category of a synthetic a-priori truth, or the soul theory is based on such a premise. In contrast, for an informed Buddhist, conceptual thinking cannot be a-priori to observation. A time span for instance, is a relational concept, built from the observation of change and not in any sense absolute as in Newtonian physics.[1]

The theory of impermanence in Buddhism is, however, something more than the mere observation of change. For the Buddhist philosopher this lack of permanence is supposedly so, even for the briefest of an observational time span (a moment). The Buddha and other accomplished individuals in the Buddhist tradition (known as *Arahantās*), are said to have observed such an overarching lack of permanence, as experienced fact. This is what is recognised by the major Buddhist schools to be the doctrine of impermanence or *Aniccā*. The Buddha and the *Arahantās,* when referring to this foundational principle of impermanence, are fully aware that normal perception and concept formation give rise to the illusion of permanency. In the *Mūlapariyāya Sutta* (The Discourse on the Root of Existence), the Buddha explains to a large number of monks who were well versed in the then prevailing philosophies, as to how an *Arahantā,* in contrast to a lay person, perceives reality.[2] This forms the first discourse in the collection of discourses by the Buddha known as the 'Middle length discourses', signifying its importance. The claim by the *Arahantās* is that direct seeing,[3] without the intervention of perception and concept formation would establish this simple observational truth. The process of normal observation for an untrained individual occurs with the formation of static pictures from a dynamic process of phenomena. This occurs at the point of perception, and concept formation is built on a collection of these perceptions, made up of static pictures. Thus, what is permanent is the concept formed from real contact with phenomena, not, may I emphasise, *actuality itself.* The point of observing phenomena directly is purely soteriological for a Buddhist, that is, for liberation from the eternal phenomena of re-becoming *(saṃsāra);* but in this paper, I claim that such a way of knowing (epistemology) has far reaching consequences for the process of scientific inquiry.[4]

Substance Theories in Science

It is apparent that all substance theories are based on a belief that reality in an ultimate sense, consists of a permanent essence. Without permanency even for a brief time span talk of a substance becomes mere tautology. Once some duration of permanence has been postulated, one may inquire as to what it is that persists? The birth of a substance postulate occurs at this point. That which persists is now given a name and entity; for example an electron in physics. Thus a scientist in training would be taught about the permanent nature of a sub-atomic particle, or an energy form, which remains unchanged from the early beginnings of the universe. The idea given here is that if one were to 'hitch a ride' on, say a Quark,[5] one would be riding on an entity, which even for the briefest of moments remained unchanged. Although, observational realities at present have resulted in contradictory evidence on this matter, almost all scientists are carefully schooled on this belief.

The second important proposition common to most substance theories is the belief in a 'self nature' to a substance entity. That is, there exists even momentarily a unique observable nature to an entity, which belongs to itself, and forms its identity. This self nature is used to form an identity independent of its relationship to an 'outside' world. I wish to emphasise that such a self nature may be momentary, and a changed condition may lead to its annihilation and the arising of a new 'thing' with its own unique self nature. Thus, this theory would say that an electron possesses a negative charge, a mass of so much, a spin in such a direction and so on. It is identified by its properties, and thus one can talk of them as being its intrinsic self nature. Thus the class of entities we know as electrons are said to have been created in the early beginnings of the cosmos, and for a while they exist as a particle, cloud or wave; or whatever its individual self nature would be, until such time as a new condition arises. The new condition may even be an investigative probe in a laboratory. This is the belief in all substance theories underlying modern science.

In the modern scientific theory on substance, there is the idea of a shared self nature amongst an identifiable class of entities. In addition to this shared self nature, each and every one of these entities may possess its uniqueness, by other attributes such as position with momentum. There was also the problem of the transformation of these particulate forms of substance into each other; with apparent rapidity as an observational fact. How could such transformations from one self nature to another occur? It was not easy to describe in philosophical or mathematical language as to how this occurred. The idea of a field is used in modern physics to explain this. One could inquire from a physicist, as to what is the shared self nature of an electron and a neutrino, and one would receive the answer that both are forms of Energy. All entities are said to be manifestations of energy, a primeval underlying substance, with its own self nature, from which the material world arises. The change of self nature from one entity to another occurs due to an exchange of this primeval substance termed energy, and the quanta of energy so exchanged should be sufficient to cause this transformation. This switch in self nature from one form to another is not simply quantitative, but a qualitative change. Thus in an atomic explosion, sub-atomic particles may change into some entirely different types due to an energy exchange between impacting particles. In this event, a residual mass of this particulate matter would be transformed into its underlying nature, that is energy, with of course devastating consequences. The properties of energy were very general, they behaved like a field, had a wave like character, and its wave front travelled at independent speed of light. Energy, the primeval underlying substance is never annihilated, only transformed into other forms of itself or particulate material entities. Thus, one can see that the modem scientific theory of substance is as expected of all concept categories firmly grounded on permanency. This in summary is the substance theory proposed by the 'conventional' modern sciences. In using the term 'conventional modern sciences', I include even interpretations of Quantum and Relativistic physics, which reduce them to a complex development of Newtonian assumptions.[6]

That which Belongs to a Self

The idea of non-self *(anattā)* or the negation of anything that belongs to a self, based on the observation of impermanence, is central to the philosophy of the Buddha. The idea of non-self refers in particular to the negation of the concept of self, that all living beings, consciously or unconsciously adhere to. Living beings not only adhere to such a self concept, but make this the central basis of their existence. In the use of the term, anything that belongs to a self, the Buddha widened its meanings to include various substance theories that were in vogue at the time. In human history this central idea took several metaphysical turns. In the west the idea of self gave rise to the concept of a soul. Thus, it was thought that although observable material forms changed, and thought appeared to be even more volatile, the indestructible soul remained impermanent. The individual tagged his name card (self) firmly on to this unobservable soul. Rene Descartes, the French Mathematician-philosopher, lived at a time when a number of these metaphysical ideas were being overthrown by an emerging youthful science. There was also the physics of Leibnitz,[7] which entirely did away with the metaphysics of self nature to substance. Descartes however grounded the idea of self on a different basis (circa 1633). The famous statement by Descartes, "I think therefore I am", was based on the argument that there has to be a thinker, behind this observable process of thinking. Despite a rather brilliant critique of the idea of self by David Hume[8] for around two centuries Descartes' philosophy became the basis of a self in the emerging sciences. Isaac Newton (1642-1727), the much celebrated English physicist, took on board the Descartian world view, and built a firm foundation for the physics to come.

In India, in many of the pre-Buddhist philosophical schools there was a similar inclination to metaphysical thinking. In Vedic philosophy the permanent entity which formed the individual was known by the name *Ātman*. When final liberation (*Vimukti)* was achieved the individual *ātman* lost his/her identity to merge with the eternal principle, or *Brahman*. Even in its individualised form, the *ātman* shared the nature of Brahman with all other individualised forms. Brahman, the eternal principle, was known as the creator, from which individual beings supposedly emerged. The whole of the phenomenal world emerged from this permanent essence (Brahman). Further, this one-ness was not material but made of an all-encompassing consciousness. Thus, matter was an epiphenomena of consciousness. The parallel with the modern scientific scheme of particulate matter and an underlying energy field is apparent to even a non-scholastic person. The basic theme of an individualised self and a collective shared nature are stunning in its similarity between the two systems of modern science and Vedic philosophy; and indicates either a cross-cultural linkage, or a universal similarity in patterns of thought. In modern science however, the role of consciousness and matter are reversed. Consciousness becomes an epiphenomena of matter, where the underlying permanent essence becomes a subtle material substance, termed Energy. Thus, modern scientific theory falls firmly into the category of a materialism; and there is an overthrow of consciousness as being the supreme principle behind an observable universe. Some interpretations of Quantum mechanics in significant ways challenge the supremacy of a non-living material substance, and brings into play the role of consciousness. [9,10] These initiatives, however, are not yet accepted by scientists working in these fields; and almost all of the major scientific programmes are based on a structure which is not much more than a complex form of Newtonianism.

The first discourse in the list of discourses credited directly to the Buddha is the Brahmajāla Sutta.[11] A stunning display of the Buddha's knowledge of the then known philosophical views is given here. The sixty two different views listed here even encompass a number of the philosophical schools and standpoints known today. Modern materialism, post-modernist meandering and the metaphysics of Descartes do not escape this rather comprehensive 'net of views'. Brahmajāla, in effect stands for the 'net of Brahman', which supposedly entangles the human mind and ties it down to the endless process of becoming *(Saṃsāra)*. The purpose here is to situate two major substantialist viewpoints known then and today, amongst this 'net of views'. It is interesting to note that in this discourse, the Buddha refers to all sixty two views as being erroneous, but treats many of the advocates of non-materialistic doctrines with great respect. Thus, the prelude to the first five viewpoints begins in this manner.

"In the first case bhikkhus!, some recluse or brahmin, by means of ardour, endeavour, application, diligence, and right reflection, attains to such a degree of mental concentration that with his mind thus concentrated, he recollects his numerous past lives..."[12] It ends by the assertion that the recluse or brahmin, having recalled his numerous past existences, argues that a self persists through these rounds of existence, and the world remains the same. That is through all of these transformations the self and the world consist of a substantive essence. In the text he asserts this position in the following manner; "the self and the world are eternal, barren, steadfast as a mountain peak, standing firm like a pillar. And though these beings roam and wander (through the round of existence), pass away and re-arise, yet the self and the world remain the same just like itself."[13]

The above views are known as arguments for Eternalism *(Śāśvatavāda)*. In eternalistic views it is argued that in both the living (self) and the non-living (world), there is a substantive essence which is permanent and unchanging for all times. This type of metaphysical speculation is commonly found in most religions, and the Vedic theory of *ātman as self* and Brahman as a principle of creation of the cosmos falls under this category of eternalism. Eternalism, as far as living beings are concerned, stands refuted by the modern scientific programme. In the sutta quoted above the reality of the memory of past lives is not refuted, which is supposedly made possible with a great deal of meditative training; only the final conclusions arrived at on the basis of such evidence is said to be erroneous. The Buddha's refutation of anything that 'belongs to a self' could be taken as with reference to the world, that is a denial of an essence in innate matter. In Buddhism both materiality and consciousness are considered to be void of substance, their ontological status therefore is best described here as null. In the Samyutta Nikāya, a text in early Buddhism, the following is stated:

"Suppose, bhikkhus, a large lump of froth was floating on this river Ganges and a clear sighted man were to see it, and properly examine it, seeing it, observing it, properly examining it, it would appear to him to be empty *(ritta),* unsubstantial *(tuccha),* without essence *(asāra)*. What essence, bhikkhus, could there be in a lump of froth?

In the same way, bhikkhus, whatsoever body, past, present or future, internal or external, gross or subtle, inferior or superior, far or near, that a bhikkhu sees, observes and properly examines it would appear to him to be empty, unsubstantial, without essence. What essence, bhikkhus, could there be in the body ?" These words, attributed to the Buddha, are repeated in a similar fashion with regards feelings, perceptions, activities and consciousness.[14]

Self in the Modern Sciences

The viewpoint number fifty one in the Brahmajāla sutta, categorised under annihilationism (*Ucchedavāda*) is closest to the modern scientific standpoint on self. It reads as follows:

"Herein, bhikkhus, some recluse or brahmin asserts the following doctrine and view: 'The self, good sir, has material form; it is composed of the four primary elements[15] and originates from father and mother. Since this self, good sir, is annihilated and destroyed with the breakup of the body, and does not exist after death, at this point the self is completely annihilated'. In this way some proclaim the annihilation, destruction, and extermination of an existent being."[16]

The philosophical move in this instance is to deny existence of an eternal self, as assumed by the eternalist, but to assert a permanent self over a limited duration of time; essentially during the period of the physical life span of an individual. This is the case made by the scientific materialist. Since he/she is unable to observe any form of continuity of life after death, the eternalist argument for self, cannot be made by a modern scientist. However, as so many commentators on science have pointed out, science like all other human endeavours is conditioned by cultural, economic and political factors.[17] I need not explain to you here, as to how central the concept of self is to modern economic and political systems, and as such it is not surprising to find that the concept of self and substance are deeply entrenched in the scientific programme. The belief then is that an identifiable self persists during a lifespan only to be annihilated at death.

The development of evolutionary Darwinism in the nineteenth century considerably weakened Descartes' assertion of 'self as the thinker'. Thinking appeared to be an epiphenomenon of matter and the soul theory as being unnecessary metaphysical baggage. However, some form of a self, entrenched within the individual, became of increasing importance to political and economic developments at the time. The search for a material self, born of the 'mother and father' as the Buddha commented, continued with increasing vigour in the biological sciences. In parallel in the physical sciences, the search for a substance essence was pursued. This search has resulted today in a bewildering array of 'fundamental particles', the 'proof' for their existence with names and classifications have now become an esoteric mathematical art form. As shown earlier, there was also the idea of a shared self nature which developed in physics. The prime concepts behind this idea in modern physics were the mathematical Space-Time in cosmology developed by Einstein's mathematics professor Minkowsky (1908), and a revival of the ancient idea of Energy. The idea of a shared self nature which comes with these entities, is closer to the Socialist political project, while that of its individualised form is closer to the now dominant 'neo-liberal' socio-economic project. It is not a mere coincidence that advocates of Space-Time as ultimate entity, such as Albert Einstein, were strong advocates of Socialism. Einstein originally derived all of the results of the theory of Relativity, without the idea of a Space-Time[18], however later he became one of the strongest supporters of the fundamental ontological status given to this mathematical space. And he spent the latter part of his life attempting unsuccessfully to derive quantum reality from Space-Time.

In modern biology there has been a retreat to reductionist theories an extreme example of which would be the theory of a selfish gene. This theory claimed that most human characteristics, including altruism could be reduced to the structure of genetic material. The theory situated 'self' squarely in the genetic material of a living being. It even claimed that intelligence was an innate property of this 'self' and transmitted through 'mother and father' to the offspring. The *"raison de'tre"* for existence was declared to be the maximum spread and survival of its genetic type; a Darwinism of the 'selfish gene' was thus born. This theory was roundly attacked in the west by eminent biologists (insiders) such as Stevan Rose and by Feminist critiques, and even the statistical data used by these theorists shown to be flawed. This was in the seventies; however, with the rise of the neo-liberal project and the initial 'successes' of bio-technology, there appears to be a revival of this reductionist programme. This suites very much the individualised version of the Self, which neo-liberalism would support. To identify a candidate for a Self, three characteristics are required. The Self should be unique to the individual. Secondly, Self should be unchanging (impermanent) during the life term of the individual; and thirdly, important characteristics of the individual should be reducible to this Self. All of these three criteria appear to the bio-technologists to be satisfied by the genetic fingerprint resident in the cellular structure, of an otherwise ever changing individual. The rather absurd idea that the Self could be cloned arises from these beliefs. This form of the self idea has been around implicitly in most scientific programmes of biology. Alfred Tauber's excellent text titled 'The Immune Self[19] details the scientific narrative behind the theory of disease in modern medicine, and shows how central the idea of self was in describing the pathogenesis of disease. If one were to situate the biological concept of self in the spectrum of views given in the Buddhist suttas, it falls unambiguously amongst the annihilationists category, that is the belief that a unique identifiable Self persists unchanged during a human life span.

Looking Back and to the Future

The object of examining modern science from a Buddhist standpoint is two-fold. Firstly, it was to highlight the entanglement that scientific programmes have had, with substantialist viewpoints. Secondly, to examine the limitations of its claim to Universality. These are admittedly negative comments about this 'thing' we call science. I am sure that a majority of 'insiders', that is working scientists, would agree that science is heavily entangled with substantialism, but consider it to be a positive attribute. This is principally because it would bolster its claim to universality. What other local knowledge system could have unravelled the inner secrets of matter (atomic theory), or found the 'real and only causes' for the many diseases besetting humankind; and so the argument goes. The debate on the efficacy of modern science, is not what I wish to enter into here. My appeal here is simply to recognise the metaphysical foundations of modern science, substantialist in character, to be what they are. Already the ground from these metaphysical foundations of science are shifting,[20] which I consider to be positive developments from within and without, of the scientific enterprise. The shift to a non-substantialist philosophical base, however is slow in coming but would be welcome for several reasons. The idea that we as knowledge seekers, are constructing rather than discovering 'things', and therefore should leave room for others to do the same, would slowly seep through. Science as a universal project may collapse, but without its baggage of discovered substantive 'things', it would be more open than ever, to new ideas, concepts and more importantly observations. There are already developments in this direction, as the work of Australian physicists Cahill and Klinger seem to indicate. I briefly quote from a New Scientist report (Feb. 2000) on their work,

"At the core of conventional physics is the idea that there are 'objects'-things that are real, even if they don't interact with other things. Before writing down equations to describe how electrons, magnetic fields, space and so on work, physicists start by assuming that such things exist. It would be far more satisfying to do away with this layer of assumption".[21]

A word of caution here, earlier in the eighties we had a brief flirtation by physicists with 'bootstrap' theories,[22] a promising start to a relational physics, only to be abandoned for more 'conventional' approaches. The call here is not to abandon atomism, but simply to recognise its metaphysical nature. Thereby, other structures on reality will be allowed to survive.

There is the 'parable of the raft' which is credited directly to the Buddha, which indicates the direction in which non-substantialist doctrines lead to. In this parable the Buddha questions the status of his own teachings (*Dhamma*). If, he says, "a man were to assemble a raft, and make one which is sturdy and reliable and use it to cross a turbulent river and reach the other shore. What would you say if he were to be so attached to the raft that he carried it on his head and subsequently proceeded? 'Even so, monks', says the Buddha, 'is the parable of the raft, the *Dhamma,* taught by me is for crossing over not for retaining. You monks by understanding the parable of the raft should get rid of even right mental objects, all the more of wrong ones."[23]

On a non-substantialist base, 'devoid of 'things' and 'selves', with their own nature, there could be many constructions. They would as I have indicated previously be built upon Relational structures. Some would be efficacious others less so, and designed for different purposes. But, let this be decided on their ability to engage with actuality, rather than on their conformity to the modern sciences.

It is the business of science, to *'let a thousand flowers bloom',* that is, quite simply to allow for pluralism.

References

1. *Kathāvatthu Atthakathā,* trans., Shew Aung and Rhys Davids, 1915, Humphry Milford, London.
2. *Discourse on The Root of Existence (The Mūlapariyāya-Sutta),* Bhikkhu Bodhi, (Kandy, Sri Lanka, Buddhist Publication Society (BPS), 1992).
3. Using any of the six sense facilities (five senses plus mind as an additional sense facility).
4. If one were to situate Buddhist philosophy in the western philosophical tradition, it would be best described as a radical phenomenology. A phenomenology without 'essences' fits the bill for most purposes.
5. Latest candidate in physics is a foundational particle.
6. Markeley Robert, *Fallen Languages, Crisis of Representation in Newtonian England, 1660-1740,* (Ithaca & London: Cornell University, 1993), pp. 258-9.
7. Leibnitz-German philosopher-mathematician and contemporary of Newton. He was also the co-discoverer of the mathematics of Calculus and had a running controversy on this matter with Newton. His theory of Monads, a relational

'object', formed a radical break with the particle theories, which are in fashion since the time of Newton. The theory however was both difficult and culturally alien, and in the scientific milieu of his time it did not survive.

8. Hume David, *Treatise on Human Nature,* ed. Selby-Bigge, (Oxford: Clarendon Press, 1978 (org. 1888).

9. Anderson E.E, *Modern Physics and Quantum Mechanics,* New York: W.B. Saunders, 1971.

10. Von-Neumann J, *Mathematical Foundations of Quantum Mechanics,* Trans. R.T. Bayers, (Princeton: 1955).

11. *The All Embracing Net of Views, the Brahmajāla Sutta and its Commentaries,* trans., Bhikkhu Bodhi, (BPS, Kandy, Sri Lanka, 1992).

12. *Ibid.*, p. 62.

13. *Ibid.*, p. 78-79.

14. These refer to the four properties of matter as described in the ancient Indian sciences.

15. "An Anthology from the Samyutta Nikāya", trans. Ireland John D, (BPS, Kandy, Sri Lanka, 1981), pp. 47-8.

16. Einstein A, "Collected Papers (1905-09)", trans Anna Beck, (Princeton Univ. Press, USA, 1989), pp. 140-311.

17. Tauber Alfred I, *The Immune Self: Theory or Metaphor?,* (Cambridge Univ. Press, UK, 1997).

18. Dupre John, *The Disorder of Things,* (Harvard Univ. Press, Cambridge, 1995).

19. Chown Marcus, "Random Reality", report on the work of Reginald Cahil and Christopher Klinger, Flinders University Adelaide, (New Scientist, U.K., 26 Feb. 2000).

20. De Zoysa Arjuna, *Change and Reality, Beyond the Metaphysics of Common Sense*, ed. De Zoysa, Karunadasa, Ranawaka & Tillakeratne (Vidyartha and Pali and Buddhist Studies Inst., 1997, Colombo, Sri Lanka), pp. 57-78.

21. Harding Sandra, *Is Science Multicultural?,* (Indiana University Press, USA, 1999).

22. *A Passion for Physics, Essays in Honour of Geoffrey Chew,* Edit. by Carlton De Tar et. al, (World Scientific Publishing Co., 1985).

Chapter 3

An Indian Philosophy of Universal Contingency, Nāgārjuna's School

Carmen Dragonetti

The Normal Experience and the Philosophical Study of the Empirical Reality

The ordinary experience reveals to us a reality composed by beings and things which present themselves as existing *in se et per se,* as compact, continuous and unitarian, as permanent and as real, i.e. as being such as we perceive them.

The *Mādhyamika* school of Buddhism, founded by Nāgārjuna at the beginning of our era, studies the reality we perceive and reaches a conclusion regarding that reality completely different from our ordinary experience. The empirical reality is composed by beings and things absolutely contingent. In this empirical reality, in which we live, there is nothing existing *in se et per se;* nothing has a being that belongs to it by own right (*svabhāva*); in this reality everything is conditioned[1], relative[2], dependent, contingent. Moreover everything without exception is constituted by parts. No totalitary entity exists; there are only ensembles, conglomerates of parts[3], elements, constituting factors[4]. Besides that nothing is permanent, inalterable; everything is in a process of change, submitted to an evolution which proceeds under the sign of decay and deterioration. And, as a consequence of what preceeds, there is nothing which exists truly as it manifests itself before us (substantial, compact etc.). The empirical reality, as we perceive it, is only a deceitful appearance to which nothing real corresponds, something similar to a dream, to a mirage, to an illusion created by magic.

The conditionedness, the relativity, the dependence on another, the composedness, the impermanency, in a word, the *contingency* is the true nature, the true form of being of the empirical reality; and the form under which this reality appears to us is only an unreality, an illusion. So the ordinary experience is the opposite of the conclusion to which arrives the philosophical study of the perceptible world done by the *Mādhyamika* school.

Two Realities, the Reality of Concealment (*saṃvṛtisatya*), the True Reality (*paramārthasatya*)

According to what preceeds, for the *Mādhyamika* school there are two realities[5]: on one side, an apparent, phenomenal reality, the empirical reality as it appears before us (substantial, compact etc.) and on the other side, the true form of being of the apparent reality (unsubstantial, composed etc.) which is the true reality, in the same way as the serpent, under whose image we perceive the rope in the darkness, is the apparent reality, while the rope is the true reality.

The rope is a concealing reality, the threads that compose it are the true reality in regard to the rope; but at its own turn each thread is a concealing reality in regard to the filaments that compose it, and the filaments that compose it are the true reality in regard to the thread, and so on, without finding a last substantial reality.

Speaking in general modern terms, it could be said that the world as it appears to us is the concealing reality of the *Mādhyamikas* and that the atoms and energy which constitute the world are, in regard to it, the true nature of the world, the true reality. The *Mādhyamika* would add that the atoms and energy are, at their own turn, a concealing reality in regard to the elements which compose the atoms and energy, and which are the true nature of the atoms and energy, the true reality, and so on, without finding a last substantial entity.

The apparent reality, the empirical reality as it manifests itself to us is called, by the *Mādhyamika* school, "envelopment reality" or "concealment reality" (*saṃvṛtisatya*). This is an appropriate term, because the appearance under which the empirical reality is perceived by us *envelops* or *conceals* its true form of being, which is the true reality (*paramārthasatya*).

Universal Contingency: "*Svabhāvaśūnyatā*" and "*Pratītyasamutpāda*" as Denominations of the True Reality

The true reality (*Paramārthasatya*) appearing as empirical reality can be designated with the words *svabhāvaśūnyatā* and *pratītyasamutpāda*.

Svabhāvaśūnyatā means "emptiness (=absence) of an own being". *Pratītyasamutpāda* literally means "dependent origination", but in the area of the *Mādhyamika* school it can be translated by "Universal Relativitly" as Stcherbatsky rightly does[6]. Both words designate the true nature, the true way of being (conditionality, relativitly, etc.) of the empirical reality—true nature that is concealed under the false appearance of the empirical reality and which is the true reality. Both words express the basic and, from all points of view, important conception of the *Mādhyamika* school about the empirical reality: it is only *a totality of contingent beings and things,* in which there is nothing that exist *in se et per se.*

Many Western thinkers have deduced, from the contingency of the world, the existence of a non-contingent supreme principle, God. Cf. for example, Copleston in *The Existence of God. A debate between Bertrand Russell and Father F.C. Copleston, S.J.,* in Bertrand Russell, *Why I am not a Christian, and other essays on religion and related subjects* (London: Unwin Books, 1967, p. 139) ..."*Well, for clarity's sake, I'll divide the argument* (from contingency) *in distinct stages. First of all, I should say, we know that there are at least some beings in the world which do not contain in themselves the reason for their existence. For example, I depend on my parents, and now on the air, and on food and so on. Now, secondly, the world is simply the real or imagined totality or aggregate of individual objects, none of which contain in themselves alone the reason for their existence. There isn't any world distinct from the objects which form it, any more than the human race is something apart from the members. Therefore, I should say, since objects or events exist, and since no object of experience contains within itself the reason of its existence, this reason, the totality of objects, must have a reason external to itself. That reason must be an existent being. Well, this being is either itself the reason for its own existence, or is not. If it is, well and good. If it is not, then we must proceed farther. But if we proceed to infinity in that sense, then there's no explanation of existence at all. So, I should say, in order to explain existence, we must come to a being which contains within itself the reason for its own existence, that is to say, which cannot not-exist.*" Nāgārjuna's school affirms also the contingency of everything, but from such a fact does not draw the conclusion that a non-contingent supreme principle, God, exists. For him the universal contingency has had no beginning, as *anādi,* and consequently it is irrelevant to ask when, how and why did it begin. The hypothesis of a beginningless contingency has the same function as the hypothesis of a beginningless God.

The Denial of the Empirical Reality

The *Mādhyamika* school does not stop within the limits of the two tenets we have already mentioned, i.e. the opposition between the phenomenic reality and the true reality (which is nothing else than the true nature of the phenomenic reality), and the universal contingency; it carries on its analysis of the reality and reaches a more radical position, a "nihilistic" position. The school denies the true existence, the existence as it appears, of the empirical reality, of all its manifestations, of all the elements that constitute it, of all categories that manifest themselves in it, of all the characteristics which are proper to it.

The great majority of the stanzas of the *Mādhyamaka kārikās* composed by Nāgārjuna is destinated to deny the real existence of the principal manifestations and categories of the empirical reality: birth and destruction, causality, time, the sensorial activity, the elements that constitute man (*dharma*), passion and its subject, action and its agent, suffering, the consequence of actions (*karman*), the reincarnations cycle (*saṃsāra*), the ego (*ātman*), Buddha, the saving truths taught by Buddha, the liberation (*mokṣa*) from the reincarnations cycle, being and not being, etc. ... In the same way great part of the intellectual activity of Nāgārjuna's school had an identical aim.[7]

Fundamentation of the Mādhyamika Thesis

The *Mādhyamika* school has to establish and to demonstrate its "nihilistic" thesis against other philosophical and religious, Buddhist and non-Buddhist, schools, which adopt realistic positions. This demonstration is carried on in different ways.

The school adduces, of course, the texts that contain Buddha's teaching (*āgama*), which duly interpreted can serve as a basis for its thesis. For Buddhist schools these texts contain the truth, but only for them, and consequently cannot be adduced against the thesis of non-Buddhist people.

Besides that, the school uses reasoning, logical argumentation (*yukti*). The arguments developed by the *Mādhyamika* thinkers to defend their own negative conceptions and to destroy contrary thesis are contained specially in the great commentaries that accompany the works of Nāgārjuna and of the other masters that followed him. Among those commentaries it is necessary to mention the most valuable commentary of Candrakīrti on Nāgārjuna's *Mādhyamakakārikās*. This commentary reveals the parallel use of Buddha's word and logic. Generally the great masters of the *Mādhyamika* school, like Āryadeva,

Buddhapālita, Candrakīrti, Śāntideva, Prajñākaramati, faithful to the school founder, adopt the *prāsañgika* or *reductio ad absurdum* method,[8] they do not adduce arguments of their own invention; they limit themselves to show the contradictory and absurd consequences that derive from the thesis and arguments of the rival schools. For instance, if one of these schools affirms the real origination of beings and things, the *Mādhyamika* will indicate that, in that case, origination should be either out of one self or out of another or out of one self and of another or without any cause, and will show that all these alternatives are logically impossible, employing for that aim, as basic principles of his own argumentation, the adversary's own principles.

Finally, the *Mādhyamika* school utilizes the analysis of the empirical reality in order to get results which destroy the rival doctrines and which found its own world conception. The treatise *Hastavālanāmaprakaraṇa* (stanzas and commentary),[9] gives us an example of this procedure. The author investigates the empirical reality and finds that it is composed only by entities which, on being analyzed at their turn, happen to be mere appearances, which cover or conceal other entities, which happen to be also mere appearances which cover or conceal other entities and so on. This analysis reaches the conclusion that it is impossible to find something substantial, permanent and irreducible, in which one could stop and establish oneself. The thesis of the real existence of the world becomes in this way untenable and the place becomes free for the *Mādhyamika* conception of the illusory character of the world.

The True Nature Comes forth as a Result of the Abolition of the Empirical Reality. Śunyatā as a Denomination of the True Reality

As a result of this abolishing and negative process we have referred to, we have the *impression* that, where the empirical reality previously existed, a huge "voidness", "emptiness" is being done, is coming forth, is remaining. That "voidness", that the abolitive analysis *seems to* leave behind itself before us, is absolutely different from the empirical reality, since in it there exist, no element, no manifestation, no category, that are proper of the empirical reality and which one by one have been eliminated by the abolishing *Mādhyamika* dialectic. That "voidness" is the true reality, that has manifested itself after the elimination of the false appearance which constitutes the empirical reality.

On the basis of the experience that has been described, the word *śūnyatā* ("voidness") serves also to designate, as a metaphor of course, the true nature of the empirical reality or, what is the same, the true reality. From all the terms that designate that true reality, *śūnyatā* is most commonly used and it is the one we shall employ.

The "Voidness" Exists Previously to the Abolitive Analysis

We have said that we have the *impression* that, as a consequence of the abolitive analysis, the "voidness", i.e. the true reality, comes forth before us. This impression is caused by the fact that the abolitive analysis is realized by the discursive reason, which in its analysis and elimination of all the elements, factors, manifestations, categories, etc. of the empirical reality must proceed gradually; and so in our minds the idea is formed that the "voidness", the true reality, *is being created* step by step. This impression does not correspond to the truth, because the "voidness" *has been, is,* and *will be* always there, independently from our analysis, previously to it, although it has not been perceived.

Using the comparison of the modern conception of world already referred to, we could say that the atoms and energy exist previously to the experiment that reveals them.

The true reality, the "voidness", extreme end to which the abolitive analysis cannot reach, can only be grasped *tota et simul,* in its total and absolute integrity, only in an act of intuitive yogic knowledge, which is reserved to the great *buddhas.* The contingency realized in its extreme point reveals to us the voidness in its extreme form.

The Doctrine of Universal Sameness (*samatā*)

A well known stanza (*kārikā*) of Nāgārjuna (*Mādhyamakakārikās* XXV, 19 and also 20) and its commentary equally well-known, by Candrakīrti, express that there is no difference between the *saṃsāra,* the empirical reality, and the *nirvāṇa.* Both effectively are only voidness, *śūnyatā.*

We have seen that in order to find the true nature of the *saṃsāra,* it is necessary to eliminate through a rigorous abolishing analysis everything that manifests itself to us as forming part of the *saṃsāra.*

We must act in a similar way to find the true nature of the *nirvāṇa.* The *nirvāṇa* is what is completely different from the empirical reality when this one is considered not in its true nature, the *śūnyatā,* but under the false appearance under which it presents itself before us. In order to discover what the *nirvāṇa* is we must also abolish everything that constitutes the empirical reality, specially being and not being.[10] That abolishing process, carried into its last consequences, total and absolute, will present to us the same *śūnyatā,* that we have found on applying to *saṃsāra* the same method.

Using the comparison of the modern conception of world again, we could say that all beings and things that form the world, are identical among themselves, since they all are, in their last essence, atoms and energy: the uniformity is also an universal attribute.

Primitive Buddhism is built on the opposition, on the insuperable difference between *saṃsāra* and *nirvāṇa, nirvāṇa* being considered as the full extinction of *saṃsāra.* For Nāgārjuna there is no difference: *saṃsāra* and *nirvāṇa* are the same, since both are voidness.

We think that this is the only way to understand the idea of sameness between *nirvāṇa* and *saṃsāra:* That sameness has as its support the abolition of everything that is presented to us in the empirical level by our senses and our reason. It is impossible to understand that the sameness between both is based on the *saṃsāra* and *nirvāṇa* having as a common characteristic the *svabhāvaśūnyatā* and the *pratītyasamutpāda,* i.e. the total contingency, since *nirvāṇa* is precisely the unconditioned one, what is beyond contingency, beyond conditions and causes.

Empirical Reality, a Mere Mental Creation

We have said that for Nāgārjuna's school two realities are opposed: on one side, the true reality and on the other side the false one, which disappears with the abolishing analysis and which conceals or covers the first one. This second reality is a mere illusion in the common sense of the word, a mere mental creation, which is superimposed on the true reality, concealing it, in the same way as the illusory idea or image of a serpent which is superimposed on the rope seen in the darkness; in the same way as the illusory idea or image of a rope is superimposed on the conglomerate of threads which compose the thread, and the illusory idea or image of the thread is superimposed on the filaments that compose that thread and so on. The existence of the empirical reality as we normally see it is nothing else than the existence of an illusion, devoid of a true existence.

Using the same comparison as before, it is possible to say that, since the world is only atoms and energy without the empirical attributes of colour, taste, etc., the manifold variety of the world in terms of colour, taste, etc., is only a construction of our mind and senses, of our subjectivity and sensibility.

We find here the great function which the mind possesses in Nāgārjuna's school, as in all the Mahāyāna schools: the empirical reality is only a series or succession of illusions, of imaginations, of ideas, which our mind creates incessantly above the infinite abyss of universal voidness. And this succession of mental creations has had no beginning, according to the *anāditva's* postulate which is essential in Indian thought.[11] Of course it can come to an end through the method taught by Buddhism, and on that day, together with the cessation of the imaginary creations of the mind, the empirical reality will also disappear and there will remain only the universal emptiness, which it concealed and which constitutes the true way of being of everything.

The great function, which the mind possesses in Nāgārjuna's school, must not induce us to be mistaken about its true nature: the mind which through its activity creates the illusory empirical reality, and which through the abolishing analysis gives us a glimpse of the absolute voidness–the mind itself belongs also to the empirical reality and as such is also contingent, is also void. In the terms of the comparison referred to, the mind and the senses themselves, constituted by atoms and energy, are not something apart from the world they create; they are nothing else than atoms and energy.

Irrelevant Questions

Questions that naturally come to mind are: why, when and how the series of mental creations, which constitute the empirical reality, did begin? But these questions are irrelevant, because the series of mental creations had no beginning and therefore nothing can be said about the cause, the moment and the manner in which that series began to flow, in the same way as these questions are irrelevant in references to *Brahman,* also beginningless.

Liberation

Empirical reality, according to what we have expressed, is just an illusion, a mental creation, and of the same nature are bondage to reincarnations and liberation from that bond. Consequently, the man who wishes to liberate himself from reincarnations (the supreme goal of all religious and philosophical systems in India) has not to destroy anything really existent, but to put an end to the series of mental creations which constitute the empirical reality and the series of reincarnations, that is to say he has only to stop mind functioning, which is the source of those illusory creations.[12] This is the great goal to be reached.

This is not an easy task, because the essence of the mind is precisely the mental creativity. The destiny of man, while he is immersed in the empirical reality, is its infinite reincarnations, is to originate incessantly a series of mental creations. The overcoming of that destiny can only be obtained adopting the ethical and intellectual method that is fixed by Buddhism, with extraordinary effort, endeavour, and energy. When the mental creations ceased, ceases *ipso facto* the empirical reality which they constitute, and the reincarnations which are a part of the empirical reality.

Everything is Nirvanized ab aeterno

In Primitive Buddhism *nirvāṇa* was something completely different from the empirical reality; its abolition, its negation. The *Mādhyamika* school does not abandon this conception as it affirms that *nirvāṇa* is *śūnyatā,* voidness, and consequently is the negation of all the elements, manifestations, categories of the empirical reality.

To the *śūnyatā,* negation of all, as the true reality, is opposed the empirical reality, which is a mere illusion, an erroneous mental creation. As a consequence of this *saṃsāra's* nature, there is not, there has never been and there will never be a *true* and *real* forthcoming of anything and therefore no real transmigration, no real destruction, nothing real. And this state of things that means a complete negation of everything, is precisely the universal voidness or, what is the same: *nirvāṇa.* Therefore nothing has ever really abandoned the *śūnyatā* or *nirvāṇa* state.

Finally, in the terms of the general modern comparison we are using, since the atoms and the energy never transform themselves into the beings and things of the world we perceive, assuming the empirical attributes with which they appear before us; and since the world is only a creation of our mind and senses, we can say that nothing has really departed from its atoms and energy, that it has always remained in that state, that is to say, that everything has been "nirvanized" *ab aeterno*—in Buddhist terminology.

If there was a *real* forthcoming, transmigration or destruction, there would be negation of *śūnyatā,* to which something *real* would be opposed. But as something *real* has never existed, does not exist and will never exist, the only thing that remains is the total *śūnyatā.*

It is not possible to argue that the uniqueness of *śūnyatā* is nullified by the illusory world which is opposed to it, because for Indian thought the uniqueness of a *true* reality that is postulated as unique, can only be destroyed by another *true* reality; the existence of an *illusory* reality, opposed to the true reality that is postulated as unique, does not eliminate the uniqueness of that true reality.

References

1. Everything comes forth through the cooperation of a series of causes (*hetu* and *pratyaya*).
2. A thing is *high* in relation to another one that is *low* in regard to it; a person is a *father* in relation to his *son* and *vice versa*. In the same way as 'high', 'low, 'father, 'son' exist, so exists everything in the empirical reality.
3. A rope is composed by threads; each thread by filaments and so on. Man is only a conglomerate of material elements, which form the body, and of sensations, perceptions, volitions, acts of consciousness. In the same way as the rope and man are only conglomerates of parts, so is everything in the empirical reality.
4. One of the great thesis of Buddhism is that the whole as such does not exit, that only the parts exist, and the parts at their own turn can be analyzed into other parts and so on. Cf. Fernando Tola and Carmen Dragonetti, "Dignāga's Ālamabanaparīkṣāvṛtti", in *Journal of Indian Philosophy,* ed. Bimal K. Matilal (Dordrecht: Holland/Boston: USA: D. Reidel, June 1982), Vol. 10, No. 2, pp. 105-134, note 6 in page 129.
5. The *Mādhyamika* school does not admit another reality besides the empirical illusory reality as it appears to us, and the true reality, which is the true nature of the former.
6. Th. Stcherbatsky, *The Conception of Buddhist Nirvāṇa* (London-The Hague Paris: Mouton & Co, 1965), *passim.*
7. For instance see Nāgārjuna's *Dvādaśadvāra* and Āryadeva's *Śatasāstra* and *Catuḥśataka*.
8. The *Mādhyamika* school was called skeptical by its rivals, because it refrained itself from emitting judgements. This suspension of judgement was a consequence of the conviction that the school has that any thesis, when it is duly analyzed, falls into contradiction and that the true reality cannot be reached by human reason.
9. See our article "The Hastavālanāmaprakaraṇavṛtti", in *'The Journal of Religious Studies'* Vol. VIII, No. 1 (Patiala, India: Punjabi University, Spring 1980), pp. 18-31.
10. This abolishing method corresponds to the method which the Hellenistic thinkers called *'aphäiresis'* (Albinos, Didaskalikos X, p. 165 ed. C.F. Hermann; Plotinus, *Enneades* VI, 7 (18), 36; Plutarchus, *Quaestiones Platonicae* 1001 E, who also uses *'périkopé'*) or 'analysis' (Clemens Alexanddrinus, *Stromata V,* 11, p. 374, 5 ed. O. Stāhlin; Kelsos *apud* Origenes, *Contra Celsum* 7, 42 P.G. II, col. 1481 (−p. 188 ed. R. Bader). Cf. John M. Whittaker, "Neopythagorismus and Negative Theology", in *Symbolae Osloenses* 44 (1969), pp. 109-125 (German translation in: *Der Mittelplatonismus,* herausgegeben von Clemens Zintzen, Darmstadt: Wissenschaftliche Buchgesellsschaft, 1981, pp. 169-186).
11. Cf. Fernando Tola and Carmen Dragonetti, "*Anāditva* or beginninglessness in Indian Philosophy", in *Annals of the Bhandarkar Research Institute.*
12. Death does not stop the series of mental creations; this series continues after death in the new following existence, without interruption, although with the oblivion of the past experiences, and in a new body.

Select Bibliography

Ames, William L., "The Notion of *Svabhāva in the Thought of Candrakīrti"*, in *Journal of Indian Philosophy,* Vol. 10, No. 2, June 1982, pp. 161-177.

Bhattacharya (Chakrabarti), Bhagwati, "The Concept of Existence and Nāgārjuna's Doctrine of śūnyatā, in *Journal of Indian Philosophy,* Vol. 7, No. 4, December 1979, pp. 335-344.

Bugault, Guy, "Logic and Dialectics in the *Mādhyamakakārikās*" in *Journal of Indian Philosophy,* Vol. 11, No. 1, March 1983, pp. 7-74.

Chakravarti, Sitansu, "The Philosophy of Non-Involvement of the Mādhyamikas", in *Journal of Indian Philosophy,* Vol. 10, No. 4, December 1982, pp. 397-403.

Chakrabarti, Sitansu, "The Mādhyamika *Catuṣkoṭi* or Tetralemma", in *Journal of Indian Philosophy,* Vol. 8, No. 3, September 1980, pp. 303-306.

Chatterjee Sastri, H., *The Philosophy of Nāgārjuna, as contained in the Ratnāvalī,* Part I, Calcutta: Saraswat Library, 1977.

Conze, E., (i) *Buddhist Thought in India,* London: G. Allen & Unwin, 1962; (ii) *Thirty Years of Buddhist Studies,* London: O. Cassirer, 1967.

Crittenden, Charles, "Everyday Reality as Fiction—A Mādhyamika Interpretation", in *Journal of Indian Philosophy,* Vol. 9, No. 4, December 1981, pp. 323-333.

De Jong, J.W., *Cinq Chapitres de la Prasannapadā,* Introduction, Paris: P. Geuthner, 1949.

De Jong, J.W., "Le probléme de l'absolu dans l'école Mādhyamīka", in *Revue Philosophique de la France et de l'éitranger* CXL, 1950, pp. 323-347.

De Jong, J.W., "The Problem of the Absolute in the Mādhyamika School", in *Journal of Indian Philosophy,* Vol. 2, No. 1, December, 1972, pp. 1-6.

De Jong, J.W., "Emptiness", in *Journal of Indian Philosophy,* Vol. 2, No. 1, December 1972, pp. 7-15.

De la Vallèe Poussin, L., "Mādhyamīka, in *Mélanges chinois et bouddhiques* 2, 1932-1933, pp. 1-146.

De la Vallée Poussin, L., "Buddhica", in *Harvard Journal of Asian Studies* III, pp. 146-158.

De la Vallée Poussin, L., "Note sur les corps du Bouddha, in *Le Muséon,* 1913, pp. 269-272.

Della Santina, Peter, "The Division of the Mādhyamika System into the Prāsangika and Svātantrika Schools", in *The Journal of Religious Studies,* Vol. VII, No. 2, Autumn 1979, Punjabi University, Patiala (India), pp. 40-49.

Dutt, N., "The place of the Āryasatyas and Pratītyasamutpāda in Hīnayāna and Mahāyāna", in *Annals of the Bhandarkar Oriental Research Institute,* Poona Vol. XI, January 1930, Part II, pp. 101-127.

Fatone, Vicente, *El Budismo "nihilista",* in *Obras Completas* II, Buenos Aires: Sudamericana, 1972, pp. 16-156. There is an English translation of this work, published in Delhi, by Motilal Banarsidass.

Fenner, Peter G., "A Reconstruction of the *Madhyamakāvatāra's* Analysis of the Person", in *The Journal of the International Association of Buddhist Studies,* Vol. 6, No. 2, 1983, pp. 17-34.

Frauwallner, Erich, *Die Philosophie des Buddhismus,* Berlin: Akademie Verlag, 1969.

Gomez Rodrīguez, Luis O., "Consideraciones en torno al Absoluto de los Budistas, in *Estudios de Asia y Āfrica,* Vol. X, No. 2, 1975, pp. 97-154.

Huntington, C.W., Jr., "The system of the Two Truths in the Prasannapadā and the Madhyamakāvatāra: A Study in Mādhyamika Soteriology", in *Journal of Indian Philosophy,* Vol. 11, No. 1, March 1983, pp. 77-106.

Ichimura, Shohei, "A New Approach to the Intra-Mādhyamika Confrontation over the Svātantrika and Prāsaṅgika Methods of Refutation", in *The Journal of the International Association of Buddhist Studies,* Vol. 5, No. 2, 1982, pp. 41-52.

Ichimura, Shohei, "A Study on the Mādhyamika Method of Refutation and its influence on Buddhist Logic", in *The Journal of the International Association of Buddhist Studies,* Vol. 4, No. 1, 1981, pp. 87-95.

Ichimura, Shohei, "A Study on the Mādhyamika Method of Refutation, Especially of its Affinity to that of *Kathāvatthu*", in *The Journal of the International Association of Buddhist Studies,* Vol. 3, No. 1, 1980, pp. 7-15.

Jones, Elvin W., "Buddhist Theories of Existents: The Systems of Two Truths", in *Mahāyāna Buddhist Meditation: Theory and Practice,* ed. by Minoru Kiyota, ass. by Elvin W. Jones, Honolulu: The University Press of Hawaii, 1978, pp. 3-45.

Kajiyama, Yuichi, "Later Mādhyamikas on Epistemology and Meditation", in *Mahāyāna Buddhist Meditation: Theory and Practice,* ed. by Minoru Kiyota, Ass. by Elivin W. Jones, Honolulu: The University Press of Hawaii, 1978, pp. 114-143.

Koseki, Aaron K., "Later Mādhyamika in China: Some Current Perspectives on the History of Chinese *Prajñāpāramitā* Thought", in *The Journal of the International Association of Buddhist Studies,* Vol. 5, No. 2, 1982.

Lai, Whalen W., "Non-duality of the Two Truths in Sinitic Mādhyamika": Origin of the "Third Truth", in *The Journal of the International Association of Buddhist Studies,* Vol. 2, No. 2, 1979, pp. 45-65.

Lai, Whalen W., "Chou Yung vs. Chang Jung (on *Śūnyatā*): the *Pen-mo Yu-wu* Controversy in Fifth-Century China", in *The Journal of the International Association of Buddhist Studies,* Vol. 1, No. 2, 1979, pp. 23-44.

Lamotte, Etienne, *L'enseignement de Vimalakīrti,* Introduction, Louvain: Institut Orientaliste de Louvain, 1976, Tome IV, pp. 1995-2042.

Lancaster, Lewis ed., *Prajñāpāramitā and Related Systems: Studies in honor of Edward Conze,* Ass. Ed. Luis O. Gomez, Korea: Berkeley Buddhist Studies Series, 1977.

Lindtner, Chr., *Nagarjuniana, Studies in the Writings and Philosophy of Nāgārjuna,* Copenhagen: Akademisk Forlag, 1982.

Matilal, Bimal K., *Epistemology, Logic and Grammar in Indian Philosophical Analysis,* The Hague: Mouton, 1971, pp. 146-167.

May, J., *"Candrakīrti's Prasannapadā Mādhyamakavṛtti",* Introduction, Paris; Maisonneuve, 1959;

May, J., "Kant et le Mādhyamaka, A propos d'un livre récent", in *Indo-Iranian Journal* 3, 1959, pp. 102-111;

May, J., "La philosophie bouddhique de la vacuité", in *Studia Philosophica* (Basle) 18, 1958, pp. 123-137;

May, J. "On Mādhyamika Philosophy", in *Journal of Indian Philosophy,* Vol. 6, No. 3, November 1978, pp. 233-241;

May, J., "Chugan (Mādhyamika), in *Hōbōgirin. Dictionnaire Encyclopédique du Bouddhisme d'aprés les sources chinoises et japonaises,* Cinquiéme Fascicule, Paris-Tōkyō : Maisonneuve-Maison Franco-Japonaise, 1979, pp. 470-493.

Murti, T.R.V., *The Central Philosophy of Buddhism,* London: Allen & Unwin, 1960.

Nagao, Gadjin, "From Mādhyamika to Yogācāra, an Analysis of MMK, XXIV and MV, I.1-2", in *The Journal of the International Association of Buddhist Studies,* Vol. 2, No. 1, 1979, pp. 29-43.

Nagao, Gadjin M., "What Remains in Śūnyatā: A Yogācāra Interpretation of Emptiness", in *Mahāyāna Buddhist Meditation: Theory and Practice,* ed. by Minoru Kiyota, Ass. by Elvin W. Jones, Honolulu: The University Press of Hawaii, 1978, pp. 66-82.

Panikkar, R., "The "Crisis" of Mādhyamika and Indian Philosophy", in *Philosophy: East and West,* Vol. XVI, Numbers 3 and 4, July-October, 1966.

Quiles, I., "El absoluto budista como "vacīo" (śūnya), segun Nāgārjuna", in *Stromata* 22, 1966, pp. 3-24.

Ramanan Venkata, K., *Nāgārjuna's Philosophy,* Delhi: Motilal Banarsidass, 1975.

Robinson, R.H., *Early Mādhyamika in India and China,* Madison: Wisconsin University, 1967;

Robinson, R.H., "Some logical aspects of Nāgārjuna's System", in *Philosophy East and West* 6, 1957, pp. 291-308.

Ruegg, David Seyfort, "Mathematical and Linguistic Models in Indian Thought: the case of *śūnyatā",* in *Wiener Zeitschrift für die Kunde Südasiens und Archiv für indische Philosophie,* her. von G. Oberhammer, Band XXII, 1978, pp. 171-181.

Ruegg, David Seyfort, "The Uses of the Four Positions of the *Catuṣkoṭi* and the Problem of the Description of Reality in Mahāyāna Buddhism, in *Journal of Indian Philosophy,* Vol. 5, Nos. 1/2, September/December, 1977, pp. 1-71.

Ruegg, David Seyfort, *"The Literature of the Mādhyamaka School of Philosophy in India,* Wiesbaden: Otto Harrassovitz, 1981 (A History of Indian Literature, ed. by Jan Gonda, Vol. VII, Fasc. 1).

Samdhong Rinpoche ed. and C. Mani Ass. Ed., *Mādhyamika Dialectic and the Philosophy of Nāgārjuna,* with an Introduction by T.R.V. Murti, Sarnath (India): A Tibetan Institute Publication, 1977 (The Dalai Lama Tibetan Indology Studies, Vol. 1).

Schayer, St., *Ausgewāhtte Kapitel aus der Prasannapadā,* Krakōw: Polska Akademja Umiejetności, Prace Komisji Orjentalistycznej, No. 14, 1931;

Schayer, St., "Das Mahāyānistische Absolutum nachder Lehre der Mādhyamikas", in *Orientalischer Literaturzeitung* XXXVIII/7 July, 1935, pp. 401-415.

Siderits, Mark, "The Mādhyamaka Critique of Epistemology. I", in *Journal of Indian Philosophy,* Vol. 8, No. 4, December 1980, pp. 307-335.

Siderits, Mark, "The Mādhyamaka Critique of Epistemology. II", in *Journal of Indian Philosophy,* Vol. 9, No. 2, June 1981, pp. 121-160.

Sprung, Mervyn, "Non-Cognitive Language in Mādhyamika Buddhism", in *Buddhist Thought and Asian Civilisation: Essays in Honor of Herbert V. Guenther,* ed. by Leslie S. Kawamura and Keith Scott, Emeryville, California: Dharma Publishing, 1977.

Stcherbatsky, Th., *The Conception of Buddhist Nirvāṇa,* The Hague: Mouton & Co., 1965;

Stcherbatsky, Th., "Die Drei Richtungen in der Philosophie des Buddhismus", in *Rocznik Orjentalistyczny* 10, 1934, pp. 1-37;

Stcherbatsky, Th., *Madhyānta Vibhañga,* Introduction, Calcutta: Indian Studies, 1971.

Streng, F.J., *Emptiness: Study in Religious Meaning,* Nashville, New York: Abingdon Press, 1967.

Sweet, Michael, "*Bodhicaryāvatāra* 9:2 as a Focus for Tibetan Interpretations of the Two Truths in the Prāsangika Mādhyamika", in *The Journal of the International Association of Buddhist Studies,* Vol. 2, No. 2, 1979, pp. 79-89.

Takakusu, Junjiro, *The Essentials of Buddhist Thought,* London: Routledge & Kegan Paul, 1963.

Thurman Robert A., "Transcendence and the sacred in the Mahāyāna Middle Way", in *The Journal of Religious Studies,* Vol. VIII, No. 1, Spring 1980, pp. 32-50.

Tola, Fernando and Dragonetti, Carmen, "Nāgārjuna's Conception of 'Voidness, (Śūnyatā)", in *Journal of Indian Philosophy,* Vol. 9, No. 3, September 1981, pp. 273-282;

Tola, Fernando and Dragonetti, Carmen, "The Hastavālanāmaprakaraṇavṛtti", in *The Journal of Religious Studies,* Vol. VIII, No. 1, Spring 1980, pp. 18-31;

Tola, Fernando and Dragonetti, Carmen, *Budismo Mahāyāna. Estudios y Textos,* Buenos Aires: Editorial Kier, 1980;

Tola, Fernando and Dragonetti, Carmen, "*Anāditva* or beginninglessness in Indian Philosophy", in *Annals of the Bhandarkar Oriental Research Institute,* Vol. LXI, Parts I-IV, pp. 1-20.

Tola, Fernando and Dragonetti, Carmen, "The *Yuktiṣaṣṭikākārikā* of Nāgārjuna", in *The Journal of the International Association of Buddhist Studies,* Vol. 6, No. 2, 1983, pp. 94-123.

Tuxen, P., "In what sense can we call the teachings of Nāgārjuna negativism?", in *Journal of Oriental Research* 11, Madras 1937, pp. 213-242.

Vaidya, P.L., *Etudes sur Āryadeva et son Catuḥs'ataka,* Paris: P. Geuthner, 1923.

Vetter, T., "Die Lehre Nāgārjunas in the Mūla-madhyamaka-kārikās", in *Epiphanie des Heils,* Wien, 1982, pp. 87-108.

Wayman. A., "Contributions to the Mādhyamika School of Buddhism", in *The Journal of the American Oriental Society'* Vol. 89, No. 1, 1969, pp. 141-152.

Williams, Paul M., "Some Aspects of Language and Construction in the Mādhyamīka", in *Journal of Indian Philosophy,* Vol. 8, No. 1, March 1980, pp. 1-45.

Yamakami, Sōgen, *Systems of Buddhistic Thought,* Calcutta; University of Calcutta, 1912, pp. 186-209.

Chapter 4
Emptiness in Aesthetic Experience

Kenneth K. Inada

Introduction

There is art appreciation and there is art creation. Where the former refers, generally speaking, to the viewer of the art, the latter refers to the artist or creator of the art. When the concept of aesthetics is introduced, we casually assume that it covers both the viewer and the creator because both are concerned intimately with artworks and creators of all kinds. But the applicable range of the nature of aesthetics is too wide and deep. For out of all this, we have witnessed the rise of different theories of aesthetics covering the whole spectrum of disciplines and the consequent delineation of different types of experiences. There is no need to examine them at this point but suffice it to say that the field of aesthetics has blossomed due to the contributions made from the various disciplines. But now it is time to examine the nature of aesthetics seriously and return it to its proper mode of human experience. In attempting this, I am siding with the latter view that aesthetics is concerned with the creator of the art. This will be amplified later but for now it should be noted that the main reason for siding with the creator, not the artwork, is that the creator always looms above the artwork by his or her fresh dynamic activity. An artwork is not something passively existing out there; in reality its essence must be seen or captured in the creative act. Needless to say, the creation is the result of a function, a sustained novel and unique dynamics of action by the creator. In an attempt to understand the function, it challenges us to communicate directly with the creator's action by means of one's own action. This is not mere imitation but instead it is to be in close sync experientially with the action that created the artwork. On the other hand, it would not be fruitful to pursue the artwork, the finished product. Why? It is because it would only focus on a past function and all that it entails, placing certain limitations but worst of all, it would be a recession, a move away from the nature of the dynamic function.

What is most important in aesthetics is to seek out and retain the original nature in sense experience. This idea belongs to the early Greeks. In brief, aesthetics has to do with our senses, i.e., how they function in their purest form. In this, we are really focusing on the origins, the primal nature of sense experience. In stark contrast to a mind-oriented view on things,[1] this experiential view goes deep into our ontological condition, its primordial nature that is pure and unadulterated. This primordial state in perception can for now be referred to as the *aesthetic nature.* Its realization is a desideratum for the beginning of any moment of experience, although it is rather difficult to understand and implement it, much less sustain it, as a vital basis of our creative experiences. We must therefore proceed to expand on this crucial concept of the *aesthetic nature.* But first, a few words on the contributions of western science as prelude to eastern thought.

In looking at the past periods of renaissance, explorations, modern science, and industrial revolution, the huge contributions made by pure science are at the forefront and remain a bellwether in human endeavor and advances in living. It has been the key to opening up new frontiers as well as lowering the barriers on ideological and cultural contacts. It bodes well for further interchanges and fusion of ideas as we enter the global arena.

In the early decades of the 20th century, the scientific world contributed two of the most significant theories. The first is Albert Einstein's outstanding Special and General Theories of Relativity and the second Werner Heisenberg's puzzling but equally outstanding Principle of Uncertainty. Needless to say, we live within the confines of both theories but, unfortunately, the ordinary layperson is far from acknowledging their import on his or her life, although the scientific community has long come to terms with those theories. This means that there is a huge gap or lag existing between the scientific and common sense worlds. It is time to close the gap or lag.

There are of course a variety of gaps or lags but the one I wish to focus on has to do with the relationship of human beings in the world. We have for the most part isolated ourselves from the world we live in rather than becoming more intimate and direct with its extensive nature. The obsession with objects, numbers, statistics, etc. has had its toll on human existence in terms of bifurcating or dichotomizing things, including one's own existence. The "divide and conquer" mentality did successfully separate humans from the world but at a costly price that is now having a whiplash effect, the other cutting-edge of the sword, in terms of creating a global environmental crises. Ideologically, the high point was reached when Friedrich Schelling first enunciated the famous question, "Why is there something rather than nothing?" This question, subsequently asserted by not a few thinkers, shows the solidification of the substantive-view of perception. Within a century, however, thinkers began to doubt this simplistic stance on perception. And surely enough, the deathblow came with Einstein and other process thinkers.

Both theories by Einstein and Heisenberg reveal the hidden character of the cosmos or the nature of things. Up to the 19th century, we had rushed to understand the world in which we live. But as we quietly probed deeper and deeper into the nature of nature itself, we, especially the scientists, began to feel the limiting power of finiteness that humans as observers of the world must cope with. And there came an awakening that there is a subtle but pervasive involvement of the finite and the infinite nature of things. Not being conscious of this involvement is perhaps the beginning of the gap or lag between human beings and the world. It can be labeled the *ontological lag in existence.* Both Einstein and Heisenberg tread the same path, cosmically concerning the world as well as ontologically concerning human nature. In a sense, Heisenberg's theory can be considered an extension of Einstein's in that it makes more obvious the involvement of entities in the nature of relativity. In brief, then, they are both interpreting the entities in terms of the dynamics involved. So whether the dynamics is in reference to the relativity of things or the uncertainty of perception, the nature of reality is a total involvement that exhibits traits of mutuality and identity that are at once complex, profound and elusive.[2]

Take the Uncertainty Principle. In essence, it says that perception is inexact because the object is changed by the very act of perception. Sounds like a very simple statement, easy to understand and accept, but in reality it isn't. The grasp of it escapes us because the dynamics involved exhibits the fact that the perceiver and the perceived are never the same at any given moment of time. They mutually change and there is no way that the two could be held at bay for any clear perception. The idea of time is not the problem; the problem here is the understanding of the dynamics of mutuality and identity. Simple idea of time does not belong here because it is the result of classical metaphysics that relates things one at a time, in lumps, e.g., past, present and future. If classical metaphysics cannot handle the condition, then we need to consider a new type of metaphysics.

Before proceeding any further, it should be pointed out that the contributions made by both theoretical physicists including others associated with them, positively or negatively, have opened up a new frontier in science. In so doing, science has opened up its doors to other non-scientific disciplines and the latter have in turn opened up its doors to still other disciplines and the process seems to go on and on. With the exposure to the east in full force in the 20th century, fortunately, the process of opening up to other cultures has had a very salutary effect. We have not seen or experienced the full effect yet but it would seem that what the scientific world has exhibited in the realm of dynamics bodes well for the future in terms of human relationship and understanding that transcend cultural borders.

Obviously, we find ourselves in a bind here due mainly to the lack of an adequate language of dynamics in its deeper nature. We do use certain dynamic terms, such as, motion, function, force, process, speed, field, interpenetration, interrelatedness, etc., but we do not understand immediately their full force in their respective dimensions. We can expand and elaborate by adding qualifying terms, such as, *the nature of mutual dynamics* or simply *relational dynamics,* but the inadequacy still remains. All this calls for a novel way of perception, a way that goes beyond the confines of ordinary perception. At times, I have used the phrase, a borderless perception of things. It simply means that perception is not restrained, limited or bounded in any way but, at the same time, it does not deny nor restrict the function of ordinary perception. Instead, it only expands the field of perception and thereby adds more content, so to speak, to realize the fullness of perception. How can we justify this paradoxical situation? Can we realize this novel perception? For some answers, we move over to the eastern sector of the world.

Enter the East

It seems that the east had always looked at the dynamics of things with very keen eyes. All of the great systems of thought, such as, Brahmanism, Jaina, Buddhism, Taoism and Confucianism, have examined individuals and their proper place in the world oriented in the dynamic flow of things. In a word, everything is in the Heraclitean flux at all times. A single most effective term to cover this state of things is *temporality.* Both east and west have this term but the east in many ways had a flying start, so to speak, in understanding and incorporating it as a viable way of individual life bound to the extensive realm of existence. So whether life is delineated as microscopic or macroscopic, finite or infinite, atomic or non-atomic, self or selfless, immanent or transcendent, one or many, objective or subjective, etc., the nature *of temporality* inheres and underlies the very dynamics of mutuality and identity that continues on and on.

There are two classic analysis *of temporality* in the east that signify the fundamental basis of philosophical discourse on reality, one Chinese and the other Buddhist. In the Chinese sector, there is the famous representation of reality by the *yin* and *yang* or, more properly, the hyphenated *yin-yang* dynamics of mutuality and identity. These polar concepts, graphically illustrated in the drawing of the shaded and non-shaded "69" figures intertwined or clasped together, depict a most perfect figure to exhibit the circularity as well as the dynamism of the whole. Each of the shaded and non-shaded figure has a respective "eye" that belongs to the other, contrasting and depicting the constant dualistic involvement that is always total and holistic. It can be said that Chinese thought, whether Confucian or Taoist, has always honored the *yin-yang* dynamics. For example, Confucian concept of timeliness *(shih-chung)* is a most powerful concept relative to the execution of human relationship inspired by human-heartedness *(jen)*. It is in brief the grasp of the dynamics of *"yin-yang temporality"* infused by *jen*. In consequence, it takes at least two persons to issue forth the nature of *jen* and, moreover, it takes two persons to sustain it. All actions are part and parcel of the *yin-yang* dynamics. Although at times the response of the other person may not be forthcoming or responsive enough as one might hope it to be, nevertheless, the accomplished person *of jen* must rise above the crowd.

In Taoist philosophy, the dynamics of things is exhibited in more graphic terms. The very first verse of the *Tao Te Ching* clearly captures the spirit of the whole work and displays the mutual dynamics thus:

The Tao (Way) that can be told of is not the eternal Tao;

The name that can be named is not the eternal name.

The Nameless is the origin of Heaven and Earth;

The Named is the mother of all things.

Therefore let there always be non-being so we may see their subtlety,

And let there always be being so we may see their outcome.

The two are the same,

But after they are produced, they have different names.

They both may be called deep and profound *(hsuan)*.

Deeper and more profound,

The door of all subtleties![3]

The dynamics of being and nonbeing is patently associated with the dynamics of *yin-yang*. Moreover, human endeavor is focused on catching glimpses of reality on the move. In this respect, there are changes and transformations going on but there is also non-differentiation or identity in the whole.[4] It should be noted that Wang P'i, the NeoTaoist, emphasizes that "Whenever activity ceases, there is tranquility, but tranquility is not opposed to activity."[5] This statement exhibits the *yin-yang* dynamics and the nature of mutual ingression whereby each side slides into the realm without any barrier or obstacle. Wang P'i also makes an illuminating point by introducing the concept of *t'i-Yung* substance/function or form/function for the dynamics. It is yet another profound insight and revelation of the dynamics of mutuality and identity.

In the Buddhist sector, the dynamics of mutuality and identity is represented in the famous Buddhist Wheel of Life. The Wheel has twelve spokes, beginning with ignorance *(avidyā)* and ending with aging-and-death *(jarā-maraṇa)*. It is ceaseless in the presence of ignorance and other defilements (basically greed, hatred and delusion) that cause the rise of suffering due to the biological phenomenon of grasping and clinging on to the objective nature of things. In the ceaseless spinning of the Wheel, the other spokes or components are equally present and involve each other to give it the full and holistic nature. The process is popularly called the Wheel of Life because of the incessant thirst *(tṛṣṇā)* that causes the Wheel to turn on and on. But the Wheel need not necessarily turn. There are two solutions available according to Buddhism. One is simple death when all biological processes cease; the other is the attainment of enlightenment *(nirvāṇa)*. *Nirvāṇa* means, literally, the cessation of the thirst of life. It means more profoundly that one could live without hankering after anything, physical or non-physical, and not clinging on to it. The dynamics involved here is not only subtle but also difficult to grasp because it involves more than our common understanding of perception. We will have more to say on the Buddhist inordinate nature of perception.[6]

An Implicate Metaphysics

We take cue from David Bohm's insightful concept of the *implicate order*[7] in the world of physics. Indeed, the concept is not only limited to the physical world but could easily include our experiential realm since we are part of the physical world at large. The implicate nature reveals that the elements in the physical and experiential processes involve as well as emerge from each other; it is an implicate dynamics where nothing is absolute in and of itself. And yet, in the very dynamics of implication, it would seem that the genesis of the process, at least from the eastern view of things, comes from the pre-experiential nature, i.e., prior to the function of the senses. On this point, however, it is interesting to note that Immanuel Kant's famous phenomenon-noumenon analysis shows the classic case of seeking the unknowable by way of the known, i.e., to infer the existence of noumenon from the phenomenon. Although this analysis seems to be solid epistemologically in that it does not break any epistemic rules or order, the process is suspect. It is suspect because it only points the way to the unknowable and closes all discourse to it; but to shut off the unknowable so facilely is a problem. Let us pursue the problem.

The western perception of things is crisp, clear and distinct, but at the same time it is cut and dried. It focuses on something and in so doing it marginalizes the rest of the content of perception. Marginalization as such is a legitimate tool, to be sure, but if it goes further to deny the very existence of what had been marginalized, then a basic fault arises in the epistemic system. To use a familiar metaphor, one sees the trees at the expense of missing the whole forest.

In another sense, the western view has relied so overwhelmingly on the atomic features of things themselves that the total or holistic nature has been sacrificed and even abandoned unwittingly. For example, we employ the concept of dynamics without really penetrating its very nature in the experiential process. We ignore or pay very little attention to what is involved in particular and concrete ways. Now, it could well be that from the western standpoint our minds are just incapable of understanding the nature of dynamism itself, i.e., capturing the full force and dimension of the dynamism involved as things are actually happening. And yet, in another sense, we know that movement or motion is real and that we must be able to accommodate it in our experiences.

In recent decades, Fritjof Capra has written a most influential work, *The Tao of Physics.*[8] It brings up to date on recent scientific theories and their contributions to the worldview, but the value and thrust of the book is an admirable exhibition of the parallels and similarities that exist in the vision of nature and its function as seen through the eyes of modern physicists and ancient Asian masters. The work of course is incomplete in the sense that the East-West dialogues are still going on, but it has laid out the significant metaphysical features that tie the two sectors together. For example, the important points of contact are lodged in such concepts as dynamics, change, field, form, void/emptiness, interpenetration and holistic universe. This is a remarkable exploration of the parallels.[9]

Let us examine what the Buddhist did to the concept of dynamics. One of the cardinal Buddhist doctrines informs us that life is transitory or impermanent. We should note that there are two distinct meanings expressed here. The first is the ordinary conception that life is all too often brief and will terminate at any moment. This is easily understood and accepted. The second, however, is much more profound and subtle and not easily understood. It refers to the fact that the life process is a series of cyclic impermanence, i.e., the units of experience are not only momentary happenings but also overlapping, continuing phenomena. The units do not singularly endure at all but continue to constantly carve out new realms of experience. The interesting point here is that we try vainly to capture these impermanent moments by the *static* "logic of things." That is, we attempt to seize them by assigning certain permanent, atomic features to them but this attempt is doomed to failure since the abstract features arise from human contrivance and have therefore no direct relationship to the moments themselves. Nevertheless, the moments are real, indeed we are the moments themselves, and we have no other recourse but to deal with them in a most direct and intimate way.

The Buddhists gave a hard long look at the moments of experience. The *Avatamsaka Sūtra* or Chinese *Hua-yen Ching,* for example, dug deep into the dynamics involved in these intricate moments and came up with profound theories on how they are interwoven and continue to behave in a certain pattern. These theories did not deviate from the original teachings of the historical Buddha and thus go directly back to the cardinal doctrine of relational origination *(pratītya-samutpāda)*. The doctrine in brief states that a moment emerges from the complex of relational dynamics that goes on in a continuum. The Hua-yen theories expound on the fact that moments are (1) non-obstructive of one another, (2) mutually penetrative and (3) mutually identifiable of one another. In short, the moments are mutually and dynamically involving one another in the temporality of human experience. Such a deep metaphysical and ontological nature of experience goes beyond any simple framework of logic or any set procedural system. The dynamics of momentary existence is both microscopic and macroscopic, interrelating and interpenetrating. Capra made a telling point here: "Like the Eastern Void, the 'physical vacuum'—as it is called in field theory—is not a state of mere nothingness, but contains the potentiality for all forms of the particle world."[10]

We are today faced with many unknown factors that do change and modify our perception of things. We are, for example, made aware of such a puzzling concept as "fuzzy logic" that gives pause to our minds and indeed taxes our imagination. It warns us of the existence of unknown factors and forces that play certain unrecorded roles in modifying the final results as presented by ordinary logic. Moreover, it sends a clear message that the logic we are familiar with is not only a human contrivance but that we need to explore human experience further in order to move forward in novel ways.

With reference to the Aristotelian three principles of logic, the Buddhist could subscribe to only the principle of identity (A is A), and would deny the principles of non-contradiction (A is not ∼ A) and excluded middle (A v ∼ A). The reason for the denial is that human experience in all its fullness does not negate nor exclude anything. As seen earlier, Hua-yen thought asserts that there is no barrier or obstruction but only blending and merging of moments or elements of being in process. There is simply no separation or differentiation of anything. Strange as it may seem, our understanding has strayed away from the experiential dynamics of things. There was a time in the past when philosophers were intent on gaining so-called positive knowledge and were intensely attracted to terms spelled out in meta-philosophy or even meta-meta-philosophy. Such an attempt, heavily linguistic in nature, may help to clear up vague or confusing concepts and their application in the name of positivism but we must be aware that it will also move us away from the reality of experiential events. In brief, we must remain true to our experiences by first turning our attention to the inner, direct and intimate dynamics of things before we proceed to understand the external, indirect dynamics of things.

A Cosmology of Aesthetic Experience

In the Buddhist text, *Udāna,*[11] a famous passage states that there is the realm of the unconditioned (Pali: *asankhāta)* and the unborn *(anuppāda),* but because of this realm there is the conditioned and the born or arisen. This passage is considered to be one of the most profound ideas in the whole of Buddhism. In many ways, it wraps up the whole Buddhist concept of the reality of things, i.e., the rise and fall of the phenomenal world within the total realm of existence. Moreover, it is the first sign of an implicate metaphysics in Buddhist thought. It is redundant to say that the historical Buddha captured this truth of existence *(Dharma)*[12] in his enlightenment *(nirvāṇa).* He suffused in it for some time and refused to reveal what he had achieved to his erstwhile friends who beseeched him time and again. He is reported to have said to his friends that they will not understand it because they are captivated by the mere empirical nature of things and continue to indulge in them. However, after a fortnight and overcome by compassion, he revealed the content of his enlightenment, and the rest is history.

The fact of the matter is that, unfortunately, we here today are still struggling to understand the *nirvāṇa*-content. Indeed, it is not an easy matter to grasp the full dimension of the content. The standard or traditional method is to take up meditation as prescribed by the Buddha. This has been followed seriously throughout every Buddhist tradition in the world and has remained one of the greatest factors in the propagation of Buddhism itself. On the other hand, alongside the meditative approach, we already have sufficient textual material from the various traditions to assess the philosophical basis upon which to understand the true nature of the Buddha's teachings. We may, for example, expand on the following:

(1) Buddhist reality *(Dharma)* is more than what could be found in the empirical or phenomenal world. It involves a deeper and wider nature of perception, one that goes beyond ordinary perception of objects.

(2) Buddhist reality is thoroughly naturalistic. It is simply the unadulterated *vision of things as they really are.* There could be no intervention or imposition on it by human contrivance, such as, conceiving and perceiving things as being isolated with clearly defined features. Human contrivance limits and narrows the natural status of things and even distorts the *vision of things.*

(3) *The vision of things as they really are* does not cancel out the realm of the empirical or phenomenal. There is no categorical (metaphysical) distinction made here between the empirical and non-empirical or between the conditioned and unconditioned, as stated in the *Udāna.* There is no separation at all in the dynamics of both realms; thus they coalesce and are co-terminous at all times. Any difference or distinction that arises comes solely from the empirical or conditioned realm. And yet to understand the dynamics, we must start from the conditioned where our sense faculties are in full force.

(4) The dynamics of co-terminality of both realms exhibits the profound aspect of Buddhist reality. Here there is an implicative interpenetration and mutual emergence of both realms; there are symmetrical as well as asymmetrical movements involved in the dynamics.

(5) At this point, we need to speculate on how the dynamics of the two realms persists. We can only begin in the empirical or conditioned realm in which our five senses inform us what is happening in particular and objective ways. This perception however is finite and limited. As the process continues, it is possible that in time a feeling of the finite and limited will arise and cause one to yearn and reach for the larger and fuller nature of things. It may well be a biological or psychological phenomenon that prompts one to reach for the whole or totality. I would like to think of this phenomenon as an existential or ontological grasp of the whole. But the conditioned realm alone does not offer an answer to this quest for the whole. In a graphic sense, the conditioned realm, due to its inherent limited fragmented perception, causes and exhibits so-called "cracks" in the realm. Like earthquake faults, they reveal the presence of more ground beneath them. In similar fashion, the conditioned realm has shown that it does not exist alone and that there is another realm as a backdrop, as a silent partner if you will, which remains unsoiled by the disruption or fragmentation within the conditioned realm. This silent partner is the unconditioned.

The experiential dynamics exhibits the co-terminous function of the conditioned and unconditioned realms. In this dynamics, we have come to what may be referred to as the aesthetic nature. I would venture to say that the aesthetic nature, though invisible, is the supreme moment that spans both realms. It is pure and non-grasping. It does not impute nor assign any feature or value to any objective component or element of the dynamics, and yet at the same time, it is that which gives substance to the objects of the conditioned realm by providing the character of belonging to the whole. That is, in a sense, it sanctions ordinary perception to be what it is as a legitimate function within the larger scheme of things. The aesthetic nature is then the vital chord or bridge in the dynamics that propels one to move beyond any restrictions and boundaries.

Let us pursue the matter by introducing certain familiar cognate concepts of the aesthetic nature, i.e., freedom and creativity Although these concepts have been around for a long time, they have never been addressed and answered fully within the context of human dynamics except in very tangential or relativistic ways. The answers by and large have centered on phenomenal matters and skirted around the real depth of the ontologically dynamic being that serves as the fountainhead of the phenomenal or conditioned realm. When we define freedom, for example, it is in terms of the movements and actions relative to things or elements that can be seen and manipulated by the individual or group of individuals concerned. The result is of course freedom in a relative sense and not absolute. Absolute freedom exists only when a movement is not restricted at all or is not influenced or manipulated by external means. It is not related to nor based on elements within the phenomenal world of action. The same analysis holds true for the concept of creativity. Again, there are both relative and absolute types of creativity. Absolute creativity, in contrast to relative creativity, is pure and unrelated to any element or elements that can be manipulated. The crucial question now becomes this: Where then is the real basis or source of absolute freedom and creativity? The answer must be sought in the dynamics of the conditioned and unconditioned where the aesthetic nature is found, i.e., in the pre-experiential or primal nature of the dynamics. The primal nature of the aesthetic is quite an uncommon conception and difficult to comprehend so long as one is oriented in the substantive realm of perception. Indeed, the primal nature is not something that could easily be conceived or perceived as in ordinary cognitive process. We could now sum up this section by asserting that as we probed into the very nature of the dynamics of being, we arrived at a cosmology of aesthetic experience which is at bottom found to be an implicative metaphysics or an implicate ontology of the conditioned and unconditioned. We need to probe much further into the nature of the aesthetic and its function by introducing other Buddhist doctrines.[13]

The Dynamics of Emptiness

Following the insight revealed in the *Udāna,* we explore further into the nature of the conditioned and unconditioned. Although we are already aware of the co-terminous nature of both, our ordinary understanding of things tend to give existential priority to the conditioned over the unconditioned. This is understandable but, in reality, it is not a question of temporal priority but one of ontological dynamics. Both are constantly involved with each other, i.e., the dynamics of two realms coming together and emerging as one, and mutually penetrating and identifying each other, *ad infinitum.*

Methodologically speaking, there is a problem of treating the two realms as separate entities and attempting to derive some answers in the analysis. This is not fruitful at all since our ordinary perception of things is loaded or burdened by a *habit of perception* we have formed from a remote past. We learn in Buddhist psychology that the habit was formed from birth, i.e., when a child is born, it immediately begins to grasp for the sustenance of its own life and attaches to things or elements of perception that give it the necessary nourishment. The biological process is unconscious at the beginning but gradually the attachment to things, elements and results is felt and the awareness of the process increases. Yet, for the most part, we pay very little attention, if any, to the presence of this *habit of perception* by being overwhelmed by the success and effectiveness of our perceptions. But the truth of the matter is that in the biological process, fundamentally, we are constantly engaged in dichotomous perception and remain unmindful of the distortion vacuity of the results that come later. For example, when we perceive things, we divide the visible from the invisible, empirical from non-empirical, being from non-being, form from formless, conditioned from unconditioned, etc. Once the division or separation is made, we concentrate on the manipulative realm – the visible, empirical, being, form and conditioned – and ignore the non-manipulative realm – the invisible, non-empirical, non-being, formless, and unconditioned. This is clearly an example of classical, metaphysical thinking at work but at the same time, more importantly, we are unmindful of its failure to account for the fuller perception and consequent understanding of things. This failure shows up clearly when current scientific field theories are applied, where the void or vacuum is not what the term ordinarily means but rather it refers to a *plenum* that is very much "alive" and potential for the field of activities of whatever kind.

Parenthetically, the Buddhist would say that the narrow type of perception is a form of suffering *(duḥkha)*. It is so because this type of perception does not take into account the real nature of life that is based on the nature of impermanence *(anitya)* and the nonexistence of an essential self *(anātman)*. These three concepts – suffering, impermanence and non-self – are popularly known as the Three Marks of Buddhism. They characterize at once what Buddhism is all about and who is the subscriber. Their meanings however come alive only when they are taken together in the dynamics, i.e., in the sense that they are seen to mutually penetrate and identify each other. Taken alone or separately, none of the marks make any real sense but only fosters vagueness and confusion; but together they present a rare insight into a philosophy of life that has withstood the times.

It should be clear by now that the locus of experiential reality lodges in the dynamics of the conditioned and unconditioned realms. For clarity sake, the realms may be separately conceived but in the strictest sense they cannot be separately perceived. They are ontologically equal only in terms of their co-terminous nature. An example of this is found in the *Heart Sūtra (Prajñāpāramitā-hṛdaya-*

sūtra)[14] where form *(rūpa)* and emptiness *(śūnyatā)* are equated. This equation, however, has been the source of much confusion and misunderstanding. It is not an equation derived, for example, in simple mathematical operation or conceived in classical metaphysical framework. Both form and emptiness are always vitally and dynamically involved with each other in their co- terminous nature. They are in constant flux and go through a process beautifully stated by Alfred N. Whitehead: "The many become one, and are increased by one."[15]

At this point, one is tempted to equate form[16] and emptiness with the conditioned and unconditioned realms, respectively. While in a way form does nestle in the conditioned realm, the nature of dynamics prevents the one-to-one relationship. The same condition holds true for emptiness and the unconditioned because emptiness is not a metaphysical but an ontological concept. Being so, emptiness in perception is what gives substance to the unconditioned realm and not the other way around. As an ontological concept, it cannot be separated from the dynamics of things, however conditioned or unconditioned it may appear to be. In sum, the dynamics of experience is at the center of all discourse.

The crucial question before us is this: What is the nature of emptiness seen in the dynamics of the conditioned and unconditioned? It has already been stated that emptiness is an ontological concept. This means that any thinker—logician or perceiver—cannot isolate oneself from the very open dynamics involved. At the same time, one needs to seek out the moorings for the phenomenal, the grounds for the alleged rise of a divided or fragmented world one has constructed or contrived. It is here that the doctrine of emptiness plays its role.

Emptiness is not sheer emptiness devoid of everything. If it were so, no further discussion would be necessary. Unfortunately, we do not have the English equivalent for the Sanskrit term, *śūnya* (empty) or *śūnyatā* (emptiness). The etymology of the term expands on its nature of swelling or growing, just like the biological phenomenon of pregnancy. It depicts at once potency, maturation and production in the microcosmic continuum of life process. But it also depicts the receptive, free and open nature that is limitless or borderless, i.e., from the microcosm to the macrocosm. In this way, emptiness is at once a "receptor" and an "initiator" for the greater realms of existence, from the conditioned to the unconditioned and vice versa. It is that which fosters and maintains the whole or holistic nature in the dynamics of things. It could thus be seen as the deepest thrust made into the nature of perceptual dynamics.

We may infer that the Buddha's enlightenment revealed to him that the conditioned realm (i.e., empirical, phenomenal, contingent) is moored in the unconditioned and that the latter is not bound to the former but indeed it is the ground for the ultimate human resolution of the tainted dynamics. The grounds, in a sense, constitute the saving truth of existence of the *Dharma*. Where the unconditioned is ever neutral, pure, and unlimited, the conditioned is always obsessive, tainted, and limited. The mix of the two is unnatural and the way out is only through the unconditioned that "receives, tames and controls" the blind forces of the conditioned and "cleanses" the tainted dynamics.

This essay thus focused on a deeper probe into our perceptual mechanism to exhibit certain limitations and incongruities in it. Experiential reality however is always fluid and in the flow, and so our perceptual process must conform to the flow rather than be attached to the static and abstract play of elements or other concepts so designed and assigned by the mind. But the flow is difficult to grasp by the mind whose dichotomous activity from the outset leads it astray from the flow itself. Indeed, it must be trained or retrained to relinquish the perceptual attachments contrived, conceived and imposed by the careless, even wayward, mind. What is to be done? Enter meditative discipline.[17]

As the Buddha had initially prescribed, meditative discipline has proved to be the standard practice to pacify, weed out or eradicate the attachments to the empirical elements that block the way to the truly holistic vision of things. We can contrive and conceive things symmetrically but we cannot do it asymmetrically since the latter consists of movements that are inclusive, fuller, deeper and open. Meditation then is the instrument by which dichotomies of all kinds are resolved in order to perceive things as they are without restrictions or borders. It is the capture here of the peace and tranquility that brings the conditioned realm under control. This state of tranquility is the aesthetic find, so-called, the aesthetic nature that exhibits the equilibrium or pure natural span of the conditioned and unconditioned nature of things. In this way, also, there is an accommodation of the conditioned and unconditioned, an accommodation that is total and pure and, strictly speaking, without distinguishing the two realms. Furthermore, the accommodation and forward thrust in the dynamics is the power, so-called, of emptiness. This is emptiness of dynamics in its fullness, wholeness and pureness. It offers the completion, satisfaction and enjoyment of experiential events in the process.

Concluding Remarks

This explorative essay has traversed difficult grounds of discourse. The difficulty lies in the main in our reluctance and resistance to question the limited nature of our ordinary perception of things. There must be a drastic turn around in our ordinary perception, a paradigm shift if you will, that would take us beyond classical metaphysical thinking with old habits and bring us to contemporary scientific perception and thinking oriented in the holistic ontological dynamics of things. This is the way to discover and intimate with the true roots of our perception that is untainted by the contrived and skewed elements of the conditioned realm.

Ch'an (Zen) Buddhism's famous *The Ten Oxherding Pictures*[18] in various presentations is a perfect example of depicting the inner dynamics of the conditioned and unconditioned realms. It begins with the sensual experience of the herder and ends with the enlightened herder returning to the market place. In sequence thus: (1) searching for the ox, (2) seeing the traces, (3) seeing the ox, (4) catching the ox, (5) herding the ox, (6) coming home on the ox's back, (7) the ox forgotten, leaving the man alone, (8) the ox and the man both gone out of sight, (9) returning to the origin, back to the source, and (10) entering the city with bliss-bestowing hands. The sequence of events exhibits the constant transformation of the dynamics from the conditioned to the unconditioned and finally to the properly conditioned. In the whole process, however, nothing is added or detracted and all events are taking place in the whole.

In sum, the aesthetic nature and emptiness realized in the dynamics of the conditioned-cum-unconditioned are the basis for the pure, unadulterated actions and activities. We, especially the artist of whatever persuasion, strive to gain the inner dynamics of being in order to achieve the purest form of art. We are then not so much interested in the finished product of an artisan as we are in the unique nature of *beauty* that exudes the mental and physical functions of the artisan in tune or harmony with the purity of the dynamics of being. This is the rare *inner beauty* so desired in the east as compared to our normal attraction to and promotion of common "external beauty" attributed to various objects of the art world.

References

1. It is difficult to date the origins of logocentrism or the emphasis on the mind as the sole center of epistemological process but in the west it probably dates back to the early Greek period. Aristotle, for example, has given us a logic that is clear and simple in operation due to its orientation in the objective or substantive

nature of things. The three rules of logic are based on this orientation, i.e., the rules of identity (A is A), non- contradiction (A is not ~ A), and excluded middle (A v ~ A). Yet, this type of logic ignores the realm and nature of the experiential that is larger and more inclusive than the realm of the mental or logic. Indeed, the success of the realm of the mental or logic had overwhelmed the nature of experiential realm such that the latter had been forgotten or permanently marginalized. Exposure to eastern thought, however, will force us immediately to refocus our vision on the larger experiential realm in which logic functions and in doing so brings to bear the holistic non-objective or non-substantive nature of things. How the objective and non-objective thrive together was a problem that the easterners did not shirk from considering and indeed they came up with a solution unique to their own traditions but also applicable to all. This paper is a mere extension of their discovery and contribution.

2. 20th century thinkers, including religious thinkers like Martin Buber and Alfred N. Whitehead, have shown keen insight into the relativistic and holistic nature of reality, especially with respect to the relationship between God and the world. Whitehead's principle of concretion is an excellent example of how both God and human beings are together in the concrescence of actual occasions. God has the primordial nature but in the involvement with the world of human beings, his function is within the realm of consequent nature.

3. Wing-tsit Chan, *A Source Book in Chinese Philosophy* (Princeton: Princeton University Press, 1963), 139.

4. Chan, 152, Verse *25*.

5. *Ibid.*, 320.

6. It should be noted that the Buddhist Wheel was earlier illustrated by a *swastika* with four wings in constant spin. Like the flight of a bird, life itself is seen in constant movement. The spin could "cease" but only in terms of resolving itself within the dynamics, i.e., by rooting out the cause of the spin and arriving at the state of "spinless spin." This is a paradoxical situation sensed and resolved by the Buddha in his profound meditative way.

7. See David Bohm's influential work, *Wholeness and the Implicate Order.* (London: Routledge & Kegan Paul, 1980). His concept of *implicate order* has been a great boon to the comparative understanding of Chinese *Yi-Ching (Book of Changes)* metaphysics and Buddhist *Avatamsaka (Flowery Splendor)* reality.

8. Fritjof Capra, *The Tao of Physics,* Second Edition, Revised and Updated, (Boulder: Shambhala Publications, Inc., 1983).

9. It should be noted that recent findings in physics, especially on the nature and function of quarks, have given rise to different views about the field concept of subatomic particles and consequent understanding of the atomic world as well as the world at large. Parenthetically, on a different matter, I must take exception to Capra's reference to "eastern mysticism." Indeed the term is used in his subtitle, "An Exploration of the Parallels between Modern Physics and Eastern Mysticism." The time to view the east in mystical terms is over. It only shows up the limitations, ignorance and even prejudice on the part of the viewer.

10. Capra, 222.

11. Edward Conze, ed., *Buddhist Texts Through the Ages* (New York: Philosophical Library, 1954); see I. B. Horner's partial translation of the *Udāna* ("*Solemn Utterances*"), 94-5. The work is an old Pali text that records some of the most profound philosophical ideas of the Buddha. It is a storehouse of early Buddhist

thought quite in tune with the original period and has become the basis for further exposition, dissemination and development in both the southern (Theravāda) and northern (Mahāyāna) traditions.

12. The word, *Dharma,* has been used for the Buddhist truth of existence or Buddhist reality. The various texts, especially the texts that deal with the nature of human experience called the *Abhidhamma or Abhidharma,* utilize the word, *dhamma/ dharma,* to depict the various factors of experience. Such factors as greed, hatred, delusion, etc., are all *dharmas.* Note that the *dharmas* are not capitalized but the *Dharma* is. Moreover, to distinguish Buddhist Dharma from non-Buddhist dharma used in other Indian systems, a compound is used, i.e., Buddha Dharma.

13. This paper will focus and concentrate on Buddhist thought to discuss and arrive at the concepts of the aesthetic nature and emptiness. It will save the Chinese contributions for another time.

14. Edward Conze, 152-53. All Buddhist schools are careful in preserving the so-called parity principle of human ontology. Early Mahāyāna thought as reflected in the *Prajñāpāramitā Sūtras* has set the stage for the famous "equation" (parity) between the conditioned and unconditioned, roughly the realms of form *(rūpa)* and emptiness *(śūnyatā).* Later on, Nāgārjuna (150-250 A.D.) will firm up the parity principle in his celebrated assertion that emptiness is the provisional designation of relational origination *(pratītya-samutpāda)* of events which is yet another designation for the middle way *(madhyama-pratipad). (Mūlamādhyamakakārikā; Verses on the Fundamental Middle Way;* Chapter 24, Verse 18) All this brings us full circle to the popular "equation:" *samsāra=nirvāṇa=samsāra.* It simply depicts the cyclic nature of life process in the fullest and purest ontological sense.

15. Alfred N. Whitehead, *Process and Reality, An Essay in Cosmology;* Corrected Edition, Edited by David Ray Griffin and Donald W. Sherburne (New York: The Free Press, 1978), 21.

16. Form *(rūpa)* is variously translated as matter, element, object, etc. However, strictly speaking, it refers to the first of the five *skandhas* (constituents of being) and thus it is an ontological term that should properly be translated as corporeal nature or corporeality. The other four *skandhas* are feeling *(vedanā),* sensual perception *(samjñā),* mental formation *(samskāra)* and consciousness *(vijñāna).* The dynamics of the five *skandhas* exhibits the function of ordinary perception by an alleged conventional self.

17. Ch'an (Zen) Buddhism as a "hard core" meditative school gave China the needed impetus to develop and propagate beyond the confines of Buddhist institutions as well as beyond the borders to Korea and Japan. Its central focus on the ontological concept of emptiness *(śūnyatā)* has had great influence on the thought and culture of all the nations of Asia proper and currently in all parts of the world. Other highly visible institutional schools, such as, Hua-yen, T'ien-T'ai, and Ch'ing-t'u also maintained and developed meditative discipline in their respective ways to preserve and spread the *Buddha Dharma* in profound metaphysical and ontological ways.

18. For an explanatory discussion of the ten pictures, see Daisetz Teitaro Suzuki, *Essays in Zen Buddhism,* First Series (New York: Harper & Brothers, 1949), 361-74.

Also, for two other sets of *The Ten Oxherding Pictures, see* D.T. Suzuki, *Manual of Zen Buddhism* (London: Rider and Company, 1950), 127-44.

Chapter 5

Encounter with Emptiness: A Study of the Early Japanese Account of the First Systematization of Buddhist Thought in China

Shotaro Iida

One of the basic questions of philosophy and religion is: In the ultimate sense, what are the modes and bases of human existence in regard to the liberation of man? And this was precisely the issue that pivoted around those Six or Seven Early Chinese Buddhist schools upon encountering the Indian Buddhist notion of *Śūnyatā* or *emptiness* propounded by the Mādhyamika school. As T.R.V. Murti says:

> The Mādhyamika philosophy claims our attention as the system which created a *revolution* in Buddhism and through that in the whole range of Indian philosophy. The entire Buddhist thought *turned* on the *Śūnyatā* doctrine of the Mādhyamika.

It was, indeed, this dynamic religio-philosophy of *Emptiness* which also inaugurated a new era of religio-philosophical climate of China, Tibet, Korea and Japan. Through the Sun-lun, Dbu-ma-pa, Sam-non and San-non schools respectively, these countries saw the beginnings of systematic philosophical investigations. Thus, China was ushered into the age of systematic philosophy by Kumārajīva, the great translator of Kuccha, an oasis kingdom of Central Asia, who with sweeping strokes of genius translated the four major Mādhyamika treatises between 401 and 409 A.D. The excitement and sense of discovery over the pages of these texts of Buddhist philosophy are eloquently expressed by Seng-jui: How vast it is! It may truly be said to put in order and make level the road to (along) the "hollow stairs" and to open out the metaphysical gate with cosmos...

Aside from such exclamations, the question that interests us is: "How was the Mādhyamika thought, a product of an Indian philosophical heritage, understood by the first Chinese who studied it?" We encounter several obstacles in attempting to answer this question. As Arthur Link used to say, "To comprehend Chinese Buddhism we must understand it not just as Indian Buddhism in China but rather as a cultural amalgam, a synthesis of Indian thought and Sinic concepts and ideals". We may add that while the Chinese had a difficult enough task themselves in trying to comprehend a doctrine promulgated in a foreign language bearing foreign denotations and connotations, they at least knew what they themselves thought, and it was simply (!) a matter of learning the abstract terms and concepts and jamming them somehow into their own comparatively more concrete and earthly language. The modern scholar is not so fortunate. Not only does he have to know what the Indian Buddhists thought (implying a knowledge of Indian language and culture) and what the Chinese translators and thinkers thought (implying knowledge of Chinese language and culture) but he also must be able to move around easily in the fields of philosophical investigations (implying not only fluency in his own language but also in the language of philosophy). It is no wonder that Western scholars continually *watch* each other's language(s)! For either they understand Indian Buddhism well and Chinese thought not so well, or Chinese thought well and Indian Buddhism not so well, or as is probably more common, they are overly linguistic or overly philosophical in orientation.

Before the advent of Kumārajīva, as there shall be occasion to state again, there was no rigorous study of Buddhist doctrine in China. The literate Chinese Buddhist would read scriptures in Chinese translation, scriptures that, in spite of the widely divergent views they might express, he took to be saying the same thing. What this was would be determined by the learning experience of the Chinese in question, an experience purely Chinese. At the time we are dealing with, the preoccupation of the Chinese thinker, as far as can be reconstructed from the literature at hand, was with 'being and non-being (*yu wu*). The latter, far from a mere nothing, seems to have had two referends, one temporal, the other conceptual. In the temporal sense, *wu* was presumed to have existed before the creation of *yu*. In the conceptual sense, non-being was felt to be, in a manner quite transcending time, space, and all particulars, pregnant with being. In other words, to the extent that we are justified in making a pronouncement—and it bears comment that *wu* is nowhere defined in the accessible literature—*wu* is potentially everything precisely because it is actually an entity called nothing, not the absence of something. The Chinese gentleman, whether religious or layman, who read Buddhist literature in translation would encounter, in the *Prajñāpāramitā* literature, the ubiquitous word *k'ung,* which as an adjective means "empty" (*śūnya*), as a noun "emptiness" (*śūnyatā*).

In the words of Tsukamoto Zenryū (see p. 380-1 in his History of Chinese Buddhism, vol. I):

The interests just mentioned gravitated more to the study of the *Prajñāpāramitā* scriptures than to anything else. The development was guided from without by the...situation of the Buddhist religion in India and Central Asia..., but it also coincided with an internal Chinese development, the rise and eventual...triumph of dark learning (*hsüan hsüeh*).

The new ideas constituted a new learned vogue, one that sought the Way—that is, the abstract, invisible Truth that constitutes the root and source of all phenomena—in Lao-tzu, Chuangtzu and the *Canon of Changes.*

The new vogue despised classical scholarship, whose aim was to be true to the traditional Confucian canon with its principled insistence on the doctrine of propriety, which latter the 'dark learners' denigrated as the study of how to deal with reality in a world of concrete, practical specifics (*shih*) or of 'being' (*yu*). In other words the new movement busied itself with the quest for and attainment of 'non-being' (*wu*), an abstract and metaphysical universal truth (*li*).

Among the earnest and distinguished *Prajñāpāramitā* scholars in the Chinese Buddhist community, there were, to be sure, a Chih Tun and a Tao-an, who, by devoting the whole of their lives to a comparative study of the Vaipūlya scriptures, contrived to come close to the early Mahāyāna notion of emptiness. Generally speaking, however, all were ignorant of the original language. Thus, as long as the Chinese intellectual—stepped in Lao-Chuang study and now showing an interest in Buddhism—had to rely exclusively on the *Prajñāpāramitā* in Chinese translation, there was scarcely any choice but to approach it through the ideas of 'dark learning' ascribed to Lao-tzu and Chuang-tzu.

Until Tao-an's time, for *Prajñāpāramitā* scholarship to be accessible to the Chinese, the mediation of the ideas of Lao-tzu and Chuang-tzu was a necessity. This was particularly true in the case of the intellectual layman, who was both fond of and thoroughly versed in the study of Lao-tzu and Chuang-tzu; who, at the same time, enjoyed listening to public readings of the *Prajñāpāramitā* by the *saṃgha;* and who understood the *Prajñāpāramitā* doctrine of emptiness only with reference to the several interpretations mentioned earlier and in the light of his own secular knowledge. The produce was, so to speak, a *ko yi* Buddhism consisting of an interpretation of the *Prajñāpāramitā* scriptures in the light of Lao-tzu and Chuang-tzu, one that of necessity removed itself from the meaning of the words contained in the original scriptures. On the other hand, it won a secure place in the hearts of many Chinese as a sort of specifically Chinese *Prajñāpāramitā* study based on scriptures now available in Chinese. As such, it liberated a host of theories that were to guide that community's spiritual life—at the very least, theories typical of persons who enjoyed 'dark learning' and 'pure talk'. This, in turn, made early Mahāyāna scriptures such as the *Prajñāpāramitā* into vehicles of specifically Chinese Buddhist thought—thought that was no longer Indian because its translated sources were not Indian but Chinese—and thus assured them a rapid spread throughout the intellectual society of the Tsin. Seng-jui, who studied under the guidance first of Tao-an and then of Kumārajīva, says, in effect—in a preface to the latter's translation of the *Vimalakīrtinirdeśa*—that Chinese *Prajñāpāramitā* scholarship before Kumārajīva, based as it was on translations rather far removed from the originals and making use of a fundamentally different vocabulary and unable as it also was to throw off the tendency to propound the doctrine with reference to the ideas of Lao-tzu and Chuang-tzu, was unable to arrive at a perfectly accurate understanding of the meaning of the *Prajñāpāramitā* originals. This could eventuate in nothing but a set of conflicting doctrines. In other words, he tells us frankly, there was no sidestepping the "the era of *Prajñāpāramitā* study by resort to *ko yi*".

On the basis of the colophon of the *Chūronshoiki,* we know that Anchō spent some five years (801-806 A.D.) working on this *magnum opus.* We also know that the work was the summary of his many years of Buddhist Studies, for he died five years after its completion at the age of fifty two years old. Moreover, we recognize that the *Chūronshoiki* was an excellent epitome of the Mādhayamika Studies unfolded in China, Korea and Japan during preceding four centuries. As the Chinese development has already been described in this study, a note is added here to sketch the Japanese background of the work.

As the Capital had already moved from Nara to Kyoto, the Heian Japan was ushered into the Ninth century with the eruption of the Mt. Fuji in 800 A.D. As a new era of the Japanese Buddhism unfolded, the focus of the Buddhist Studies also shifted from the Sanron Studies (Mādhyamika) to that of the Yuishiki-Hossō (Yogācāra and Abhidharma). The Sanron Studies already had the following three transmissions from Korea and China:

1. Ekan (Hyegwan) of Koguryo, a direct disciple of Chi-tsang arrived in Japan in 625 A.D. and introduced the Sanron at the Gangōji.

2. Chizō (625-672?), a son of Fukuryō, studied in China nearly eighteen years from 701 A.D. He engaged in the Sanron Studies at the Daianji in Nara.

Besides these three transmissions, the Daianji records of 747 A.D. mention the name of Betsu Sanron. Thus, these various Sanron transmissions preceded Anchō during the Nara period centered around Gangōji, Daianji, Saidaiji, Hōryūji and Tōdaiji monastic colleges. Among them Gangōji tradition produced a celebrated monk scholar of Sanron whose Chikō was a prolific writer on the subject. It was not, however, with these scholarly works Chikō's name went down in history, but a maṇḍala known as *Chikō mandara* which aided the individual visualization of the Pure Land. The *Nihon-ōjō-gokurakuki* (Records of the Ascendant to the Pure Land in Japan) illustrates the formation of the Maṇḍala by Chikō coincides with, as Tsukamoto Zenryū suggests, the decline of the Gangōji as a Sanron scholastic monastry, due to the transfer of the Sanron Gakushū (the Sanron Study Group) to the Tōnanin of the Tōdaiji. The ensuing financial curtailment prompted the support from the public which, in turn, shifted the emphasis of the Gangōji from the abstruse Sanron philosophy to the 'concrete' Pure Land visualization practice. Chikō also wrote a commentary entitled the *Muryōjukyō Ronshaku* (Discourse and Commentary on the Amitāyus Sūtra). Consequently, after the death of Chikō, his monastic cell was held sacred to his memory by the name *Gokurakubō* or Paradise Cell. Thus, we know the decline of the Sanron Studies, owing to the rise of the Yuishiki-Hossō Studies long before Anchō's time. The Sanron scholars, however, did not give up their hegemony without 'dharma-fights', as Hirai Shunei has shown in detail. Among them, that of Anchō and Taien exemplifies these *hōrons* or dharma-debates in the open arena of the dharma assembly (*hōe*) inside of the Imperial palace. Their heated Buddhist controversies concerning existence and non-existence representing the Sanron and the Yuishiki-Hossō, prompted, perhaps, composition of the *Chūgan-ronshoki,* which became a pyramid of the Sanron Studies together with the *Daijōsanrontaigishō* (the Essentials of the Sanron of the Mahāyana) by Genei (?-840).

Delineation of similarities and differences (*dōi mon*)

I. List of the many teachers (*shushi o ressu*

A. Catalogue of the doctrines of the Three Houses (*sanke no gi o ressu*)

1. General exposition of the doctrines of the Three Houses (*sanke no gi o sōhyō-su*)

2. Separate list of the doctrines of the Three Houses (*sanke no gi o betsuretsu-su*)

a. Doctrine of original non-being (*hommu gi*)

(1) Doctrine proper (*shō hommu gi*)

(a) Exposition of the doctrine (*homu gi o ressu*)

(b) Citation of proof to perfect the explication (*inshō shakujō*)

(2) Alternate doctrine of original Non-being (*hommu igi*)

(a) Citation of heterodox theses (*geshū o agu*)

(b) Refutation of matters in which it has gone astray (*shomei o ha-su*)

b. Doctrine of emptiness identical with visible matter (*sokushiki gi*)

(1) General outline (*sōhyō*)

(2) Separate enumeration (*betsuretsu*)

(a) Within the passes (*kannai*)

1’ Introduction to major tenets (*koshū*)

2’ Refutation of error (*hamei*)

(b) Chih Tao-lin (Shi Dōrin)

c. Doctrine of mental disengagement (*shimmu gi*)

B. Exposition of the doctrines of the Seven Schools (*shichishū no gi o ressu*)

1. YūFa-k’ai (U Hokkai)

2. Shih Tao-yi (Shaku Dōichi)

3. Yū Tao-sui/Fa-sui (U Dōsui/Hossui)

C. Citations from the “Treatise on the Three Theses” (Sanshū ron o hiku)

1. Non-emptiness of provisional designations (*fukū kemyō*)

2. Emptiness of provisional designations (*kū kemyō*)

3. Identity of provisional designations with emptiness (*kemyō kū*)

Discriminatory discussion of strengths and weaknesses (*tokushitsu o ben-zu*)

Phrase-by-phrase commentary to the treatise of the middle view by Shih Chi-tsang

Part Six, Delineation of Differences.

Originally, before the Master [Kumārajīva] arrived in Ch'angan, there were the doctrines of Three Schools. First, Shih-Tao-an declared the doctrine of original Non-being, holding that non-being preceded the myriad transformations, while emptiness was at the [very] beginning of the multitudinous forms. It is final being [according to this view] that man gets bogged down, [for] if he [would but] commit his mind to original non-being, his varied notions would at once come to rest.

Notes on the Phrase-by-phrase commentary to the middle treatise by Anchō, *śramaṇa* of the Daianji

"Part Six, Delineation of Differences". Within this sixth section, there are, broadly speaking, two major lines of thought: (I) a list of many teachers, and (II) a discriminatory discussion of their respective strengths and weaknesses. The former (I) also has three subdivisions of its own, of which the first (A) is a catalogue of the doctrines of Three Houses, the second (B) a catalogue of the doctrines of Seven Schools, and the third (C) a citation from "Treatise on the Three Theses". Again, the first [of the three] (A) has two subdivisions, of which the former (1) is a general exposition of the doctrines of the Three Houses, and latter (2) a separate list of those doctrines.

Anchō: "The Dharma-Master Jui says...". This and what follows [constitute the] second [part indicated earlier in the expression, "the latter] cites proofs, just perfecting the explication" (I.A.Z. a.1)b)). As the "Restated Meaning of [Seng-]chao's Treatise" (*Jōron jutsugi*) says in it fourth roll, citing Dharma-Master Jui's preface to the "Scripture of Pure Name" (*China ming ching hsu*), "Since the wind of wisdom has fanned eastward, since the words of the Dharma have flowed hither in song, though one may speak of centers of exegesis, the matching of meanings was askew and ran afoul of the originals, while the Six Houses were biased and not right. That is to say, the two treatises, the "Middle" and the "Hundredfold," had not yet reached this place, nor was there a perfect mirror. With whom, then, was one to make corrections? If our former Master [Tao-an] sighed despondently into the distance, thinking to resolve the discourse with Maitreya, truly it was for this reason!"

Such being the case, before Master [Kumārajīva] translated the four treatises, [current views on the] recondite doctrine were largely mistaken and, with regard to the universal truth, there was still doubt. This, and this alone, is the reason that [Tao-an] wished to await an audience with Maitreya [before] resolving [his questions].

A separate comment says, "The expression 'matching meanings' [is used by those whose] focus is the proper [meaning of the phrase being explained]. 'Runs afoul of the originals' means that [this method] has already produced a deviant interpretation. The Six Houses are the one that ascribes emptiness to provisional designations, the one that does not, and so on. 'Biased and not right' means that they were not relying on the right doctrine".

The "Restated Meaning" says, "The matching of meanings is askew..'

This means that [those who resorted to this device] mistook ideas they had not yet grasped for a doctrine they had, in [supposed] fact, understood. Where the Six Houses were concerned, Shih Pao-ch'ang, under the Liang, composed a 'Treatise on [Maintaining the] Continuity of the Dharma' (*Hsü fa lun*), in which he says, 'Shih T'an-chi, under the Sung, composed an "Essay on the Six Houses and the Seven Schools" (*Liu chia ch'i tsung lun*), a treatise that contained [reference to] six houses that he [further] divided, thus constituting seven schools. First was the School of Original Non-being (*pen wu tsung*); second was a variant school of original non-being (*pen wu yi tsung*); third was the School of [Emptiness] identical with Visible Matter (*chi se tsung*); fourth was the School of Mental Disengagement (*hsin wu tsung*); fifth was the school of consciousness contraine (*Shih han tsung*); sixth was the School of Magical Conjurings (*huan hua tsung*); and seventh was the School of the Meeting of [Causes and] Conditions (*yüan hui tsung*).

A

"First, Shih Tao-an's "Essay on Original non-being" (*Pen wu lun*) is as follows: "When the thus Come One emerged into the world, he propagated his doctrine by recourse to original non-being. This is why the multitudinous scriptures of universal scope (*fang teng chung ching* i.e., *bahulāni vaipulyasūtrāṇi*) all make clear the original non-being of the multitudinous forms. It is in final being [according to this view] that man gets bogged down, [for] if [he would but] commit his mind to original non-being, his varied notions would at once come to rest. From this, the whole can be deduced".

The "Treatise on the Emptiness of the Non-absolute" says, "Primordial inexistence"—many who feel partial to inexistence are dominated by inexistence in everything they say. Thus, "not existent" [they take to mean] "the existent is inexistent", and "not inexistent" [they take to mean] "the inexistent is also inexistent"." The Master Yüan-k'ang says, 'Under the heading [of original non-being]....' refers to the third point, the refutation of the doctrine of original non-being as expounded by Chu Fa-t'ai [who lived under the] Tsin dynasty. 'Feel partial' means that, for the most part, they felt partial to this non-being. 'In everything they said,' they turned towards non-being. 'Dominated by' means that they treated [non-being] with the honor due a guest. Guests all look toward their host. Now, by this 'thesis of original non-being' is meant that all [of its proponents] looked to non-being.

B

Chi-tsang: Second is the doctrine of [emptiness] identical with visible matter. However, there are two subschools. The former is the subschool within the passes, which declares [the following as its thesis]: [The proposition that] visible matter, just as it is, is empty is a clear statement that visible matter has no nature of its own. This is why it is worded thus: "Visible matter, just as it is, is empty," not thus: "Visible matter is empty in its original nature".

Anchō "Second is the doctrine of emptiness identical with visible matter....". This means that below is the second [division, i.e., I.A.2.b.], wherein there is a discussion having as its focus the doctrine of [emptiness] identical with visible matter. Within it, moreover, there are two [subdivisions]; (1) general outline and (2) separate enumeration. Within (2) the separate enumeration, there are also two [sections]; the doctrine of [emptiness] identical with visible matter (a) first, [as preached] within the passes; (b) second, [as preached by Chih] Tao-lin (Tun). Within the former of these (a) are yet again two [divisions]; (1') the introduction of major tenets and (2') the refutation of error. By "the former is the subschool within the passes" is meant the introduction of major tenets. The "Treatise on the Emptiness of the Unreal" says: "Identical with form' states that, because form does not make itself form, though called form, it is not form. Now, the word 'form' simply refers to [corresponds to] form *qua* form. To be form, it need not wait until form makes itself form".

The "Restated Meaning" [of the Commentary to the Middle Treatise] says: "Below is refuted the doctrine of [emptiness] identical with visible matter. The Master's [Seng-chao's?] view is as follows: Subtle matter, by coalescing, forms gross matter. When one construes it to be empty, one does so merely for gross matter, not for subtle matter. Gross matter is such only in relatively to subtle matter, for it is not matter independently. Further, white color is such only in relatively to black color, for white color is not color independently. Therefore, to speak of emptiness identical with visible matter is by no means *to* [*imply that*] there is not visible matter. If visible matter had definitive marks, then, without waiting for causes or conditions, there should exist the dharma of visible matter. Also, if gross matter had definitive marks, it would achieve completeness without dependence on subtle matter. This clarifies the principle that conventional matter is no mere void. Yet the two masters, (Yüan-) k'ang and (Hui-) ta, in the unanimous statement that this is a refutation of Chih Tao-lin's doctrine of [emptiness] identical with visible matter, are mistaken.

Chi-tsang: This doctrine [al view] was attacked by the honorable [Seng-]chao, for the latter declares, "The opponent says correctly that matter [as it is found] is not in itself matter, but he does not understand that matter [as it found] is [itself] no matter."

Anchō: "This doctrinal view was attacked by the honorable Seng-chao". The reference is to the latter [above-mentioned] refutation of error, as said in the "Treatise on the Emptiness of the Unreal". "This [school] only says that form does not make itself form but does not understand that form is non-form". The "Restated Meaning" says, "They merely understand that visible matter is not in and of itself matter, that it comes into existence thanks to cause and condition, but, ignorant that visible matter is [itself] at bottom empty, they continue to maintain conventional [provisional] existence". By "understand" (ling) is meant to "be aware" (wu).

C

Chi-tsang: Next, Chih Tao-lin (Tun) published his "Treatise on Wandering in the Mystery on Matter as Such" (*Chi se yu hsüan lun*), in which he declares that matter, just as it is, is empty, which is why he called it the "Treatise on Wandering in the Mystery of Matter as Such". It is thus no different from Master [Tao-]an's [doctrine] of emptiness by intrinsic nature.

Anchō: "Next, Chih Tao-in…". This means that what follows discusses the issue by confining itself to Master Tao-lin's doctrine of [emptiness] identical with visible matter. As one reads in the fifth roll of the "Recondite Doctrine of the Mountain School," "Eighth, Chih Tao-in published a 'Treatise on Wandering in the Mystery of Matter as Such,' which says, 'Now, the nature of visible matter is such that visible matter is not in and of itself visible matter.' Not being so in and of itself, although visible matter, it is yet empty. Knowledge, not knowing itself, albeit knowing, it yet quiescent'. Its meaning is clear. The emptiness of the dharmas of visible matter and mind is called the real [i.e., the transcendental truth], while visible matter and mind, though not unempty, are conventional [truth]". The "Restated Meaning" says, "In composing his 'Treatise on [Emptiness] Identical with Visible Matter,' (Chih Tun) was saying, 'In my view, "Visible matter in and of itself is empty. It is not that visible matter, by perishing, becomes empty". The words just quoted are perfectly descriptive of the sense. Why is this? Now, such is the nature of visible matter that there is no visible matter in and of itself. Since visible matter does not exist in and of itself, although visible matter, it is yet empty. Knowledge, not knowing itself, while knowing, is yet eternally quiescent.' Yet, if one examines the meanings of these [two, one will see that both] alike [refer to the] emptiness of the unreal, since visible matter, contingent as it is on cause and condition and owing its existence as it does to these conditions, does not exist in and of itself. This is what one calls emptiness. It need not be analyzed and demolished in order, then and only then, to be empty. Admittedly, it has been said, 'Now, the nature of visible matter is such that visible matter does not exist in and of itself, although visible matter, it is yet empty'. Yet there is here no biased statement on the side of the absence of [own-] being. Thus, "one knows that it is the very same as the emptiness of the unreal". [Roll] 3 in the "Lives of Eminent Monks" says, "Chih Tun, whose courtesy name was Tao-lin and whose secular surname was Kuan, was a man of Ch'en-liu or, as some say, a man of Lin-lü in Ho-tung. At the age of twenty-five, he left his household. Under the Tsin, in the first year of T'ai-ho (366), in the intercalary fourth month, on the fourth day, he died in his residence, his springs and autumns being fifty and three." As to *tun* (*don*), the *Yü p'ien* says that [the reading] is *d*[o-t]*on*. *Chin* is the name of a monastery. This is why the "Lives of Eminent Monks" says that, later, he returned to Wu, where he built a monastery on Mount Chih.

Chi-tsang: Third was the doctrine of mental disengagement, advocated by the Dharma-Master Wen. By 'mental disengagement' is meant that, even if one had no mentation toward the myriad things, the myriad things would never [for all that], be inexistent. They interpret the sense of this as follows: When it is said in scripture that the dharmas are empty, the intention is to bring it about that the substance of mind, being vain, is not clung to; this is the only reason that there is any talk of non-being. There is no [ascription of] emptiness to external objects—that is, the realm of the myriad objects is not taken as empty [by those who hold this view]. The Master [Seng-]chao parses this as follows: What [the partisans of this view] grasp is the quiescences of the spirit; what they miss is the vacuity of things. The refutation is as follows: [The adherents of this view] are plainly aware of the emptiness of mind; still, they maintain the existence of things. In sum, then, this [view] has advantages and disadvantages.

These four masters [i.e., Shih Tao-an, Chu Ch'ien, Chih Tun, and Chu Fa-yün, constituting a group] set themselves up in the age of the Tsin. Then, under the Sung, the Master T'an-chi of the Ta-chuang-yen-ssu published his "Treatise on the Seven Schools", still maintaining the tradition of the first four as Four Schools.

D

Anchō: "Third was the doctrine of mental disengagement, advocated by the Dharma-Master Wen." Under this third entry, one confines oneself to the doctrine of mental disengagement in one's discussion. The "Recondite Doctrine of the Mountain School", in its fifth roll, says "First, Shih Seng Wen published a 'Treatise on the Two Truths in the Light of Mental Disengagement,' in which he says, 'Being has shape, non-being has no form. What has shape cannot inexist, while what has no form cannot exist. Yet the scripture declares that visible matter is inexistent, but [when it does so] it is merely [referring to] the internal cessation of thought, it is not [ascribing] emptiness to outward matter'. This was refuted by the honorable [T'an-lyi, who, to the contrary, made it clear that [the interpretation that] mind inexists is the true construction". The "Treatise on the Emptiness of the Unreal" says: "One has no mention toward the myriad things, but they are never inexistent". The "Restated Meaning" says: "[What has gone before is] a refutation of Chu Fa-wen's doctrine of mental disengagement. The 'Treatise on the Quest for the Recondite in the Two Truths' says: Chu Fa-wen of the Tsin was a disciple of the Dharma-Master Shih Fa-shen. In composing his "Treatise on Mental Disengagement,' he said: "Now, being is what has shape, while non-being is what has no form. If this be so, then what has form may not be spoken of as inexistent, while what has no shape may not be spoken of as existent. Thus, the existent really exists; visible matter is genuine matter. When the scripture says that 'visible matter is empty', [its aim is] merely to halt that thought internally by keeping it from getting bogged down in external matter. If external matter is not preserved within the superfluous affects [of the mind], then, if not inexistent, what is it? Can this possibly mean the inexistence of visible matter in the sense of a vast formlessness?"

Within [the "Lives of] Eminent Monks", [one reads that] the *śramaṇa* Tao-heng clung to the doctrine of mental disengagement. However, in this, he was merely relying on the doctrine he had learned from Fa-wen; it was not anything he had established in his own thinking. Later, Chih Min-tu, following [in the footsteps of his predecessors], studied the earlier doctrines.

Thus, the Master Yüan-k'ang says: "[The thinkers just quoted], in attacking Chih Min-tu's doctrine of mental disengagement, sought out the tips [of the branches] but forgot the trunk". Now, as to the proposition that 'mental disengagement' means "no mentation toward the myriad things", the citations appearing in the "Treatise on the Emptiness of the Unreal" are in total agreement. The Master Yüan-k'ang says: "When the scripture speaks of 'emptiness', [its aim is] merely not to excite thought that will cling to things; this is why it speaks of their emptiness". Yet the mass of physical objects is existent and has not ever be inexistent. By "ever" is meant "at-all".

"They interpret the sense of this as follows...". The Phrase-by-phrase commentary is principally concerned with clarifying the meaning of the Dharma-Master Wen. The "Restated Meaning" says: "[The aim is to] cause the mental substratum to forget the sense objects and not to cling to them easily, which is why emptiness is spoken of. The word 'scripture' [as used] in this [context refers] to the predications of the scriptures of the Greater Vehicle."

"The Master Seng-chao parses this as follows". The "Treatise on the Emptiness of the Unreal", being in complete agreement as to quotation of text, will not be recorded here. The Master Yüan-k'ang says, "What follows is the refutation proper. For the ability not to cling to the dharmas, it is called gain; The "Restated Meaning," quoting the *"Prajñā* Scripture," says: Since visible matter is limitless, therefore, *prajñā* is limitless. 'Limitlessness' is another name for emptiness. If one is to clarify emptiness of mind, one must [first] cite the objects [of mentation]. The emptiness of the objects of mentation is made manifest from the mind. The objects and the knowledge of them complement each other, as do the halves of a tally. As long as charcoal ash has not been swept away, the notion of a tree lives. How much the less can the notion of a tree perish when branches and leaves are both flourishing!"

"The refutation is as follows". The "Restated Meaning" says: "In this master's [i.e., in Chu Fa-yün's?] opinion, it is merely that there is no excitation of the mind to cling to things, which is why there is mention of emptiness. Yet things are existent and by no means inexistent, which accounts for the expression, 'this view had advantages and disadvantage". As for "these four masters", the "Restated Meaning" says: "These four men were confined to Tsin times, not reaching into the Sung era. Therefore, since they are widely known, it is proper to cite them, whereas the last three houses are not commonly known, the Dharma-Master T'an-chi alone mentioning them".

As to *tsin* (*chin*), the *Yü p'ien* says that *chin* is read by resort to the combination *c*[ijk-ñ]*in* and means "to advance". It is also the name of a prefecture and of a state. It is also a clan name. It is also the name of one of the hexagrams in the *Canon of Changes*.

"Then, under the Sung, the Dharma-Master T'an-chi of the Ta-chuang-yen-ssu...". What follows is the second part, focused on the Seven Schools (I.B.). "Then, under..." The "Lives of Eminent Monks", in their seventh roll, at the end of the biography of T'an-pin, says: "At the time, the Chuang-yen (monastery) also had a certain T'an-chi, who, for his learning, his practice, his talent, and his fortitude, was valued by all his contemporaries. [T'an-]chi produced a "Treatise on the Seven Schools," while [T'an-]tsung published a scriptural catalogue and a forest of number[ed categories]. On this basis, one knows that [this T'an-chi] is not the master T'an-chi of the Ts'ao-t'ang-ssu on Mount Sung in the land of Wu "Then, under" means "by the time of".

Chi-tsang: Fifth, Yü-Fa-k'ai established the doctrine of consciousness contained [as stored impressions]: "The Triple Sphere is the abode of a long night, while the cognizing [activity of the] mind is the subjective agent of a great dream. The assembly of existents that one sees now are visions in a dream. Once one has awoken from the great dream, once dawn has come to the long night, straightaway the perverse and erroneous vanish from one's consciousness, and the Triple Sphere is [seen to be] totally empty. At such time, there is no source whence [anything is] produced, yet there is nothing that fails to be produced". The following objection is raised: If it be so, then, once one awakes, one no longer sees the myraids of objects. In that case, one simply loses the worldly truth. What is there, then, for the five eyes of the Thus Come One to see?

Anchō: "Fifth, Yü Fa-k'ai..." Part 5 of the "Recondite Doctrine of the Mountain School" says: "Fourth, Yü Fa-k'ai in his 'Treatise on the Erroneous Cognition of the Two Truths,' says, 'The Triple Sphere is the abode of a long night, while the cognizing activity of the mind is the subjective agent of a great dream. Once one has awoken from the great dream, the Triple Sphere is seen to be fundamentally empty, the perverse and erroneous vanish from one's consciousness, and, in rank, one mounts to the tenth stage'". We now say this: What is seen through error is conventional, while [the notion that], when one awakes, everything is empty, is real. [The remainder] can be understood by analogy. Concerning the words "awake" and "dawn," [one notes,] upon examination, [that] in the *Yü p'ien,* the upper character is read *k*[o-ṅ]*āk* (*chüeh*), meaning "to awake" or "great". The *Kauang yün* says that it is read *k*[o-n]*āk* and means "to perceive intuitively", "great", "clear", "bright", "to awake", or "to know". It is also read *k*[o-x]*āu* (*chiao*), meaning "reflect". The lower character is read *x*[*uā-l*]*eu* (*hsiao*), meaning "brightness", "dawn", "wisdom", or "to know". [The rest] may be understood by analogy. The third roll in the "Lives of Eminent Monks" says: "Yü Fa-k'ai of White Mountain [Po-shan] in Shah, [a man of the] Tsin was a man whose place of origin is not known. He served the Master [Yü Fa-]lan as a disciple. His profound thought asserted itself uniquely; unaided, he saw beyond words, skilled as he was [at interpreting the "Prajñā Scripture of the] Emission of Light" (*Pañcaviṃśati°*) and the "Lotus of the Dharma" (*Saddharma-puṇḍarīka°*). At the age of sixty-six, he died. By *yü* is meant that his clan surpassed the world.

E-F

Chi-tsang: Sixth, the Dharma-Master Yi says: "The dharmas within the worldly conception are all like magical conjurings. This is why the scripture says, 'Ever since the beginning, there has never been anything existent'". The objection is as follows: The scriptures state that the creations of a magical conjurer have neither sin nor merit. If all dharmas are absolutely the same as the conjurings of a magician, then where on earth is the difference between a real person and a conjured person? Also, the scriptures borrow the [notion of] reality. Anyone who, once the real has departed, still clings to the vacuous has not yet got the scriptures' meaning.

Anchō: "Sixth, the Dharma-Master Yi says...." The "Recondite Doctrine [of the Mountain School]" says: "First was Shih Tao-yi, who published the 'Treatise on the Two Conceptions [from the Standpoint of the] Spirit', in which he said, 'All dharmas are the same as magical conjurings; therefore, they are referred to with the name of the worldly conception. The mind and the spirit, for all that, are still real, not empty; this is the prime meaning. If even the spirit were empty, what would the doctrine have to propound? Who would cultivate the Path, get beyond the common, and achieve the saintly? Thus, one knows that the spirit is not empty'". The rest one may understand by analogy.

"This is why the Scripture says....". The "Restated Meaning", citing the "Scripture of the Great Collection ", scroll 9, says:

> All dharmas are empty and signless,
> Nor is there sequential birth in them.
> Their nature, from the very beginning, is eternally quiescent. There is no one able to create them, just as [is the case with] empty space.

We have just cited this by taking its [essential] meaning. The Buddha was pronouncing himself in *gāthās* in addressing the boddhisattva Sea-Wisdom (*hui hai, prajñasamudra? prajñāsāgara? prajnodadhi?*). "The objection is as follows: The scriptures state ..." It is as, in the thirty-eighth roll in the "Scripture in the Greater [Number of] Chapters" (*Pañcaviṃśatisāhasrikā prajñāpāramita sūtra*), the Buddha addresses Subhūti, saying, "To your mind, how is it? When a magician conjures up a variety of things, whether elephants and horses or men and women and the like, do these conjured beings have any deeds by virtue of which they descend into Hell or go from there anywhere up to and including the place where there is neither perception nor non-perception (*naivasaṃjñānāsaṃjñāyatana*)? Are there, for that matter, any among them who cultivate the Path, or are there not"? "No, O World-Honored One! These dharmas having no reality, how shall this be"? It also says, "'Subhūti, to your mind, how is it? When the Buddha conjures up a man, does this conjured man have any deeds by virtue of which he descends into the Triple Sphere'? Is there [among such men] any who cultivates the Path, or is there not"? "No, World-Honored One! These dharmas having no reality, one may not say so". We have cited this [likewise] by taking [its essential] meaning. The "Restated Meaning" says, "When something is not, then suddenly is, the sense of that is called magic or conjuring (*ke hua*). When something is and is then transformed, the sense of that is called illusion, hallucination (*maboroshi/gen/huan*). "Also, the scriptures borrow the notion of vacuity in order to smash the notion of reality". It is, as in the thirty-eighth roll in the "Scriptures of the Greater [Number of] Chapters", the Buddha says, "The bodhisattva uses *prajñāpāramitā* to create such devises as these, by the power of which he benefits the multitudinous beings, yet he does not cling with greed to this body [of his]. Why is this? The attached person, the manner of his attachment, and the object of his attachment–of these three dharmas, none can be grasped, because they are empty of any nature of their own. The empty cannot cling to the empty, for, with respect to emptiness, there is no one attached nor any object of attachment, the interior of emptiness being marked by emptiness and hence not to be grasped". On the basis of this scriptural text, [it is evident that] what is here called vacuity (*hsü*) is emptiness (*k'ung*) under another name.

The fourth roll in the "Lives of Eminent Monks" says: "(Chu Tao-yi, of the Monastery of the Rejoioing at the Auspicious (*Chia-hsiang-ssu*) north of the mountains, in Tsin [times], was a man of Wu [belonging to the] Lu clan. As a youth, he left his household and received instruction from the honorable Fa-t'ai. His contemporaries dubbed him the *Tu wei-na* of the Nine Provinces. Later, he went for a time to Mount Tiger Hill (*hu ch'iu shah*) in Wu, where, during Lung-an of the Tsin (397-401/2), he met with illness and died. He was then buried south of the mountain, his springs and autumns being seventy and one".

G

Chi-tsang: Seventh, Yü Tao-sui declares: "[the proposition that] existence is due to the meeting of [causes and] conditions is called the worldly conception; [the proposition that] the dispersal of [causes and] conditions is *eo ipso* non-existence is called the conception of prime meaning". The objection is as follows: The scriptures preach the marks of reality without demolishing provisional designation is conventional non-existence, nothing more.

Anchō: "Seventh, Yü Tao-sui...". The "Recondite Doctrine" [of the Mountain School] says: "Seventh,Yü Tao-sui published a 'Treatise on the Two Truths (in the Light of the) Meeting of [Causes and] Conditions', in which he says, 'Existence because of the meeting of [causes and] conditions is the conventional [conception]; reduction to inexistence is the true [conception]. It is, for example, just as earth and wood unite to form a house. The house, [however], having no prior substance [as such], has a name but no reality. This is why the Buddha declared to Rādha, "When the signs of visible matter have been annihilated, there remains nothing to see."," [The rest] may be understood by analogy. "The objection is as follows: The scriptures...". This is a reference to a passage in the thirteenth roll of the "Scripture in the Greater (Number of) Chapters," by resort to which the refutation is made. A full citation of the scriptural text is as given in the second roll of the record [of Chi-tsang]. We are here citing it in brief; however, the scripture says, "the marks of the dharmas," and [Chi-tsang] says, "real marks". By 'marks is meant something like 'substantial marks. The third roll in the "Lives of Eminent Monks" says: "Yü Tao-sui was a Tsin man from Tun-huang. When he reached the age of sixteen, leaving his household, he served Master [Yü Fa-]lan as a disciple.

Later, proposing to accompany [Fa-]lan to the Western Regions, he encountered illness in Chiao-chih and died, his springs and autumns being thirty and one". In the name *tun huang,* the first syllable is read *d*[o-k]*on,* the second [o-k]*uaṇ.* The Tun-huang commandery was created by Emperor Wu during the Hou-yüan years by dividing Chiu-ch'üan. Tu Lin holds that this corresponds to the ancient Kua-chou. *Sui* is read *s*[jīk-z]*ui* and means "deep".

Chi-tsang: We are now, in general, clear on these matters. Yet, rather than become the prisoner of what one's predecessors have acquired, one would do better to reject it all. If [on the other hand] one's mind has nothing to cling to and nothing to gain, and it, in keeping with conditions, one gains intuition, then anything may be used. Also, [the learned men just mentioned were] exclusively persons who took the scriptures and treatises as their authority. Shih Tao-an's 'original non-being', the honorable Chih (Tun's) 'emptiness identical with visible matter', Master Chou's emptiness of provisional designations', and the honorable [Seng-]chao's 'emptiness of the non-absolute', though [going back to] one source, yet differed in their several verbalizations. Hence, all are useful.

Anchō: "We are now, in general, clear...". There follows the second part, the judgement of the several good and bad points, which one may understand fully by analogy.

What makes the present work unique, if the word is appropriate, is that it takes a stand on the meaning of every word, both in Chi-tsang's treatise and in Anchō's commentary.

Here, I have made an exposition in the manner of a chorus of distant echoes on the controversy among the great masters, who have voiced [the abstruse points] of emptiness.

Chapter 6

Buddhist Meditation

Alex Wayman

1. The Two Situations of Buddhist Meditation

The world-wide influence of Buddhist meditation practice began in India some 2500 years ago. It is part of India's profound investigation of the human psyche. To establish the nature of Buddhist meditation it is useful to first allude to its two situations, namely, the not-two and the two. A thoughtful article by D.C. Ahir that appeared in The Maha Bodhi Magazine, 1960, remarks: "Since Buddhism is social, all embracing, if man is alone he need not practise Dhamma but wherever there are two persons Dhamma is a necessity."[1] This important observation needs some explanation. The word 'Dhamma' (Skt. Dharma) here means the rules for right and wrong, and these rules are established by the mind. The Buddhist classic *Dhammapada,* in its initial famous verse, points out: "The *dhammas* are preceded by mind, are chieftained by mind, are made of mind." If it is granted that Dhamma is necessary when there are two persons, why is it not necessary if man is alone? The eighth century Buddhist commentator Buddhaguhya appears to answer this question when he writes: "A cave is a place for seclusion of body (*kāya-viveka*). A monastery, constituting seclusion of thoughts (*citta-viveka*), is not seclusion of body, but better, a place for seclusion of the mind."[2] Now, both these cases are found in Buddhist meditation. The retreat to an isolated place is allowed; and this isolation is suggested to apply to the body, but not to the mind. But especially praised is the restriction of mental activity in the context of Dhamma, practiced jointly by the monks, aided by the spiritual guides (*kalyāṇa-mitra*). Why is this regulation of mind in the situation of social relations called 'better' than the retreat to a cave? The reason must be that it is primary, whether or not one also resorts to a cave. As an example, in Tibet the story of the poet-yogin Milarepa is celebrated. He was first the disciple of the translator Marpa, making two persons initially. Then he meditated in a cave; so the non-two (*advaya*) came afterwards. Thus, the one who goes into a retreat with seclusion of body, does not need Dhamma, because previously he practiced Dhamma along with other persons, and proved his mastery of Dhamma. Having trained his mind, he could proceed to the advanced case of solitary practice.

A scripture, the *Akaṅkkeyya-sutta* (D, I, 33), suggests that the meditator can go back and forth, i.e. forth from the monasterial situation, to the solitary abode; and then back to the personal and social involvement with other monks:

> "Monks, if a monk should wish: 'May I be agreeable to my fellows in the pure life, liked by them, revered and respected,' he should be one who fulfills the moral rules (*śīla*), who is intent on calming the mind (*ceto-samatha*) within, whose meditation (*jhāna*) is uninterrupted, who is endowed with discerning (*vipassanā*), a frequenter of solitary abodes (*suññāgāra*)."

The above distinction of stress on 'body' in the non-two case, and on 'mind' in the two-or-more case appears consistent with the Pāli Abhidhamma work *Puggla-paññatti,* translated as *Designation of Human Types.*[3] Here Chapter I presents the division of human types by one. We find fifty descriptions of persons in terms of their individual progress on the Buddhist path and their partial or complete success toward supernormal faculty, liberation, or enlightenment. Then Chap. II, the division of human types by two, goes into the good and bad natures, with twenty-seven paragraphs, starting "What sort of person is angry? What then is anger?" Āsaṅga is his *Śrāvakabhūmi* uses the term 'embodiment' (*ātmabhāva*), when saying, "Only by oneself does the embodiment achieve..."[4]

The distinction is alluded to somewhat mystically in Candrakīrti's *Madhyamakāvatāra:* "The one whose mind is thwarted must do it in immediacy with the body."[5] The context in which this was cited has to do with the ordering of ritual in the Buddhist Tantras; but there is also the suggestion that eventually one must leave the social situation of the monastery, the superior conventional life, for the isolated retreat, the non-two that is philosophically the absolute. There is a further suggestion that this resort to the body—mystically said to be in a 'cave'—is the beginning of what centuries later would become the tāntric stress on the body.

2. Stations of Mindfulness in Theravāda and Elsewhere

In a discussion of Buddhist meditation, some technicalities are unavoidable; otherwise we would only have some glad sentiments about the greatness of the practice. The *Dasuttara Suttānta* (D, III, 273) says there are two natures (*dhamma*) that help much, namely 'mindfulness' (P. *sati;* S. *smṛti*) and 'awareness' (P. *sampajañña;* S. *saṃprajanya*). From early Buddhism these have been two important terms about meditation. According to Asaṅga's north India school, 'mindfulness' means the non-slipping-away of the meditative object by constantly recalling it to mind – that meditative object being the precept-entity, the mental recitation, obtained from the *guru*. 'Awareness' is what recognizes subtle faults, especially the 'fading away' (*laya*) or the energetic 'scattering' (*auddhatya*) of the meditative object.[6]

The kind of Buddhist meditation that has been most popular in the Theravāda of the Southern or South-east Buddhist countries is the 'stationing of mindfulness' (P. *sati-paṭṭhāna;* S. *smṛty-upasthāna*), following the *Sati-paṭṭhāna Sutta* (*Majjhimanikāya,* no. 10).[7] These stations of mindfulness are four in number: 1) mindfulness of bodies; 2) of feelings (*vedanā*); 3) of thoughts (*citta*) or states of mind; 4) of mental objects (P. *dhamma;* S. *dharma*). It is the meditation on these four over the centuries since the Buddha first preached this scripture that has made Buddhist literature a grand source of precepts about the mind of man. Now I shall present sentences of this scripture, interspersed with comments from other texts or studies.

According to this *Sati-paṭṭhāna Sutta* 1. the monk who would practice 'mindfulness of body' should proceed to a forest, or to the root of a tree, or to a solitary abode. [While the theory of twelve or thirteen ascetic practices called the *dhutāni* is not canonical, it does discuss what kinds of trees are appropriate and so on.[8]] Then he should be mindful of his breaths. So practicing, while breathing out he experiences the whole body and tranquilizes the activity of the body. [According to Buddhaghoṣa, this counters delusion, *moha;* according to Āsaṅga, it counters conjecture, *vitarka.*[9] This also is the topic of the discourse *Ānāpānasati Sutta,* M, no. 118, and has been well treated by modern authors.[10]]. He may contemplate the various kinds of bodies, his own and others. [Asaṅga's *Śrāvakabhūmi,* lists thirty-five kinds of body (*kāya*), starting with his own and others, including also those of beings in the five destinies, i.e., hell being, etc.[11]] He is advised to be mindful of his bodily postures, whether walking, standing, sitting down, or lying down. [The *Mahā-Suññatā Sutta,* M, no. 122, combines these four postures with contemplation of voidness, internally and externally; and uses the term 'awareness' (P. *sampajañña*); accordingly, when walking, etc., the monk has awareness that he is not invaded by evil, unvirtuous natures]. This mindfulness extends to his setting out and returning; carrying his outer cloak, begging bowl, and robe; eating and obeying calls of nature. [And *Dhammapada,* 299: "The disciples of the Buddha are always well awake; their mindfulness (*sati*) is always, day and night, stationed on their body (*kāyagata*)."] Besides, he may visualize his bodily parts from the soles of the feet up and from the crown of the head down, noticing that all these parts are full of impurities. [The scripture's list is counted as thirty-two parts of the body, beginning with 'head-hair'; again countering 'lust' (*rāga*).][12] He analyzes the body into the four elements of water, earth, fire, and wind. [This promotes skill (*kauśalya*) in the elements; according to Āsaṅga countering pride (*māna*).][13] He may contemplate the decaying corpse in the charnel ground. [Buddhaghoṣa and Āsaṅga agree that this counters lust.[14] According to the great *Prajñāpāramitā,* a Mahāyāna Buddhist scripture, the traditional nine contemplations of decaying corpse counter respectively nine cravings, beginning with 'idea of corpse swollen with putrefaction' counters 'craving for shapes'.][15] [Besides, M, no. 119, the *Kāyagatā sati Sutta,* after presenting approximately the same statements as above about mindfulness of body, lists ten advantages to be gained from the full practice of body mindfulness: (1) one conquers aversion and attraction; (2) as well as fear and dread; (3) one can bear cold, heat, hunger, thirst; touch of insects; harsh words, and fierce pains; (4) one easily attains the four Jhāna (S. *dhyāna*) [i.e., the four levels of the 'realm of form' (*rūpaloka*)]; (5) also the faculty of magical change (S. *ṛddhi*); (6) as well as divine hearing; (7) knowledge of others' minds; (8) and of one's past lives; (9) the divine eye, which sees beings going to various destinies according to *kamma* (*S. karma*), (10) in the present life one eliminates the fluxes (*āsava*) and realizes the liberation in mind (*cetovimutti*) and liberation in insight (*paññāvimutti*)].

Then the *Sati-paṭṭhnāna Sutta* refers to 2. 'mindfulness of feelings'. When a monk is experiencing a pleasant feeling, he well knows "I am experiencing a pleasant feeling". Likewise, if the feeling is unpleasant or if it is neutral. And well knows of these three kinds of feelings (*sukha, dukkha, adukkha* and *asukha*) whether they are for material or for immaterial things; whether they are personal or external; whether they are 'origination natures' (*samudayadhamma*) or 'dissolution natures' (*vaya-dhamma*) or 'origination-dissolution natures' (*samudayavaya-dhamma*). Or, he thinks, "There is feeling," without relying on anything in the world, but just for knowledge and for mindfulness. ['Origination-natures' refers to the second Noble Truth, the source of suffering; 'dissolution-natures' refers to attaining the summit of the formless realm called 'cessation of notions and feelings' (*saññāvedita-nirodha*); 'origination-dissolution natures' refers to the position of 'feelings' in Buddhist 'dependent origination. (S *pratītya-samutpāda*) where it is no. 7 concluding the first seven members, the determinate series, hence 'feelings' here are the passive enjoyment, pain, or neutral feeling—the person cannot help but have them; it is sometimes taught that *Nirvāṇa* is attained by transcending feelings.][16]

The *Sati-paṭṭhāna Sutta* goes to 3. 'mindfulness of thoughts (or, states of mind)'. When the monk has a state of mind 'with lust' (*sa-rāga*), he knows, "It is state of mind with lust". Knows the one free from lust as free from lust. And so on, with the states of mind, with hatred, free from hatred; with delusion, free from delusion; contracted, dispersed; become great, not become great; with a superior to it, without a superior to it; equilibrized (*samāhita*), unequilibrized (*asamāhita*); liberated, not liberated. Or he dwells, experiencing the state of mind in the mind internally, externally, or internally and externally. Or he dwells, experiencing 'origination natures', 'dissolution natures', or 'origination-dissolution natures' in the mind. Or, he thinks, "There is a state of mind," without relying on anything in the world, but just for knowledge and for mindfulness. [The scriptural remark about 'internally', etc. may well be a reference to the theory of the 'Liberations'—the yogin's attainments in the 'realm of form'.[17] And 'origination-dissolution natures' may well be a reference to 'impermanence' (*anityatā*)].

Finally, this scripture treats 4. 'mindfulness of mental objects (*dhamma*)'. The monk contemplates his mental objects, knowing them as present when they are. First the five hindrances: (1) sensuous lust, (2) ill-will, (3) torpor and sleepiness, (4) mental wandering and regret, (5) doubt. [Of these five, it is taught that 'mental wandering and regret' is a hindrance to 'calming (the mind)' (*śamatha*), 'torpor and sleepiness' and 'doubt' are hindrances to 'discerning (the real),' (*vipaśyanā*), while 'sensuous lust' and 'ill-will' are hindrances to both.][18] As previously, the monk should be mindful of 'origination natures', 'dissolution natures', and 'origination-dissolution natures' among these mental objects.

[As *dhamma-s* (S. *dharma*) they are all held to arise dependently.] The monk should contemplate the mental natures in the five grasping aggregates [=the five personal aggregates, called 'grasping' because they pile up]; the mental objects in regard to the six personal and the six external sense bases (*āyatana*); the mental objects in regard to the seven ancillaries of enlightenment (S. *bodhyaṅga*) [according to Āsaṅga's *Śrāvakabhūmi,* the ancillaries of enlightenment, the cathartic (*praśrabdhi*), deep concentration (*samādhi*), and equanimity (*upekṣā*) are in the category of 'calming' (the mind); the ancillaries, analysis of the doctrine (*dharmapravicaya*), striving (*vīrya*), and joy (*prīti*) are in the category of 'discerning' (the real); while mindfulness (*smṛti*) is in both categories].[19] Then the mental objects in regard to the four Noble Truths. Here the monks know as it really is, "This is suffering;" as it really is, "This is the source of suffering;" as it really is, "This is the cessation of suffering;" and as it really is, "This is the path leading to the cessation of suffering." And in all these, as previously, the monk should be mindful of 'origination natures,' etc. Or, he thinks, "There are mental objects," without relying on anything in the world, but just for knowledge and for mindfulness. [Naturally, I have abbreviated the scripture. Asaṅga's *Śrāvakabhūmi* states that the lord established the four kinds of mindfulness to oppose the four contrarieties (*viparyāsa*), namely, to oppose the contrariety that the impure is pure, he established the station of mindfulness toward bodies; to oppose the contrariety that suffering is happiness, he established the station of mindfulness towards feelings; to oppose the contrariety that the impermanent is permanent, he established the station of mindfulness toward states of mind; to oppose the contrariety that non-self is self, he established the station of mindfulness toward mental objects].[20]

Śāntideva's *Śikṣāsamuccaya,* Chap. XIII is devoted to the Mahāyāna Buddhist formulation of the four stations of mindfulness. The citations stress the impurity and regular decay of the body, with a fleeting reference to the Tathāgata's incorruptible body. As to the feelings, the Bodhisattva engenders great compassion (*mahākaruṇā*) for the beings under the sway of feelings. The station of mindfulness on the states of mind finds them to be like illusions. Passing to the mental objects, there is agreement with Āsaṅga's point that this contemplation establishes non-self, because a citation stresses that there is no living being in these mental objects.[21]

Even the Buddhist Tantras did not lose sight of the stations of mindfulness. Thus, the *Sarvarahasya-tantra* in the section dealing with the imagination of the *maṇḍala,* verse 123ab, mentions: "The four stations of mindfulness are understood as the four courtyards." Then the commentary on the same Tantra, its verse 182, states that in the outer courtyards are the sixteen Bodhisattvas, the four in the East, white; the four in the South, yellow; the four in the West, red; the four in the North, green.[22] The tantric imagination makes the stations of mindfulness the palace grounds, here inhabited by the sixteen Bodhisattvas; and in the case of other *maṇḍalas ṛṣi-s* or other spiritually powerful persons are assigned to this location.

Thus the four stations of mindfulness constitute an excellent example of the continuance of early Buddhism into the Mahāyāna and tantric

Buddhism. It may be the case that the early type of Buddhist meditation of the four stations placed the station of mindfulness on bodies in the solitary retreat, and the stations of mindfulness on feelings, states of mind, and mental objects in the monastery—such would be the conclusion consistent with our first section on the two situations of meditation. Śāntideva's *Śikṣāsamuccaya* appears to preserve the early 'body' meditation and to exert the Mahāyāna on the other three. However, in their tantric survival, the four stations of mindfulness become symbolical.

3. Buddhist Meditation and Worship

It is well known that the Buddhists take refuge in the three Jewels (of Buddha, Dharma, and Saṁgha). After the passing of the Buddha, the Dharma was the authority for the monks. Therefore, from the outset it was the monks who were the exponents of the Dharma, the doctrine of Buddhism; and we have already observed that it was the monks themselves, who constitute the core of the Saṁgha, that furnished the meditators in the two situations as was discussed above. But it seems to have been the Buddhist laymen who worshipped the Jewel of the Buddha in the form of the *stūpa* which they honored by circumambulating.[23] Therefore, in the beginning Buddhist meditation and Buddhist worship were two separate matters. It appears to have taken some centuries before the monks would also circumambulate *stūpas;* and taken still longer before laymen could also become expert in the Dharma and practice Buddhist meditation. In short, there came a time when worship and Buddhist meditation were combined, sometimes by monks, sometimes by devout laymen.

The early form of Buddhist art was aniconic. Buddha could be worshipped in various forms of this art, the *stūpa,* the Buddha footprint, and so on. About the first century, A.D. the Buddha image appears, along with the Bodhisattva ideal, and these Bodhisattvas can be lay or monk. Later with the rise of Buddhist tantrism, the *gurus* and candidates could be laymen as well as monks. So now the two situations were the home and the monastery.

After the creation of the Buddha image, and the multiplication of Buddhas to derive Amitābha, etc., there arose a group of celestial Bodhisattvas, such as Mañjuśrī and Avalokiteśvara, as well as fierce and mild deities. It was possible to become a follower of one or more by daily serving the deity, and in the case of the great Bodhisattvas reciting the 108 names. This shows worship, but not necessarily meditation. Meditation necessarily enters in what is called the seven-membered rite of 'supreme worship' (*anuttarapūjā*) of Bodhisattva ritual: 1. praising the deity; 2. offering of flowers, etc.; 3. confession of sins before an imagined celestial Bodhisattva or (more difficult) the thirty-five visualized 'Buddhas of Confession'; 4. sympathetic delight with the merit of Buddhas and Bodhisattvas; 5. entreaty for the Buddha to continue to teach in the world; 6. generating in the Mind of Enlightenment, done ritually; and 7. transfer of merit, namely, to all the sentient beings.[24]

Meditation practice is mandatory for some kinds of tantric worship. This is when these rites involve identification with the deity, or imaginary generation of the deity in front, sometimes with his (or her, i.e., the 'goddess') retinue. Such rites operate in three avenues: body with symbolical gestures called *mudrā* ('seal'), speech with incantations (*mantra*), and mind with deep concentration (*samādhi*). These three, when coordinated, are held to affiliate the performer with the three mysteries of the Buddha (his Body, Speech, and Mind).

Samādhi is optimum for the general tantric rite. Mandatory is 'conviction' (*adhimukti*) for making any rite 'work', to achieve the results that are promised. Indeed, whenever the directions of materials to be put in flasks, etc. involve items, such as jewels, that are unobtainable, it does not matter, if the performer is convinced that such items are present in the flasks, etc; and it appears that if the performer is not convinced of such things, his imaginative power is not equal to the task of performing the ritual effectively.[25]

This information suggests that the tantric rites with their kind of meditation, sometimes involving imagination of a deity with multiple arms each of which carry in hand a different emblem, make advanced demands on the meditator. Ordinarily, one should have succeeded in an easier meditation, such as those presented above as the four stations of mindfulness. It is explained that when the disciple has been given a meditative object by his *guru* he should continue on this same object until he is successful to some degree in meditation, perhaps taking six months for it (a frequently mentioned period).[26] His success in the *samādhi* is indicated, according to the classical accounts, by a sensation of lightness called *karmaṇyatā* and a sensation that a purifying 'wind' called *praśrabdhi* courses through his body and mind. These are signs that the performer has surmounted the 'realm of desire' (*kāma-dhātu*) and has arrived at the threshold of the 'realm of form' (*rūpa-dhātu*) in which he may develop a certain amount of supernormal faculty.[27] It is explained that when someone has succeeded in any meditative object in this manner, he can go on to any other meditative object, even tantric worship, with the prospect of success. Given this prior attainment of a Buddhist *samādhi,* one can take up such tantric *samādhi* as imagination of the *maṇḍala,* both the residence or hallowed place, and the residents or the deities that are invited to take their places on the lotus petals, etc.

To illustrate this tantric kind of Buddhist meditation, I now translate the brief text no. 173 in the *Sādhana-mālā,* among the evocations (*sādhana*) of the goddess Kurukullā.[28]

> At first the *mantrin* (i.e., the tantric performer) seats himself in a comfortable seat. By means of rays from the seed syllable in his own heart, he draws toward him in front, the Lordess as well as Buddhas and Bodhisattvas and worships them, and should perform the set beginning with triple refuge. Thus (i.e., how it is done), being convinced of voidness, and being empowered by the *mantra,* he should imagine (in the void) an "A", from it a moon arising, thereon a "TĀM" which has a garland of rays. He sees that changing into the Lordess Kurukullā who is red, seated with diamond posture on a solar seat which is on a red eightpetalled lotus. She has six hands. In the first right and left hands she bears the seal (*mudrā*) 'Victory over the Three Worlds'. In the second right and left hands she bears a hook and a red lotus. With the remaining two hands she extends a bow and arrow 'up to the ear'. She wears a red garment. Has the five Tathāgatas (i.e., Buddhas) in her crest. In the heart of the performer (*sādhya*), on the seed vessel of a red lotus, on a moon-disk, he should contemplate a "TĀM" colored red, and that elevated on a wind-disk. With her hook she pierces him in the heart and draws him near. Having entered his heart, she pierces the performer again and again by arrows made of red lotus buds. He should recite the *mantra:* OM KURUKULLE HRIH AMUKAM ME VAŚAM ĀNAYA HOH, SVĀHĀ "Om. Kurukullā, reduce me, named so-and-so, to thy subjection! Hoḥ Svāhā."
>
> Then, having seen him trembling, brought to subjection, fallen at her feet, she dismisses him. In that way, she brings to subjection even Śakra (i.e., Indra, lord of the gods).

I have in the foregoing presented only a small indication of Buddhist meditation in its vast array of *samādhis* over the many centuries. These precepts, as so many pearls handed down from the Indian gurus, have a sublime message for this world plunged in a morass of material pursuits. It is indeed a privilege for me to have been permitted a small glimpse into these spiritual practices that began in India so long ago.

References

1. As reprinted in *Buddhist Digest; English Series* 7 (Young Buddhist Association of Malaysia, May, 1984).
2. Buddhaguhya's commentary on the *Vairocanābhisambodhi-tantra,* Japanese photo, edn. of Tibetan canons, Vol. 77, p. 162-5, line 4.
3. Bimala Charan Law, *Designation of Human Types* (Pali Text Society London, 1922).
4. Alex Wayman, tr., *Calming the Mind and Discerning the Real* (Columbia University Press, New York, 1978), p. 33.
5. Ferdinand D. Lessing and Alex Wayman, trs., *Mkhas grub rje's Fundamentals of the Buddhist Tantras* (Mouton, The Hague, 1968), p. 239.
6. Wayman, tr., *Calming the Mind,* p. 124.
7. Cf. Nyanaponika Thera, *The Heart of Buddhist Meditation* (The Citadel Press, New York, 1969), pp. 11-12.
8. P.V. Bapat, *Vimuttimagga and Visuddhimagga, a Comparative Study* (Poona, 1937), Chap. III.
9. Alex Wayman, "Aspects of Meditation in the Theravāda and Mahīśāsaka," *Studia Missionalia,* Vol. 25, 1976, pp. 4-5.
10. For example, *Ñāṇamoli* Thera, tr., *Mindfulness of Breathing: Ānāpānasati* (Buddhist Publication Society, Kandy, 3rd ed., 1973); Buddhadāsa Bhikkhu, tr. by Bhikkhu Nāgasena, *Ānāpānasati* (*Mindfulness of Breathing*) (Sublime Life Mission, Bankok, 1971).
11. Alex Wayman, *Analysis of the Śrāvakabhūmi Manuscript* (University of California Press, Berkeley, 1961), p. 97.
12. Bhikkhu Khantipālo, *Bag of Bones; a miscellany on the body* (Buddhist Publication Society, Kandy, 1980), pp. 11-13.
13. Wayman, "Aspects of Meditation", pp. 4-5.
14. Wayman, "Aspects", pp. 4-5.
15. Wayman, tr., *Calming the Mind,* p. 444, n. 41.
16. Cf. Nyanaponika Thera, *Contemplation of Feeling* (Buddhist Publication Society, Kandy, 1983), notes, p. 37.
17. Cf. Paravahera Vajirañāṇa Mahathera, *Buddhist Meditation in Theory and Practice* (M.D. Gunasena & Co., Colombo, 1962), p. 62: or, Wayman, "Aspects", p. 20.
18. Wayman, tr., *Calming the Mind,* p. 451, n. 147.
19. Wayman, *Analysis,* p. 101.
20. Wayman, *Analysis,* p. 98.
21. Cf. Cecil Bendall and W.H.O. Rouse, *Śikṣā-samuccaya* (John Murray, London, 1922).
22. Alex Wayman, *The Sarvarahasyatantra* (Studies of Mysticism in Honor of the 1150th Anniversary of Kobo-daishi's Nirvāṇam, *Acta Indo-logica,* Volume VI, 1984), pp. 521-569.
23. Akira Hirakawa, "The Rise of Mahāyāna Buddhism and its Relationship to the Worship of Stupas," *Memoirs of the Research Department of The Toyo Bunko,* No. 22 (1963).

24. Alex Wayman, "Buddhism, *Historia Religionum II* (E.J. Brill, Leiden, 1971), p. 402.
25. Lessing and Wayman, *Mkhas grub rje's,* states this in many places for example, p. 297.
26. Wayman, tr., *Calming the Mind,* p. 115.
27. Wayman, tr., *Calming the Mind,* pp. 148-153.
28. Benoytosh Bhattacharya, ed., *Sādhanamālā,* Vol. II (Oriental Institute, Baroda, 1968), text, pp. 350-351.

Chapter 7
Buddha's Message of Universal Compassion and Altruism

S.R. Bhatt

The advent of Śākyamuni, the Buddha, the beacon light of India and the entire world, has been a significant event in the history of world culture and civilization. Born in a princely family with all material prosperity and physical comforts, he was awakened by the pain and suffering, finitude and evanescence of the mundane life. After intensive study, deep reflections and profound meditation he gained insight into the nature of reality and the phenomenal world. Having attained enlightenment he did not remain self-centered. He was not contented with his own emancipation and strived for the liberation of the suffering beings. He showed to the humanity the sure path of *Nirvāṇa*, a way to eradicate suffering and to escape from the labyrinth of the cycle of birth and death, which consisted of a symbiosis of wisdom and conduct, ethics and meditative practice. He realized the 'Four Noble Truths', practiced them in his own life and subsequently enlightened people about it. That is why he was regarded as a great healer (*Bhaiṣajya Guru*) and a liberator (*Tāyin*).

The concept of *Mahākaruṇā* (Universal compassion) plays a pivotal role in the Buddhistic mode of thinking and way of living. The Buddha advised the fellow monks as follows:–

"O Monks! Move around every where for the well-being of every one, showering compassion on the entire world; for the good, for the welfare, for the happiness of divine and human."

But the *Mahākaruṇā* is not just to be taught or talked about, but it is to be translated in action through proper and adequate endeavor (*upāya kauśala*) fructifying in enhancement of quality of life and attainment of excellences (*pāramitās*).

Like the Buddha, the Bodhisattvas also exhibit *Mahākaruṇā* by resolving to suffer the torments of others, by striving for the enlightenment of others (*sarvamukti*) and by postponing one's own *Nirvāṇa* till such time every one else also gets *Nirvāṇa*. They are happy in the happiness of others and unhappy when others are unhappy. They are 'Engaged Buddhists' actively participating in social upliftment. They are manifestations of *Dharmakāya* whose all motives, efforts and actions pivot on the furtherance of universal welfare without distinction or discrimination.

A Bodhisattva is comparable to a *Sthitaprajña* of the Bhagavadgītā who has *samatva* (equanimity of mind) and *samadṛṣṭi* (realization of similarity and commonality of experience with all sentient beings), and who is *sarvabhūtahiterataḥ* (constantly engaged in benevolent activities for the well-being of all beings) Benevolent temper permeates his life in a natural way. A Bodhisattva practices four psycho-physical modes of value-oriented living known as *Brahmavihāras*, viz., *Maitri, karuṇā, muditā* and *upekṣā*. *Maitri* stands for love, respect and care for all lives. It is lived through the concreteness of loving kindness based on the feeling that just as our life is precious to us so also is the life of others. *Karuṇā* is universal compassion. *Muditā* is altruistic sympathetic joy. It is happiness in the happiness of all. *Upekṣā* stands for equanimity of mind, impartiality and compassion to all beings without discrimination. Such a mode of thinking and living helps in the cultivation of selflessness or egolessness that provides a basis for widening of the self.

In the Jātakamālā there is a story that needs to be meditated and practised particularly by those who aspire to be the rulers either as politicians or legislators. It is very much pertinent and relevant to modern times. In one of the previous births the Śākyamuni was a monkey-chief living in deep Himalayan forests. His abode was a big banyan tree bearing in abundance large, juicy and deliciously sweet fig fruits. One branch of that tree hung over a stream that flowed towards the plains. The wise and farsighted monkey-chief warned his tribe not to allow fruits to be born on that branch as that will one day give rise to the situation in which they will never be able to eat the fruits of other branches as well. The fellow monkeys paid heed to his advice and acted accordingly. But eventually one fig fruit grew up unnoticed by them under the cover of a large leaf. The ripened crop was swept away by the water of the stream and reached the hands of a royal lady in the plains. She presented it to the king who ate and relished it so intensely that he longed to eat more of such fruits. So along with his troop he set forth towards the mountain in search of the tree which yielded that fruit. He could spot out the tree on which monkeys were feasting on the fruits. Angrily the king ordered his troop to drive away or kill the monkeys. The soldier started attacking the monkeys. When the monkey chief saw this calamity and witnessed his distressed and endangered people who called for his help and protection his heart melted with compassion. He was wise and valiant. He immediately climbed to the top of the tree, sprang to the peak of the mountain, picked up a cane lying there, tied its one end to his leg, jumped back to the tree, threw back the other end over to the peak of the mountain and commanded his tribe to cross over to the mountain for safety. The fellow monkeys in haste and panic rushed over his body to escape but he did not mind it. He continued to suffer pain and wound on his back till every one crossed over. His back had broken and he was seriously injured.

The king who was witnessing the scene from below wondered about the wisdom, compassion and self-sacrifice of the monkey chief. He asked his troop to spread a net beneath the seriously injured monkey chief, very carefully cut through arrow the cane tied to his leg so that he was not hurt any more. The monkey chief fell on the net. He was put on a coach and given medical treatment applying healing oil. The king, overcome with admiration, approached him with great respect and wonder. He inquired from the monkey chief as to why he did he sacrifice his life for the sake of other monkeys to save them. The monkey chief replied, "All the monkeys had given me the responsibility of being their ruler. It was a onerous and burdensome job but I accepted it. So I was duty-bound to save them cherishing the affection of a father for his children". The king foolishly asked that it should be the other way round. The people are meant to serve the ruler and the ruler has only to rule over them. With a bright face and joy the monkey chief replied, "This is a degenerated political wit. This is not wisdom. For a wise person it is not possible to overlook suffering even if the sufferer is a stranger. In this case all are my people. Since I alleviated the distress of those whom I ruled and who showed me affection and reverence, I am happy to embrace death for their sake. It is a great occasion for me as I have saved all of them." The monkey king gave departing advice to the human king that it is the duty of the ruler to endeavor wholeheartedly and selflessly to endow his people with happiness and well-being. Only then he can be really happy and prosperous. Otherwise he enjoys only sadistic pleasure.

Chapter 8

Buddhist Compassion as a Principle of Reconciliation

S.K. Kim

1

Western civilization in laying more emphasis on material progress, has brought about a disparity between the theory and the practice of philosophy, and has kept science apart from religion, and metaphysics from ethics. This dualistic attitude of the west has been responsible for the social crisis and political conflicts that have disrupted the normal life of individuals and have brought man to the brink of committing atomic suicide. In spite of man's mastery over the nature, the common man of the world is not at peace. Doubt, despondency and fear are rife in the world today. The most progressive countries are in the greatest danger of meeting doom if war breaks out. In the face of these circumstances the need of the hour is the spiritual regeneration of human society. There is no doubt that the ethical ideals laid down by Indian sages thousands of years ago are universal standards that can be followed at all times, and are a lasting cure for the evils which have crept into modern society. This is true because these ideals were never regarded as mere theories of morality, but as modes of spiritual life by adopting which the individual and society could develop in a reconcilable manner. This need can be met only when Buddhist Compassion as a Principle of Reconciliation is carried out.

2

The aim of present chapter is to illuminate the real meaning of Buddhist compassion.

Compassion (*karuṇā*) has been the first and foremost among the five-fold virtues, which form the core and essence of Hindu ethics and are known by various names, such as *pañcaśīla, pañcayāma* or *pañca-mahā-vrata*. Compassion, in its wide sense, is defined as abstention from a desire to harm any creature in any circumstance in any manner, by action, speech or thought. Positively speaking, it is universal love. The Buddhistic preaching about compassion (*karuṇā*) has a universal appeal. The *Dhammapada* defines nobility as harmlessness to creatures. It recommends compassion on the basis of self-analogy.

In the *Pāli Tripiṭaka* a regularly mentioned precept is abstinence from killing any living being. In the physical realm of existence this meant that any slaughter of animals, from the grub-worms in the earth to the majestic elephant, was the result of violence and should be avoided. One should not kill a living being out of hate, out of fear for one's self, or to accumulate wealth (*artha*). In general, the ideal of compassion (*karuṇā*) has been an important ethical norm throughout Buddhist history.

Besides restrictions on harm and killing, there were positive noble emotions that all people were to cultivate: friendliness, compassion, sympathetic joy at the happiness of others, and equainimity. In the "Mettāsutta" of the Sutta-Nipāta, for example, we read the following admonition:

> As a mother at the risk of her life watches over her own child, her only child, so also let everyone cultivate a boundless (friendly) mind, above and below and across, unobstructed, without hatred, without enmity.

This notion of compassion applied not only to all beings but also to one's own self. Absence from overt violent behavior was not enough; rather, a spiritual attitude required the effort to pervade all beings with thoughts of loving kindness. Such a social emotion was itself a prescription of the Buddha's teachings for one could, thereby, experience a reduction in the pseudo-isolation of a self caught in fear and anxiety, or exhausted by the strain of maintaining self-sufficiency. The act of caring for others could be a condition for a new self-awareness.

It is in the *Mahāyāna* Buddhist literature, beginning with the *Prajñāpāramitā-sūtra*, that compassion is central to attaining the supreme enlightenment. Showing 'great compassion (*mahākaruṇā*)' is a manifestation of the bodhisattva's perfect insight into the emptiness of all existing things. In The Large *Sutra* on Perfect Wisdom, for example, the extreme case of enduring animal aggression through fulfilling great compassion is given:

> When confronted with those who struggle to kill him, the bodhisattva renounces himself with supreme patience for the

> sake of those very beings and does them no harm. In this way ....you should know that the bodhisattva, when he fulfills the great compassion for the sake of beings, is even on the way to his supreme enlightenment, reborn as an animal, but is not tainted by the faults of animal life.

Loss of one's own life for the sake of someone else is seen as the supreme test of patience and a serene mind. The compassion expressed without hope of reward for oneself manifests a consciousness that is balanced and unwavering. A bodhisattva voluntarily participates in the world; he "becomes ill" because of his vow to save living beings who are subject to illness. Not one being in the universe exists by itself. All beings depend on one another, help one another, and reform themselves constantly in order to maintain reconciliation between them. Such a phenomenon may be referred to as people living in the great compassion of the *Tathāgata*, religiously. Likewise, when one surveys the Buddhist's ethics from the point of the law of the *Pratītyasamutpāda* the essential idea of Buddhist's ethics is to manifest the great compassion of the *Tathāgata*.

One cannot expect illness or violence to go away in our present world; through great compassion and insight, however, one need not fear, and one can be in the psychological, political, commercial, intellectual realms and even in the world of religious institutions without being bound by the distorting forces found there. The solution to violence in light of great compassion is not escape or retaliation; it is a transformation of distorted forces into a reconciliation of movement.

3

Today, violence prevails all over the world. As stated above, the *Mahāyāna* Buddhism's particular character is the practice of the mind of a Bodhisattva which may be successfully performed through a movement to work for others with body and soul. *Mahā-vaipulya-buddha-avatamsaka-sūtra* teaches us that providing the necessities of life to those who are poor, preaching the truth to those who suffer from agony, and giving guidance to those who are ignorant is the ultimate of practicing compassion. Social orders can not be established when violence prevails as in modern society. Should we not make every effort to reestablish social order based on the spirit of a *Mahāyāna* Bodhisattva's compassion, to restore mutual cooperation between families, between societies, and between nations, and to realize a society and a nation of co-existence and co-prosperity, of mutual aid, and of interdependency?

Chapter 9

Ecological Significance and Contemporary Relevance of *Dhammacakkappavattanasutta*

S.R. Bhatt

The seminal and foundational text of *Dhammacakkappavattanasutta*, containing the first sermon of Śākya Muni, the Buddha, delivered at Sarnath in India, is not only the base and the starting point of all *Budhavacanas* but also has various such dimensions, both theoretical and practical, which have great academic importance and contemporary relevance. All significant and basic Buddhist doctrines and practices stem from it and therefore its value is both historical and doctrinal. It is no doubt the first discourse of the Buddha after having attained enlightenment; it is also the essence of Buddha's teachings and a point of reference for all subsequent expositions of Buddhist thought and culture. It is rightly regarded as the foundation on which the entire edifice of Buddhism is erected. All the three *Piṭakas* and the subsequent literature are nothing but elaborations and expositions of the fundamental ideas enunciated in this text. Since all basic doctrines of Buddhism spring and emanate from this first and foremost *Sutta*, it occupies a unique place among the *Buddhavacanas*. In the contemporary times its message for ecological thinking and mode of living is highly relevant and significant. The present chapter attempts to work it out by giving a general background of the *Sutta*.

The contents of this *Sutta* are multifaceted and varied touching different facets of empirical life and reality, but they are all interwoven in a holistic and integral understanding and realization, a symbiosis of *prajñā* and *karuṇā*, *śīla* and *samādhi*. Therefore its multidimensional nature admits of diversified treatment from different perspectives in accordance with the temperaments, needs, aspirations and value-pursuits of different ages and different societies. The contents of this text are addressed not to a particular section of humanity at a particular time but they have universal appeal, importance and value. The adjective *chakka* symbolizes its perennial significance and relevance. It also suggests its all round permeation and pervasion in all spheres of life and reality. The word *pavattana* implies that *dharma* and its *śāsana* (promulgation) need to be propagated again and again incessantly. Every word of this caption has to be understood in its proper and exact connotation. Then only its real meaning and significance can be worked out and practiced. A fresh look at and analysis of this significant *Sutta* is the need of the contemporary times as the Buddhist ecumenism has the capacity to provide newer insights and fresh pathways to the present day suffering humanity provided it is approached in an unbiased manner with *samyagdṛṣṭi* free from all narrow considerations.

II

In this text the Buddha taught loving care and respect of nature and natural objects. The physical and mental ecological considerations are quite prominent in the Buddhist thought and mode of living. The path shown by him, known as *madhyama pratipad*, consisted of a symbiosis of wisdom and conduct, ethics and meditative practices. He visualized the 'Four Eternal Truths' and practiced them in the form of 'Eightfold Eternal Path' in his own life and being assured of their veracity he moved around to enlighten people about it. The *nidāna* (diagnosis) and the *upāya* (cure) put forth by him were so efficaciously redeeming that people revered him as *Bhaiṣajya Guru*. During his life time itself he was regarded as *Tāyin* ('Great Saviour'), *Buddha* (an Enlightened Seer), *Sarvajña* (Omniscient Person) and *Sugata* (i.e., one who has visualized and realized the *summum bonum* of life).

The Buddha has been one of the finest products of Indian culture. He was an inheritor of an old tradition as well as a creator of a new outlook. He inherited a rich and varied cultural tradition of a very high order and formulated and established a new culture out of it which was theoretically enlightening and practically redeeming from the labyrinth of suffering, imperfection, impermanence and vicissitudes of life. He showed an old path, a middle path, which avoided all extremes and which attracted the elites and the masses alike. In his own words, "Even so have I O Monk! seen an ancient way, an ancient road, traversed by the supremely enlightened ones of the older times." (Samyutta Nikāya, I, p. 106)

The Buddha was a very well read and well-versed person with a critical bent of mind, subtle logical acumen and deep understanding of human nature and psychology. He was well steeped in the traditional Indian wisdom and drew his ideas and inspirations from it. He was fully exposed to the rich and varied cultural milieu of his times. He was not born in an intellectual void and his ideas did not grow in a cultural vacuum or in isolation from his social surrounding. In fact they also sprang up as resurgent thoughts protesting against the distortions in and deviations from the Vedic lore that crept in later on in the vast temporal canvass of Indian history. In the words of Mrs. Rhys Davids, "He was the greatest, and wisest, and best of that long line of reformers who have tried to infuse new strength into the religious life of India." (Buddhism, p. 83).

The Buddha had an open and assimilative mind and accommodated all those noble and sublime ideas available in the intellectual and meditational environment of his time that were agreeable to his experiences. But the way he reformulated them was innovative and attractive and that is why he could impress upon and command respect and following of millions of people. He was a wise and practical person fully knowledgeable of human psychology. He not only discerned the inner cravings of human heart and intellect, he also knew the logic and language in which he was to communicate with fellow human beings.

The Buddha was a path breaker and a path setter. He founded a new monastic order known as samgha and gave a novel turn to the institution of *samnyāsa* directing it for universal well-being and happiness. He not only formulated newer objectives and new techniques, he also provided them newer modes of living in mutual care and share with a spirit of cooperation and sacrifice, with compassionate love and tolerance. He advised the fellow monks to come out of their narrow shells, move around and work for the universal good and happiness. His famous and well-known exhortation to the members of the *saṃgha* is as follows:

"Caratha bhikkave cārikam, bahujana hitāya bahujana sukhāya, lokānukampāya atthaya, hitāya, sukhāya devamanussānam".

i.e., "O Monks! Move around for the well being of every one, for the happiness of every one, showering compassion on the entire world; for the good, for the welfare, for the happiness of divine and human." (Vinaya Piṭaka I, 23)

His popularity spread far and wide and his teachings provided solace and succour to the distressed people. He wandered from one place to another along with his disciples conversing with people in the language and idiom familiar to them. He mastered the art of discussion and debate and spread the radiance of his enlightened knowledge and conduct without taking rest out of loving mercy and compassion for the suffering beings. He convinced people with his wit and wisdom, selfless service and painstaking benevolence. Though he did not write anything his teachings were preserved and subsequently codified by his disciples who very diligently and intelligently collated and compiled them with mutual consultation. His teachings were not theoretical and were exemplified in his conduct and in that of his disciples. Because of their practical nature it was easy to remember and recapitulate them.

The origin and spread of Buddhism has been a landmark in the history of Greater India the boundaries of which covered a large part of Asia. Its introduction, preservation, propagation and furtherance in entire Asia in ancient times and in Europe and America in modem times have been significant events in the cultural history of humankind. It would be interesting and academically important to reconstruct the story of this wonderful phenomenon. It is a huge task, a matter of research and teamwork. I hope some day it may see the light of the day.

III

The *Dhammacakkappavattanasutta* is a concise encyclopedia of Buddhist thought and culture. It contains the essential and fundamental teachings of the Buddhist way of thinking and living. The Four Eternal Truths and the Middle Path, the doctrine of *pratītyasamutpāda,* the *trilakṣaṇas* of *anityatā, duḥkkha* and *anattā* of the empirical world along with *nirvāṇa* known as '*catvāri dharmapadāni*', the doctrines of *karma* and *samsāra*, of *dhyāna* and *śīla*, of *prajñā* and *karuṇā*, of *pañcaskandha* and their *samghāta* all are contained in this tract in some form or the other.

Buddha's teachings of eradication of egocentricity and cultivation of existential openness and universal sameness based on the principles of dependent origination, interdependence, interconnectedness and essenselessness of all phenomena enunciated in the famous doctrine of *pratītyasamutpāda* are remarkable and the most distinguishing features of Buddhism that have great relevance and significance in contemporary times and in the new millennium to bring about universal peace, harmony, prosperity and well being. It is rightly characterized as *yuktirāja, guhyakośa, gambhīra, prajñābhūmi* etc. to highlight this fact. The doctrine of *pratītyasamutpāda* has three facets of *idampratyayatā* or *hetupratyayatā* (causally dependent origin of all phenomena), *nissvabhāvatā* or *śūnyatā* or *prapañcarūpatā* (essenselessness of all phenomena) and *parasparāśrayatā* (interdependent and interrelated existence of all phenomena). It is not any one of them alone as has been sometimes misunderstood by some scholars. Any controversy in this regard is misplaced and unwarranted. The significance of this doctrine lies in this that it presents both the *nidāna* (diagnosis) and the *upāya* (cure) of the miseries and evanescence of the empirical world. It makes us realize the truth that all existences and experiences are relative and conditional. Nothing has absolute and independent or exclusive existence. The mistake lies in regarding them as otherwise. In the world phenomena are mutually exclusive as well as interdependent. The reality, thought and language abide by the regulation of *apoha* according to which every one is *svatovyavartaka*, i.e., complement of its compliment and negative of its negative.

There are different formulations of the doctrine of *pratītyasamutpāda* in terms of nine, ten, eleven or twelve *angas* but the last one is most popular. The difference is only from the point of view of *upāyakauśala* (expediency). It is also classified in terms of *trikāṇḍas* or *trayadhvikas*, the first two pertaining to the past, the last two to the future and the remaining eight to the present time. It is also classified as *avidyā, tṛṣṇā* and *upādāna* giving rise to *kleśa, samskāra* and *bhava* to *karma*, and *nāmarūpa, vijñāna, āyatana, sparśa, vedanā jāti* and *jarāmaraṇa* to *duḥkha*. Another classification is in terms of *kṣaṇika, prākarṣika, sāmbandhika* and *āvasthika*. All these details are useful in proper understanding of the nature of the empirical world and the phenomenal existence. One who understands this gets rid of all suffering and afflictions. This is *nirvāṇa*. This is *paramam sukham*, which is the sumum bonum of life. This is the wish expressed in the saying, *"Sabbe sattā sukhi hontu"* (Let all creatures be happy).

The doctrine of *pratītyasamutpāda* is really very *gambhīra* and not very easy to understand. It is not just to be studied or analyzed or appreciated as the most fundamental or central etc. Its real meaning and connotation is to be understood which would automatically fructify into practice. *Prajñā* has to be accompanied by *upāya*. Then it would provide a ground for individual, social and cosmic change for betterment and for universal well-being. By pointing out causal origin of *kuśala* and *akuśala dharmas* it points out the necessity of removal of pathological causes and cultivation of those that are conducive to good. The same is the case with other Buddhistic doctrines propounded in this Sutta.

IV

The "Four Eternal truths" and the doctrine of '*pratītyasamutpāda*' as a corollary there from, have deep ecological significance. From the

Second Eternal Truth it follows that all empirical phenomena have causal origin. Nothing is self-existing. Everything is caused by a set of causal conditions. Given the causal collocations the phenomena occur and in the absence of them they cannot take place (*Asmin sati idam bhavati*). The Third Eternal Truth entails that by the removal of causal collocation the effect also gets removed. The Majjim Nikāya (Pali Text Society, London, Vol. I, p. 134) says, "When that exists this comes to be; on the arising of that this arises. When that does not exist, this does not come to be. On the cessation of that this ceases." This implies that both ecological equilibrium and disequilibrium are causal happenings. They are caused by human conduct. Human being is the most evolved species in the cosmic evolution and he has acquired the capacity to preserve nature or harm nature. So all ecological disturbances and environmental pollutions are our making. We are responsible for this. Since we are the most evolved we are the most responsible being. We therefore carry a universal responsibility not to create ecological imbalance and to rectify whatever imbalance we have made because of our folly. Our entire actions stem from our consciousness, says the Buddha. If we have pure consciousness (*kuśala citta*) our actions will be good and conducive to well-being. If we have impure consciousness our actions will certainly be bad and they will lead to all miseries and sufferings. Through our actions we help or harm others and ourselves. All our thoughts, words and deeds are results of our past actions and shape our experiences of the present and the future. What we shall be depends on what we are at present and how we behave in the present. We have therefore to cultivate *samyak dṛṣṭi* (right attitude) towards life and reality. We have to follow the Middle Path. We have only to cater to our needs and not to feed our greed. We have to avoid extremes of indulgence and abstinence. We have become too much selfish, consumerists and exploitative. We have ceased to respect our authentic existence and also the authentic existence of others. Nature has its intrinsic value as well as instrumental worth. We have forgotten the intrinsic value of nature and have taken it as merely instrumental. We forget that we are products of nature and we are sustained by nature. Instead we try to conquer nature and have mastery over it. This is our ignorance, our *mithyā dṛṣṭi*. Lord Buddha always respected and loved nature and wanted to be in the lap of nature. If we care for nature, nature will care for us. If we destroy nature, nature will destroy us. This is the simple principle of interdependence. So it is saner to preserve and protect nature, rather worship nature as a spiritual entity. Nature is beautiful and bountiful. It is full of joy and it gives joy to us. Let us appreciate and preserve this quality of nature. Nature is to be approached with respect and gratitude. This is Buddhist ecology. The western ecology is utilitarian, materialistic and mechanical but Buddhist ecology is spiritual and teleological. In the teachings of the Buddha we have both surface and deep ecological thinking but their meanings are different than the ones understood by the western thinkers. By deep ecology the Buddha would mean that we have to attend to the functioning of our mind. The Buddha has said, *"Cetenā bhikkave kammo vadāmi"*. We should have *kuśala citta*. The very opening lines of the Dhammapada emphasize the role of mind in the cosmic process. All good and evil proceed from the mind. Mind occasions our conduct and makes it good or bad. So we should educate our mind first. This is the foundation of all ecology. This is the real deep ecology that pertains to inner environment. The surface ecology pertains to our actions that constitute outer environment. We feel affected by our actions. They alone are visible and tangible. But they are not basic. They only result from our thinking. Their roots are in our thinking. So *prajñā* is the basis of *śīla*. Knowledge and conduct are two sides of the same coin, but knowledge is more basic. In the Eternal Eight-fold Path the Buddha began with knowledge as a starting point. The point is that ecological consciousness is fundamental to ecological conduct. Consciousness operates at the deeper level and actions are its outward expression at the surface level.

There is another dimension of Buddhist deep ecology. Because of its spiritual orientation it talks of essential unity of all existences. All entities exist in the same *Buddhakṣetra* and share the same *Buddhabhāva*. All existences have mutuality and participatory being. As Ui-sang, a famous Korean monk, in 'Ocean seal of Hua-yen Buddhism' writes, "Since dharma–nature is round and interpenetrating, it is without any sign of duality. All dharmas are unmoving and originally calm. No name, no form; all distinctions are abolished. It is known through the wisdom of enlightenment, not by any other level. The true-nature is extremely profound, exceedingly subtle and sublime, It does not attach to self-nature, but takes form following (causal conditions). In one is all, in many is one. One is identical to all, many is identical to one. In one particle of dust are contained the ten directions and so it is with all particles of dust. (quoted from 'Buddhist Ecology' (eds.) Martine Batchelor & Kerry Brown, p. 16).

From the doctrine of interdependent origination of all phenomena it follows that Buddha's approach to reality and hence to ecology is holistic and integral. He does not entertain human-nature or nature-culture or body-mind or heredity-environment or theory-praxis or thought–action dichotomy. Further, his approach is spiritualistic and teleological. From his teachings we get a vision and an approach to cosmo-centric eco-ethics, a widening of moral sensitivity as they view human actions in a cosmic context. In modern times we need such eco-conduct to solve eco-crises. From Buddha's teachings we learn another lession that ecology is not a mere matter of theorizing or sermonizing but something to be practiced. So all of us have to be 'Engaged Buddhists' irrespective of our religious affiliation, whether we are Buddhists or not in faith. The Buddha did not propound any religion of his own but only pointed out a way to eradicate all miseries and sufferings. This is important and relevant for us. In this sense Buddha's message is perennial and eternal. This is enlightenment.

The Buddha has been one of the most revolutionary thinkers and the holiest persons ever lived on the earth. He has been a bacon light not only for India or Asia but also for the entire world. His advocacy of pursuit of *prajñā* with practice of *karuṇā*, his vision of self-sameness of all existences and zealous longing for eradication of sufferings of others as one's own cross all barriers of race, creed, country and even humanity. His benevolent teachings of universal compassion and cosmic goodwill, his emphasis on noble virtues of *maitri, karuṇā, muditā* and *upekṣā* known as *brahmavihāras*, i.e., living and working for totality, all these have a significant message for the present day distracted humankind suffering from exhaustion of spirit and languishing in the narrow and rigid confinements of ego-centricism, parochialism and disastrous materialistic consumerism. A time has come for the beginning of a cultural renaissance for which the teachings of the Buddha can play a vital and pivotal role. The Buddhistic truths are of great relevance and significance in contemporary times and in the new millennium to bring about universal peace, prosperity and well-being. These should be our guiding lights for our ecological thinking and doings. If we have to draw eco-syllabus for eco-education it has to be on Buddhist foundation to be meaningful, efficacious and practical.

Buddhism and Ecology

The aim of the present write up is to point out as to how the doctrine of *pratītyasamutpāda* (Interdependent Origination), which is the central doctrine of Buddhism, provides a foundation to an environmental perspective to be offered to humanity to meet the present day crises that are endangering and threatening all existences human as well as non-human. It also deals with the cardinal Buddhist teachings that can help in bringing about an ecological lifestyle. Ecological thinking and ecological living go hand in hand and a symbiosis of the two has been the keynote of the Buddhist view and way of life. Concern for the well-being of the mental and the physical world has been an important element though out the history of Buddhism. Human existence and destiny are inextricably linked with environments. Recognition that human beings are essentially dependent upon and interconnected with their environments has given rise to instinctive respect and care for mind and nature.

Buddhism has come into existence as a problem solving exercise both in terms of prevention and of cure. Śākya Muni, the Buddha, was rightly regarded as the Supreme Physician (*Bhaiṣajya Guru*) as he has provided us a methodology (*nidāna*) to solve all sorts of problems. Awakened by the evils and vices, pain and suffering, finitude and evanescence of mundane life, after intensive study, deep reflections and profound meditation he gained insight into the nature of reality and the phenomenal world. Having attained enlightenment he did not remain self-centered. He was not content with his own emancipation and longed and strived for the liberation of all beings. He showed the sure path of eradication of all evils, which consisted of a symbiosis of wisdom and conduct, ethics and meditative practice. He advised the fellow monks in the following words, "O Monks! Move around for the well-being of every one, for the happiness of every one, showering compassion on the entire world; for the good, for the welfare, for the happiness of divine and human." (Vinaya Piṭaka I, 23). He was the 'Engaged Buddhist' who wanted the well-being of all (Sarvodaya). He prayed, as "*Savve sattā sukhi hontu*" and preached *Siladharma* accordingly. He exhorted, "O Monk! A wise person does not intend harm to self, harm to others or harm to both self and others. Thinking in this way, such a person intends benefit for self, for others, for both and for the whole world. Thus is one wise and of great wisdom." (Anguttara Nikāya II.179).

The doctrine of *pratītyasamutpāda* follows from the second and the third Noble Truths. In its causal form it states that the entire empirical world is a conglomeration of events that are caused by the preceding conditions the presence of which gives rise to them and their absence thwarts their origin or eliminates them. (*Asmin sati idam bahvati, Asmin na sati idam na bhavait*). The Majjim Nikāya Vol. I, p. 134) states, "When that exists, this comes to be; on the arising of that, this arises. When that does not exist, this does not come to be; on the cessation of that, this ceases."

Further all the events and phenomena of the world are our own making. The Samyutta Nikāya says, "*Cittena niyati loko*" I, 39). The Dhammapada (1&2) puts this very aptly as follows,

Mind precedes all things
Mind is supreme, produced by mind are they.
If one should speak or act with mind defiled,
Suffering will follow,
Just as wheel follows hoofs of the drawing ox.
Mind precedes all things,
Mind is supreme, produced by mind are they.
If one should speak or act with purified mind
Well-being will follow,
Like a never parting shadow.

If we have *kuśala citta* (righteous mind) we perform good deeds and virtues spread. But if we have *akuśala citta* (vicious mind) we indulge in bad deeds and vices spread. Delusion (*avidyā*) produces greed, hatred and all other vices. Moral degeneration results in pollution within and without. The point to be noted is that no event and no phenomenon, good or bad, is self-existent or eternal. As Nāgārjuna puts it, nothing has *svabhāva* and every thing is *svabhāva śunya. (Yah pratītyasamutpādaḥ śunyatām tam pracakśmahe)*. The implication to be derived is that all ecological pollutions have a causal origin and annihilation and all these are caused by human mind and resulting actions. The Buddha said, "*Cetanā bhikkave kammo vadāmi*." Since we have caused the evils and consequent undesirable suffering, it is our responsibility to eliminate them. This is what is referred to by His Holiness Tenzin Gyatso, the Dalai Lama, as 'Universal Responsibility'.

There is another dimension of the doctrine of *pratītyasamutpāda* which Chandrakirti, the commentator of Nāgārjuna, has pointed out. The entire cosmos is a network of mutuality of events characterized by universal interdependence, interpenetration, interconnectedness and interrelationships (*parasparāpekṣā*). In this undivided world everything miraculously supports everything else. This insight is beautifully expressed by the Avatamsaka sūtra in the metaphor of 'jwelled net of Indra' which exhibits 'mutual interpenetration and interfusion of all phenomena'. In the words of Ui-sang, a Korean monk, it means,

In one is all, in many is one.

One is identical to all, many is identical to one.

In one particle of dust are contained the ten directions.

And so it is with all particles of dust. (Ocean seal of Hua-yen Buddhism)

This text of Avatamsaka Sūtra has been explained as follows:

"If you sit in one jewel then you are sitting in all jewels in every direction, multiplied over and over again. Why? Because in one jewel there are all jewels. If there is one jewel in all jewels then you are sitting in all jewels too. And the reverse applies to the totality if you follow the same reasoning. Since in one jewel you go into all jewels without leaving this one jewel, so in all jewels you enter one jewel without leaving this one jewel." (Tr. Thomas Cleary).

The Zen master Dogen puts it as follows:

"There are myriads of forms and hundreds of grasses through out the entire earth, and yet each grass and each form itself is the entire earth" ('Moon in Dewdrop' Ed. Kazuaki Tanahasi, Elements Books Shaftesbury, 1988, p.15). The contemporary Vietnamese monk Thich Nhat Hanh also writes in the same vein as follows:

"When we look at a chair we see the wood, but we fail to observe the tree, the forest, the carpenter, or our own mind. When we meditate on it, we can see the entire universe in all its interwoven and interdependent relations in the chair. The presence of wood reveals the presence of the trees. The presence of the leaf reveals the presence of the sun. Meditators can see the one in many, and the many in the one. Even before they see the chair they can see its presence in the heart of living reality. The chair is not separate. It exists only in its interdependent relations with everything else in the universes. It is because all other things are. If it is not so, then all others are not either. (The Sun My Heart, Parallax Press, Berkeley, p. 90).

A corollary of this view is that all existences share the same essence, the same Buddha-nature. All exist in the same *Buddhakṣetra*. All partake in the same *Dharmakāya*. As the Avatamsaka Sūtra (Trans. Thomas Cleary) puts it,

All lands are my body
And so are the Buddhas living there'
Watch my pores,
And I will show you the Buddha's realm. (p. 14)
Just as the nature of earth is one
While beings each live separately'
And the earth has no thought of oneness or difference
So is the truth of the Buddha. (p. 302)

The point is that there is wholeness of life, self-sameness of all existences and therefore we must cultivate universal love, universal compassion, universal kindness and respect for all lives and all existences. One of the early Buddhist texts (quoted by Martine Batchlor in 'Buddhism and Ecology, p. 2) exhorts us to cultivate loving kindness in the following words,

In joy and safety let every creature's heart rejoice,
Whatever breathing beings there are,
No matter whether timid or bold,
With none excepted, long or big,
Or middle-sized or short,
Or thin or thick,
Or those seen or unseen,
Or whether dwelling far or near,
That are or that yet seek to be.
Let every creature's heart rejoice.
Let none betray another's trust
Or offer any slight at all,
Or even let them wish in wrath
Or in revenge each other's ill
Thus as a mother with her life
Will guard her son, her only child,
Let him extend without bounds
His heart to every living being.

This feeling of oneness is not physical or geographical but mental and psychological. The root cause of suffering is delusion (*avidyā*). The consequence of it is feeling of separateness, fragmentation, a sense of separate and independent existence. We are a conglomeration of five elements which are in constant flux. But we feel as if we are a lasting self. We feel separated from each other, separate from the environment that sustains us and separate from the things we are inextricably related with. The ecological crises we witness today is the result of this delusion which gives rise to greed, hatred and stupidity.

The physical and external pollution is due to mental and internal pollution. As stated earlier, it is due to *akuśala citta*. This moral degradation affects the individual as well as his or her surroundings. The remedy lies in recovering the lost vision of wholeness and practicing *śīla* in the form of '*Brahma vihāras*'. This is enlightenment. This is *Buddhatva*.

Apart from loving all living beings the Buddha has always advocated love and respect of nature. All living beings are creatures of nature. Nature provides them physical form and sustains them. Nature environs them and provides them nourishments. It is joyful and joy-yielding. Śāntideva in Bodhicaryāvatāra (VIII, 25) voices this idea as follows,

When shall I come to dwell in forests

Amongst the deer, the birds and the trees.

That say nothing unpleasant

And are delightful to associate with.

A life in the lap of nature is a mark of spiritual freedom. It is freedom from all restraints, physical and mental. It is widening, deepening and heightening of spirit. It is a life of purity, internal and external. Life in nature is natural life. We should ideally lead a life of middle path as a 'green monk' caring for nature and sharing the bounties of nature. If we care for nature, nature will care for us. If we pollute nature it adversely affects our existence. Nature is an 'Embodied Love' and 'Embodied Benevolence'. For example, trees do not exist for themselves, they stand in the sun and provide shadow not to themselves, and they yield fruits and other benefits not for themselves. They do so for the sake of others. The same is the case with rivers, mountains and other objects of nature. In this respect nature is a great master and a teacher practicing and teaching *maitri* (loving kindness), *karuṇā* (compassion), *muditā* (sympathetic joy) and *upekṣā* (equanimity).

All natural objects have a spirit residing in them. They are our co-inhabitants. As we have a right to live, they also have a right to live. It is therefore a sin to harm or pollute or destroy them. Zen Master Dogen writes, "It is not only that there water in the world, but there is a world in water. It is not just water. There is also a world of living beings in clouds. There is a world of living beings in the Air. There is a world of living beings in Fire. There is a world of living beings on Earth. There is a world of living beings in the phenomenal world. There is a world of living beings in a blade of grass. There is a world of living beings in a staff." ('Moon in a Dewdrop' Ed. Kazuati Tanahasi, Element Books, Shaftesbury, 1988 pp. 106-7). This sort of panpsychism is an outcome of spiritual approach to reality and life. It also reveals the interconnectedness and interpenetration of all phenomena.

Further, in loving all beings and nature there has to be a life of collectivity, a *samgha jīvana*. The real meaning of life is to be found in the midst of this network of collectivity, a network of interrelationship we call 'life'. Life is to be lived meaningfully in the spirit of cooperation, of mutual give and take, with love, compassion and respect for all.

Buddhist ecology is based on conservation ethics of mutual care and share. Love, compassion and concern for others should be as natural and instinctive as it is for our own selves. The cardinal principle of Buddhist eco-ethics is, "In joy and safety let every creature's heart rejoice". Śāntideva uses two very catching and apt words for this idea. He talks of '*parātma samatā*' and '*parātma parivartana*', feeling of sameness with others and identification of one self with other selves. He writes,

I should dispel the miseries of others

Because it is suffering, just like my own,

And I should benefit others

Because they are living things, just like myself.

There is another reason for respecting the life of all living beings. The Buddha has advocated the doctrine of cycle of birth and rebirth. This implies kinship with all creatures. We may take rebirth as any of such creatures depending upon our karmas. These creatures could have been our parents or sons or daughters in their previous births.

While concluding it should be reminded that human being is the climax of evolutionary process. He possesses vast potentials for betterment or devastation. He can be a super-being or super-malignancy. He has a choice and also the capacity of judicious discrimination. Since he is the most evolved he should be the most responsible. He has not only to voice environmental concern but also to cultivate environmental consciousness. For this we need environment friendly value system and a suitable code of conduct. Through proper education alone this is possible.

Chapter 10

Philosophical Foundations of Ecological Ethics

(Based on Buddhist Traditions)

V V Mantatov

Entirety and Interdependence of Ontological Reality

Global scales of crisis which destroyed our planet requires the united measures and efforts of East and West in formation of ecological ethics. East and West are two parts of mankind's consciousness. If a man realizes this he can become a perfect human being. And only after that he can solve those global problems of surviving, which mankind is facing now.

The fundamental idea of all Buddhist philosophy is the inseparable unity of subject and object, man and nature, substance and mind. The Buddhists consider world and man as a dynamic psychophysical entirety. It's character and direction, which is called stream (*santāna*), that makes a principle of absolute change (*anityatā*).

Anityatā is of a deep ecological importance. It raises a problem of uneternity of psychocosm's spheres and an image of its being destroyed. According to Buddhist religious doctrine the category "*anitya*" must occupy a certain position in each analysis. Speaking of a statement it is important to take into consideration its change and movable character. Only stable and permanent efforts of all living beings make this world better and without this direction for making kindness our world can become worse and suffering permanent characteristics of *saṃsāra* can acquire rude and vulgar forms. Besides simple constatation of change *anityatā* says about non-reversibility of former conditions. It is impossible to reverse one's life. It is impossible to return to the history of a country back as well as impossible to make the planet evolution come to beginning.

The Principle of Emptiness *(śūnyatā)*

Buddhism denies the inherent existence of things and phenomena. If you take away the reasons and conditions of existence of something then it will disappear itself because it doesn't have inherent existence. A thing exists only through dependence on others. Emptiness of a thing is its interdependence and unsubstantiality, it isn't unexistence. It exists but not absolutely. Changing the nature, man deprives many kinds of living beings their existence conditions, and they die out. It's absolutely impossible to restore them; in this example we can see that there is no law according to which any kind of living beings can exist eternally.

Principle of Interdependence of all Entities

Our inter-relations with the world are very complicated, and isolated existence is impossible. Every phenomenon has as a reason a number of many others. We see interdependence of the world even in human curiosity. Why do we turn on the radio and TV in the morning and listen to news from all over the world? It's important for us to know how other people live, we feel existential connection with others.

All these three principles lead us to the main principle of Buddhist philosophy. The principle entirety of the Universe is described in one of the most significant texts of Buddhism—*Avatamsaka-sūtra*. Analyzing the ecological laws of nature discovered by modern scientists, we see much in common with ideas of *Avatamsaka-sūtra*. Comparative analysis of *Avatamsaka-sūtra* promises many perspectives in investigation of Buddhist original texts from the point of view of modern science. Modern Buddhist philosophers Tenzin Gyatco Dalai Lama XIV, Chogyam Trungpa, Djampa Tinley suggest the conformity of the Buddhist philosophy in accordance to the modern science. Buddha says in sūtra:

"Monks and scientists have to consider my words, as gold that needs to be of checked by means of melting, cutting and grinding and only then accept them." This sutra attracts our attention by its inner uncontradiction of its ideas, the absence of irreconcible oppositions, the harmonic entirety about world outlook. The basic principle of inter-relation of creatures, things, phenomena is cooperation. The absence of inherent existence of phenomena doesn't mean to deny the present world, but connects phenomena with the Universe. Getting rid of the conceptual duality gives realization of inseparable entirety, which is unknown to the usual mind and opens only the level of the universal consciousness.

Universal consciousness brings into beings the feeling of participation with everything that is going on in the Universe. It is called omniscience, but it doesn't mean the knowledge of every detail; it means knowing true nature of every phenomenon, being able to see a single unity. To reach this level of consciousness it's necessary to develop *Bodhichitta*. Geshe Djampa Tinley called it "philosophically damped kindness and compassion." Without *Bodhichitta* any knowledge is considered to be meaningless and useless. Kindness and compassion should be inducing motives of cognition of the world.

Ecological Ethics of Buddhism

An ecological problem is global not only because it contains danger for mankind but also because its solution requires tremendous and general efforts. This problem is a sort of a challenge to the mankind and every single man. Today it is necessary to wake up in people the feeling of unity with nature and other people, the feeling of participation with everything which is going on Earth. Many ecological problems arise not because there are some wicked people who want to ruin the planet but because detachment and division of labour have led to the break of motivational psychological level.

Karma

Realization of law of karma helps to overcome the gap between actions and their results. Law of karma states that all our activity, words and ideas form conditions of our existence in future. So law of karma convinces man to accept responsibility for the recent position, and also for all his lives in future. The law of karma shows how from small trivial, daily routine, man's life is being built, the history of the country, mankind's way of development, global ecological situation. Karma is divided into mental, active and verbal. Actions and words are brought into being first in mind, mind is considered to be the main form-making factor. Thought is a personal destiny creator and a creator of the whole world and that's why moral degradation of the society is the reason of physical degradation of the world. "The world begins in everybody from us."

Ahimsā

"The greatest killer on Earth is man", who kills and takes another's life in order to keep his own one, said Herder. The principles of *ahimsā* became quite an expression of this deep metaphysical shame. This principle contains the requirement of non-doing harm to other creatures in an allegoric form-prohibition of letting one's blood on to the ground. *Ahimsā* was born in the foundation of the Indian culture and belongs to all directions of the Indian Thought. Buddhism adopted this spiritually high note and widely spreaded it to other countries and culture. Many Buddhist terms have a sign of negation "a". It speaks that Buddhism doesn't accept acsiological foundation of morality of the society. In the world of *himsā*-violence, it speaks of non-violence. In the world of stability it speaks of change and development. In the world of static essence existing next to each other it speaks of common interdependence. In the world of private interests it speaks of personal responsibility for own destiny and the destiny of the whole world.

What principles of Buddhist philosophy are most the important for formation of ecological paradigm of mentality: First: vision of world in dynamics, development. Second: the system of relative truth, which is the negation of dogmas. Third: moral foundation of scientific knowledge. Fourth: non-violent thinking and the absence of repressive scientific methods. Fifth: progressive movement of intellect to Universal consciousness which postulates the unity of microcosm and macrocosm.

The comparative analysis of laws and principles of modern ecological science and basic statements of Buddhist thought points out to their common intentional direction. The Buddhist philosophy declares creative participation of man in the united world synergetical process and forms the foundation of altruisticaly marked ecological ethics.

Chapter 11

The Dialectic of Śūnyatā As the Trans-cultural Basis of Cultures

Shohei Ichimura

I. Introductory Remarks:

During the first quarter of twentieth century, scholarly interest, for the first time, took up the subject of Mādhyamika Studies in conjunction with that of Buddhist Logic. It was Stcherbatsky who initially rendered the term 'dialectic' to the Sanskrit term *'prasaṅga-vākya'*, known as the Mādhyamika method of refutation, and it was he who also gave to it another translation as *'reductio-ad-absurdum argument'*, which in fact comes to be nearest to the meaning of its actual form.[1] This *prasaṅga-vākya*, however, was not simply a method of refutation, but was primarily designed by Nāgārjuna to communicate the insight of *śūnyatā*. In this paper, therefore, I shall consider 'Buddhist dialectic' as a method of communicating the Buddhist insight of *śūnyatā*.

Secondly, I am considering 'Buddhist dialectic' as a method of resolving so-called *communication breakdown* which arises from cultural, religious, or ideological differences. The term 'dialectic' was regarded by the 19th century theorists either as the order of *Geist*, or its contrary, as the order of *Dinge*. 'Dialectic' was regarded as the only way to express dynamic spirit or dynamic nature. In this paper, however, I am considering it as the process underlying every use of linguistic symbols, or more simply speaking, the mental process underlying every act of *naming*. In this sense, I propose to say that Buddhist dialectic shares methodology rather with the 20th century theorists who discarded both of the 19th century metaphysical principles and have instead carried out logical enquiries into the nature and function of language.

Thirdly, I am considering 'Buddhist dialectic' not as confined to the Indian Mādhyamika form, such as, introduced by Nāgārguna, but as extended to the Chinese Mādhyamika form, such as, innovated by Seng-chao (374-414) quite differently. For, Seng-chao, and following him, Zen Buddhist thinkers in later periods, did not resort to the *reductio-ad-absurdum* method, but to the method of paradoxical assertion and negation. Though unique to Chinese Buddhists, this paradoxical method nevertheless can be proven as an authentic Mādhyamika, especially, as to the way it discloses the same dialectic underlying language and culture.

Since culture is definable as 'a system of meaningful symbols.'[2] the way of using linguistic symbols, or more simply, the act of naming, is of paramount importance to every culture, precisely because it underlies every cultural activity which, in turn, is ultimately identical with naming. With this definition of culture at hand, the problem of communication breakdown can easily be explained as arising from the very *discrepancy* between the *naming* and the *named*. The purpose of this paper is to determine how and why Buddhist dialectic can be regarded as the method of resolving the so-called 'problem of communication breakdown' caused by cultural, religious as well as ideological differences, and for this purpose, to reconcile the *reductio-ad-absurdum* method developed by Indian Buddhists and the paradoxical method innovated by Chinese Buddhists of the Classical Period in terms of Buddhist dialectic, and finally, to indicate a significant parallel between the interest in Mādhyamika Studies in the post-world-war era and the contemporary theoretical trends, such as, represented by Cognitive Structuralists and Generative Grammarians.

II. Nature of Communication Breakdown and Buddhist Logicians' Approach to its Solution

Professor Arnold Kunst once made an interesting observation regarding how Buddhist logicians of Medieval India dealt with the intra-Hindu controversy exchanged between the Naiyāyika and Mīmāmsaka schoolmen over the nature of *śabda* (vocal word).[3] The Naiyāyika sohoolman defined it in syllogistic argument as:

Pratijñā:	Śabda is impermanent	(*śabda anityaḥ*);
Hetu:	Because it is a product	(*kṛtakatvāt*);
Dṛṣṭānta:	Just as a pot is	(*ghaṭavat*).

The Mīmāmsaka schoolman, on the other hand, countered it as:

Pratijñā:	Śabda is permanent	(*śabdo nityaḥ*);
Hetu:	Because it is audible	(*śravaṇatvāt*);
Dṛṣṭānta:	Just as anything that is audible	(*śabdatvavat*).

Professor Kunst commented three points: First, Buddhist logicians lay emphasis on the respective arguments (i.e., the Hetu-statement), namely: "Because *śabda* is a product" by the Naiyāyika, and "Because it is audible" by the Mīmāmsaka, but not on their syllogistic forms as a whole, because each syllogism is valid in the light of inferential rules, such as *anvaya* and *vyatireka*. Second, Buddhist logicians accepted the simultaneous validity of the two theses within each system of philosophical presuppositions respectively expressed in their *vyāptis*;

> Whatever is a product is impermanent (the Naiyāyika);
>
> Whatever is audible is permanent (the Mīmāmsaka).

For the Naiyāyika, an utterance (*śabda*) is a temporary modification (*guṇa*) produced upon a permanent substance (*dravya*), like a pot which is a mere product out of a substance clay. The Mīmāmsaka, on the other hand, maintained that any audible, that is, communicable, sound carries its transcendental ideation as its essence, which, for them, is permanent. Third, Buddhist logicians shifted both the mental process and the logical meaning on to a different plain from that of those logical laws, so as to resolve an existing conflict between the two schoolmen.

It is evident that Buddhist logicians intended to resolve the controversy in the trans-empirical plain, not only because it is impossible within the domain of logical convention to determine validity or invalidity for the two seemingly contradictory assertions, but also as Prof. Kunst suggested, because, in order to accomplish this goal, Buddhist logicians did not apply the so-called objective criterion independent of human mind, but sought it in the mind making reality only partly a function of external phenomenon.

III. Genesis of 'Buddhist Dialectic' as the Method for resolving Communication Breakdown

Earlier I proposed that the Mādhyamika dialectic had its origin as a method of resolving the problem of communication breakdown ensued among the pre-Classical Abhidharmist schoolmen.[4] As the *Kathāvatthu* recorded, the Theravādin and the Pudgalavādin confuted over the status of reality of *pudgala*, but were unable to determine logically as to whether *'pudgala'* is real or unreal. The essential points which I am obliged to make here as related to this controversy is three-fold. To explain the general condition in which the two schoolmen were engaged in debate, the Theravādin set forth two concomitant statements which are supposed to be verified by the class members of transcendental *dharmas* (i.e., *sapakṣa*), but to be falsified by the contra-positive class members, such as, any empirical things like *pudgala* (i.e., *vipakṣa*). The following are the two statements together with Mrs. Rhys Davids' translation as respectively transcribed by symbolic notation:[5]

"p": (x) "is known in the sense of a genuinely real thing";
puggalo upalabbhati saccikaṭṭhaparamaṭṭhenāti

"q": (x) "is known in the same way a genuinely real thing is known".
yo saccikaṭṭho paramaṭṭho tato so puggalo upalabbhati saccikatthaparamatthenāti

First of the the two concomitant assertions: "p" and "q" of both parties ended up *to violate the logical boundary* between the class of *pudgala* and that of *non-pudgala*, here meaning that of *dharmas*. The resulting forms or expressions the two schoolmen respectively arrived at are as-"p.q" (the Theravādin's) and "p.-q," which obviously lead to logical indeterminancy. The following is the chart of the entire fivefold refutational session or the two schoolmen:[6]

I	II
Theravādin Refutation	*Pudgalavādin Rejoinder*
Pudgalavādin thesis "p.-q"	Theravādin thesis "-p.q" is
is false, because $P \supset q$;	false, because $-p \supset -q$;
"p.-q" is false,	"-p.q" is false,
because $-q \supset -p$;	because $q \supset p$;
Thererore, Pudgalavādin	Thererore, Theravādin thesis
thesis "p.-q" is false.	"-p.q" is false.

III	IV
Pudgalavādin Refutation	*Pudgalavādin Application*
Theravādin thesis"-p.q"	Our thesis "p.-q" is not
can be refuted,	falsified, and
because $-p \supset -q$;	Your refutation "-(p.-q)" is
Nor can "-p.q" be	not acceptable,
refuted because $q \supset p$;	because $p \supset q$ and $-q \supset -p$;
Therefore, Theravādin thesis	Therefore, your refutation
"p.q" can be refuted.	"-(p.-q)" is not acceptable.

V

Pudgalavādin Conclusion

Our thesis "p.-q" is not refuted,

because "p.q" is not compelled;

Your refutation "-(p.-q)" is not convincing,

because "-q.-p" are not compelled;

Because "p.q" and "-q.-p" are not compelled,

our thesis "p.-q" is not refuted.

The dual rules of *anvaya* and *vyatireka* are clearly expressed as "p then q" (position) and "-q then -p" (contraposition), and both parties accuse each other as faulty by referring to or paralleling with, valid formulas: "p ⊃ q" and "-q ⊃ -p".

Second, the problem of this indeterminacy arises from the very observational context where both parties are equally addressing to what is called *'pudgala'*. Despite the fact that they refer to one and the same thing by name, their respective variables are indeed different, and this difference is sharpened by the referential force of the mind. Thus, it was the task of the Buddhist dialectic to resolve this antithesis, and this was accomplished by *total juxtaposition of these two variables* in reference to that transcendental observational context as indicated by the adverbial term: *saccikaṭṭhaparamaṭṭhena*.

Third, this principle of juxtaposition which can be accomplished by total identification of two contrary or contradictory statements is what Nāgārjuna's *reductio-ad-absurdum* method as well as the Chinese Mādhyamika paradoxical method equally accomplish for the sake of communicating the insight of *śūnyatā*. In this respect, 'Buddhist dialectic' is *the method of restoring communication breakdown,* for it restored the original meaning of *anātman* in terms of *dharma-nairātmya,* namely, universal Emptiness.

IV. Buddhist Dialectic Expressed in Nāgārjuna's Reductio-ad-abs urdum Method

There has been some reservation as to whether the Indian Mādhyamika insight and method were correctly understood by the Chinese Mādhyamikas, such as Seng-chao. W. Liebenthal, for-instance, implicated his skepticism as to Seng-chao's understanding in stating that "a wall of misunderstanding separated the Chinese understanding of Buddhism from that of the Indian".[7] On the other hand, R.H. Robinson determined that Seng-chao was a representative Chinese

Mādhyamika for his fairly accurate understanding of the doctrine and the dialectical method. Nevertheless, he underestimated Seng-chao's logical argument as immitative and his paradoxical method merely rhetorical.[8] In this respect, I proposed at the 194th AOS meeting that his method is an authentic Mādhyamika and equally a Buddhist dialectic.[9] The reason that Seng-chao and Chinese Buddhists in general did not resort to the Nāgārjunian *reductio-ad-absurdum* method was primarily due to the difference of the two languages. I shall elaborate this point in the following.

Sanskrit and its derivatives in the Indian subcontinent are known to have been Indo-European cognates, having the sentential structure *action-centered,* and the parts of speech highly inflected, and endowed with other intricate grammatical word classes. In this respect, the Chinese language is an independent system as it is mono-syllabic, lacking inflection, copula, and other equivalent grammatical word classes. As Polish logician, Janusz Chmielewski points out, the latter language, especially Classical Chinese, is the only known language which possesses intrinsically calculational qualities to an extent of implicit formal logic, because, besides those other qualities, its sentential structure consists of *topic* and *comment* as equivalent to logical subject and predicate.[10] Nevertheless, in our confined subject of interest, such as, the Mādhyamika Buddhist communication, there was a set of problems standing in the way of perfect translation and communication. Introducing one such problem, I am obliged to call attention to Nāgārjuna's critique of the Kāraka categories, the essential norms of sentential structure in Sanskrit,[11] as implicated in the second chapter of his major work *Mūlamādhyamakakārikās*. (i.e., Gatāgataparīkṣā).

What Nāgārjuna essentially accomplishes in this chapter is twofold: (1) to examine the abstract scheme of *kārakas* in reference to actual motion or time passage, and (2) to demonstrate why the system or language cannot really cope with actual motion. We know that even a simple sentence '*gamyamānam gamyate*', for instance, involves a whole set of the underlying schemes, not only *kārakas,* their case endings, etc., but also those of all verbal declensions. By confining our attention to the scheme of syntactical categories (i.e., *kārakas*), Nāgārjuna analyzes three basic *kāraka* categories in the said chapter: (1) *gantṛ* or the goer as a nominative agent, (2) *gamyamāna* (or *gantavya*) or the referential passage or destination of motion as an accusative object, and (3) *gamana* or the act of going as an instrumental motion. Along with convention, Nāgārjuna asserts that an act of going or a motion (*gamana* and *gati* synonymously used) is concomitant with bodily action (*ceṣṭā*) and is inherent in the referential point of its passage (*gamyamānam*),[12] and using these schematic elements, which are taken for granted in convention, he executes a series of arguments for inducing absurdity:[13]

1. If 'gamana' (going) is to be found in 'gamyamāna' (referential point of passage), this view *ipso facto* commits to an erroneous consequence, such that there would be two *gamanas*: the one *gamana* by which 'gamyamāna' is produced, and the other *gamana* which is inherent in 'gamyamāna' (as its property).
2. If there are two *gamanas,* there should be also two goers (*gantārau*), because it implicates two *gamanas*, because no motion is possible without its agent, and *vice versa*.
3. The similar predicament is also at hand by a simple statement: "the goer goes" (*gantā gacchati*), because it implicates two *gamanas*, namely, the one *gamana* which indicates its agent and the other *gamana* which it produces.

So much so, Nāgārjuna culminates his arguments to Kārikās 19 and 20 of the chapter as follows:

> If the goer (*gantṛ*) is identical with the act of going (*gamana*) there follows an absurdity, such that oneness of *kartṛ* (the agent of action or nominative case) and *karman* (the object of action or accusative case) ensues.
>
> If they are imagined as different entities, there follows another absurdity, such that an act of going (*gamana*) is without its agent and *vice versa*.

The point which I am obliged to emphasize here is that the foregoing *reductio-ad-absurdum* arguments, which are directed to the grammatical scheme of *kārakas*, could not be communicated to the Chinese native speakers for creating an equal impact upon their mind as was successfully done upon the mind of Indian linguistic subjects, precisely because there is no equivalent system of *kārakas* in the Chinese language, nor is there any sustained practice of *entification* as to such categories toward the level of metaphysical being (*svabhāva*).[14] Thus, Kumārajīva, the foremost of all Buddhist translators, despite his profound insight of *śūnyatā* and excellent knowledge of both languages, just could not render the term '*gamyamānam*' (i.e., reflexive or passive progressive form of 'to go' *gam*) by an exact equivalent,[15] nor could his native disciples fully fathom the Nāgārjurā's *reductio-ad-absurdum* arguments as applied to the *kāraka* scheme without a sense of triviality. It is, therefore, more than natural for the Chinese Mādhyamika not to follow the Nāgārjunian method for communicating the insight of *śūnyatā*, but consistently applied the paradoxical method to express the same meaning of dialectical critique to the mind of Chinese linguistic subjects.

V. Buddhist Dialectic Expressed in Seng-chao's Paradoxical Method

Seng-chao, one of the ablest disciples of Kumārajīva, wrote an essay with the title "The Doctrine That Things Do Not Move",[16] in which he treats the same subject as that of *Mūlamādhyamakakārikās* II. The primary difference of his method is that by passing the procedure for analyzing the *kāraka* scheme with which his language is not equipped, he immediately matches the word meaning 'motion' with its contrary 'stillness' or the word of 'passing' with that of 'abiding'. I shall quote a few passages which attest the way Seng-chao applies his paradoxical method:[17]

> If we want to express the real, we go against convention. If we follow convention, we fail to express the real.
>
> By 'motion', people mean that things are in motion and not at rest, because (they think) past things do not reach the present. For the same reason, however, I claim that it is 'stillness', (by which I mean that) things are at rest and not in motion. (People think that) because things are in motion and not at rest, they do not come (to the present). I think (however, that) because they are at rest and not in motion, they do not pass away (from the present).
>
> When people say that things are 'abiding', I say that they are gone. When they say that things are 'gone', I say that they are 'abiding'. Though 'gone' and 'abiding' are different in expression, what they mean is one reference.

Both the method of *reductio-ad-absurdum* argument and that of paradoxical one are equally based on the law of (non-) contradiction, which generally expressed as "-(p.-p)". But contradiction occurs not only with the conjunction of two contrary statements of which one differs from the other merely by negation {i.e. -(p.-p)} but also with any pair of statements of which one implies the negation of the other. [i.e., -{p.q. (q -p)} or-{p.q.(p -q)}]. Thus, Seng-chao's paradoxical arguments can be shown as containing both of these cases. The following passage, for instance, is the typical form of his paradoxical expressions:[18]

Thus, things are said to be permanent and yet not abiding; they are said to be passing and yet not changing. Because not changing, things are passing and yet always at rest. Because not abiding, they are at rest and yet always passing. Because things are at rest and yet always passing, they are passing and yet not changing. Because they are passing and yet always at rest, they are at rest and yet not staying).

By transcribing as "p"; and as "-p"; and as "Q"; and as "-Q" we can arrive at the following formula:

P.-P; Q. -Q; -Q(Q.P); -P(P.Q); P.Q.(Q.-Q); Q.P.(P.-P).[19]

As obvious, every formula contained in the series constitutes contradiction, hence logically appears to be meaningless.

Seng-chao's paradoxical method can, however, be defended as an authentic Mādhyamika by comparing it with Nāgārjuna's another favourite dialectic applied to be relationship between 'light' and 'darkness'. It is well known in the history of Indian philosophy that Nāgārjuna made this metaphorical relation the subject of his critique in order to refute the Naiyāyika notion of *pramāṇa* and *prameya*.[20] For, the fact of vision is taken for granted in convention as arising from the contact of visual faculty (*pramāṇa*) and incoming stimuli (*prameya*), just as the fact of illumination is believed to originate in the contact of light and darkness. It is such concrete example, powerful and persuasive, on the basis of which Nāgārjuna justifies his dialectical juxtaposition of any two correlatives in reference to the spatio-temporal sphere of interaction. As I proposed in the paper presented at the 31st International Congress of Orientalists in 1983,[21] this *juxtaposition feature* embodies one of the two fundamental criteria to authenticate Mādhyamika dialectic, precisely because it reveals the universal nature of self-contradiction as inherent in convention. On the one hand, light and darkness are clearly differentiated in convention as separate entities, while, on the other hand, in this very convention, their identification is also *a-priori* accepted in terms of their interaction for explaining the fact of illumination. In short, Nāgārjuna's dialectical treatment is designed to demonstrate (1) that in order to make our convention work, this self-contradictory feature must be simultaneously accepted, to the effect that 'light' and 'darkness' are simultaneously identical and yet also different, and accordingly (2) that our linguistic convention invariably has its reference as '*dual natured*'. The latter constitutes the second, but equally important, criterion to authenticate Mādhyamika dialectic.

Now, Seng-chao's method of paradoxical expressions can be ascertained as authentic Mādhyamika by disclosing these two features in them. As quoted before, Seng-chao not only invokes the first criterion (i.e., juxta-position feature) by matching up correlatives, but also does not fail to express the presence of dual natured reference, quoting:[22]

> We want to say that *dharmas* exist, but their existence is not real production. We want to say that *dharma*s do not exist, but phenomenal forms are already configurated. Phenomenal forms cannot be said as 'identical with nothing' but we only say that anything unreal is not a real existent. It follows that the meaning of 'Emptiness of Whatever is Unreal' is thus revealed. Accordingly, the *Pañcaviṇśatisāhasrikā-prajñāpāramitā-sūtra* says : "*Dharmas* are called metaphorically as 'unreal' just as a magically created man is. For, we cannot say that there is no magically created man, but that such is not a real man".

Seng-chao, then, summing up his understanding of *śūnyatā*, goes back to the problem of discrepancy between the *naming* and the *named*, and claims that no naming is possible for expressing things as they really are; i.e., their being simultaneously identical with others as well as different from them, quoting:[23]

> Though we look for things by names, they do not match the real to which names refer. Though we look for names by (matching) things, no names obtain the efficiency things bear. Since things do not match the real to which names refer, they are not real things. Since names do not obtain the efficiency things bear, they are not real names. Because of (all) this, names do not match the real nor does the real match the names. Names and the real do not match, (and yet) milliads of things abide as they (really) are.

VI. Conclusion as to Trans-Cultural Function of Buddhist Dialectic

From the foregoing examples of the Mādhyamikā dialectic as demonstrated by Indian and Chinese Buddhists, there emerges the characteristic function of Buddhist dialectic as twofold: (1) On the one hand, it discloses the workings of innumerable schemes and categories of the mind in terms of simultaneous identity and difference underlying every act of naming or use of symbols; (2) On the other hand, it also discloses the fact that this naming has no objective referent as such, except the dual natured reference, which transcends the sphere of empirical experience.

As a system of meaningful symbols, every culture is based on foundation frameworks, such as, cognitive and linguistic. While these schemes and categories serve as the skeletal framework, linguistic symbols act as catalysts to or tools for, developing the world of experiences external as well as internal. Some of the contemporary theorists, such as Cognitive Structuralists and Generative Grammarians have explained quite convincingly how and why cognitive and linguistic schemes, which may genetically be coded in every new born baby, develop and expand themselves into a vast network as the infant grows, through his accumulation of information over cognitive and linguistic schemes as experienced with particular instances, and also through his application of these schemes not only to mapping the external world but also to orienting the internal conscious world.

It is indeed the use of language, act of naming, which influences upon human culture not only in guiding schematic foundations, but also providing those schemes whose development they direct. Thus, linguistic symbols enable societies to insure not their languages but also institutions, intellectual attainments, cultural orientations through generation to generation. In the light this understanding, to critically examine such underlying schemes and ways we use linguistic symbols becomes the crucial task for the goal of greater communication between different cultures as characterized by their respective cognitive and linguistic schemes. It is here, I see reason as to why there has been a sustained interest in Mādhyamika Study within the holding of Buddhist Studies in the West ever since the 1920's.

As to the question for those of us who are concerned with the philosophical study of religion, namely: "Whether human religiosity transcends cultural differences", the Classical Sino-Indian forms of Buddhist dialectic provides a positive answer as an excellent paradigm, vindicating the cases of successful communication for the insight of *śūnyatā*. It remains to be seen, however, whether Buddhist dialectic fares equally well in the West, and in this matter, in the Middle West as well, where, unlike the pre-Buddhist Chinese culture, theistic belief systems and their linguistic usages culturally sway the minds of the majority.

References

1. Cf. Th. Stcherbatsky, *The Conception of Buddhist Nirvana* (pub by the Academy of Sciences of USSR, Leningrad, 1927), Indo-Iranian Reprints, VI, 1965; p. 35, p. 65, p. 94, and so on.
2. This definition of 'culture' has its advantage for cross-cultural studies as advocated by social scientists and anthropologists. For the same reason, it is also useful for the discipline of comparative religion. Cf. Geertz, "Religion as a Culture System", *Anthropological Approaches to the Study of Religion*, ed. by M. Banton, ASA Monographs 3 (London: Tavistock Pub. 1966), p. 4.

3. Cf. "The Concept of the Principle of Excluded Middle in Buddhism", *Rocznik Orientalistyczny* XXI, 1958, p. 146. The example quoted here is found in the *Nyāyapraveśa* by Śankarasvāmin (*GOS*, 38 (1930), pp. 3-4).
4. Cf. Ichimura, "A Study of the Mādhyamika Method of Refutation, Especially of its Affinity to that of *Kathāvatthu*", *Journal of the International Association of Buddhist Studies* III, 1 (1980), pp. 7-15.
5. *Kathāvatthu*, ed. by A.C. Taylor, PTS: 1984-7; p. 2f; *Kathāvatthu: Points of Controversy,* tr. by S.Z. Aung and Mrs. Rhys Davids, PTS: 1915; p. 8f.
6. Duplicated from the chart given in Ichimura's "A Study of the Mādhyamika Method..., *loc. cit.*, p. 12.
7. *Chao-Lun: The Treatises of Seng-chao*, trans. with introd., notes and appendices (Hong-Kong: Hong-Kong Univ. Press 1968), p. 22.
8. Cf. *Early Mādhyamika in India and China*, Univ. of Wisconsin Press 1967, pp. 130-134.
9. Ichimura; "Is Seng-chao's Paradoxical Method of Demonstration an Authentic Mādhyamika?" presented at the 194th Annual Meeting of American Oriental Society, 1983, and will appear in *the Professor L.M. Joshi Memorial Volume,* ed. by Samdhong Rimpoche, the Central Institute of Higher Tibetan Studies, Sarnath, Varanasi.
10. Cf. "Notes on Early Chinese Logic IV", RO XXVIII, 2 (1965), 87-111, esp., p. 103ff.
11. The Kārakas (syntactical cases are the corollary system of the action-centered structure of sentential construction. For the definition, see Pāṇini, *Aṣṭādhyāyī*, Bk. I, Chap. IV, 23 (on *Kāraka*), or in S.C. Vasu, (trans.), *The Aṣṭādhyāyī of Pāṇini*, Vol. I, (Delhi: Motilal Banarsidass, 1962), pp. 327ff.
12. *MMK* II, k. 2.
13. Respectively, *MMK* II, k. 5; k. 6; k. 11.
14. 'Entification' means to derive nominal formation from properties and actions by affixing derivational endings, such as abstract suffixes: *tā, tva*, etc. Sanskrit literature has a wealth of this kind of practices, whereas the Chinese language is said to have hardly any equivalent practice before Buddhist literature was introduced. In short, the term 'entification' involves a degree of more theoretically extracted categorization regarding qualities and attributes, which is a decisive step toward meta-physization.
15. Kumārajīva translated '*gamyamānam*' as 'passing moment' and hence, '*gamyamānam gamyate'* as 'passing moment passes'. *Taishō*. Vol. 30, e.g. k. 2 (p. 3); k. 4 (p. 4), and so forth, Prof. H. Ui, also gives it in similar term as (*Tōyō no Ronri*, Tokyo: Aoyama Shoin, 1950, p. 252). I am obliged to mention my indebtedness two decades ago to the late Prof. J.A.B. van Buitenen for correcting my preconception based on the Chinese translation and thereby acquiring the proper understanding of the expression on the basis of Sanskrit grammar.
16. *Taishō-shinshū-daizōkyō*, Vol. 45, p. 151; one of the four short essays collected in *Cho-lun* or *The Treatise of Chao,* Taisho. No. 1858.
17. *Ibid.*, respectively, p. 151 a (15-18); a (22-26); c (10-12).
18. *Ibid.*, b (18-21).
19. As I do *not* think that the relationship between antecedent and consequent, for instance, "Because not changing, things are passing and yet always at rest",

constitutes conditional implication, I transcribed it as conjunction in the sense of juxtaposition as having been discussed. There is a question, however, as to whether the serial order of arguments Seng-chao presents here has any logical meaning. It remains to be examined.

20. Cf. *Vigrahavyāvartanī,* esp. *kārikās,* 36-39, of which Vātsyāyana defended the Naiyāyika position in his *Bhāṣya* II, i, 15-16, on the basis of the semantic power (*samākhyānimittam*) of *kāraka-śabdas.* Cf. Ichimura, "An Analysis of Mādhyamika dialectic in terms of the Logical Principle of *anvaya* and *vyatireka*" in *the Professor P.V. Bapat Felicitation Volume* (Motilal Banarsidass, 1985), esp. Sect. IV, which includes my transcription of the above *kārikās* into symbolic notation. (A similar chart is also given in Ichimura's "A Study on the Mādhyamika Method of Refutation and its Influence on Buddhist Logic", *JIABS* IV, 1(1981), pp. 94-95).

21. Ichimura, "Buddhist Dialectical Methods and their Structural Identity", (See the résumé appeared in *the 31st CISHAAN Proceedings,* Vol. I, pp. 149-50), which appears in *the Dr. S.V. Sohoni Felicitation Volume* for *JBRS.*

22. This passage is found in another essay by Seng-chao: "The Doctrine that whatever is Unreal is Emptiness"; *Taisho.* p. 152 c (15-20).

23. *Ibid.,* c (20-23).

Chapter 12

Tāntric Buddhism (in Eastern India)

Bijayananda Kar

Introduction

Tāntric Buddhism has a long established tradition. After the *Mahāpari-nirvāṇa* of Lord Buddha, major Councils were held at Rajagṛha and Vaiśāli. Dispute and controversies arose concerning the teachings and messages of the Lord. It is said that even during the life time of the Lord, there were occasional debates and disputes among the disciples and, as a result, the Lord left the assembly of the disciples and remained silent. After few weeks of the passing away of the Lord, the first Buddhist Council was held at Rajagṛha and Mahākāsyapa was the chairperson of that Council. Some settlement over the disputes was made possible and teachings of the Lord were practised and propagated for sometime without any serious obstacle. But gradually again controversies among the disciples as well as followers were found quite serious and, as a result, the second council was held at Vaiśāli after hundred years almost. There was found to be explict division among the Buddhist followers on the theoretical as well as practical issues. Some remained firm to the established tradition and were identified as orthodox. Others were found to be somewhat progressive and wanted some modifications on the traditional setting. They formed a separate school of their own, known as Mahāsaṅgha, while the orthodox ones were identified as Theravādins or the elders. Later on this division among the Buddhists had been named as Hīnayāna and Mahāyāna meaning thereby that the theravādins, being orthodox and not prone to change and progress, followed the Low Path (*yāna*) and the Mahāsāṅgikas, being progressive and dynamic, followed the Great Path. It is said that the terms like *hīna* and *mahā* were originally coined by Mahāsāṅgikas. It is remarked that while the Theravādins remained bound by the canon and mostly became confined to the principles of *Dhamma* in a rigid form without having any scope for investigating into the theoretical and rational foundation of different dharmic practices, the Mahāsāṅgikas were engaged in revealing the theoretical basis of Buddhistic teaching resulting thereby different speculative formulations on the basis of reason. In other words, philosophical and metaphysical theorisations of Buddhist teaching were made possible by the effort of Mahāsāṅgikas and thereby important schools like Vijñānavāda, Svatantra-Vijñānavada and Śūnyavāda were brought to focus under the banner of Mahāyāna.

Both the sects, i.e., Hīnayāna and Mahāyāna continued to have their followers quite impressively. But, in due course, it was found that the impact of elders was not so strong among the masses primarily because, the elders were found quite rigid and radical in respect of following the diverse practices. Some such practices were found to be not easily accessible to the ordinary folk. Probably, on account of that, the principle of Theravāda did not attract the popular mass impressively and also members of Theravādins left the country to propagate their views elsewhere, particularly among the people of South-east region. After the great Kalinga War (261 BC) the emperor, Aśoka embraced Bauddha dharma and changed from Caṇḍāśoka to Dharmāśoka. He convened the third Buddhist Council at Pāṭaliputra and patronised Buddhism outside India by sending his own children, Buddhist monks and followers. That is how one finds large number of Hīnayānists remaining today in Srilanka, Thailand, Myanmar, Cambodia and other countries.

The Mahāsāṅgikas, being progressive and less puritanic were found to be more accessible to the demands of popular front. They introduced very many changes in the realm of established practices and, in this connection, had introduced theoretical background of certain Buddhist practices they retained. By introducing the theoretical foundation, their stand became more convincing among the laity. But, again, this optimistic note remained for a short-while. Very soon it was realised that too much emphasis on theorisations had also given rise to much of speculative surmises and the original Buddhistic emphasis on the observance of moral codes and conduct at the practical plane became pushed to the background. That also was not favourable to the mass. The doctrinal differences between different philosophical schools of Buddhist Mahāyānists became so rigid and acute in due course, the common mass found the whole enterprise as least appealing. The heir-splitting debate over the issue whether *Vijñāna* or *Śūnya* is ultimately real did not carry any impact on the popular front.

Further, the Buddhists' silence and non-commital attitude towards issues like theistic Lord, creation of the world and the status of the individual in relation to the theistic God did not attract the then common mass who were already well tuned with a theistic temper. The conception of Iśvara, he being reincarnated in form of different *avatāras* from time to time to establish dharma by way of wiping out the evil and establishing the good were found to be some such vital notions that attracted the mass quite considerably. Consequently, two courses were found available. Either Buddhism, in its own setting having no compromise with theism and creation, had to be confined to a limited few intelligentia or it was to be assimilated into the traditionally rooted Vedic and also non-Vedic āgamic current and thereby some of the cardinal features of Vedic/Vedāntic doctrines and non-Vedic āgamic beliefs were to be accepted within the Buddhistic fold so that Buddhism would continue to retain its stand among the common mass. Those who remained confined to the set Buddhistic pattern without making any compromise with the age old Vedic and āgamic stand became small in number and, in due course, that form of Buddhism with its separate and independent status could not flourish in the country and, in some way, that trend of Buddhist thought found its way outside the country. Its message was heard in different countries of northern region like Tibet, China, Japan and even Korea. Buddhism had to thrive by accommodating their indigenous culture, belief and faith to a considerable degree. The other move that was out to make a synthetic harmony with age-old Vedic beliefs and practices became well acceptable to the common-folk. Consequently, Lord Buddha became deified. The *prajñāpāramitā* (3rd/4th century A.D.), composed by Asanga (the elder brother of Vasubandhu) has the mention of the worship of Buddha. Buddha was adored as one of the *avatāras* in Jayadev's famous *Gīta Govinda*. Buddhists moral preachings and norms were entertained within the theistic formulation and resulting thereby a synthesis between Vedāntism and Buddhism.

II

It is at this stage, Tāntrism has crept into the fold of Buddhism. Like Hīnayāna and Mahāyāna, Tantrayāna has come to the forefront. It accepts the philosophical background of classical Buddhism but at the same time has introduced certain peculiar practices to realise the theoretical objectives. Those practices are mostly identified as tāntric in nature.

Now, before dwelling upon the salient features of Tantrayāna, let us briefly touch upon the meaning and significance of the term: *'tantra'* itself. This word has been used in several senses. The word is from the etymological point of view, derived from the root: *tan* meaning that which spreads. It stands for knowledge that is spread or propagated. *Tantra* is used as referring to some form of abbreviation of expanded version. It is also treated as pointing to certain philosophical system or darśana-śāstra. In that way, one comes across such expressions like *Ṣaṣṭhi-tantra, Kapila-tantra* (of Sāṅkhya), *Gautama-tantra* (of Nyāya), *Pūrva-tantra* (of Mīmāṁsā) *Uttara-tantra* (of Vedānta), *Vaināṣika-tantra* (referring to the Buddhist stand) and soon. *Tantra* is also taken as synonym of *Āgama* in contrast to *Nigama* that is (sometimes) applied to the Vedas. According to *Kulārṇava tantra, Vedic* is for *Satya Yuga, Smṛti* is for *Tretā Yuga, Purāṇa* is for *Dvāpara Yuga* and *Tantra* or *Āgama* is for *Kali Yuga*[1] In this way, *Tantra* is accepted in certain circle as the fifth Veda.[2]

The founder of *Tantra* is said to be Lord Śiva who is acclaimed as *ādiguru, mahāyogī* and *mahākauḷa.* From this angle of vision, there is the rise and spread of *Śaiva tantra* and in similar plane there has also been the formation of *Sākta, Vaiṣṇava. Saurya* and *Gāṇapatya tantra* wherein the authorship of *Tantra* is said to have been attributed to Devī, Viṣṇu, Śūrya and Gaṇapati respectively.

There is also another dimension which requires to be touched upon in this context. It is already indicated here that *Tantra* has been taken as *Āgama.* In the pre Vedic *āgama* sources there are found references of tāntric practices of worshipping both father and mother deities. A specific recension of *Atharva Veda: Paippalāda Saṁhitā* contains *Ugratārā* and *Tāpīnī Upaniṣads* which have definite tāntric element while the subtle dārśanic thoughts and ideas continued to attract intellegentia, and the people of higher class, the ordinary common man particularly the people of aboriginal and tribal type did not find much interest in such theoretical dialectics. They were more moved by some popular element of faith and occult practices. In this way, there is the evidence of two modes of spiritual activities: one mode being engaged in tracing as well as evolving divergent form of dārśanic standpoints based on subtle intellectual standard and at the same length another mode being confined to certain set of religious faith and beliefs with some form of esoteric practices with the supposition that sincere execution of such practices would give rise to the attainment of the highest (*parama siddhi*).

So far as Buddhism is concerned there is found to be a parallel movement. As already indicated, both the Theravādins and the Mahāprāsaṅgikas had been engaged in interpreting the sayings of Lord Buddha (*Buddha-vacana*) according to their respective dārśanic formulations. In that way, certain theories (*Vādas*) came to the focus.

Though such theorisation continued to inspire and encourage the intellectual group, those had no such appreciable impact among the popular mass. Ordinary, simple, unsophisticated mind would rather move forward to subside his difficulties by some tangible procedure which would supply prompt result. Such mind used to have no patience to wait for a distant future. The observance of rigorous moral code and conduct prescribed for both monks and householders were supposed to be visionary and impractical. Radical control of desires and passions gave rise to some form of obsession and dejection.

It was in this background, tāntrism was crept into Mahāyānic mode of meditation (*upāsanā/dhyāna*). Tāntric elements, i.e., *dhāraṇī, mantra, yantra, mudrā* and *maṇḍala* were introduced. Scholars like, B. Bhattācārya holds that despite his critical outlook to Vedic ritualism in form of animal sacrifice, magical spell, superstitious dogmatic beliefs, Buddha did not object to *tantra* in Buddhistic trend, specially the introduction of *mudrās* and *maṇḍalas*.[3]

During the period of 3rd/4th century A.D., the important Mahāyānic treatise: *Mañjuśrimūlakalpa* was composed in which description about *mudrā* and *maṇḍala* was presented. Such poses and diagrams were supposed to be necessary for worship and performance of specific tāntric rituals. Later on, there was the composition of another important tāntric treatise within the Buddhist fold, i.e., *Gūhya Samāja-tantra* (300-400 A.D., attributed to Asaṅga as its author by B. Bhattacarya) which contains detailed account of the attainment of Buddhahood by means of acknowledging the importance of *Śakti* (divine-energy) and its realisation through *yoga* and *Samādhi*. The theory of five *dhyāni* Buddhas was introduced in the treatise. Following the direction prescribed in the *Gūhyasamāja-tantra,* in and around 1200 A.D. Advayavajra brought out *Tattvaratnāvali* in which there is the mention of two division of Mahāyāna: *Pāramitānaya* and *Mantranaya,* the former dealing more with the dialectical theorisation and the latter more with tāntric element giving thereby scope for formulation of Vajrayāna, Kālacakrayāna and Sahajayāna.

According to Tārānātha (the famous Tibetan scholar) tāntric elements in Buddhism were prevalent during the time of Nāgārjuna (200 A.D.). Basing on this, the modern scholars hold that Nāgārjuna is the founder of esoteric Tāntrism so far as Buddhism is concerned.[4] But, according to another Tibetan source, there is another Nāgārjuna (700 A.D.) who was initiated to Tāntric Buddhism by Sarahapāda, the well known Siddhācarya.[5] Taking both the findings, the scholars in recent times have more or less accepted the version that earlier Nāgārjuna was the famous *darśanajña* of Mādhyamika Śūnyavāda and the later Nāgārjuna of 700 A.D. was the famous tāntric who propounded *Tantra darśana* on Tantrayāna. Though there are differences of opinion among prominent researchers like Waddell, Winternitz, Sylvain Levi and others regarding the inclusion of tāntric mystical traces in the early Buddhist sources like Asaṇga's *Mahāyāna-Sūtrālaṅkāra,* one thing remains almost certain that tāntrism, so far as Buddhism is concerned, has a long tradition. It is originally, of course, in the rudimentary form (as usual) and subsequently it has been developed into matured form during 700-1100 A.D.

Researchers are often found to differ amongst themselves on the issue whether Vedic *tantra* has any impact on Buddhist *tantra* or vice versa. It is, as already hinted earlier, held in certain quarters that the non-Vedic source had the original *Śakti* based tāntric practices. The Vedic *tantra* is said to have been more or less based on *Śaiva* footing. *Śakti* is, according to this tradition, treated as *māyā* (unreal or illusory). Buddhist *tantra,* in its original setting, did not show any linkage with *Śakti*. But a careful study would reveal that the origin as well as development of *tantra* in all these three sources have different facets at different stages. In non-Vedic source there are the traces of both Śaiva and Śākta elements and the same is also found in Vedic as well as Buddhist sources. To say that Buddhist tantra is only having Śaivite trace and no trace of Śāktism is not correct. At the subsequent stage (which will be discussed later in detail), there is the inclusion of *Yoginī* cult within the Buddhistic tāntric fold. It is rather more plausible to hold the view that all these three sources (non-Vedic, the Vedic and the Buddhist) have been found as assimilating both Śaivite and Śākta elements and that has profoundly contributed to the rise and development of tāntrism itself.

From the aforesaid discussion, it seems some what clear that *tantra* in its non-intellectual popular magical or miraculous spell has become quite attractive among the down-trodden particularly the aboriginal and tribal primitives, so far as the eastern region of the Indian sub-continent is concerned. Since early time (even today) there are considerable regions which are primarily inhabited by the tribals. So the impact of *tantra* is found to be more conspicuous in this region than in other places. Even in the age of epics, *Smṛtis* and *Purāṇas,* the eastern region was mostly being identified as the hilly, mountaneous, forest areas and the primitive people used to have their settlement. As already stated, a portion of *Atharvaveda* dealing with *tantra,* was discovered from Uḍradeśa, i.e., Orissa. The old name of modern Orissa is determined by the scholars as Uḍiyāna, Oḍvisā, Uḍra and so on. Aṅga is identified by historian as the southern Bihar (specially the areas relating to modern Bhagalpur and Ranchi). Aṅga, Baṅga and Kalinga roughly refer to Bihar, Bengal and Orissa. The greater Assam of the previous days, comprised of Nagaland, Mizoram, Manipur, Arunachal Pradesh and Meghalaya primarily has tribal population. The hilly areas of greater Bengal of the previous era are found to be quite thickly inhabited by the aboriginals.

While both Hināyana or Śrāvakayāna and Mahāyāna were found to be somewhat distant from the popular mass on account of their sophisticated intellectualism as well as prescription of rigid code and conduct, Buddhism had to survive by making some form of reconciliatary and compromising move to attract the mass, particularly the down-trodden and the primitives respecting their sentiment, set-beliefs and prejudices. The general temper of theistic outlook mixed with miracle and magic has to be incorporated within Buddhistic theory and practices so that it could gain some solid ground in such communities. And that is how there is the transition of Mahāyāna to Tantrayāna in general. And the different formulations of tāntric Buddhism in form of Vajrayāna, Sahajayāna, Kālacakrayāna have become possible in this eastern belt and that has given rise to a new form of Buddhism which has become greatly assimilated with original Vedic and non-Vedic sources.

Around 800 A.D. number of Buddhist tāntricas appeared who evolved various tāntric practices/rituals and were known as *Sādhakas*. They were said to be composer of *Sādhanamālās*. The protective magical spells usually identified as *dhāraṇīs* and the chanting having a magical effect (*parittas*) figured most in such Sādhanās and number of manuscripts belonging to 600-700 A.D. containing those have been discovered from central Asia. The Mahāyāna texts like *Mahāsannipāta-Sūtra* and *Saddharma-puṇḍarīka* of 100 A.D. have distinct reference to such *dhāraṇīs*.

The tāntric Sādhakas affiliated themselves to Mādhyamika or Yogācāra *darśana*. They all held that phenomenal world and the ultimate reality are identical. There is no difference between *saṁsāra* and *nirvāṇa*. They subscribed to the *Oneness* of the universe (*tathatā/samatā/śūnyatā*). For them, there is no basic difference between *pravṛtti* and *nivṛtti,* so also between *saṃvṛti* and *paramārtha*. They prescribed number of activities for attaining the highest e.g. *caryā* (tāntric practices), *dhyāna* (meditation), *homa* (offering of oblations), *japa* (muttering of prayers), *kriyā* (rites), *mantras* (magical spells), *mudrā* (figure poses), *niyama* (austerities), *śaucācāra* (cleanlines in performing rituals) and *śila* (moral sanctity). All these were aided by *haṭha-yoga* or *concentration* acquired by means of artificial aids and also the addition of the process of *prāṇāyāma*. The tāntric Bauddha was to have a formal initiation (*abhiṣeka*) and was to be guided by a *guru* (spiritual mentor).

The Tibetan tradition of Buddhism which has been well preserved in the documentation made by Tārānātha reveals that Tāntrism had its origin since the time of Ācārya Asaṅga in whose time there was the practice of *Anuttarayoga* (i.e., the tāntric meditation of realising the truth) giving more prominence to *yogatantra* instead of *Karma tantra*. During the famous Pāla kings of Bengal of 800 A.D. there were practices of *yogasiddhis* and there were about 84 prominent Siddhācāryas widely spread in some parts of Kashmir and the eastern India (Bengal, Bihar specially Magadha), Assam and Orissa. According to Tārānātha, king Devapāla of Bengal (810-850 A.D.) was a staunch Buddhist and during his time, Bālaputradeva of the Sailendra dynasty granted five villages to endow a monastery at Nalanda. Devapāla appointed Buddhist priest of Nagarahāra (Jalalabad) as the Head of the Nalanda monastery.

The element of Tantra is noticed in some early Buddhist sources. In the *Mahāvagga,* there is the mention of magical power and the *chullavagga* has the references of Bhikkhus carrying human skulls as bowls. But all such references are so meagre that it is quite difficult to trace the matured form of Buddhist Tāntrism before 700 A.D. There are two primary Buddhist treatises, viz., *Gūhyasamāja tantra,* and *Tathāgata Gūhyaka Sūtra* which deal with *tantras*. The *Mahāyāna Sūtras* were gradually supplimented by *tantras*. For instance, the *mañjuśrī mūlakalpa* which is also named as *Mahā Vaipulya Mahāyāna Sūtra* was rendered as *Tantra* in the Tibetan source. The *prajñāpāramitā Sūtra* was commonly used as a *dhāranī* and the *Prajñāpāramitā Hṛdaya Sūtra* that is preserved in Japan (Horiuzi monastery) is said to have alleviated all pains. In chapter VIII of the *Sukhāvati Vyūha* (of 100 A.D. and translated into Chinese in 200 A.D.), *dhāraṇis* were received by persons who enjoyed the pleasures of Sūkhāvati. In the *Laṅkāvatāra Sūtra* (400 A.D.) magical spells for protecting men against snake, demons and ghosts are enumerated.

Thus it seems plausible that Mantrayāna, in due course, evolved from Mahāyāna and has attained almost an independent status comprising of mystic practices like *Mudrā, Maṇḍala, Abhiṣeka* and *Samādhi*. The six forms of esoteric rituals called *abhicāra* are: *māraṇa* (killing), *mohana* (enchanting), *stambhana* (paralysing), *vidveṣaṇa* (envying), *ucchāṭana* (exciting) and *vaśīkaraṇa* (subducing). Those are accompanied by five further steps called as *Pañca makāras,* viz, *madya* (wine), *māṁsa* (meat), *matsya* (fish), *mudrā* (coin) and *maithuna* (sexual intercourse). Introduction of all these practices into the fold of Buddhism has paved the way for the origin and development of Tantric Buddhism and thus the former moral and philosophical temper of Buddhist thought found in Hīnāyāna and Mahāyāna has been found declined to a considerable degree.

Vajrayāna

Though, as hinted before, Tantrayāna broadly includes Vajrayāna, Kālacākrayāna and Sahajayāna there appears to be certain distinctiveness as far as these three formulations are concerned. Vajrayāna technically connotes the path of perfect void (*Śūnya*) by means of which the immutable nature of *ātman* and of the *dharma* can be attained. The *Advaya Vajra Saṁgraha* holds that *Sūnyatā* is *Vajra*. It is further held that *Sattva* means pure awareness (*Jñāna mātratā*) and the identity of *Vajra* and *Sattva* stands for *Vajrasattva*. According to the *Guhya Samāja-tantra,* an authoritative text of Vajrayāna, Vajrasattva is the symbolic representation of the *Abhūtaparikalpa* of the Yogacarcins where *Śūnyatā* and *Vyāvahārika jagat* in the form of pure experience (*Vijñapimātratā*) are realised as one and the same. Vajrayāna is generally classified into four types of tantra, viz., *Kriyā tantra, Chrayā tantra, Yoga tantra* and *Anuttara tantra*. The first two of these are meant for the beginners while the last two for the matured scholars. According to *Sādhanamāla,* there are four tāntric *piṭhas:* Kāmākhyā (identified as Kāmarūpa of Assam), Srihaṭṭa (identified as Sylhet of Bengal), Pūrṇagīri and Uḍḍiyāna. Some scholars attempt to identity Pūrṇagiri as Poona but that is not accepted by other scholars.[6] In the *Tantrasāra,* Pūrṇagiri is described as Uḍiśānāth and on that basis, scholars (cf. N.K. Sahu) identify it as Jagannātha pītha[7] and others (cf. S.N. Rajguru) refer to Śrī Kūrma of Andhra on the basis of the name *pūrṇakoṭi* occuring in the stone inscription on the Simāchalam temple.[8] About Uḍḍiyāna, there have been differences among scholars, which is also named as Oḍḍiyāna, Oḍiyāna, Oḍṛyāna and so on. H.P. Sastri takes it as belonging to Orissa.[9] M. Winterntiz also accepts Orissa as Uḍḍiyāna, but with a question mark.[10] R.M. Nath identifies it as Hojai of Assam[11] and N.N. Dasgupta identifies it with Chittangang of Bangladesh.[12] But Waddell,[13] Sylvaṁ levy[14] and Bagchi[15] identify Uḍḍiyāna as the Swat Valley of Kabul. Now, in view of the rise of tāntric Buddhism in the eastern region of India (where its traces are very much present in conspicuous form), identification of Uḍḍiyāna with Kabul very much away from all the other three *pīṭhas* which are located in the eastern region, seem to be highly dubitable. By now, there is more or less agreement among the scholars regarding the use of Oḍra, Uḍra as relating to Orissa. Uḍḍiyāna is evidently close to Oḍra/Uḍra. So, the identification of Uḍḍiyāna as Orissa is more probable where there is much tāntric Buddhistic archeological findings with the availability of tāntric texts.[16] Thus the identification of Uḍḍiyāna with Hojai or with Chittagang (Bangladesh) is rather remote in comparison with Orissa. Further, there are findings of number of *Vajrayoginī* status and centres of *yoginī-sādhanā* brought to light by way of excavation in different parts of Orissa. The identification of Uḍḍiyāna as Swat also appear to be quite doubtful in view of the fact that there is no point of similarity between the two words, and the non-availability of any archeological evidences on form of yoginī status and the places of yoginī sādhanā in the Swat Valley. Recently Lokesh Chandra in his article "India and China: the Beyond and within"[17] has just read Uḍyāna as Swat but has not established his point of identification by any reasoning. From all this discussion, it seems more plausible to identify Uḍḍiyāna as Orissa.

Kālacakrayāna

It is said to be a coarse tāntric evolution of the Ādi Buddha doctrine coupled with mystical touch of *mantras* and it is set to explain *sṛṣṭi* and the *śakti* of nature by the union of *kāli* not only with dhyāni Buddhas but also with Ādi Buddha. *Kāla* means time, death and destruction. Thus kālacakra is the wheel of destruction. It is the wheel of time where a yogic process is prescribed to protect oneself from the influence of kāla. According to kālachakra *tantra* and Tantrāloka, it is a system of yoga which moves the universe in the body of man and introverts the macrocosmic forces of time in the process of human organism. In other words, it identifies the universe with human body and that of explaining *kāla* with reference to the functions of the vital air spread through the whole nervous system.

Sahajayāna

Though *Sahaja* literally the means easy and *yāna* means path, in the technical Buddhist sense it defies all definitions. According to Tillopāda, *Sahaja* is a state where all thought is exhausted and the *prāṇa* or the vital air comes to a cessation. The idea of *sahaja* is explained by the *siddhas* negatively discarding all positive descriptions. The state of *Sahaja* is, composed with that of *tathatā* of Aśvaghośa, Śūnyatā of Nāgārjuna, Vijñāprimātratā of Vijñānavādins, *Vajrasattva* or *Vajradhātu* of Vajrayānis. In addition to all these philosophical suggestions, *Sahaja* is also treated as the fulfilment of primitive instincts and desires. According to Luipā, a prominent Sahajayānist, meditation has no fruitful consequence. He recommends for giving up of all austere yogic practices. The *Sahajans* repudiate all gods and goddess advocated in Mahāyāna and Vajrayāna. Buddha, according to Sahajayāna, resides in body only. Thus worshipping of the physical body is in tune with the propitiation of natural instincts including sex. *Sahaja Yoga* consists of embracing the female *Śakti* variously called as the *Cāṇḍāli, Doṁbi, Savarī, Yoginī, Nairātmā Sahaja Sundari*. The bliss that is said to have been derived from this sexoyogic practice is generally classified into four stages: *ānanda, paramānanda, Viramānanda* and *Sahajānanda* which is also termed as *mahāsukha*. It is like the vacant sky and yet cool and sweet.

As hinted earlier, Nālanda had come into prominence in and around early 9th century so far as Buddhist learning is concerned. It had not only been established by the patronage of the *Pāla* rulers of Bengal and Bihar, it had also attracted the Buddhist monks and preachers for a steady settlement from the Buddhist orthodox point of view, but it also had great attraction for the *dārśanikas*, and *sannyāsis*, from different parts of the entire sub-continent including foreign scholars and Pundits from the other parts of the Asiatic world. The Chinese travellers like Yuan Chwang, Hiouen-Thsand, Fa-Hien had good deal of references about this great citadel of Buddhist learning of philosophy, religion, culture and art. Nālanda was considered to be the topmost Buddhist centre of learning in the whole of Asia during 800-1000 A.D.

So far as Tāntric Buddhism is concerned, Nālanda also had its prominent share in discussing as well as spreading the tāntric religio-philosophic message to different concerned areas with positive consequences. There is difference of opinion among the scholars about the origin of *Tantra*. According to Mm. H.P. Sastri, *Kubjika Tantra* was of Chinese origin and it was from there it came to India. But from the Tibetan tradition (source *Pag-Sām-Jon-Zang*), Tāntric Buddhism first developed in Uḍḍīyāna. Of course, Mm. H.P. Sastri has identified Uḍḍīyāna as same as Orissa. It is interesting to note that, the earlier referred to *Kubjikā Tantra* mentions *Virajā* as the tāntric goddess of Uḍḍīyāna[18] and that is identified as the famous *tāntric pīṭha* of *devī* cult, Jajpur, near which there was the establishment of the famous Buddhist monastic University: Ratnagiri in 800 A.D.

Between 100-700 A.D., Mahāyāna Buddhism got its spread all over Orissa. The great *pīṭhas* where Buddhist monasteries were built where Parimalagiri (at the border of Bolangir and Sambalpur Districts-known also as Gondhamārdanagiri)[19], Suravagiri (identified as the Dhauligiri – 8 K.M. away from Bhubaneswara city in South), Bhorasaila (Near Delānga of Puri District); Che-li-ta-lo (identified) by Cunningham as Puri) where Bauddha dharma and *darśana* were discussed.

In Orissa, Mahāyāna had two formulations: Mādhyamika and yogācāra. While Mādhyamika was studied and propagated at Parimalagiri, for Yogācāra, Ratnagiri (about 20 K.M. away from Cuttack in North-east) was the main centre by 500 A.D. Nāgārjuna and Āryadeva were prominent Buddhists in Parimalagiri. According to Tārānātha,[20] Pitopāda was greatly associated with Ratnagiri and Bodhiśri and Nāropa were his two disciples.

In Orissa, gradually the Mādhyamika Buddhism had been considerably modified. Attempt was made to deify Lord Buddha. The Gods and Goddesses of the Vaidic dharma were also assimilated into Bauddha dharma. In this context, Mahāyāna was also modified into Tantrayāna. The tāntric esoteric practices were included within the Buddhistic fold and, as a result of which, Vajrayāna, Sahajayāna and Kālacakrayāna were formulated in the land of Orissa, being well patronised by the then Buddhist rulers (Bhaumakaras).

The Buddhist Tantrayāna had also strong impact on the psyche of Orissans. Its early exponent Saraha (633 A.D.), according to the Tibetan source, was born in Oḍivāsā (Orissā)[21] and composed *dohās*[22]. His disciple, Nāgārjuna (790 A.D.) was born at Kanchi and resided in Sriparvata in Andhra. He was a great Tantric and practised *Sādhanās* like *Mahāmāyā, Kurukullā* and *Mahākāla*. He was also the worshiper of Vajratārā and was a Vajrayānist. His disciple, Sabāripāda (657 A.D.) was very much associated with Orissa. He attained proficiency in Kurukullā[23] *Sādhanā* and Vajrayogin cult. Savaripāda's description of Savaragirl, her dress and ornaments (in Cariyāgīti-28) are found to have been similiar with the description given in Sāralā *Mahābhārata* (*Madhyaparva*)[24] "The state of mind as restless (*cañcala citta*) needs to be stable" is recommended in *Cariyāgīti*—21. The same also has been depicted by Oriya poet of later times (Acyutānanda's *Brahma Śaṅkuli*).[25]

Luipā (669 A.D.), according to *Pag San Jon Zang* source,[26] was from a fisherman's family in Uḍḍiyāna (somewhere near river prāchi). Apart from some of his treatises in Sanskrit Language (*Vajra Sattva Sādhanā,* and *Buddhodaya*) he is credited also with some practices in Oriya (like *Tattua Suabhava dṛṣṭi, Dohākośo gītīka* and *Luipāda gītīka*).[27]

The Tantrayāna, with its esoteric rituals and practices, introduced theism into the fold of Buddhism. It was advanced that the supreme Lord is the Ādī-Buddha. It was further speculated that Ādi-Dharma/ Adi-prajñā forms a part of Ādi-Buddha and thus constitutes the basis for the whole universe. It is from Ādi Buddha, five Dhyāni-Buddhas emanate and each Dhyāni-Buddha is to create a *Bodhi-Sattva*. According to another tradition, each Dhyāni-Buddha is attached with a *Śaktī*. Thus, the Dhyāni-Buddha and *Śakti* together bring forth number of *Bodhisattvas* for the purpose of both creation and maintenance of the universe. The five Dhyāni Buddhas are: Vairocana, Ratna Sambhava, Amitābha, Amogha Siddhi and Akṣobhya.

One of the important formulations of Tantrayāna is Sahajayāna. While in Vajrayāna *Śūnyatā* is identified with *Vajra*[16] and Kālacakreyāna is found to have given special emphasis on esoteric practices (*gupta sāddhanas*) and holds that creation is possible due to the co-operation and union between Kāli and Buddha, Sahajayāna is, mainly, found to have been propagated by *Laxmikarā*, the sister of Indrabhüti. She has the support from Jālandharipāda and his disciple, Knupācārya and Kṛsnacārya/Kahnupāda. All these Sahajayānists hold that the whole universe (*brahmāṇḍa*) is within the body (*piṇḍa/śarīra*). As such, great importance is given on human body, for it is viewed as the microcosm of the whole universe.

The great Tantrayānī, Saraha was the high priest (*ācārya*) of the university of Nālanda. About Saraha/Sarahapāda/Rahukbhadra, the Bsṭ āñ-ḥgyur plate mentions that he belongs to Uḍḍiyāna while according to Tārānātha, he was born in Oḍiviśā. It is needless to mention that scholars have identified Uḍḍiyāna and Oḍiviśā as Orissa. Saraha is attributed with the authorship of at least 25 tāntric works including 4 *Dohās* in *Chariyā*. Scholars like Cordier suggest that there are more than one Saraha. In any case, it is held that one Saraha belonged to 800 A.D. during the reign of Subhakaradeva I of the Bhaumakara dynasty in Orissa and other, as the author of *Dohās* belonged to 1000 A.D.

The disciple of Saraha was Nāgārjuna (700 A.D.) who was a great tantrayānist who was born at Kohara (near Kanchi's south) and educated under tutorship of Saraha. He practised the *Sādhanā* of *Mahāmāyurī, Kurukullā* and *Mahākālā*. He was credited with number of super-natural powers and magical spells. Two of his sādhanās are preserved in the *Sādhanamālā* that relate to the worship of Vajratārā and Ekajaṭā. He also composed some works on *Gūhyasamāja tantra*.

Savaripā was the disciple of tāntric Nāgārjuna and was the tutor of Luipā. According to Rāhula Sāṁkaṛtyayana, Luipā belonged to Magadha (769-809 A.D.). Of course there is a reference about another younger Luipā in the *Abhi-Samaya Mañjarī* composed by Śāntarakṣita who was said to have been born in Chandradvipa of Bengal and the scholars have firm reason to associate the younger Luipā with the origin of Nātha cult.

According to Tārānātha, the other Luipa had a disciple; Vajraghanṭa who, after attaining *siddhi,* propagated the *Gūhyatantra* and converted number of people to Tantrayāna. It is Kambala who is identified as one of the most prominent disciples of Vajraghaṇṭa. According to Rāhula Saṁkṛtyāyana, Kambala flourished during the reign of Dera Pāla (of Bengal 810-850 A.D.) and it is said that he wrote six works on *Heruka Sādhanā,* besides a collection of *Dohās* entitled: *Kambala-gītikā.* According to Tārānātha, Kambala and his associate, Padmavajra jointly introduced *Hevajra-tantra,* an offshoot of Vajrayāna in an important respect. Padmavajra is famous for composing the important work: *Gūhyasiddhi.*

Anangavajra, the disciple of Padmavajra was famous for his work: *Prajñopāyaviniscaya-Siddhi,* an expository work on Vajrayāna. Indrabhūti, the king of Uḍḍiyāna, was the disciple of Anangvajra according to Binoyatosh Bhattacharya. His famous work *Jñānasiddhi* expounds the doctrīne of the five Dhyanī-Buddhas. His associate, Padmasambhava, according to Rāhula Saṁkṛtyāyana, accompanied Śāntarakṣita in his sojourn to Tibet. He remained in Tibet during 180-195 A.D. and established a great monastery at Bsām-ye, after the model of Odantapurī Vihar in Magadha. It was after him, the followers of Bon-pā religious cult of Tibet developed a synthetic Indo-Tibetan mysticism called as Lāmāism.

Indrabhūti's sister, Laxmikarā was revered as one of the 84 siddhas and was responsible for introducing *Sahajayāna*, a definite departure from the trend of Vajrayāna. She gave a turning point to Tantrayāna by introducing such changes from the worship of Dhyānī-Buddhas to the emphasis on the physical gratification.

There were other *siddhas* like Jālandharipāda, Virupā etc. who contributed to Sahajayāna without being hostile to the practices of Vajrayāna and in their own way to the cause of Tāntric Buddhism. Some of their writings are preserved in the Tibetan translation in the Bsṭāñ-hgyur. Rāhul Saṁkṛtyāyana holds that the disciple of Jālandhara was Kahrupā (Kṛṣṇapāda) who was living at Somapurī (during the reign of Devapala) 900-950 A.D.). He is held to be the author of number of Buddhist tāntric works, preserved in the list of Bsṭāñ-hgyur. In this connection, a reference about the work *Bauddha gāna O Dohā* needs to be mentioned which embodies the philosophical aspects of Tāntrism. The work contains: *Caryā-Carya Viṁseaya Dohākośa* of Sarojavajra, *Dohākośa* of kṛṣṇāchārya (identified as kahnupāda by Dr. S.K. Chatterjee) and portions of *Dākārṇava.* The language of the *Bauddha gāna O Dohā* is variously viewed by the linguists. Dr. Suniti Kumar Chatterjee[28] treats it to be a form of ancient Bengali, Dr. Karunkar Kar[29] holds it to be early form of Oriya and Rāhula Sāṁkṛtyāyana[30] declares it to be old Bihari (Maithili). Of course, the reason for such diversity of opinion seems to be the point that the early Pāli language was gradually evolving itself into different forms and that were noticed in this work as a whole. So the findings of the linguists (cited above) have a definite point of significance.

Conclusion

Religion is a social phenomenon. People continue to get inspiration, solace and peace out of different religious faiths and beliefs. But, at the same time, it is marked that when such beliefs or faiths are found to be too much imaginary/speculative creating some obstacle for the smooth-functioning of normal living, people move in the opposite direction to either root out such beliefs and faiths or to advance suitable modification in that. Religion, therefore, cannot survive without popular basis. We have hinted earlier that the early phase of Buddhism could not remain intact and, as a result, there were the rise of modification and reformation. In order to suit the religious expectation, the dārśanic foundation were correspondingly reformulated. Different theorisations were advanced to make changes and, at the same time, to preserve the original religious stand in some form or other.

In Buddhism, the rise and development of Tāntrism is not, in that way, an unexpected outcome. When the speculative theorisations based on intellectual dialectic were found to be too much away from the common ordinary expectations and also while the prescriptions of radical disciplinary measures were insisted upon under the plea of some sort of impractical moral footing, the religio-philosophical standpoint no longer attracts the sizable section of the man and, as a consequence, there is change and reform. Tāntrism gave importance to the need and requirement of living at the earthly plane. *Nirvāṇa* has to be understood in terms of *saṁsāra,* moral preachings must be practically pleasable and visionary idealism in that respect has to be restricted. Magical spell is an immediate device to attract the ignorant man; so that has to be retained. Theistic faith is deep-rooted in human-psyche; so that need not be brushed aside. At least that was the demand of that period. It is because of that in Buddhism, theistic deification had been introduced to attract the ignorant, simple mind, magical spell and some form of esoteric practices were introduced. Under the garb of that tendency, cheap sentimental appeal in term of meeting the carnal desires was encouraged and, as a result, sexological devices were brought in. All such introduction were found to be again moving in the opposite direction and were proved to be degenerate and unsocial movements. Gradually, therefore, Tāntrism lost its early impact and Tāntric Buddhism now is found to be at least not so strong in the public mind.

References

1. *Kṛte Śrutyukta ācārastretayām Smṛti sambhavaḥ dvāpare tu purāṇoktaḥ kalāvāgama* sannath – *Kuḷārṇava tantra.*
2. M. Rene Guenon "*Tantra:* The Fifth Vedas" in *Indian Culture,* Vol. V, p. 85 ff.).
3. Vide his *Buddhist Esotericism,* Chaukhamba Edn., p. 48.
4. L.A. Waddell: *Buddhism* and *Lāmāism of Tibet,* New Delhi, 1979, p.15.
5. S.C. Sarkar: "A Tibetan Account of Nāgārjuna" in *the Sino-Indian Journal,* December, 1948.
6. B. Bhattacharya (Ed.): Sādhanamālā, 2 vols., Baroda, Gaekwad's Oriental Series, 1925, 1928.
7. N. K. Sahu: *Buddhism in Orissa,* Utkal University Publication, 1958.
8. S.N. Rajguru (Ed.): *Inscriptions of Orissa,* Vol. II, Bhubaneswar, 1960.
9. B. Bhattacharya (Ed.): *op. cit.,* p. xxxvii.
10. M. Winternitz: *History of Indian Literature,* Vol. II, Calcutta University, 1933.
11. R.M. Nath: *Journal of Assam Research Society,* Vol. V, 1937.
12. N.N. Dasgupta: *Indian Historical Quarterly,* Vol. XI.
13. L.A. Waddell: *Buddhism and Lāmāism of Tibet,* New Delhi, 1979.
14. Sylvain Levi: *Journal of Asiatique,* 1915.
15. P.C. Bagchi: *Studies in the Tantra,* Calcutta University, 1975.
16. S.K. Moharana: *Tāntric Buddhism,* Delhi: Aryan Books International, 2001, pp. 66-67.
17. Published in *Sandhān* 'Journal of Centre for studies in civilisation': (Ed. D.P. Chattopadhyaya), Vol. I, No. 2, July-December, 2001.
18. N.K. Sahu: *op. cit.*, p. 146.
19. According to Hieun Tsang, Nāgārjuna's monastery is called Po-lo-mo-ki-li which is identified as Parimalagiri by historians like N.K. Sahu, *op. cit.*
20. Vide Bhupendranath Dutta: *Mystic Tales of Lāmā Tārānātha,* Calcutta: 1941, p. 49.
21. *Tārānāth's History of Buddhism* in India (tr. by Lāma Chimpā and Alaka Chattopadhyaya (Ed. by D. Chattopadhyaya) Simla, 1970, p. 8.
22. Ed. by Rahul Sāṁkṛtyāyana, Bihar Rastrabhasa Parishad, Patna, 1957.
23. Kurukullā is known from Tibetan source as a goddess of Uḍḍiyāna.
24. S.N. Moharana, *op.cit.*, p. 165.
25. *Ibid.*
26. *Pag. Sam. Jon Zang,* Index, p. cxv.
27. Dr. Bhagvan Panda "Bauddha Tantra" in *Oḍiśāra Bauddha Dharma O Sanskṛiti,* Bhubaneswar: Kedarnath Gavesana Pratisthana, Granth Mandir, Cuttack, 2000, p. 66.
28. Vide his *Origin and Development of the Bengali Language,* 2 Vols., Calcutta University Publications, 1962.
29. Vide his *Āścarya Caryācaya* (Oriya), Bhubaneswar, 1969.
30. Vide his *Dohakośa* (in Hindi), Patna, 1957.

Chapter 13

The Uniqueness of the Buddhist Way of Thinking and its Encounter with West To-day

Guy Bugault

1. First of all Please Excuse my English and my own Translation.

I shall start with the uniqueness of some utmost Buddhist ways of thinking in two texts of the Prajñāpāramitā Literature and Mādhyamīka School, the *Vajracchedikā* and the *Mādhyamikakārikās*. This will give me the opportunity of discussing with two eminent scholars, late Professor Conze and Professor David Seyfort Ruegg.

Thereafter, I shall give a hint to a contemporary hypothesis of connecting causal logic with dependent origination (*Pratītyasamutpāda*). Finally, I shall deal with Buddhism and Western thinking today.

1.1 The Way of Thinking in the Vajracchedikā

The *Vajracchedikā* makes use of a paradoxical process, in which two terms, that are not only opposite but contradictory, are linked together as if identical with each other, through the instrumental word *tena,* or *tad* in Pargiter's manuscripts, rarely *tasmāt* as in the *Hṛdaya-Sūtra*. The expression *tenocyate, tenocyante,* works as a logical but paradoxical cliche. For instance, *tat kasya hetoḥ? buddhadharmā buddhadharmā iti Subhūte 'buddhadharmāścaiva te Tathāgatena bhāṣ itāḥ, tenocyante buddhadharmā iti* (ed. Conze, 98).

The same click works for a lot of other pairs. Among them: *lakṣ ana/alakṣaṇa, kṣetravyūha/avyūha, puṇyaskandha/askandha, saṃjñā/ asamjñā, sattva/asattva, ātmabhāva/abhāva, dharmadeśanā/ na...dharmadeśanā*. And last but not the lest, *prajñāpāramitā/ apāramitā*.

Let us focus on *tena:* 'therefore'. Professor Conze asks explicitly whether one must understand 'that is why, for that reason' or 'that is how, in that manner, in that sense'. Practically, he translates 'therefore' most frequently, but reading the whole of his translation one has rather the impression – if I have not misunderstood – that he is slightly closer to the strong and abrupt interpretation, viz., 'for that reason'.

Whatever it may be, he concludes, perhaps falsely: 'by abrogating the principle of contradiction, the logic of the Prajñāpāramitā differs from that of Aristotle in at least one fundamental point'.

I am not sure that it is necessary to invoke the abrogation of the law of contradiction. Firstly, Aristotle's logic is concerned only with life in a city, social intercourse, and above all with a debate between opposite partners. Now, Subhūti is by no means an opponent, he is the echo of the *Bhagavant*, with all due reverence 'his master's voice'. There is actually no discussion between them.

Secondly, the most paradoxical passages can be explained with the help of a trans-symptotic dialectics, a sort of *passage ā la limite* (passing beyond limits, out of bonds) as in mathematics the squaring of the circle, or when an infinite curve is asymptotic to a straight line. This is an example quoted from nicolas de Cues. Another enlightening example is that of the parabola on the Cartesian plane. When one continues to advance on the axis of *x,* the same curve, without breaking its continuity, meets at a certain time a point from where it retrogresses on the axis of *y.* This makes me think that in the carrier of a *bodhisattva* there is a similar reversal of his intentionality.

Now, let us read *Vajracchedikā* 13 a: *'tat kasya hetoḥ? yaiva Subhūte prajñāpāramitā Tathāgatena bhāṣitā saiva, apāramitā Tathāgatena bhāṣitā. tenocyate prajñāpāramiteti.'* One may interpret, it seems to me; it is because *prajñāpāramitā* includes its own contradiction that it deserves the name of *pāramitā.* Conze translates 'Wisdom which has gone beyond'. My humble comment would be 'insight out of sight'.

The same kind of argument, in its double expansion, states in the case of a *bodhisattva:* 'after beings have thus been led to *nirvāṇa,* no being at all has been led to *nirvāṇa.* And why ? If in a *bodhisattva* the perception of a being would take place, he should not be called a *bodhisattva.* And why ? He who has set out in the *bodhisattva*-vehicle, he is not one of the dharmas' (17 a). As it were, in the word *bodhisattva, bodhi* cancels *sattva.*

1.2 Dialogue with Professor D.S. Ruegg About the Law of Excluded Middle in the Mādhyamakakārikās.

Nearly opposite to Professor Conze's interpretation postulating the abrogation of the principle of contradiction in the *Vajracchedikā* is Professor D.S. Ruegg's point of view—if I have not misunderstood his very important article 'The uses of the four positions of the *catuṣ koṭi* and the problem of the description of reality in Mahāyāna Buddhism' (*Journal of Indian Philosophy,* 5, 1977). For, Professor Ruegg endeavours to account for Nāgārjuna's *prasajya* negation in keeping with Aristotle's two-valued logic, as far as possible. After the publication of my own article 'Logic and Dialectics in the Mādhyamakakārikās' (*JIP,* 11, 1983), we had a passionate discussion, writing twice to each other. The main point was the principle of excluded middle. After having read his article again, especially pp. 50-51, *and his letters, I think I see* better. Aristotle's statement 'οὐδὲ μεταξὺ ἀντιφάσεως' involves two commitments. Of two contradictory propositions, one can accept one at most, one must accept one at least. Regarding the first commitment, *tertium non datur,* there is no problem. It works relentlessly in the *Mādhyamakakārikās*. But Nāgārjuna, as *prāsaṅgika,* is not at all concerned by the second commitment. Hence the final scruple and caution of Professor Ruegg (pp. 50-51): this happens in the case of a 'nonfulfilment of referential presuppositions', if the opponent's proposition 'is not semantically well-formed'; if the subject of the sentence 'is in fact null'.

But I naughtily add: it is always the case for any entity, for any *bhāva*.

As a matter of fact, Aristotle never expressed such an additional semantical condition, as it is not relevant to a formal logic. In this respect, a great deal of difference remains between Nāgārjuna's and Aristotle's dialectics. So let us provisionally conclude that the third value is rather a non-value. There are, in fact, not only in Nāgārjuna but already in the *Caturdaśāvyākṛtavastūni,* although implicitly, three cases: true, false, meaningless or irrelevant.

2. *Causal Conditional Logic and Dependent Origination*

Another opportunity of pointing out the uniqueness of Buddhist way of thinking is its possible encounter, now a days, with causal logic, which is in a way a by-product of modal logic.

This topic is far beyond my competence, but I have been recently acquainted with a French mathematician, Mr. Pierre Basso, working in a team, on Artificial Intelligence. Besides, stimulated by some readings like Professor Mac Dermott's studies on Ratnakīrti, he is trying to make a connection between causal conditional logic and dependent origination.

2.1 Let us Remember the Statement of Dependent Origination

'imasmiṃ sati idaṃ hoti imassuppādā idaṃ upajjati imasmiṃ asati idaṃ na hoti imassa nirodhā idaṃ nirujjhati' (Majjhimanikāya, III, p. 63): 'This existing, that exists; this appearing, that appears. This not existing, that does not exist; this ceasing, that ceases'—that is, as far as I know, the oldest formulation of the idea of function or law in world literature. Nothing but for this reason, Buddhism is an all-important event in the development of human knowledge.

2.2 The Aim of Causal Conditional Logic

Now, giving up the logic of identity, the aim of Mr. Basso's project is to elaborate a logic of universal flux. It is not to make, once more, a mathematical transcription of logical operators in various Buddhist schools, for he believes that such a transcription is necessarily metaphorical. He wishes to work out a formal design of the notion of interacting existence, of being through causes and conditions. In his opinion, the statement of *pratītya-samutpāda* is right away a meta-language, some kind of *vāda,* for it is the mutual relationship between terms that is *a priori.* The terms themselves, of course *bhāvās* and even *dharmās,* are *a posteriori.*

Hence, the aim of such a causal conditional logic would be to formalize a logic of non-substantiality (*dharma-nairātmya*), instead of the logic of predicates which postulates a real *bhāva* as a subject: snow is white.

2.3 Its Tools and Basic Concepts

The most elementary concept is that of *punctor,* which denotes no more an object in-itself but its conditional identity through dynamic series. It is no longer an entity with definite semantic contents. Its import depends on a context. When one says that lotus is blue, *blue* has no ontic referent, since the flower is going to fade, and *blue* can equally qualify the sea, sky, etc. There is no inherence-relation between blue and lotus. *Blue,* as a *punctor* is a *kṣaṇikā kriyā* in a *santati.* In Buddhist terms, a *dharma* is not a *bhāva.* In CCL language, a *punctor* is an empty compartment, the characteristic of which is its *E-ity.* This is the second basic concept of *E-organization:* for instance, the nominal unity of the chariot (*ratha*), is the assemblage of its parts. This concept should not be mistaken for that of set or class. Then comes the concept of *I-ity* or efficiency condition, corresponding to *pratyaya.*

Therefore, causal determination would be different from referential determination. While an axiomatic theory of sets depicts its objects from inside, in other words from contents, the theory of 'categories' depicts objects from outside, from their connecting links. A category is different from a set, it is rather a coming-to-be resulting from a concourse of causes and conditions (*hetu-pratyaya-sāmagrī*).

I am not capable, and perhaps it is too early, to estimate the success of Mr. Basso's project. But one thing is certain. His attempt reveals a real affinity between the idea of law expressed in the *pratītya-samutpāda* and recent developments of modern logic.

3. *Buddhism and Western Thinking Today*

Now, let us have a look on some other fields of a fruitful cross-cultural encounter between Buddhism and Western ways of thinking today.

3.1

Generally speaking, a common feature is noteworthy between Buddhist approach and scientific approach: viz. analysis leading to reduction. When one sees, *prima facie,* unity, one should try to find out plurality. In this respect, how easy is the situation of a Buddhist facing the various trends of contemporary sciences. Let us consider, for instance, the fresh results of neuro-physiology. Professor Changeux, member of Institut Pasteur and College de France, recently published a book the title of which is 'L Homme neuronal' (neuronal man). It depicts human mind as a collection of neurones. Some philosophers and humanists, imbued with spiritualistic and theistic tendencies, were quite shocked and they protested against it. On the contrary, a Buddhist reader is not disturbed at all, he keeps serene and gives an ironical smile for the simple reason that he does not believe in a self.

Roughly speaking, I think that Buddhism, being neither spiritualism, theism, nor materialism, is in a privileged position to fit in with modern world of science and technology.

3.2

Social change is also a feature of modern times. In this respect, it was an event to read an important cross-cultural and cross-scientific publication of Serge Christophe Kolm, a well known French economist. In this book of 637 pages, entitled *Le Bonheur-Liberte'* (Happiness-Freedom), subtitled *Bouddhisme profond et Modernite'* (Profound Buddhism and Modernity), Paris, P.U.F., Dec. 1982, the author strives to apply to the Western world social perspectives derived from Buddhism. Although I read it with some critical distance, on account of some simplifications and exaggerations, nevertheless it is a fact that such a book is symptomatic of our time. It was unimaginable a few years ago.

3.3

Owing to all these scientific, technological and daily life changes, most of the religions are more or less falling into decay. I think that Buddhism, if understood not as a religion but as *Śīla, Samādhi* and *Prajñā,* not depending on revelation but mainly on experience and reason, is in a very good position to fill up the space previously occupied by religious or ideological systems. This cannot happen, however, at a mass-level, because actual lived-experience, on both sides, Buddhist and Western, is too opposed, particularly regarding the self and the impression of being *kartṛ-bhoktṛ*. But, for small intellectual groups, it is quite different. And their impact may be important in course of time.

3.4

Let me introduce, now, just two or three remarks concerning my own field, metaphysics. As a *madhyamā pratipad* between *astīti* and *nāstīti* – let us refer to the *Kātyāyana-Sūtra* – Buddhism is in a position to arbitrate between two trends of contemporary philosophy: metaphysical and anti-metaphysical. As I wrote in my thesis "Mahāyāna Buddhism is a metaphysical act transcending all metaphysics; so to speak, a metaphysical challenge to all metaphysical speculations".

It could also resolve the old quarrel, still alive in Europe, between the two theses of immanence and transcendence. How is it possible to transcend transcendence? That is, in a sense, Heidegger's and Prof. Jean Wahl's interrogation. The latter adds in the same spirit: "Dialectics will be fully dialectic provided it is amenable itself to dialectics" (Traite' de Metaphysique, p. 714). Now, in a way, dialectization of dialectic is precisely the whole Mādhyamaka.

3.5

I would have liked to tell you a few words about my experience with my students, Eastern and Western, from a psychological point of view. Among my students acquainted with the manifold varieties of Hinduism, some turn out better, it is for them a very enriching achievement. Others let themselves carried away by their personal whims. On the contrary, I have never seen, till now, students well initiated in Buddhism, turning out worse. For them no danger of *prajñāparādha,* probably because Buddhist medicine cures, depending mainly on experience and reason. This shows the pedagogical uniqueness of Buddhism.

4. Conclusion

It is high time to conclude.

4.1

I believe that a limited but deep encounter between Buddhist and Western ways of thinking can be fruitful today. In particular, Western knowledge, while keeping rational, could become more meditative and supple imbued with a good deal of *dhyāna* and *mṛdutaruṇacittatā.*

4.2

We have seen two examples of that suppleness. First, while considering the style of reasoning of the *Vajracchedikā,* especially the import of *tena,* we caught a glimpse of this. When one goes to the very end of any entity whatever it may be, one goes beyond. *Pūrṇā prajñā* is *adhiprajñā.*

Then we found out that a third value, or more exactly non-value, let us say a third case, is in accordance with the spirit of the *Caturdaśāvyākṛtavastūni.* It is also present, as a void, in Nāgārjuna's merely purgative, releasing dialectics. In this respect, the cross-cultural dialogue between Buddhist and Western ways of thinking is less upsetting, since Lukasienvicz and Post have enlarged the two-valued logic of Aristotle.

4.3

After the failure of philosophical systems, modern science too has given up the claim of enclosing the universe in one system. Concerning this, the last sentence of Mr. Basso's project is very suggestive. Raising an objection against himself, he asks: "does causal conditional logic claim to be a universal system involving others?" He answers: 'It would be the case if causal conditional logic would claim to be the first "determinant" of any system. In fact according to the emptiness of emptiness (*Śūnyatā-Śūnyatā*), it is a way of stating that there is no universal system.'

4.4

Here again, the trends of modern scientific mind do agree with the practice of inner patience, the Buddhist *dharmakṣānti,* viz. assenting to the Tathāgata's profound Law, even if one does not understand it yet. *Kṣāntipāramitā* is *Prajñāpāramitā.* In this light, a system is nothing but a symptom of mental impatience.

In the same way, the middle path can soothe metaphysical anguish of some modern minds and induce them to mental peace.

So my last words will spontaneously be *dharma-kṣānti, śānti.*

Chapter 14

Buddhist Ecumenism and National Cultures

Hajime Nakamura

I. Aspects of Original Buddhism

It is generally admitted that early Buddhist Philosophy is set forth in the Pāli Nikāyas and their corresponding Sanskrit and Chinese texts. But the Pāli Nikāyas themselves consist of various earlier and later layers which derive from different periods.

The Theravāda Tripiṭaka, now preserved in the Pāli language, is certainly one of the most authentic, in the sense of trying to preserve the discourses of the Buddha in their wording as recognized probably before schisms.

But in the Buddhist texts there is no word that can be traced with unquestionable authority to Gotama Śākyamuni as a historical personage, although there must be some sayings or phrases derived from himself. So, selecting older parts among the voluminous scriptures of Early Buddhism, scholars of critical approach try to elucidate the true purport of the teachings of the Buddha. According to text-critical studies it has been made clear that some poem (*Gāthā*) portions and some phrazes represent earlier layers. They are Gāthās of the *Suttanipāta* (especially the Aṭṭhaka-vagga and the Pārāyana-vagga), of the Sagātha-vagga of the *Saṃyutta-Nikāya,* of the *Itivuttakas,* of some Jātakas, the Udānas in the scripture named the Udāna, and some Gāthās and sentences rewritten from Gāthās into prose. There must be some more. Based upon these portions of the scriptures we can construe aspects of early Buddhism. The picture which we can get therefrom is fairly different from that as we can get from the Pāli scriptures in general.[2] That is to say, Buddhism as appears in earlier portions of the scriptures is from what is explained by many scholars as earlier Buddhism or primitive Buddhism. Main Points are as follows:

(1) Those words or phrases which are regarded by scholars as peculiarly Buddhistic or what are said to be technical terms of Buddhism are seldom noticed in earlier Gāthā portions or stock expressions in prose.

(2) A special kind of nuance which reminds us of later Buddhism is less; on the contrary those phrases and words which remind us of the Ājivaka religion and Jainism are often used. They are quite similar to those as are used in the edicts of King Aśoka. It means that many sentences in prose sections of the Pāli scriptures were fixed after the reign of King Aśoka.

(3) The life of Buddhist ascetics in its incipient stage was fairly different from the monastic life of monks in later days. It was quite close to the life of hermits as is mentioned in great epics, such as the *Mahābhārata* and the *Rāmāyaṇa*. In these epics ascetics are mentioned as hermits (*ṛṣis*), and in Gāthās of earlier texts of early Buddhism, Buddhist recluses or hermits are also referred to as *ṛṣis* (The Pāli form of the Sanskrit *ṛṣis*), whereas in the prose sections explaining Gāthās, the word *ṛṣis* disappears and the word *bhikkhu* is used in its place.

(4) Buddhist recluses lived lonely in solitude, chiefly in woods, forests, and caves.[3] Many Buddhist recluses lived in huts thatched with straw (*kuṭī*, *kuṭikā*).[4] A story is told that in the past hermits (*ṛṣis*) lived in thatched huts (*paṇṇakuṭī, assama*) thatched with leaves. The dwelling where Buddhist recluses lived were called *assama,*[6] as in the cases of Epic hermits.

    Some monks lived together with their fellow ascetics (*sabrahmacarin*,[7] *sādhivihārin*)[8]. But the common livelihood of monks in monasteries (*Vihāras*), as was conspicuous in later days, is scarcely mentioned.[9]

(5) In the earliest stage of Buddhism nuns did not exist.[10]

(6) When earlier *gāthās* were composed, the fully developed form of disciplines (*pātimokkha*) as can be seen in the Pāli and Chinese versions of the Book of Discipline (*Vinaya-piṭaka*) did not exist, for it is not mentioned in entirety in *gāthās*, and the *pātimokkha* as is mentioned in the Suttanipāta is very simple.[11]

(7) Gotama the Buddha was looked upon as an excellent personage, and was not defied, but deification of Gotama the Buddha was going to take shape gradually.

Buddhism is the teaching to have one become a Buddha, and also the teaching which was set forth by a Buddha (or Buddhas). But 'the teaching which was set forth by Buddha' does not necessarily mean 'the teaching which was set forth by 'Śākyamuni'. Besides Śākyamuni many other Buddhas were supposed to exist.[12] There did exist some Buddhists who declined to worship Śākyamuni.[13]

II. The Attitude of Ecumenism

(a) The Fundamental Attitude

In the earliest phase of Original Buddhism as is mentioned above, the possible attitude of ecumenism can be noticed. In the oldest layers of Early Buddhist scriptures also the ecumenical viewpoint can be noticed.

Buddhism has been regarded by Indians as a philosophy (*darśana*) and also a religion (dharma). Although it was not a rationalistic philosophy achieved by ratiocination alone (*ānvīkṣikī*), Buddhism has developed a variety of philosophical systems in different countries of Asia. However, the problem of man has played the central role in Buddhist philosophy. What might be called 'dogmas' of Buddhism are seldom taught in the incipient stage of early Buddhism. Dogmas (*diṭṭhi*) of any religious or philosophical school are refuted. Rather sceptical attitude about dogmas is expressed. In this respect it was closer to the attitude of Sañjaya, the sceptic, and to the theory of *naya* (viewpoints) of early Jainism.

In early Buddhism metaphysical speculation concerning problems not related to human activities and the attainment of Enlightenment was discouraged, these problems being such as 'whether the world is infinite or finite,' 'whether soul and the body are identical with, or different from, each other' or 'whether a perfect person exists after his death or not', etc.

How, then, should we view the wrong metaphysical views prevalent in those days? The Buddha said:

> "On such points Brahmins and recluses stick; Wrangling on them, they violently discuss; Poor folk! They see but one side of the shield."[14]

This means that all metaphysical views are only partial apprehensions of the whole truth which lies beyond own cognition, beyond rational analysis. In scripture we also find the famous parable of the blind men and the elephant.[15] Here we can locate the ecumenistic attitude in the outset.

According to Buddhism personal behaviors and activities should be brought into harmony with the universal norms, the universal laws which apply to all existence, regardless of time and space. Theoretically it is supposed that they apply not only to human existences but also to all other living beings. Buddhism claims to have made clear *dharmas,* which are valid in different periods and among various peoples, regardless of the difference of race.

The word *dharma* is often used as meaning the Doctrine of the Buddha; in the sense dharma is not dogma, but is rather the Path. Buddhism claims to be the Path which is regarded as the universal norm of all mankind, conformity to the nature of the universe. A Buddha is simply one who has trodden this Path and can report to others on what he has trodden this Path and can report to others on what he has found; the person who understood the truths and norms in Buddha. Buddha means the person who received the truth, the person who was awakened to the truth, the person who understood the absolute norm and became norm itself, the teacher and the person to be respected. We can interpret the appellation Tathāgata as one who has gone thus, way farer in this sense. His standpoint was practical. Buddhism theoretically admits the existence of many Buddhas. The theory taught by the Buddha is called "Buddha Teaching".

Buddhism sought reform of Brahamanism rejecting the authority of established religions which arose before the Buddha, and teaching an independent morality in the ethical sense.

The authority of Brahmanism, Jainism, the ājīvakas and other religions was denied and also, the attitude of reliance upon authorities of their own religion has been comparatively weak among Buddhists.

The acceptance of rational analysis of the nature of human existence has been a continuing characteristic of Buddhism, but it should be noted that metaphysical speculation concerning problems not related to the attainment of Enlightenment have not been considered to be a proper part of Buddhist ecumenism. Considering these features, we should say the Doctrine of the Buddha is not a system of philosophy in the Western sense but is rather a Path. The Buddha taught many doctrines which later scholars elaborated. Some of them contradict each other. However, all Buddhists, whether Theravāda or Mahāyāna, agree that they aim to teach the way to realize an ideal life. In Buddhism the entire stress lies on the mode of living, on the purification of life, on the removal of vices. A merely theoretical proposition, such as "there is not ego," would be regarded as utterly sterile and useless.

All Buddhists follow the Buddha in wanting to be taught how to lead a selfless life. Rational analysis is no more than a tool which is justified in its products. That is why there are so many teachings even on one subject, such as "Dependent Origination," "the Four Noble Truths", etc. Their sentences may differ, but their aim is the same.

The Buddha's doctrine is called a "vehicle" in the sense that it is like a ferryboat. One enters the Buddhist vehicle to cross the river of life from the shore of worldly experience of non-enlightenment, the shore of spiritual ignorance (*avidyā*), desire (*kāma*), and suffering to the other shore of transcendental wisdom (*vidyā*) which is liberation (*mokṣa*) from bondage and suffering. Suppose a man builds a raft and by this means succeeds in attaining the other shore. "What would be your opinion of this man," asks the Buddha, "would he be a clever man if, out of gratitude for the raft that carried him across the stream to safety, he, having reached the other shore, should cling to it, take it on his back, and walk about with the weight of it?" The monks replied, "No". The Buddha then concludes, "In the same way the vehicle of the doctrine is to be cast away and forsaken, once the other shore of Enlightenment (*nirvāṇa*) has been attained."[16] Teachings can be compared to rafts. Once the goal has been attained, they become useless, they can be no more than inappropriate burdens.

The conceptions that constitute the doctrines communicated to people are, from the standpoint of the Enlightened One, without corresponding ultimate realities. They are part of a raft, which is helpful for the crossing of a stream of ignorance and indispensable for disciples on the way, but they are devoid of meaning for the accomplished master whose crossing is over.

Religious dogmas are nothing but expediencies leading one to the ideal state at the end and therefore religious dogmos should be forsaken. This attitude can be seen already in Early Buddhism and Mahāyāna of India, but it has been most emphatically stressed by Zen Buddhism.

Just as the difference in shape, weight, and materials among rafts does not matter, difference in teachings does not matter. This point of view is set forth both in Southern and Northern Buddhism. Buddhism is nothing but "the path leading to release" (nibbānagamana-magga), or 'the path leading to immortality' (amatagāmimagga).[17] Even contradictory sayings are, virtually and practically, not contradictory in their eyes, all these aim at the same end.

(b) Mahāyāna Ecumenism

While such an attitude toward the teachings of Buddhism seems quite contradictory, this attitude can be justified. If one says something, it is justified only by what is called "skill in means". Words like *enlightenment, ignorance, freedom,* and *attachment* are preliminary helps, referring to no ultimate reality, mere hints or signposts for the traveller on the Path, serving only to point out the goal.

In Mahāyāna this kind of philosophical knowledge is called "the Perfect Wisdom" or "the Transcendental Wisdom" (*Prajñāpāramitā*).

The wisdom which is sought in Buddhism is not the wisdom of conflicting metaphysical systems, it is the wisdom of Enlightenment as to the true nature of human existence, to show us how to live. It was especially stressed in Mahāyāna scriptures. The true Wisdom is not a doctrine. A disciple Subūti said: "Difficult to be attained through Awakening is the perfect Transcendental Wisdom, O Venerable One!" The Buddha replied: "That is the reason, O Subhūti, why no one ever attains it through Awakening."[18]

All Buddhists believe that even a most vicious person can ultimately attain Enlightenment. In Theravāda, the attainment must come through his own free will and efforts; in Mahāyāna the efforts may be aided by the help given by Buddhas or Bodhisattvas. There is no concept of the eternally damned, although that does not mean that Buddhists deny the existence of many people who are in fact very difficult to save.

Mahāyāna Buddhism developed the concept of the realization of *Nirvāṇa* through the recognition of the true nature of one's existence. In Mahāyāna, everyone is entitled to become a Buddha finally, although he might have to pass through many births. In this connection it is the Lotus Sūtra (Saddharma-puṇḍarīka-sūtra) that set forth the ecumenical idea most lively.

In this Sūtra the Buddha gives his believers a single "vehicle," the "Buddha vehicle," which carries them to their final goal. Everyone who has merely heard the Buddha's preaching, and who has performed any kind of meritorious actions, can become a Buddha. It is only for the sake of expediency that there are three "vehicles," namely that of the disciples, that of the Pratyeka-buddhas, and that of Bodhisattvas, by means of which *nirvāṇa* can be attained. In the Lotus Sūtra the One Vehicle (*ekayāṇa*) means the Buddha Vehicle (*Buddhayāna*) and the Bodhisattvayāna means one of the Three Vehicles.

Mahāyāna Buddhism admitted principally three different levels of understanding among its believers. The idea of expendiency (*upāya* or *upāya-kauśalya*) was exceedingly esteemed.

So all people are entitled to be called Bodhisattvas. Well-known Bodhisattvas such as Mañjuśrī, Samantabhadra, Bhaiṣajyaguru, etc., play subsidiary roles, whereas those who were newly given qualification to attain Enlightenment and those who appeared on the earth (by which the Eternal Buddha is meant symbolically) are important as Bodhisattvas of essential significance.

In the Lotus Sūtra all living beings are called 'children of Buddha.' Its teaching centers on the faith in Śākyamuni Buddha. The intelligence and intuition of Buddha were greatly extolled.

The thought of the Three Vehicles can be traced in the literature before the Lotus Sūtra, already in the Abhidharma-Mahāvibhāṣā-śāstra. The Three Vehicles are called with various names. The practice of pratyekabuddhas in the Three Vehicles can be traced to non-Buddhist (Jaina etc.) origin. *Śrāvakas* were tolerated in some Mahāyāna Sūtras. The thought of setting forth prophesy (prediction) that someone will attain perfect enlightenment in the future (*vyākaraṇa*) originating in early Buddhism, culminates in the Lotus Sutra.[19] The Mahāsatya-nirgrantha-pūtra-vyākaraṇa-sūtra[20] and its prototype are scriptures in which the conciliatory character of the Lotus Sūtra has been further expanded and made thorough-going. It came into existence later than the Lotus Sūtra. Here the spirit of tolerance is conspicious, with a Jaina ascetic as the preacher of Buddhist teachings.[21]

The *Lankāvatāra-sūtra* which has been very important for Zen Buddhism in China and Japan set forth the theory that all discriminated entities are mind-only. According to this Sūtra the fundamental principle or truth is called *siddhānta* or *siddhāntanaya* (*tshong* in Chinese; *Shū* in Japanese). It should be known intuitively by oneself. However, various religious teachings (*deśanā*, *śāsana* or *deśanānaya; kyong* in Chinese; kyō in Japanese) are given in different forms.[22] Different ways of teaching are admitted as based upon the fundamental self-realization. Zen inherits this attitude. In Zen Buddhism the famous comparison to fingers pointing to the moon is very often set forth. The truth is compared to the moon, whereas fingers of different persons pointing to the same moon are compared to the different doctrines of the Buddha, or occasionally to various religions.

Esoteric Buddhism (*Vajrayāna*) and some Chinese and Japanese sects developed the concept of the Great Self (*Mahātman*), which idea had especially been emphasized in the *Mahāparinirvāṇasūtra* of Mahāyāna, whose Sanskrit original has been preserved only in fragments, and which became very important in Chinese Buddhism. This idea is not found in Theravāda Buddhism and was criticized by some Buddhists as well as Non-Buddhists as being very close to Vedānta philosophy.

(c) Ecumenical Justification of Various Teachings in China and Japan

In ancient China attempts were made to expound and coordinate the various and, at times, contradictory teachings promulgated in the voluminous Buddhist scriptures. The theory of Five Periods and Eight

Kinds of Teachings as propounded by Master Chih-i (6th century) is the culmination of these attempts in China. The Eight Teachings of the Buddha which are described by the adjectives "sudden, gradual, secret, undetermined, collected, developed, distinguished and accomplished" are assigned to the Five Periods of the Buddha's lifetime in which the Buddha progressively revealed his full and mature philosophy to his believers. Different Buddhist schools are assigned to each of the stages with the Tendai doctrine as typified by its interpretation of the Lotus Sūtra occupying the ultimate stage of Perfection. Master Kukai was the first Japanese to unify all the known philosophies of his time into a comprehensive system.

His synthesis was more comprehensive, for he assumed a conciliatory and tolerant attitude towards other faiths besides Buddhism: his system incorporated not only Buddhist doctrines but also the teachings of Taoism and Confucianism, which he considered manifestations of the basic principles of the Mahāvairocana Buddha.

Esoteric Buddhism of Japan assumed the Fundamental Buddha of the universe who is called the Mahāvairocana Buddha. Even heretics and demons are outcomes of the Mahāvairocana Buddha.

The Esoteric Buddhism recognizes that the Mahāvairocana Buddha is everything and everything is Mahāvairocana. Nothing exists apart from the Mahāvairocana, and aside from the Mahāvairocana there is nothing. Master Kukai conceived of the ten stages of spiritual progress, including within them the prehumanistic vehicle of passion and appetite, the humanistic vehicle of Confucianism, the heavenly vehicles of Hinduism and Taoism, Hinayāna, Mahāyāna and the One Vehicle School of Buddhism, through which he attempted to describe the modes of encompassing and the movement of spiritual horizons. When Amane Nishi (1829-1897), the Japanese philosopher, wrote a treatise entitled *Hyakuichi Shinron* this title represented the idea that Hundred Teachings including Confucianism, Buddhism and various philosophical systems of the West converge in One. He aimed at the eternal and universal principle. Generally speaking, among Asians there prevails strong antipathy to the Western use of 'ism' to represent individual religions, saying 'Buddhism is not an 'ism' or 'Hinduism is not an ism", just dharma.

Dharma could mean 'religion', but that dharma is beyond the differences of established religions. It should be universal to mankind, but not to be restricted to any particular religion. When we think this way, we can say that the concept of dharma as is held by South Asiatics to mean 'religion' is quite close to the idea of 'shū' (or siddhānta) as has been held by Buddhists of the Far East.

III. The Relevance of the Ecumenical Religion to National Cultures

As Buddhism is a universal religion and ecumenical character has been essential to this religion, it has spread among many nations of the world. However, cultural forms or aspects as Buddhism has displayed in various countries have been quite varied, multifarious. They differ with nations.[22]

When Buddhism was introduced into China, it underwent great change. Buddhism in China was essentially the same as that in India, but its outlook became highly different.

Whereas Indians tended to esteem abstract ideas of universal concepts, Chinese were apt to emphasize the perception of the concrete; concepts were expressed by means of concrete expressions, and explanation of Buddhist concepts by means of perceived symbols was resorted to especially among Zen priests. Chinese intellectuals didn't like to discuss the relationships between genus, species and individuality. Although Indian logic was introduced into China, it didn't develop, and finally vanished. That is the reason why Buddhist logic did not develop in China's adjacent countries, such as Korea, Japan and Vietnam. In sayings by Chinese Zen masters non-logical character is quite conspicuous.

On the other hand the attitude of emphasis on particular instances is quite conspicuous among Chinese, and explanation of Buddhist abstract ideas and ethical values or rules was given by way of citation of particular instances. That is why many historical works describing the development of Buddhism and biographies of Buddhist high priests were composed by Chinese Buddhist writers, whereas in India and its adjacent countries works of this kind are almost lacking.

Chinese are the people who don't want to be entangled in metaphysical speculations, quite different from the tendency among Indian Buddhists who earnestly maintained the idea of transmigration in the mundane world (*saṁsāra*). Chinese Zen priests did not discuss the problem of after-life or transmigration, although they maintained these ideas very dimly, faintly. This peculiarly Chinese attitude was inherited by peoples of the Far East, i.e., Korea, Japan and Vietnam.

Buddhist ethics was introduced into China in such a way as would not infringe on the traditional ethical value of filial piety, esteem of seniority, conciliation and other ethical values.

Among Chinese the attitude of esteem for nature has been prevalent, and among Chinese Buddhists conformity to nature was taught. Among Chinese Zen thinkers the acceptance of phenomenalism to regard the phenomenal world as absolute can be noticed, and this tendency came to be more and more emphasized by Japanese and Korean Buddhists.

The above-mentioned features of Chinese Buddhism have been preserved by Korean, Japanese and Vietnamese Buddhists to a more or less extent. However, in Japanese Buddhism some other features are noticed. The most predominant one is the tendency to emphasize a limited social nexus. In Japan there exist many distinctive sects which are exclusive to each other, whereas in Korean Buddhism synthetic or conciliatory character is more conspicuous. In China and Korea for the last several centuries the governments encouraged Confucian ideology and suppressed Buddhism, whereas in Vietnam Confucianism, Taoism and Buddhism were encouraged alike; intellectuals were required to study them all. In countries of South Asia, i.e., India, Sri Lanka, Burma and Thailand Buddhist monks were not allowed to engage in physical labour. However, Chinese Zen monks came to engage in physical labour, such as tillage, digging, making faggots etc. Finally in Japan physical labour and rendering service to others was extolled to a great extent. This was encouraged as part of *dhyāna*. Some scholars explain that this is the reason why Japan has made such a rapid progress of industrialization in the last eleven decades.

It is very difficult to estimate synoptically the features of Tibetan Buddhism, which is different from Indian as well as Chinese Buddhism. It seems to me that such features as consciousness of the individual, discovery of the absolute in man, absolute submission to a religiously charismatic individual, absolute adherence to the Lamaistic social order, Shamanistic tendency etc. are salient.

Nepalese Buddhism is not the same as Tibetan Buddhism. It is essentially *Vajrayāna*. *Vajrayāna* which is this-wordly is professed in both Nepal and Japan. It is only in Nepal and Japan, that marriage of Buddhist priests is officially admitted, their status being hereditary.

In Central Asia Buddhism flourished before the Muhammedan invasion. It is likely that Buddhism there was introduced partly from South Asia, partly from China, and partly from Tibet, so various features were coexistent.

Throughout the long history of the development of Buddhism various cultural aspects and features have been displayed. It is very difficult to summarize systematically in a simple way. Such cultural richness is solely due to the fundamental attitude of ecumenism of the Buddhist religion. It will pave the way to world peace and coexistential beautitude of mankind eventually and finally.

References

1. A.K. Warder: *Indian Buddhism,* Delhi, etc: Motilal Banarsidass, 1970, p. 296.
2. Text-critical studies on the scriptures of early Buddhism were fully discussed by Hajime Nakamura in his *Genshi Bukkyo no Shiso* (=The thought of early Buddhism), Vol. 2 (Tokyo: Shunjusha Press, 1971).
3. The fact that early Buddhist recluses lived in huts can be evidenced from Jaina sources also. Sāriputta, who was regarded as the representative ascetic of Buddhism by Jainas, is said to have lived in a cosy abode (assama) (*Isibhāsiyāim* 38, 13).

   Insofar as early poems (*gāthās*) go, the above-mentioned way of life was predominant, but in due course of time the assertion that recluses need not spend such an inconvenient life appeared among Buddhist recluses. One of the persons who made such a set-out seems to have been Sāriputta. His saying is conveyed in a Jaina work:

   "What use of forests and huts (*assama*) for the hero who has conquered his senses? Wherever one feels happy, there one finds a forest. That place is also his hermitage.

   Medicines are useless for those whose diseases have been healed.

   For the one who has disciplined oneself well forests of treasures (in villages) are vain. The whole (world) is for his meditation".

   (Isibhāsiyāim 38, vv. 13-15.)

   Śāriputta asserted that ascetics need not necessarily live in forests or hermitages. Based upon such an assertion ascetics came to live in villages, and finally in monasteries. Recluses became monks.
4. A monk said, "I should lie down with a roof of thatch, like others in comfort." (Theragāthā 208). Another Buddhist recluse said,

   "My hut was made of three palm leaves on the bank of the Ganges. My bowl was only a funeral pot, my robe a rag from a bust-heap." (*Therag.* 127). "I made a small hut in the forest, and I am vigilant, zealous, attentive, mindful, (*Therag.* 59).

   A monk named Sarabhañga said,

   "Having broken off reeds with my hands, having made a hut, I dwell there; therefore by common consent my name was Reed-breaker (=Sarabhañga)." (*Therag.* 487).
5. Saṁyutta-Nikāya, vol. 1, pp. 226-227, prose.
6. A very early poem which encourages donation of huts to recluses depicts the Buddhist life in a hut in its earliest stage:

   "An intelligent person, even if of low birth, should embody forbearance and meekness, act rightfully, and worship holy persons. He should make a comfortable and pleasant huts (Karaya assame ramme).

He should establish wells and springs in waste land and roads in steep places, and give foods, beverages, foods to chew, clothes, beddings to rightful persons with faithful mind (SN.I. p. 100 Gāthā).

7. Sabrahmacārin, *DN.* II, p. 27; III, p. 241 ff; *MN.* I, p. 101; *AN.* II, p. 97 *SN.* 973.; *Theragāthā,* 387-392.

8. Sādhivihārin, Sānchī Inscriptions, ed. by Buhler, I, No. 209. This corresponds to the Pāli *saddhivihārin.*

9. The term *vihāra* is mentioned in the Suttanipāta only once (v. 391), but in this passage vihāra means just 'abode', not 'monastery'. In the *Theragāthā* (477) and the *Therīgātha* (68; 115; 169 etc. *vihāra* in the sense of 'monastery' is mentioned.

   Early Buddhist recluses lived in forests, caves and practised meditation there, even in grave-yards. (They claimed themselves to be *vanavāsins,* those who live in forests. This picture exactly corresponds to that given by Megasthenes, the Greek traveller to India around 300 B.C.).

10. Legend has it that it was with Mahāprajāpatī, Buddha's mother-in-law, that women took order to become nuns. However, it is likely that, when Magasthenes, the Greek ambassador sent to India by Seleucus, the king of Syria in about 300 B.C., came to the court of Candragupta, Buddhist nuns did exist, for Megasthenes relates with surprise that in India 'lady philosophers' existed, (It is almost certain that Jaina nuns came into existence later than in Buddhism).

11. To the question: "which are the precepts and vows (sīlabbatāni) for a resolute bhikkhu?", the Suttanipāta (v. 961) sets forth the regulations for the way of life especially the diet and clothing, of bhikkhus. In Buddhist literature in general *sīlabbatāni* were refuted as being set forth by other religions, but here they were set forth for Buddhist ascetics, which sounds very strange for those who have knowledge of Buddhist literature. This can be explained away only in this way. Early Buddhism in the process of formation did [not] have special technical terms peculiar to Buddhism. Therefore Buddhists used the terms current throughout all religions, and were in common with other schools.

    After describing regulations about dwelling, the *Suttanipāta* lays injunctions:

    "Let him not commit theft,

    This is substantially close to the teaching of Chāndogya-Upaniṣad (III, 17, 4)

    let him not speak falsely,

    let him touch friendly what

    is feeble or stong,

    What he acknowledges to be the

    agitation of the mind, let him

    drive that off as a partisan of

    Kanha (i.e., Māra.) (V. 967)"

    Here we can find three among the five precepts of Buddhism, mentioned in the *Chāndogya-Upaniṣad* and the Suttanipāta. It means Buddhism inherited these precepts from early religions, and later systematized them in a fixed form.

"Let him not fall into the power of anger and arrogance; having dug up the root of these, let him live, and let him overcome both what is pleasant and what is unpleasant."

Jainism also teaches the same thing. (A monk should forsake arrogance and anger. Dasav/IX, 3, 12)

12. In Jaina scriptures also those who have perfected their religious practice are all called 'buddha'.

    A person who has attained enlightenment is called *'buddha'* in Jaina scriptures also. Buddhism just inherited it. According to the "Words of Sages" (*Isibhāsiyāim*), a Jaina scripture, non-Jaina sages were also called 'buddha', such as Uddālaka and Yājñavalkya, the Upaniṣadic philosophers and some sages who appear in great epics. Before deification of Śākyamuni began, all excellent ascetics of Buddhism were called 'buddhas'. For example, the term 'buddha in the Suttanipāta (513; 517; 523; 622; 643; 646 etc.) means simply 'an excellent ascetic', not the glorified and deified Buddha.

    The term 'buddha' did not mean a single person. Theoretically we are led to the conclusion that the teachings which enable us to become buddhas could exist besides the teaching by Śākyamuni. It was only that they were not conveyed to posterity under the name of Buddhism (*Buddhaśāsana, Bauddha*).

13. Devadatta is hated nearly in all Buddhist scriptures, although the teachings ascribed to him are contradictory to each other. This much was common to all versions of his legend. He was a dissenter, although he wanted to become a Buddha and to have others become Buddhas. He was also a Buddhist and established a Buddhist order, which continued to exist till late periods, and which differed with the Buddhist order of Śākyamuni. Fa-hien (4th century A.D.), the Buddhist pilgrim, when he travelled to Śrāvasti, found the Buddhist order residing there and worshipping the three Buddhas in the past, but not worshipping Śākyamuni).

    "The Biography of Fa-hien the High priest", Taisho Tripiṭaka, vol. LI, p. 861a).

    Hsuan-tsang relates that the monks of the Buddhist order of Devadatta living in three monasteries, didn't take milk and butter, ("The Travel Records of Hsuan-san", vol. X, *Taisho Tripiṭaka,* vol. LI, p. 861a). It is said that "they follow the posthumous teachings of Devadatta".

14. Udāna VI. 4. F.L. Woodward, trans. Udāna: Verses of Uplift and Itivuttaka; As it was said. The Minor Anthologies of the Pāli Canon, Pt. II. Sacred Books of the Buddhists, Vol. VIII (London; Oxford University Press, H. Milford, 1935), pp. 81-83.

15. Udāna VI. 4. *ibid.* the Chinese version of the Arthavargīyasūtra (Taisho Tripiṭaka, Vol. 4, p. 178 a-c,). This parable of the blind men and an elephant (andha-gajanyāya) is a favourite one for both Hindu and Jaina philosophers (M. Winternitz; *op. cit,* Vol. II, p. 88n.).

16. *Majjhima, Nikāya.* Vol. I, pp. 134-135, Chinese *Madhyamakāgama,* Vol. 54 (Taisho Vol. II, p. 764 b-c); *Aṅguttarāgama,* Vol. 39 (Taisho, Vol. II, p-759 c-760 b), Chinese *Abhidharma* Kośa, vol. 28 (Taisho, vol. 29, p. 119c), *Vajracchedikā.*

17. *Saṁyutta Nikāya,* XLV, 7, Vol. 8.

18. *Aṣṭasāhasrikā-prajñāparamitā,* 8.

19. Studies on this sūtra in this line are mentioned in Hajime Nakamura's *Indian Buddhism.* A Survey with Bibliographical Notes (Hirakata, Osaka Kansai University of Foreign Studies, 1980).

20. Nanjis catalogue 178; 443 A.D. Wogihara: Index, p. 123. Translated in Chinese by Guṇabhadra in 435-38.

21. *Ibid.*, p. 192.

22. According to the *Laṅkāvatāra-sūtra* (ed. by Bunyin Nanjo), Kyoto at the Otani University Press, 1956, p. 148 f. p. 172) Shū and kyō are set forth in coordination (i) Shu's Sanskrit original is *siddhānta* or *siddhāntanaya*. It is beyond conceptualisation. It should be known intuitively by oneself. (p. 147f.) D.T. Suzuki translates this as 'realization'. In abridgment it is called 'pratyātma' ('self-attainment'), which might be translated as 'inner intuition'. In this case the Buddhist term '*siddhānta*' is quite different from the Hindu concept of 'siddhānta'. Kyō is various teachings.

    Thus, these two concepts are explained in the Lañkāvatārasūtra as follows (I cite from D.T. Suzuki's The Lañkāvatāra Sūtra, Prajna Press, 1978, pp. 127f.; p. 148f): Bodhisattva raised question "What is the characteristic of the realisation by which I and other Boddhisattva-Mahāsattvas, becoming thoroughly conversant with its meaning, may quickly attain the highest enlightenment and, relying upon themselves, will not be led away by any speculations or philosophies (sarva-tārkika tirthakarāṇām).

    Said the blessed One: Then listen well, and well reflect within yourself; I will tell you.

    There are two ways of characterising the realisation (dvividham ....siddhāntanayalakṣaṇam) attained by all the Śrāvakas, the Pratyekabuddhas, and the Bodhisattvas, the realisation itself sidhāntanaya and the teaching (about it deśanānaya).

    "Now by the realisation itself is meant that it is the realm of inner attainment: its characteristic features are that it has nothing to do with words, discriminations, and letters; that it leads one up to the realm of non-out-flows; that it is the state of an inner experience; that it is entirely devoid of philosophical speculations and (the doing of) evil beings; and that, destroying philosophical speculations and (the doing of) evil beings, it shines out in its own inner light of attainment. These are the characteristics of the realisation."

    tatra siddhātanayo...yaduta pratyātmādhigamaviśe salakṣaṇaṃ vāg-vikalpa-akṣara-rahitam anāśravadhātugatiprāpakaṃ pratyātmagatibhumigatisvalaṣaṇaṃ sarva-tarka-tīrthya-māravarjitaṃ vinihatya ca tāṃs tīrthyamārān pratyātmagatir virājate. etan....siddhāntanaya-lakṣaṇam. *Laṅkāvatāra,* p. 148.

    "Now what is meant by the teaching (concerning it)? It is variously given in the works pertaining to nine divisions of the doctrines; it keeps one away from the dualistic notions of being and non-being, of oneness and otherness; first making use of skilful means and expedients, it induces all beings to have a perception (of this teaching) so that whoever is inclined towards it, may be instructed in it. This is the characteristic of the teaching".

    tatra deśanā-nayaḥ katamo yaduta navāñgāsāsanavicitropadeśo nyānanyasadasatpakṣa-varjita upāyakuśalavidhipūrvakaḥ sattveṣu darśanāvatāro yad yad yenadhimucyate tat tasya deśayat, etan..........deśanānaya-lakṣaṇam.

    v. 15. Realization and teaching, self-attainment and doctrinal instruction—those who have an insight into the difference will not be led away by philosophical authorities.

    v. 16. There is no truth in any object that is imagined by the ignorant; deliverance is where there is no objective world; why is this not sought by the speculators.

    v. 15: siddhāntaś ca nayās cāpi pratyātmasāśanañ ca vai/

ye paśyanti vibhāgajñā na te tarkavaśam gatāḥ//

v. 16. na bhāvo vidyate satyaṃ yathā bālair vikalpyata/abhāvena tu vai mokṣaṃ kathaṃ necchanti tārkikāḥ//

In this case teachings of religion are admitted, but philosophical speculations by means of reasoning are repudiated.

In another passage also it is said as follows:

"Further the ignorant and simple-minded keep on dancing and leaping fascinated with their wrong reasonings, falsehoods, and self-discriminations, and are unable to understand the truth of self-realisation (svasiddhāntanaya) and its discourse in words (deśanā), clinging to the external world which is seen of the Mind itself, they cling to the study of the discourses which are a means and do not know properly how to assertain the truth of self-realization (svasiddhāntanaya) which is the truth unspoiled by the fourfold proposition."

The Bodhisattva asked the Buddha:

"Pray tell me, Blessed one, about the characteristic features of the truth of self-realization and about the discourses on it (deśanā-siddhāntanaya), whereby I and other Bodhisattva-Mahāsattvas in future time, understanding what they are, may keep ourselves away from the wrong logicians (kutārkika) such as the philosophers (tirthaṅkara) and those who belong to the vehicles of the Śrāvaka and the Pratyeka-buddha."

"The Blessed One said this to him; Mahāmati, there are two forms of teaching the truth attained by the Tathāgatas, Arhats, Fully-Enlightened ones of the past, present, and future. They are, the teaching by discourses, and the teaching by the establishment of self-realization. What is meant by the studying of the discourses is this, Mahāmati, there are various materials and canonical texts and discourses by which sentient beings are taught according to their dispositions and inclinations."

So far is the realm of dogmatics or theology.

But the realm of intuition is quite different.

"What then is the truth of self-realization (siddhāntanaya) by which the Yogis turn away from discriminating what is seen of the Mind itself? There is an exalted state of inner attainment which does not fall into the dualism of oneness and otherness, of bothness and not-bothness; which goes beyond the Citta, Manas, and Manovijñāna; which has nothing to do with logic, reasoning, theorising, and illustrating; which has never been tested by any bad logicians, by the philosophers, Śrāvakas, and Pratyeka-buddhas, who have fallen into the dualistic views (*antadvaya*) of being and non-being—this I call self-realization (*siddhānta*)".

So, to summarize, there are two aspects of religion:

(1) self realization and (2) discoursing on it.

"This, Mahāmati, is what characterises the truth of self-realization and discoursing on it, and in this you and the other Bodhisattva-Mahāsattvas are to discipline themselves. So it is said:

I have two forms of teaching the truth: self-realization and discoursing. I discourse with the ignorant and (disclose) self-realization to the Yogin."

This problem has been discussed in full detail by Hajime Nakamura in his *Ways of Thinking of Eastern Peoples* (Honolulu: East-West Center Press, 1964).

Chapter 15

Interface of India with other Asian Lands

Lokesh Chandra

A Chinese poet says: "The empires crumble, mountains and rivers remain". The mountains of transcendence and the rivers of perenniality, spirituality and sensitiveness of Asia's Eternal peep through millennia. In the Garden of Blessings are planted our seeds. India has symbolized profound necessities of the spirit, a vision of the infinite in an unbroken sky, the plenitude of the void, the embrace of the one and the zero, the union of abstraction and sensuality in art and life, intellection and meditation, an aesthesis beyond the eyes and reason, the universe as a working of mysterious and impersonal laws or as the Atharvaveda 19.53 says: "Time (*Kāla*) created the Lord of Creatures (Prajāpati)". The solitary contemplative Arhats and Theras and Bodhisattvas who have renounced *nirvāṇa* to help living creatures have been the bread and being of Buddhist Asia. Dharma has been a radiant promise to the millions of Asia, the Truth of Life. The barefoot light of their centuries has been the gods and goddesses, not as such, but as images of the Divinity of Man. Time has opened its doors to their soul, ablaze in the steps or seats of divine beings on lotuses. The entire cultural interflow has been a sharing of dreams, rather than borrowings or influences.

The inmost force that undergrids the symbiosis of Asian lands is the harmony of the human and the cosmic, or in the words of Goethe: *"Was die Welt an innersten zusammenhält"*. The ephemeral and eternal are endowed with a luminous consciousness. It finds varying intellection in accord with the texture of different ethnicities and ages. It is the blending of wisdom and life in the symbolism of three planes: *saṁskāra, saṁskṛta* and *saṁskṛti*. *Saṁskāra* is the inner consciousness where the collective psyche and individual experiences are the inexhaustible soul of the highest. *Saṁskṛta* is its verbal (*vācika*) expression so that the interior light, the *antarjyoti* of the Upaniṣads, flows uninterrupted over spans of time to be inherited and enriched by the future. Its expression in concrete visual terms is *saṁskṛti*, the embodiment (*kāyika*) of the Eternal in the visual, verbal and performing arts: as sculptures in the round, as paintings in the flat, as prose and poetry, as music, dance and theatre. This trinity or *triveṇī* of *saṁskāra, saṁskṛta* and *saṁskṛti* is the confluence of luminous nature.

The introduction of Buddhism into China was due to Emperor Ming of the Eastern Han dynasty who dreamt that a golden man came flying into the palace. When told by his courtiers that he was Buddha, the Sage of the West, he sent an embassy to India to bring *sūtras* and *śramaṇas*. He returned in A.D. 64 with Kāśyapa Mātaṅga and Dharmarakṣa. It was on Chinese initiative that the long pilgrimage of Buddhism began in her thought, literature and visual expression. It was a flux and reflux of two cultures with a new personality of its own.

The Chinese writer Tuan Ch'êng-shih (en A.D. 800 – 863) narrates a legend about the foundation of the city of Balkh in Tukhara. The Tocharians share linguistic features with the Celtic language as well as the textile technology of the Celts. Hundreds of Tocharian mummies have been found in the Tarim Basin and most of them have been dated to about 1000 BC, while the earliest ones from Loulan were buried as early as 2000 – 1800 BC. The Beauty of Loulan with blue eyes and light brown hair is dateable to 2000 BC. Hsüan-tsang speaks of the Tocharian kingdom (Beal 1884: 1.37) and says that the literature, customs and money used in commerce in Bamiyan were the same as those of the Tukhara kingdom. It seems that the Tocharians had settled in this region very early, and were migrating to Central Asia. The Bamboo Books record the travels of Emperor Mu of the Chou dynasty, who ruled for forty five years, 1001 – 945 BC. He crossed the Flowing Sand Desert on the North, ascended the K'un-lun Mountain to pay a visit to the Queen Mother of the West (Xiwangmu). Prof. Dr. Wang Bangwei of the Peking University told me that she is Goddess Umā. It seems that the Udīcya region or North West India was in contact with Central Asia and China as early as the second millennium BC and these contacts increased in the first millennium BC.

The introduction of Buddhism into China was a *novum*. It meant a new intellectual elite in which persons of diverse origins could engage. The monastic ideal created a new form of social organization in which the rigid class boundaries were effaced. The Chinese word, 寺 ssu for a Buddhist monastery originally meant a "government office". The transcription of Buddhist terms into Chinese followed the system in the Accounts of the Western Regions in the Annals of the Han and later Han dynasties. Sanskrit masters entered China on Serindian horses sought after by Chinese emperors. In A.D. 148 the Parthian prince-monk An Shih-kao arrived at Loyang and initiated intense literary activity that lasted for a millennium. *Sūtras*, sculptures and paintings coming from the Buddhist kingdoms ushered new perceptions in the Chinese mind. An Shih-kao began an era of transcreations of Sanskrit works into Chinese, which became an impressive achievement of the Chinese intellectuals from *all* walks of life in contradistinction to the Confucian class of mandarins. Palace Culture was invigorated by a new Peoples' Culture wherein brilliant monks came to the mainstream of cultural and intellectual life without any class distinctions. The *śramaṇas* and *sūtras* on horses led to a symbolism in which superior horses were equated with superior human beings. The noble steed in Chinese polity and poetry was "Power and Virtue", as the State was conditioned by the value systems of the *Sūtras*. The translation of the Sukhāvatī-vyūha by An Shih-kao left China spell-bound: (i) firstly by the genius of a non-Han, (ii) secondly by the deeper realms of wisdom wherein Avalokiteśvara saw that the five *skandhas* in their own-being were empty (*ārya-Avalokiteśvaro bodhisattvo.....svabhāva śūnyān paśyati sma.* Nothingness is the fragrance of the beyond); and (iii) thirdly that there are many universes where definitions disappear, and the undefined reigns. It was a new awakening, in which the classical Confucian sino-centrism was enriched by polycentrism, the non-Han barbarian emerged as a magnetic center, the peripheries became universes in their own right, the Central Kingdom had a counterpart in the Western Paradise of Sukhāvatī. Sukhāvatī became vivid as beauties of Iranian Parthia danced in the joyous tenderness of their vibrant movements. Buddhism was associated with fiery steeds of victory, with caravans laden with affluence, with the passionate beauty of life, and with the enlightenment of the mind.

All the four accounts of the foundation of Khotan (two in Chinese and two in Tibetan) associate it with the son and ministers of Emperor Aśoka in the third century BC. A collection of coins of the first centuries A.D. from Yotqan the ancient capital of Khotan bears Chinese legends and Prakrit legends in Kharoṣṭhī. The Chinese used to get jade for Imperial rites from Khotan. The ideogram *yü* 玉 for jade is a metaphor for purity, nobility and beauty. A jade woman 玉人 means a beautiful woman. This phrase refers to the charm of Iranian ladies of Khotan who must have come to the Imperial Court along with jade, with their jade-smooth skin. The Chinese were fascinated by the beauties, by the music and by the dances of the Serindian peoples of Central Asia. As early as the Chou, which is 1027-256 BC, the Chinese got music of the Western Barbarians and played it on special occasions to vaunt their political might. Jade, the product of Heaven itself, traveled from Khotan to China. Khotan was also famous as a center of Buddhism and of Sanskrit texts. The Chinese expression 'to obtain the doctrine' meant to procure Sanskrit *sūtras*, e.g. Chinese monk Chu Shih-hsing undertook the arduous journey from Loyang to Khotan to get a copy of the Pañcaviṁśati-sāhasrikā Prajñāpāramitā. In the fifth century eight Chinese monks traveled in search of sacred texts. They reached Khotan at the time of the *pañcavārṣika* ceremonies held every five years. Here the most distinguished *bhikṣus* from all over Central Asia embroidered their sermons with parables. The Chinese monks put them together at Turfan on their way back to China in 445, under the title "*Book of the Wise Man and Fool*". This was translated into Tibetan and Mongolian, and, was widely read in the Lamaist world. In the mural at shrine II of Dandan Uiliq, Hārītī has Sino-Khotanese features.

The westward probing and expansion of China led to the introduction of Buddhism after the consolidation of the centralized state in 221 BC. The Xiongnu raids were a constant threat to China's agricultural border regions. The Chinese formed alliances with people further west to establish bases in their rear. They exported goods of sinic gracious living to corrupt the simple martial spirit of the Xiongnu. Han garrisons were stationed all along the route to Khotan that occasioned cultural contracts. The first millennium culminated in the tenth century, when Buddhism ushered in the beginning of modern times with large-scale printing in the Song dynasty. The first printed Buddhist Tripiṭaka started in Chengdu in 971 arrived at Tun-huang around the year 1000.

Kabul, as a great center of Buddhism, had the unique honour of sending the largest number of eminent Buddhist teachers to China to translate *sūtras* into Chinese. The first teacher was Gautama Saṅghadeva who arrived at Ch'ang-an in A.D. 383 and rendered Āgama and Abhidharma texts. Saṅghabhūti of Kabul translated the Buddhacarita into Chinese in A.D. 381-385. The Chinese monk Shih Chi-yen came to Kabul to obtain Sanskrit texts. Guṇavarman, a son of the King of Kabul, came to Nanking in A.D. 431 and translated ten works.

The Fa-t'a stūpa, dominating the oasis city of Shantan in the Kansu province, contains a Hair of King Aśoka. A stone inscription of the T'ang dynasty at the Mo-gao Caves at Tun-huang states that its first cave was constructed by an Indian monk Lo Ts'un in A.D. 366 and was called the "Cave of Unequalled Height". It may have been inspired by the colossi of Bamiyan. The Northern Wei emperors were not of Han origin. These barbarians demonstrated their cultural excellence to the Chinese through the magnificent cave temples, the grandeur of colossal statues at Yun-kang, and the profound thought of the Buddhist *sūtras*. The sinocentric view of the Chinese underwent a new realization of the existence of other cultural universes, at times deeper and more subtle than their own. The first series of caves 16-20 at Yün-kang, begun under the supervision of T'an-yao in 460 for the Northern Wei sovereigns, are reminiscent of Bamiyan. Buddhist sculpture and painting gave a new ambience to China wherein funerary bas-reliefs were replaced by glowing divine forms, smile on their faces, youthful features endowed with serenity of compassion, drapery falling in subtle and gracefully flowing lines. Buddhist art spread with rapidity endowing the vast spaces of China with the glory and grace of the divine, accessible to the nobility and literati as well as to the humblest and lowliest in the land. The caves of T'ien-lung-shan, which date before 750, display influences of late Gupta style.

In A.D. 490 Hsieh Ho established the "Six Aspects" of painting. They have remained the criteria for Chinese art criticism. They echo the six elements of painting in the Kāmasūtra (*rūpabheda, pramāṇa, bhāva, lāvaṇya-yojanā, sādṛśya, varṇikā-bhaṅga*). They impart a vital tone and atmosphere that is moving and alive, in a rendering of 'bones' (essential structure) and essence, rather than mere outward aspect. The divine and human become one, dissolving into ripples of the mind.

In the seventh and eighth centuries, the Chinese were fascinated by the new science of astronomy, calendrical know how and mathematics in Sanskrit texts which were known as the '*P'o-lo-men* or *Brahmin Books*'. Indians were appointed Presidents of the Imperial Board of Astronomy, for instance, Kāśyapa headed it around A.D. 650. It is a paradox that we owe to Gautama Siddha the greatest collection of ancient Chinese astronomical fragments. He introduced from India the symbol of the zero, an early form of trigonometry and other innovations. To the Chinese, Sanskrit was the language of Exact Sciences, of statecraft, of military tactics, and of surveying the sidereal locations of cities from Tashkent to Vietnam. An emperor of the T'ang dynasty sent a military mission against the king of Champa (on the coastal region of modern Vietnam) to bring his library of 1350 Sanskrit manuscripts as war booty to China.

Dance, music and musical instruments are resplendent in the depiction of the Western Paradise of Amitābha. The angels dancing in

Sukhāvatī paradise have been painted all over East Asia, for the last two millennia. Some of the finest murals at Tun-huang (the Ajanta Caves of China) are of dancing goddesses in the joyous tenderness of their vibrant movements. These dancing angels are Indian for they wear no raiments on top. Tun-huang caves show three types of female dresses: (i) the flowing drapery of Chinese ladies, (ii) the tight wear of Central Asian beauties, (iii) and the sensuous elegance of the bare bodies of Indian belles who bid the on-looker to accompany them into worlds of luminous beauty.

Sketch of a dancing scene in Sukhāvatī in Tun-huang Cave 113 of the 8-9th century

The origins of printing in China also go back to Sanskrit. The first printed sheet has the goddess Pratisarā in the center with *mantras* in Sanskrit letters written concentrically around her. It is dated A.D. 757 and was excavated in 1944 from a grave near Beijing. The technology of printing developed in rapid strides for the immense project of the publication of the Buddhist Tripiṭaka. As large quantities of paper were required for the extensive Tripiṭaka, paper industry flourished to such an extent that the use of paper became universal.

The earliest known manuscript with stanzas from the three mahākāvyas of Kālidāsa was preserved in the P'u-an monastery in China. The great Chinese master of *dhyāna* Pao-chang got it from India in A.D. 1057.

There are five Chinese inscriptions at Bodhgaya, the only ones in India, which were put up in the 10/11th century by a mission sent by the Chinese emperor to pay homage to the holy places in India.

On 6 June 1988 Christie's offered for sale a blue-and-white Chinese bowl, which was sold for £ 209,000 to Mr. C.C.Teng of Taiwan. It was made for the personal use of the Ming Emperor Hsüan-te who ruled from 1426-36. It has a Sanskrit benediction and *bījas* all around as a ritual jar:

rātrau svasti, divā svasti, svasti madhyandine sthite /

svasti sarvam ahorātram triratnāni bhavantu vaḥ//

A Princess of Ayodhyā arrived from India to Korea in A.D. 48 at Kimhae aboard a ship, with the Three Treasures of statues, *sūtras* and *śramaṇas* (monks). She became the Queen of the founder of the first Korean state of Karak. She established the first national capital and named it Gaya. From a tribal order Korea emerged as a state. In gratitude to the Sea that allowed safe passage to the Queen to his shores, the King built Haeunsa 'Temple of Sea Grace' that stands to this day near the top of Punsongsan Mountain.

Buddhism was officially introduced into Korea during the period of the Three Kingdoms: Koguryo received it in 372, Paekche in 384, and Silla in 527. The Indian Master Mallānanda brought Buddhism to Paekche in 384. It gave the Three Kingdoms a new meaning: they became civilization. In its first energy and freshness it filled the country with benefits, nourished art, diffused education, made roads, established resting places, promoted beneficence and multiplied comforts in thousand forms. It made vivid and tangible the presence of a profound social and cultural order.

In 535 the first great cathedral of Buddhism was founded and called Pulguksa. It is the oldest surviving Buddhist monastery of Korea, that has determined the tonality of Korean life for centuries. The most skilled workmen were summoned to make it a monument of restrained dignity and quiet peace. To this day, newly married couples begin their conjugal life by seeking the blessings of Pulguksa.

The pensive images of Maitreya's disciples are coeval with the period of the consolidation of the Korean state. Maitreya cult was practiced at the Silla court by young aristocratic warriors who formed a fraternity known as the Hwarang 'Perfumed Followers of the Dragon Flower'. This name is an allusion to the *nāgapuṣpa* tree under which Maitreya Bodhisattva will become a Buddha. They had an enormous importance in the government both during the Three Kingdoms and Unified Silla dynasty. They were responsible for national unity. The Buddhist kingdom of Silla accomplished the unification of the Three kingdoms and formed the nation-state of Korea for the first time in history. Ever since, Korean Buddhism was the destiny and defence of the land. Monk Wolkwang formulated the "Five Worldly Commandments" to form the basis of a national ethos.

The Korean monk Hyecho became a disciple of the Indian teacher Vajrabodhi as a youth of sixteen years. Later, he traveled to India by the sea route and returned in December 727 via Central Asia. In Samarkand he records one Buddhist monastery with one monk. Hyecho is the last pilgrim on the Silk Route (or better Sūtra Route) before the monasteries and monks perished in the Islamic onslaught. He details this wounded time in his Travel Records which are on par with those of his celebrated predecessor Hsüan-tsang.

To ward off the Mongol invasion, the King of Korea had 81,258 wooden blocks of the Tripiṭaka Koreana engraved. Completed in A.D. 1251, they have been preserved in perfect condition to this day at the Haeinsa monastery on Mount Gaya. They reflect the glory of national unity. This Tripiṭaka done for the defence of the country, is a marvel of Korean technology eight centuries ago. As the evening mist pervades the valleys and mountains dull into darkness, the windows of the monastery are lit one by one by monks preparing to cross over the 108 passions to the sea of Buddha's wisdom.

The last Indian Ācārya to visit Korea was Chikong (Dhyānabhadra). He arrived in Korea in the 1340s and established the Juniper Rock Monastery on the pattern of the Nalanda University. Its foundations can be seen near Seoul. He wrote Sanskrit *dhāraṇī-mantras* on the gigantic Yonboksa Bell for the liberation and peace of the Korean people from Mongol domination. An inscription at the Juniper Rock Monastery dated 1378 records the life and work of Dhyānabhadra and informs us that the King of Kanchi was his nephew. It gives a glimpse of Buddhism in India in the 14th century, from Kanchi in the South to Jalandhar in the North. The mill for making *sattu* installed by Dhyānabhadra still lies at the site of this Monastery.

In 1446 the sage-like emperor Seijong invented a new Korean alphabet and moveable printing types. This alphabet continues to this day as the Hangul or "Proper Writing". Dr. Kei Won Chung in his dissertation to the Princeton University says that the Korean alphabet was composed on the principles of the Sanskrit alphabet. With the new alphabet, learning became accessible to a large mass of people.

Seoul has the only Buddhist Broadcasting Station in the world. A restaurant called "Perfume of Grasses" recalls the cuisine of Ācārya Dhyānabhadra. It serves "tea of honey-stick". Honey-stick is *madhu-yaṣṭi* or liquorice (*muleṭhī* in Hindi).

In 1991, Korea dedicated the world's largest bronze image of Maitreya at Popchusa monastery. This 100 feet high statue embodies the aspirations of the Korean people for national re-unification. The

Popchusa was built in 553. Two centuries later, in 776, monk Yulsa erected a 40 feet gilt bronze Maitreya for national prosperity and unity of the people. During the Eye-Opening Ceremony in April 1991, three rainbows appeared in the clear sky: "Isn't this a sign that we can even move heaven when we are truly devoted? When we build an image of Maitreya in our hearts too, all lives on earth will turn into lotus flowers, and the very world around us will become a pond of joy" (Chief Abbot Yu).

In 552, Buddhism was officially introduced into Japan when the King of Paekche (Kudara) sent a gilt bronze image of Lord Buddha and *sūtras*. A host of secular technologies accompanied the new Buddhist order: writing, administration, weaving, metallurgy, calendar & architecture. Shotoku Taishi (574-621) is rightly acclaimed as the builder of Japanese civilization. As a thanks giving to the new order, he created Shitennoji at Osaka in A.D. 593, an architectural achievement of the age. This temple to the Four *Lokapālas* (Shitenno) symbolized unity of the east, south, west and north of Japan as a nation-state. He promulgated the first written Constitution of 17 articles in A.D. 604 in which the *Triratna* gave a humanised face to administration. He gave birth to Japanese literature by his commentaries on Hokke (Saddharma-puṇḍarīka-sūtra), Yuima (Vimalakīrti-nirdeśa), and Shōman (Śrīmālā-sūtra). Japan had wrought a miracle in the short span of half a century. Her literature and Imperial palaces were on par with those of continental China. Japan emerged as a state when Prince Shotoku substituted tribal rivalries by a centralized system of Japan as a *Buddha-kṣetra*.

From the Buddhist monasteries established by Prince Shotoku, the Horyuji "The Temple for the Flourishing of Dharma" (*Dharma-vardhana-vihāra*) still stands as the most ancient wooden building in the world. Its kondō or golden hall is adorned with murals, whose style has close affinities to that of India. It reflects the artistic achievements of the seventh century. In the years A.D. 643-646, 648-649, and 657-661 the entourage of the Chinese envoy Wang Hsüan-ts'e copied the frescoes on the walls of monasteries in India. Later on these paintings were compiled in 40 fascicules. Some of them were taken to Japan by the Korean artist Honjitsu, and they became the models for Horyuji murals. The Buddhas and Bodhisattvas of Horyuji, with a rich patina of centuries, evince a particular purity of line, surface and decoration and a desire to see humanity, flesh and blood, fused in most abstract of deities. The Horyuji monastery has yielded one of the most ancient Sanskrit manuscripts of the Uṣṇīṣavijayā-dhāraṇī in the Gupta script.

As early as the sixth century, an Indian yogin lived in the Kataoka village by begging alms. Shotoku Taishi wrote a poem on him. In the middle of the seventh century Dharmabodhi came via China and settled in Hokkezan. He had a small image of Thousand-armed Kannon. He restored the Emperor to health, when all the royal physicians had failed. In 651 he instituted the Festival of the Tripiṭaka (Daizoe).

The Japanese state found an invigorating stabilization in Buddhism. The Daibutsu at Todaiji was the culmination of Japanese resourcefulness and technology. It was consecrated by the Indian Bodhisena who reached Osaka in 773. He taught Sanskrit at Daianji that showed the way to a phonetic system to suit the needs of the Japanese language.

The *vīṇā* under its Japanese form *biwa* is an integral characteristic of the Japanese Sarasvatī. The most ancient *biwa* known today is preserved in the Shosoin Repository, dating to A.D. 757.

In A.D. 799 an Indian was washed ashore somewhere in the Mikawa province. A young man of twenty years, with nothing to cover his body except a straw coat and short drawers, he was stranded in a country where none understood him. Years later when he became conversant with Japanese he said that he had come from India. He had seeds of cotton with him. He lived at the Kawadera temple at Nara. Two ancient chronicles Nihon-koki and Ruiju-kokushi mention that he introduced the cultivation of cotton which became the most important clothing material. The Japanese words *wata* or *hata* for cotton are derived from Sanskrit *paṭa* (पट).

With the advent of the ninth century, Japanese life had been transformed by assimilation with Buddhist civilization. The blossoming of the great continental culture in insular surroundings reached its culmination in the personality of Kobo Daishi (A.D. 774-835), who visited China to drink at the purest springs of Dharma. Kobo Daishi's new denomination of Shingon or Mantrayāna was a new moral conscience of the country. He proclaimed Buddhahood to be the potential privilege of all as against the predestined few. He became an outstanding genius in Japan's cultural evolution. For the first time he founded a school for the children of common people. Till then the academies were open only to children of families above the fifth rank. To achieve this historic democratisation, he created the Japanese *kana* syllabary of fifty sounds: *a i u e o, ka ki ku ke ko*, etc. based on the Sanskrit alphabet. It was to spread education to the common man. The new syllabary was a revolutionary step in Japan's civilization: what was hitherto the prerogative of the pre-destined few became the potential privilege of all. The entire alphabet was woven into a poem wherein every syllable occurs once. This poem is called *Iroha*. It is based on the Mahāparinirvāṇa-sūtra.

The Japanese have longed to be pilgrims to India. In A.D. 818 Kongo-sammai (Vajrasamādhi) came to India via China. He makes a realistic observation that millions of flies swarmed the dining rooms of Nalanda but disappeared when the monks settled down to eat. In the 850s Hōdo undertook a hundred day long meditation. On the 70th day a beautiful lady entered the room and he fell in love. In remorse, he travelled to China and thence to the Vulture Peak in India to expiate his sin. The monk Myoe Shoin (1163-1122) was unable to visit India. He consoled himself by giving the Sanskrit name Prāgbodhi to the hill in front of his monastery and calling the stream flowing by as Nairañjanā. In the Tokugawa period, a great scholar of Avataṁsaka Hotan washed his feet in sea water at a beach in the thought that the water extended to the shores of the motherland of Buddhism.

Near Kyoto is the Golden Pavilion (Kinkakuji) which was the hermitage of Ashikaga Shogun Yoshimitsu as a Zen monk. It is a picturesque pavilion sitting in the pond, lending grace to the garden of Rokuonji temple. Here arises the ethereal pavilion of *nirvāṇa* overlooking the ocean of existence (*bhava-sāgara*). It recalls the Golden Temple of Amritsar. The Kinkakuji in the center of the pond is the emergence of Brahmā from the primal waters.

The wonderful art of Ikebana, which means putting living plants in water, is to love flowers as living beings and to tend them with kind feelings. The Japanese bow before the flowers after they have arranged them. An aesthetic creation is the essence of life itself. It is pervaded by the warmth of the human heart, whereby one gives expression to the universal heart. Japanese tradition speaks of "Indian monks who, in their universal love, were the first to pick up plants injured by the storm or parched by the heat, in order to tend them with compassion and endeavour to keep them alive".

India's austerity was Japan's elegance: minimum of lines to express plenitude of form. It is the aesthetic appreciation of stark poverty, of austere form, "the *saṁnyāsa* of rūpa". Haiku is the incarnation of loneliness, of minimal words. The dusty leaf-hut of India is an abode of meditation in Japan with not a single particle of dust. The Ryoanji garden with its naked expanse of white sand acting as a setting for stones takes us back to the sea, to the ocean of existence (*bhava-sāgara*). This supremely abstract monument, the *kare sansui*, the "dry landscape" garden, was designed in the late fifteenth century. The rocks, tiny mounts Fuji, simply mean *fuji*, not two, that is, peerless, the abolition of all distinctions, the *advaya*. They are both literal levels and symbolic tangents thereof, crossing the sea of illusion towards the shore of *satori* "illumination", to cross over the dry sandy ripples of the ocean of existence, the *bhava-sāgara*.

Zen is a product of the Chinese and Japanese soil from the Buddhist seed of Enlightenment, India's hut and Japanese bamboos, India's sophisticated thought and Japan's bizarre koans: all leading to self-reliance (*jiyū*) and self-being (*jizai*).

Along a road stands an egg-like rock on a flat roundish base of another rock, with the Sanskrit monogram RO, Sanskrit letters implying deeper levels. A modern Japanese girl in mini, her hair dyed blonde and perhaps with styrene injection for a rounded feminine form, stops by, graciously puts a tangerine on a piece of paper as an offering to the planets (*nava-graha*): RO is the symbolic *bījākṣara* for *nava-graha-pūjā*. Such are the frozen levels of culture echoing at different strata of existence and consciousness.

In our own times, the Japanese Okakura Tenshin stayed at the home of poet Rabindranath Tagore in 1902. It led to the cultural renaissance of India. Out of his talks with the Indian poet, Tenshin crystallised his essay on *The Ideals of the East*. The pioneers of modern Indian painting, Abanindranath Tagore, Nandlal Bose, and others, used Japanese brushes and colours and reflected the diaphanous aura of Japanese paintings in their new creativity. This cultural encounter left a deep impression on our national ethos. Some of our revolutionaries sought refuge in Japan. The heroic struggle of Tenshin prevented the wholesale destruction of the cultural heritage of Japan in the orgy of foreignism sweeping the country. Yet, he spoke of humanity; in his own words "humanity has met in a tea-cup".

Let us go to South East Asia. Emperor Aśoka sent his son Mahinda and daughter Saṅghamitrā to King Devanampiya Tissa of Srilanka in the third century BC. In the list of gifts, as recorded in the Dīpavaṁsa, sent by Aśoka is *nandyāvarta* whose meaning has been debated. It has been interpreted as a type of jasmine, or a gold vessel in the shape of crow-claws, or a gold flower. Nandyāvarta is an architectural term: it is a six-storeyed palace in the Mānasāra 24.24 or a pavilion with 36 coloumns in the Suprabhedāgama 31.103. Aśoka sent eighteen guilds of artists, craftsmen and painters along with Mahinda, well aware of the power of art to attract people to Dharma. By the time Mahinda died there was an art gallery (*cittasālā*) in the capital of Anuradhapura. Promoting piety through painting has lingered throughout the centuries. Mahāvaṁsa mentions painted vases in the reign of

Devanampiya Tissa in 307 BC. A very early extant painting of the second century BC showing the Vessantara-jātaka has been found in the relic-chamber of the Ruvanveli Seya from the period of King Dutugemunu (161-137 BC). There are other paintings of the second century BC in the Karambagala cave (ancient Kurandaka Lena), which are mentioned by Buddhaghosa in the Visuddhimagga.

The world famous paintings in the rock citadel of Sigiriya (Skt. Siṁhagiri) were done during the reign of King Kassapa I (479-497), who had come to the throne by murdering his father. He ruled the kingdom for 18 years surrounding himself with lissome women, trying to forget his aching conscience. The twenty one figures of sensuous ladies at Sigiriya bear a close resemblance to the art of Ajanta. Benjamin Rowland compares these maidens to the sculptures of Amaravati, whence Srilanka derived its sculptural style.

King Kassapa, who transformed it into the most impregnable fortress, identified himself with Kubera, the God of Riches, who was then held in high veneration. The abode of Kubera is on Mount Kailaśa. On Sigiriya and its environs King Kassapa tried to create the verisimilitude of this Mount, especially after the lyrical Meghadūta of Kālidāsa. The gallery is a 500 feet long concavity which has been constructed to accord with the passage of the cloud in the Meghadūta, where the cloud is told to proceed northwards on its flight to Kailāśa through an aperture in the Krauñca mountain. The high polish of the Mirror Hall of Sigiriya mirrors the heavenly damsels of the poet Kālidāsa. The artistic treatment of the world-famed damsels, depicting them waist above clouds, together with their location in the Rock, portrays the lightning and clouds in the region of cloud-land above which rises the peak of Kailāśa where Lord Kubera resides. Actually, this part of the rock is girdled by clouds in December and early January. The Princesses of Lightning or *vijju-kumārī* are fair and the Cloud Damsels or *megha-latā* are dark. These marvellous paintings precede their immortal counterparts at Ajanta. These damsels could be goddesses bringing blessings of heaven to assuage the gnawing remorse of patricide in the heart of King Kassapa.

When Sigiriya passed out of eventful history, Anuradhapura came into its own. It was here that Dutthagamani, the national hero reigned. It was here again that the Buddhist works were committed to writing in Aluvihara or the Caves of Illumination. In the heart of this city is the venerable Bo tree with a recorded history of over two and a quarter thousand years. It is a branch of the tree at Bodhgaya under which Lord Buddha gained Bodhi.

In March 1917, Sir John Marshall wrote to the Acting Director of the Colombo Museum, to make copies of two paintings in the Gal Vihara, Polonnaruva, which are of the 12th century, because "we have scarcely any painting in India of this period".

The Simhala language is in line with Hindi, Gujarati, Marathi, Bengali and others. Simhala has even preserved interesting words which are lost or have become obsolete in modern Indian languages. While Sanskrit *aśva* is nearly forgotten in modern Indian *tadbhavas*, Simhala has *as* in the literary language and in several compounds like *as-govva* 'horse-keeper', *as-hala* 'stable'. The Simhala language is important for understanding the evolution of modern Indian languages in their time-context: for in it we are able to follow the development through more than two thousand years, first in inscriptions and then in literary works. It affords time-points to locate the histories of words.

The interface of the cultures of India and South East Asia was, in the words of Paul Mus' "India seen from the East". The famous Chinese writer, Lady Han Suyin, speaks of the Indian initiative in South East Asia, as narrated in the Chinese dynastic annals. She writes: "One night two thousand years ago, a god visited a youth in India and said to the young man, named Kauṇḍinya: "Find a bow, board your boat, sail toward the rising sun". Kauṇḍinya went to the temple next morning and there found, on the floor, a bow with a quiver full of arrows; he embarked and the god-driven wind blew him across the elephant-backed sea to a shore where Willowleaf, the beautiful queen and leader of the Khmer amazons, reigned. The queen launched her war canoe to repel Kauṇḍinya, but the youth shot it through with his arrows, and she submitted to him. They were married, and thus was born the dynasty of the first Khmer kingdom".

Thus the kingdom of Funan was founded by sage Kauṇḍinya, who married the Nāgī queen Somā. This kingdom is referred to in Chinese texts from the third to the seventh century. Sanskrit was the official language of Funan. The use of the Pallava script speaks of the cultural majesty of the Pallava kings.

Cambodia is the only country named after a *ṛṣi* or sage: Kambuja kings were descendants of Kambu Svāyambhuva and Merā.

Jayavarman II came to the throne in the ninth century. He liberated Cambodia from Javanese vassalage. There is an unbroken line of rulers from him to modern times. He founded Angkor around the fertile area of the Great Lake of Tonle Sap that is inundated by the Mekong. The word Angkor is the Cambodian pronunciation of Sanskrit *nagara*. The Cambodians believe that Angkor was built by Indra who moulded the city in clay, poured over it a sort of icing whereby it solidified. Great Indra looked upon his favourite land of the Khmers, noted that its King and Queen were childless. He gave a son to the Queen and showed the child glories of his Tāvatiṁsa paradise. The son ruled over the Khmers and copied the heavenly realm at Angkor. Great Indra visited the earth for the coronation of his son, to give to his child's realm its name of Kambuja, and to give the Sacred Sword which is the Lightning of Indra. It is kept to this day in the royal palace, and used in coronation rites. The coronation ceremonies are events of great pomp. The King is robed in the colour of the day (purple if it is a Tuesday). He is received in the palace by the Grand Master of the Order of the Baku, carrying an image of god Viṣṇu. The royal feet are washed in coconut juice and perfumed essences by the Prea Reamea Reachea Thippedi (Rāma-rājya-adhipati). The Grand Master hands the statues of Śiva and Viṣṇu in the right and left hands of the King. When he hands over the Sacred Sword, he proclaims the formula: "Take, for thou art the Lightning of Indra".

Angkor flourished for six hundred years. The city was captured in 1431 by the Thais, and a curtain of darkness descended upon Angkor and the entire Cambodian civilization.

The Cambodian kings transferred their capital to Phnom Penh, then called Chadomukh. With the advent of the new dynasty in the 15th century, the construction of temples and writing of Sanskrit inscriptions ceased, as the elite had been wiped out. When King Ponhea Yat founded the capital at Phnom Penh he gave it the imposing title:

Krong chadomukh mongkol sokkala kampucheathipdei

चतुर्मुख मंगल सकल कम्बुजाधिपति

sereisothor parava intaputta borei rattharachasema mohanokor

श्रेष्ठ परम इन्द्रप्रस्थ पुरी राष्ट्रराजसीमा महानगर

Over a thousand Sanskrit inscriptions in ornate kāvya style reveal the religious, social and political life of Cambodia. The Sanskrit inscription of Jayavarman VII reveals the magnitude of the Rājavihāra of Ta Prohm where the king set up an image of his mother as Prajnaparamita. It had 439 professors and 970 scholars, and 66,625 people were employed to serve the deities of the temples. The inscription further relates that there were 798 temples and 102 hospitals in his kingdom.

Indravarman (877-889) laid out the network of irrigation channels, whereby land produced in abundance. It reached its culmination in the huge sandstone temple of Bakong. Yaśovarman (889-900) executed tremendous hydraulic works that made prosperity and Angkor synonymous. Angkor was an immense hydraulic system with supply channels, dykes, reservoirs, field runnels to store fresh water, collect rain-water, and to distribute it. The uncertainty of nature was replaced by a vast economic potential so that Khmer art could find expression in superb Pre Rup with its colossal terminal towers, or the Phimeanakas of Jayavarman V (968-1001) with its continuous galleries, or the colossal dimensions of Ta Keo, or the delicately chiseled jewel of a stone temple like Banteay Srei (968), or the supreme image of Khmer art in Angkor Vat, one of the largest temples ever raised by man.

Even today, fairy-stories are wide-spread with *yakṣiṇīs*, Indra's paradise, kings and queens, which are spun into long dramas with the water-music of the bamboo xylophones. The folk songs of Cambodia are of poignant beauty, living and so changing:

> I plunge into the forest thickets
> Searching my beloved.
> And then suddenly I see her
> Drawing water from the spring...
> But it is not she, it is not she,
> It is the morning star
> Drinking on the edge of the misty sky.

The first Sanskrit inscription of South East Asia comes from Champa. It is the Vo-Chanh Rock Inscription dated to the second or third century A.D. on paleographic grounds. The Sanskrit epigraphic records are confirmed by Chinese sources. The history of Champa has been reconstructed from A.D. 192 on the basis of inscriptions and Chinese annals. They were a major catalyst of culture in Asia. Champa was a renowned centre of Sanskrit and Buddhist learning. A Chinese military mission was sent against King Śambhuvarman to bring 1350 Sanskrit Buddhist works as war booty to China. In 752 Emperor Shomu of Japan invited Buddhasthira from Champa for the sumptuous consecration ceremony of the Daibutsu Roshana (Rocana Buddha) at the Todaiji monastery. He introduced Sanskrit music and dance in Japan and it is part of imperial repertoire to this day. The Chams had no resources of population and they succumbed to the unequal collision of population in the 19th century. Fragments of their enchanted glory can be seen in folklore, which is still full of stories of Indra, called Yan In or 'God Indra'. He is associated with the construction of a dyke above the valley of Song Luy, which magically dams up the celestial waters. In years of severe drought, the Chams pray to him to release the waters.

The rise of culture in the Indonesian isles is attested by seven inscriptions of King Mūlavarman, dated to ca A.D. 400 on paleographic grounds. By this century, the tradition of *yajñas* must have been fully established as the King donated thousands of cows to brahmins, established hospitals, and created an extensive irrigation system. The inscriptions were discovered on the *Mahakam* River, a name that can reflect the *kāmadhenu* that secured the march of civilizing influences and material affluence. He erected a light-house (*ākāśadīpa*) that indicates a developed infrastructure for transnational commerce. It was the dynasty of Kuṇḍuṅga which has left the imprint of its glory in the Chinese name K'un-lun for the SE Asian region. The inscriptions of Pūrṇavarman, King of Tārumanagara, from West Java, are of the fifth century. They reveal the use of the Pallava script of South India: Tāruma is the Tamil spelling of Dharma. The concept of the king as an incarnation of Viṣṇu and *nagara* tokens the idea of a state with a social system leading to concentration of political power that enabled large irrigation works to bring about economic prosperity. The interaction of Hinduism and Buddhism with Java and Kalimantan led to a higher state of civilisation with an alphabetic culture, effective administrative machinery, a powerful system of vast public works for economic prosperity, development of metallurgy and sculptural techniques and implements for sculpting divine images, and sophisticated architectural complexes of temples. Temples led to contemplation: beyond mere physical seeing it was the visualization of the Divine. Paintings, sculptures and architectural structures enhanced meditation. The sculptures and architecture of the chandis represent the glory of classical Indonesia. The chandis Borobudur, Prambanan, Kalasan down to the 15th century Sukuh and Ceṭo are pearls of the heritage of the emerald string of the Indonesian archipelago. The world of the narrator, bard and poet is represented by Old Javanese literature, like the lexicon Chandakaraṇa which includes metrics, grammar and *alaṅkāra*, the great *parwas* of the Mahābhārata, kakawins like the Rāmāyaṇa, philosophical texts like the Bhuvanakośa and San Hyang Kamahāyānikan. For instance, King Śrī Dharmavaṁśa Têguh Ananta-vikram-ottuṅga-deva initiated the auspicious undertaking of putting the Mahābhārata into Javanese (*mañjāvākna*) so that the tradition lives in the future. While this king carried out conquests, his queen presided over the creation of literature that became immortal fame. Local genius created a new cultural idiom of Hindu-Buddhist culture and civilization in all its manifestations.

Indo-Asian cosmosophy with its many gods and goddesses represents pluralism which has also to be the new sensibility. It is the openness to multiple forms of reality. They are the many structures of meaning and being in which we constantly live. Theo-diversity gives depth, a resonance of the transcendant function. It teaches a reverence for the variousness of ourselves and of others. Life can have no rigid fences or boundaries. It needs horizons to purify, perfect and ennoble our existence. Buddhism has kissed this world with compassion, enwoven light and love in the hearts of men, kindled lamps in the forlorn recesses of somber shades of life, offered flowers and lit lamps in place of rituals of slaughter. Buddha, the Prince of Peace, brought silence to the arid heart of man who ceaselessly runs in furious chase of victory. From the surging centuries of noise rises the prayer of love immeasurable: "Let Buddha be my refuge".**तन्मे मनः शिव-संकल्पमस्तु!**

Chapter 16

Buddhism in Asia: Tolerance and Syncretism: A View from the West

George A. Sioris

The best approach by me to this eminent and distinguished audience should be an open and sincere "triple" disclaimer. The present speaker is not addressing you in his official capacity as his country's representative to India nor as a real scholar of Buddhism, and certainly not as a specialist in comparative religion. The few thoughts that follow are solitary and modest paths of study of an outsider who happened to become fascinated by this great religion of tolerance, serenity and inner bliss, during twelve years of stay and travel in the Far East, from Japan and Korea, to China, to India and to South East Asia, in areas permeated by the influence of both Theravāda and Mahāyāna teachings.

The present writer is the first to realize that his few remarks are just drops in this vast ocean of Buddhist tolerance, unable to exhaust a subject as inspiring as it is broad.

I hope that I shall have your indulgence if the tone of these remarks is more personal than scholarly, more simple than academic.

The first observation from the very beginning of my exposure to the religious horizons of Asia was doublefold. The extreme spirit of tolerance of Eastern religions and their enormous capacity of synthesis, amalgamation and syncretism.

Two texts I find of paramount importance in this connection. One is more lengthy, extremely well researched, a model of academic excellence. It is a jewel of Thought within a larger, bold, breathtaking, comparative attempt. It is the chapter "Meeting of Religions" in Radhakrishnan's monumental work "Eastern Religions and Western

Thought".[1] The other is a voice straight from the heart, a warm appeal for a universal religion based on action, love, mysticism and philosophy, launched by the great Swami Vivekananda.[2] Both, although from different angles, converge on the simple truth enunciated by the Mahatma. Man is capable of adoring God in all his various aspects.[3]

A distant echo of the above ideas we find in the most glorious period of classic Greece, although the undertones in this case are more political than religious: "We listen gladly to the opinion of others and do not turn our faces on those who disagree with us",[4] exclaims Pericles praising his illustrious city, Athens. We find it also – in a religious sense – in almost every page of the works of one of the best known – if not the greatest – writers of modern Greece, Nikos Kazantzakis. There are many paths to ultimate Truth. What counts in the final analysis is not the path that one takes, but the sincerity and the determination of his pursuit.

Again in classic Greece, we have a unique illustration, combining, in a strange way, both reactionary intolerance with liberal spirit and exploration of new horizons and ideas. The condemnation of Socrates has been historically vindicated. One of humanity's greatest thinkers has defied through his death the intolerance of his executioners.

Since we are still talking about the West, I suspect one more remark is legitimate. I would touch very briefly upon it, since I am conscious here of the temptation to slip in another area, in another huge independent subject. Religious fanaticism in East and West. My basic impression is that the western world is not fully aware of the endless reservoires of tolerance of eastern religions. In 1951, a brilliant thesis defended by a Greek scholar[5] before the Sorbonne, examines thoroughly the phenomenon of fanaticism, be it religious, political, social, scientific or aesthetic and tries to explain it through the study of various factors. In the chapter on religious fanaticism, classic antiquity is examined, the Jewish tradition, primitive Christianity, Byzantium, Catholicism, the Inquisition, Protestantism and Islam. But the Orient is absent from this brilliant analysis! Only in the introduction there is one mention of Buddhism, simply with the purpose to argue that we in the West may judge the acts of a Buddhist as fanatic in the same way the acts of a Christian may be judged fanatic by a Muslim and vice versa. The totally different religious landscape of the East – despite its unavoidable but scarce fanatic shadows – it overlooked.

All these ideas, and their various formulations in East and West, are fascinating indeed. I would have, nevertheless, to narrow, somehow, our field of vision and try to concentrate a little more on Buddhism.

This great Religion extended to every part of Asia characterized through the centuries by a unique capacity of assimilation. Some frictions did occur, but in general the faith either absorbed pre-existing beliefs or was harmoniously incorporated in the religious frame of far away countries, to a point that clear distinction becomes often difficult, if not impossible.

Buddhism never refuted local gods, says Professor Bernard Frank.[6] It has only limited itself in explaining that even these gods are caught in the movement of universal transmigration and therefore transitory. In Japan, he adds, Shinto keeps silent as far as Death is concerned and it is precisely this vacuum which is filled by Buddhism. In this connection, the subject may be even stretched to the point of assuming a political dimension, explaining Buddhism's support by Japanese feudal lords. The Buddhist teaching of rejection of "frail world vanity" in order to achieve the state of *Nirvāṇa*, necessary for man's transformation into Buddha, argues Sladkovsky,[7] "gave the feudal lords a functional ideological weapon in support of their role over the populace". This of course is one peripheral aspects which can be debated. Personally, I am more inclined to think, following Eliot[8], that the absence of a non-organized, non-Buddhist literary class corresponding to the Confucianists – as in China – was a decisive factor for the spread of Buddhism in Japan. The truth of the matter is that syncretism did take place, as it is asserted by both Shinto and Buddhist sources.

It is further characteristic that this syncretism is reflected in the sect of Shingon, the most esoteric and with close Tibetan affinities, sect which elaborated the system of "honji-suijaku", uniting Bodhisattvas and Kamis.[9]

Moreover, it should not be forgotten that, in Japan, Buddhism not only encountered Shinto but also another faith, Shugendo, a unique offspring of both Tendai and Shingon, the little known doctrine of the Yamabushi in the heart of Japanese Middle Ages. "Buddhism", writes one of the rare Western scholars of Shugendo,[10] "assimilated Shugendo in the way it assimilated Shintoism, allowing a certain autonomy to these beliefs and at the same time leaving its "mark on them".

Another point worth stressing, while we deal with the destiny of Buddhism in Japan – is, in my opinion, the extraordinary interaction of tolerance and amalgamation which gives a special dimension to the whole syncretic phenomenon. Ryobu-Shinto means a twofold effort aiming at compromise and harmony, both from the Buddhist and the Shinto side. Buddhism embraced the pre-existing creed with tolerance but Shinto priests also "considered such a union (with Buddhism) as desirable".[11] Eliot's conclusion on this point is most enlightening. "Indeed, if an amicable arrangement had not been made, if Buddhism had struggled with Shintoism as Christianity and Islam struggled with paganism in Europe and Africa, it is probable that the victory would have remained with Buddhism". Such was the radiation of this religion in the Empire of the Rising Sun.

In China, we witness several phenomena. Overlapping of Buddhism, Taoism and Confucianism,[12] syncretism within Chinese Buddhism itself,[13] encounters between Tao and Buddhism,[14] Confucianism and Buddhism,[15] a spirit of tolerance in general and towards Christianity in particular. Mou Tzu, the philosopher, insisted that although he had become a Buddhist, "he had not ceased to be a Confucian".[16] According to Nakamura,[17] Tsung-mi declared: "Confucius, Lao-tzu, and Śākyamuni all attained sainthood. They preached their doctrines in different ways in accordance with the time and place. However, they mutually helped and benefited the people by their teachings". Or, to say it more poetically, along with Li-Shih-Chien: "Buddhism is the sun, Taoism the moon, and Confucianism the five stars".[18]

Another event which I find of particular importance as far as the history of Christianity in Asia is concerned is the Edict proclaimed by the Chinese Emperor upon the entrance to China of the first Nestorian Christians. After having studied their book "concerning the one God", the Emperor said: "The Way has more than one name. There is more than one Sage. Doctrines vary in different lands, their benefits reach all mankind. After examining these doctrines we find them profound and pacific.....".[19]

In India, land of tolerance from time immemorial, the encounter of Hinduism and Buddhism is so harmonious that one almost forgets that it takes place in a frame of continous and broader religious synthesis, from the times of Aśoka to Akbar's Din-i-Ilahi to Bhakti and Sufism to the very origins of Sikhism. Naturally, here also there have been instances of antagonism, but the cornerstones are solid: "All sects deserve reverence for one reason or another. By thus acting, a man exalts his own sect and at the same time does service to the sects of other people", proclaims the edict of Asoka.[20] This is indeed the uniqueness of Indian tolerance, taken "...not merely in a negative, but in a positive sense, that is an appreciation of other faiths...", in the words of Radhakrishnan.[21] The soul of India is based on this belief, sublime in its simplicity: "Numerous as creeds be, they are impermanent. Truth is but one on the earth", epitomizes poetically the seventeenth century Telugu saying of Vemana.[22]

The fascination of this subject is such that the Western student tends to become prisoner of the illusion that he may capsule in a few pages the vast religious horizons of the past. Before we slip into this trap, let us just try to condense our field of vision to only two smaller countries, one belonging to Mahāyāna and one to Theravāda sphere of influence, Korea and Burma. (I hope that Korean and Burmese delegates here present will view these remarks with indulgence, not as an intrusion into their heirlooms by an outsider but rather as focal points capturing a westerner's attention and interest). Let me also add that if other venerated cradles of Buddhism like Tibet, Sri Lanka, Mongolia, Thailand etc., are omitted, the reason is certainly not irreverence but the necessity to condense in a few pages a religious panorama of extraordinary dimensions. In all of these countries the same spirit of calm assimilation prevails. When Samye temple was built, writes Stein,[23] "The lower part is said to have been in the Tibetan manner, the middle with a Chinese roof and the upper part with an Indian roof...

Indeed, an illustration common everywhere in Asia.

The basic currents in Korea, cultural bridge between China and Japan, are three: The animistic and the Shamanistic beliefs of the oldest times, Buddhism as it reached there after receiving the impact of great China and Confucianism which easily "migrated" to the peninsula from its neighbouring cradle. How were all these elements combined?

At the beginning, during the 4th century, Buddhism assimilated a lot from pre-existing shamanistic beliefs. The mighty of the land appeal to Buddhists, as well as to the spokesmen of animistic tradition and to the spirits of mountains and rivers to bring along rain.[24] Shamans combine Buddhist as well as Taoists beliefs with their own polytheistic system. By the progress of time, primitive ideas recede and the vacuum is filled by Buddhism, especially in the years of T'ang glory in neighbouring China, spiritual destinations of many Korean monks.[25]

Moreover the syncretic character of Korean Buddhism is witnessed in the field of synthesis among Buddhist sects themselves, as in the days of King Mundjong's son, prince Ei-C'on.[26]

Buddhism's encounter with Confucianism which came to Korea in the 8th century, was not without complications. Eliot[27] calls the latter "a tremendous opponent" of the former and portrays vividly the persecutions of Buddhists by Confucianist scholars.

Studying Korean history we witness the destinies of Buddhism sometimes in the rise, in other instances declining, according to Confucianist influence in the court.[28] But apart from some isolated deviations in the Buddhist camp, nowhere do we witness traces of fanaticism in Buddhist circles.

Korean historians[29] maintain that Confucianism provided "new political principles denying the primitive correlation between Government and religion" whereas Buddhism, "put down its roots deep in the Silla soil". But even later, in the times of Li (1392-1410), Buddhists play an important part in social life, whereas some literati, along with the common people, abandon the Confucianist confrontational attitude and become more friendly to Buddhism.[30]

Other scholars, underline the syncretic tendencies, stressing in particular the teachings of "Hwarengdo".[31] It was blend of Confucianist ideas of filial piety, Buddhist abstention from taking of life and local beliefs of partiotism and "eastern chivalry". In addition, it is stressed that Korean Buddhism overstepped the limits of religion and philosophy and was finally identified with korean culture, covering also the realm of mythology, literature and art.

Closer to our time, Herbert[32] reminds us of the Tong-hak school which, originating in 1859 as a reaction to the aggressive Christian missionary activity, was a blend of Confucianism, Buddhism and Taoism.[33]

All these syncretic tendencies are reflected in the work of a writer who studied and loved the Peninsula: Homer Hulbert, missionary, educationist, linguist, journalist and diplomat lived there for 21 years from 1886 to 1907. Writing about Korean religion of that period Hulbert[34] maintains that Koreans feel Confucianists when they consider themselves as part of society, Buddhists when they philosophize and animists when they feel in danger. (In this last one are included shamanism, fetishism and nature worship.)

Another witness of Korea in those days, was a lady with tremendous sensitivity: Isabella Bird Bishop.[35] She thinks that Korean Shamanism is characterized by softness in comparison with Shamanism in other parts of North Eastern Asia which can only be attributed to Buddhist influence.

Burma is a country little known to the West, inhabited by one of the kindest and most smiling peoples on earth, where Buddhism's imprint is ever present. At this racial crossroads where so many races intermingle, Khmer, Chinese, Indian, sino-Tibetan, the preaching of Buddha found the widest echo. So deep is Buddhist influence here, that we can hardly talk of syncretic encounters, although they are not completely inexistent.

In any event, Burmese tolerance in general is proverbial. If we may momentarily make a slight digression from the religious to the diplomatic field, we could recall the historic episode referring to Kublai Khan's Ambassadors in the year 1273. The Great Mongol sent then an Embassy to Pagan requesting Burma's submission. The Ambassador's attitude was really insulting, a fact which obliged King Narathihapati to execute them. This cruelty cannot be considered an isolated case in those years or in that country. But what should be particularly stressed is the reaction of the King's Counsellors who did every thing they could in order to avert such a terrible punishment. It is true, they said, that the Ambassadors did not observe protocol, but "may Your Majesty adopt a conciliatory tone...Your ancestors, the Kings, have never executed foreign envoys. May Your Majesty retain wisdom and calm"...[36] The appeal had no avail. Nevertheless there are few parallels in world history where royal Counsellors express themselves in such a wise and restrained way.

A deeper study of Burmese character reveals further aspects of moderation and tolerance. In this country, writes a Japanese scholar[37] quoting writer, the administration was based on arbitration rather than power. In this way a solution was always found.

Again, behind all this, we encounter the traditional, tolerant and patient Burmese reaction, as it emerges from centuries of Buddhist influence. "The Burmese", writes Welty,[38] "claim that the teachings of Buddha on the relationship that should exist between husband and wife, parent and child, teacher and student, employer and employee, friend and friend has been a major factor in the preservation of harmonious relationships among the Burmese. Buddhists can be violent, like all men, but Buddhism has mitigated men's aggressiveness". Reading these lines, one is not only admiring the Burmese for achieving harmony, but is also tempted to substitute the word "Confucius" for the word "Buddha", insofar the above parallel relationships are concerned, to demonstrate once again the convergence between these two great religious streams of Asia.

The first encounter of Buddhism in Burma was devotion to the primeval "Nats" which had left their animistic imprint through generations and centuries.[39] The first characteristic of this encounter is "conciliation".[40]

Nats, protectors of villages, spirits of woods and rivers, are always on Buddha's side! It is to be noted that even the Gautama was born as a Nat in one of His endless re-births.[41] In Schwezigon Pagoda, numerous Nat statuettes bend piously their heads towards Buddha, because, as was stated by King Anawrata, people will not adhere to the new faith. Let them worship their old Gods and in this manner they will progressively follow the Dharma.[42] What wisdom, what moderation, what gentleness, behind these words. Free from fanaticism, Gautama's teaching, respecting pre-existing beliefs, proceeds contrarily to proselytism, aiming at voluntary adherence. We witness here traces of "a surprising religious syncretism".[43]

Every young Burmese is taught the interrelations between Nats and Buddha, how to worship the former's altars and the latter's temples. On the dying's deathbed, a Buddhist monk prays so that malevolent spirits do not hinder the soul's departure to the Beyond.[44]

An interesting study on Buddhism and Nats is the "Observations" of E. Michael Mendelson[45] based on a trip to Central Burma in 1859. Here we witness not only the assimilation process between early tradition and Theravāda, but also a broader analysis of the inter-relations between religious and secular power in old Burma. It is also shown that each time Buddhism grew stronger, belief in Nats became weaker and especially so when Buddhism was supported by a strong central authority. On the opposite, Nats became stronger in times of rebellions, so frequent in Burmese history. Mendelson observes that there are numerous theological and monastic schools with free pursuit of ultimate Truth, so that the monk is finally responsible to himself alone.

One can also note an encounter between Nats and Brahmanism.[46] Burmese Kings, although protectors of Buddhism, also adopted the brahmanical dogma of absolute monarchy. This created some social disturbance, since the popular masses were more inclined to Buddhism. Finally, as monarchy's power receded, Buddhist faith spread, although without big upheavals.

In addition there was a coexistence of various Buddhist sects, always under Theravādin predominance. Mahāyāna teachings and even Lamaist tantrism came with Burmese tribes which penetrated through the sinotibetan plateaus.[47] But King Dhammaceti tried to bring all these currents to the mainstream of Theravāda.

The only known case of anti-Buddhist persecution in Burma was between 1525-1530, when believers were slaughtered and temples burnt on the order of a cruel King, Thohanbwa.[48] But this persecution led to the dynasty's overthrow, few years later. So great was the abhorrence of peaceful Burmese to what had occurred.[49]

It would be presumptous to try after this "bird's eye view" of the immense 'Buddhist' landscape in Asia to deduce some conclusions. This would not be anything new in the world of Buddhist scholars. Buddhism is indeed a magnificent religion of tolerance, yielding to syncretism whenever it can. But it is also a fact that the overall religious climate of Asia is such that assimilation and encounter are very often encouraged. A soil fertile in conciliation. Human nature being basically the same, this does not mean that friction was unknown in Asia. Religious dissension *did* exist in all times. What is nevertheless noteworthy is that, as in the case of the 18th century India observed through the eyes of Abbé J. Dubois,[50] these dissensions "do not set the whole country ablaze or occasion those crimes of all kinds which were for centuries the result of religious fanaticism in Europe...".

At the end of this paper it would perhaps be more appropriate to remind some of the basic ideas of Prof. Nakamura[51] while examining the spirit of tolerance and conciliation: "Buddhism is not a special religion which conflicts with other religions but is in itself the Absolute Truth. Heretics are nothing but an off-shoot manifestation of the ultimate truth".

"...Buddhism, in spreading over the Asian countries caused less friction among the indigenous faiths of the people who received it. Native or traditional faiths and customs were scarcely destroyed by Buddhists and could easily survive; so long as they were seen as ethical from the Buddhist point of view, they were able to remain in existence side by side with the newly arrived Buddhism and sometimes were absorbed in Buddhism".

Finally, let us go back to Japan, to the pages of one of the greatest interpreters of Japanese Shinto to the West, Jean Herbert,[52] who relates the harmonious fusion of Kamis and Boddhisatvas, the cruel separation attempted in the years of Meiji Reform and the triumphant return to harmony to the point that one is not always sure, visiting sacred places, whether one prays before Shinto or Buddhist divinities...How many times I was myself confronted with this wonderful hesitation, in my pilgrimages through Japan, one of the many countries of the East permeated by a spirit of tolerance, where Buddhism, upon entering it, in the year 552, was seen in the very words of Nihongi as "the best among all doctrines".[53]

References

1. S. Radhakrishnan: *Eastern Religions and Western Thought,* New Delhi, 1983.
2. Swami Vivekanand: 'La Religion Universelle', in *Vision de l'Inde,* New Delhi, 1982, p. 35.
3. Gandhi: Kanyakumari, in *Vision de l'Inde* New Delhi, p. 61.
4. Quoted in Radhakrishnan, *op. cit.*, p. 315.
5. G. Iconomacos: *Le Fanatisme,* Athens 1961.
6. Bernard Frank: 'Le mystere Japonais', in *Le Monde,* 21.6.81.
7. M.I. Sladkovsky: *China and Japan,* 1975, p. 14.
8. Sir Charles Eliot: *Japanese Buddhism,* London 1969, p. 207.
9. René Sieffert: *Les Religious du Japon,* Paris 1968, p. 70.

10. G. Renondau: *Le Shugendo,* Paris, p. 141.
11. Eliot, *op. cit.*, p. 243.
12. Radhakrishnan, *op. cit.,* p. 309, Hajime Nakamura: *Ways of Thinking of Eastern Peoples,* Honolulu 1964, p. 287-291. Jean Herbert: *Introduction a l'Asia,* Paris 1960, p. 129 etc.
13. Nakamura, *op. cit.*, pp. 288-290.
14. G. Tucci: *Religioni Asiatiche,* p. 61.
15. J.M. Kitagawa: *Religions Orientales,* p. 61.
16. James Feibleman: *Understanding Oriental Philosophy,* New York 1977, p. 133.
17. Nakamura, *op. cit.,* p. 287.
18. Nakamura, *op. cit.*, p. 291.
19. Bernard Martin–Shui Chien-Tung: *Makers of China, Confucius to Mao,* Oxford 1971, p. 69.
20. G.N.S. Raghavan: *Introducing India,* New India 1983, p. 25.
21. Mahatama Gandhi, 100 years, New Delhi 1968, p. 3.
22. Raghavan, *op. cit.*, p. 31.
23. R.A. Stein: *Tibetan Civilization,* London 1972, p. 283.
24. Li Ogg: *Historie de la Coree,* Paris 1969, p. 62.
25. John Pow-Key, Kim Chol-choon, Hong Yi-Sup: *The History of Korea,* Seoul 1970, p. 59.
26. Li Ogg: *op. cit.,* p. 63.
27. Eliot: *Hinduism and Buddhism,* Vol. III, p. 337.
28. Cornelius Osgood: *The Koreans,* Tokyo 1969, p. 247.
29. John Pow-Key, *op. cit.*, p. 69.
30. Li Ogg: *op. cit.*, p. 81-82.
31. *Korea: Its Peoples & Culture, Thought & Religion,* p. 137.
32. Herbert: *op. cit.,* p. 133.
33. Osgood adds also Shamanism, *op. cit.*, p. 252.
34. Homer Hulbert: *The Passing of Korea,* Seoul 1969, p. 403.
35. Isabella Bird Bishop: *Korea and Her Neighbours,* Seoul 1970, p. 401.
36. Philippe Aziz: *Angkor et les Civilizations Birmane et Thaie,* Paris, 1976, p. 240.
37. J.M. Kitagawa: *op. cit.,* ref. to Margaret Mead, p. 185.
38. P.T. Welty: *The Asians,* Tokyo 1972, p. 294.
39. Le Buddhisme, Compil, R. de Berval, p. 234.
40. Herbert: *op. cit.*, p. 126.
41. Ulrich Zagorski: "Burma", p. 134.
42. Aziz, *op. cit.*, p. 219.
43. E. Guillonc Delachet: "Birmanie", Paris 1975, p. 51.
44. Kitagawa, *op. cit.*, p. 24.

45. E. Michael Mendelson: *Observations on A Tour in the Region of Mount Popa, Central Burma-France-Asie. N'* 173, p. 780.
46. Kitagawa: *op. cit.,* p. 172.
47. Aziz, *op. cit.*, p. 208—Eliot: *op. cit.*, III, p. 51.
48. Kitagawa, *op. cit.*, p. 171.
49. Eliot, *op. cit.*, III, p. 61.
50. Abbé J. Dubois: *Hindu Manners, Customs and Ceremonies,* Oxford 1928, p. 120.
51. Hajime Nakamura: *op. cit.*, p. 169.
52. Jean Herbert: *Aux Sources du Japon,* Paris, 1964, pp. 77ff.
53. Nihongi: Aston, Tokyo 1972, Vol. II, p. 64.

Chapter 17

Philosophy and Practices of Charity in Thai Buddhism

Ven. Phra Samran Nandapañño

Introduction

Thai people adhere to the Theravāda form of Buddhism in which social charity or charity has played a prominent role in the regulation of Thai life. Thai society recognizes charity as a merit making and complete monastic life is based on it. The laity does not only give charity to the monks but also monks contribute to the laity in the shape of preaching Dhamma. The kingdom of Thailand, formally known as Siam, took its present name in 1939 under the leadership of Marshal Phibul Songkham.[1] Thailand lies in South East Asia. It is bordered to the west and north by Myanmar (Burma), to the north east by Laos and the south east by Cambodia. Thailand extends southwards, along the Isthmus of Kra, to the Malay Peninsula, where it borders Malaysia. The isthmus, shared with Myanmar, gives Thailand a short coastline on the Indian ocean, and the country also has along pacific coastline on the Gulf of Thailand.[2] The predominant religion is Buddhism, mainly of the Hīnayāna (Theravāda) professed by more than 95 %.[3]

Definition of Charity (*Dāna*)

Buddhism defines *charity* as "a gift to which the recipient has no claim and for which he renders no return; it is made purely from pity and desire to remove human need"[4]

Dāna occurs in Dhammapada in several passages.[5] The five right ways of giving are:

(i) to give in faith,
(ii) to give carefully,
(iii) to give quickly,
(iv) to give firmly and
(v) to give so as not to injure oneself or other.

Another five set of giving are: to give carefully, to give thoughtfully, to give with one's own hand, to give discardedly and to give with the hope that the donee will come back. The theory is that the merit of a gift grows in proportion with the merit of the donee.

On the other hand Hindu *dharmaśāstra* defines charity as, "something is given according to *Śāstric* rites so as to reach a receiver who is a fit recipient". When one gives alms if no *mantra* is chanted, and then it will not be considered as charity by Hindu Śāstra. The things which are given according to śāstric rites is called Dharmacharity and this is the best kind of charity.

The essence of true charity is to give something without expecting anything in return for the gift. If a person expects some material benefit to arise from his gift, he is only performing an act of bartering and not charity.[6]

The self-reflective motivation in almsgiving remains an issue in the discussion of alms or charity; is the benefit, in moral sense, to redound principally upon the giver, or does almsgiving provide a moral incentive, somehow, to the recipient? In Buddhism the merit to the giver was stated in such a manner as to be clearly to provide the principal motivation. This concept was apparent in the viability of the second group to benefit from alms. The wandering male or female ascetics, who had taken vows to renounce the world, could no longer participate in the customary social life.

In Buddhism the monastic order or the Sangha becomes the focus of distribution of charity. The laity has provided the resources, over the millennia of Buddhist history, for monks and nuns (*Mae chii*) to live without works in order to seeks *nirvāṇa* within a highly structured cenobitic community. Through redounding the good Karma upon the donors, such laity would be given subsequent, improved opportunities (perhaps in another life) to seek *nirvāṇa*.

The laity could also gain merit by succoring the indigent and suffering in humanity at large, and by showing pity towards the need of animals.

Thai Buddhism

After two centuries, when the Indian Emperor Aśoka came on the scene Buddhism had already caught the imagination of the people in that part of the century. After his own conversion, he supplied his mind to the organization and propagation of Buddhism on a scale unknown to the world of those days. This process went on for centuries and in addition to monasteries, big educational institutions for training monks came to existence.

The king Aśoka, sent missionaries to foreign countries, for preaching the Dhamma, to Suvannabhumi Burma, under Arhats Sona and Uthara. The neighboring country of Thailand (Siam), Cambodia and Laos, also have a similar tradition.[7]

Buddhism is the state religion of Thailand. It has unique and distinguishable feature. Its purest practitioners may define Thai Buddhism as a rationalist and indeed thoroughly agnostic philosophy. It operated on more than one level. On the popular level, it is by any definition a great religion with a vast canonical liturgy, powerful independent priests and huge body of devoted followers who find in the observance of temple rites and other manifestations of their faith a strong emotional satisfaction. Thais very generally feel that their lives are ordered rather by planetary deities than by the planets as cosmic principles.

Thai Buddhism is entirely based on the concept of the doctrine of *karma and rebirth*. The actions of living being are regarded as having a special or causal effect which determine his future spiritual conditions, both in this life and in succeeding ones. These effects are known as the "fruits" of action. Good deed lead to the progress towards liberation (*nirvāṇa*); bad ones to regress from this goal. Usually present status, disease, prosperity and so forth are thought to be consequences of action in previous lives. Thus, karma is an ethically oriented condition of its effectiveness. By removing craving through the purification of one's motives one can find release from rebirth.

In Mahāyāna Buddhism, the theory of the transfer of merit involves the benefit that the otherwise unworthy individual can be given merit by Bodhisattva (Buddha-to-be) out of latter's infinite store, acquired through many lives of heroic self-sacrifice on behalf of living being; thereby the individual qualifies for rebirth in paradise (where the conditions for attaining *nirvāṇa* are peculiarly favorable). Thus the operation by *karma* is short-circuited by grace and faith. The *karma* is regarded as an invisible force so that the need to postulate and observable mechanism can be evaded.

For Thais, Buddhism is a way of life and a means of finding inner peace. In former days, young Thai boys served in the monasteries where they were given instruction in reading, writing and simple arithmetic as well as in the religion and morals. Through traditional ordination that is still observed today, they are bound to order by ties of experience on close relationships with the monks. At least they live in the Buddhist environment in which they are linked with the religion by ties of custom, by attending religious ceremonies and temple festivals, or by benefiting either directly or indirectly from some activities and spiritual influences of religious institutions. Some of them later get disrobed and serve the nation in different official levels.

Buddhism is the national heritage, the glory of the country which we feel bound to preserve. Even those who are Buddhist merely by name benefit from, and are influenced by, Buddhism in some or other ways. The cycle of life turns around activity: directly or indirectly connected with Buddhism. We go regularly to the monasteries to hear sermons and observe additional precepts. There are also Buddhist discussions or sermons on radio, which one can listen to. Some of the monasteries hold special programmes on Saturday and Sunday, the official holidays of the week, so that working people may be able to benefit. Many boys and girls go to attend classes at Buddhist Sunday School which are conducted in monasteries both in Bangkok and in the provinces of Thailand. The first of the Buddhist Sunday School was founded at *Mahachula Buddhist University* in 1958. Now it is held all over Thailand in two decades, its number has increased to 297.[8]

Buddhism in Thailand has been characterized by some people as an ascetic religion for dealing with some basic morals, observance of rituals and participation in religious ceremonies and worship. However Phra Rajavaramuni has contradicted this view. Asceticism is a kind of belief and practice that existed before the time of the Buddha which was rejected by him after attaining the Enlightenment.[9] Thai intellectuals consider it a unique system of psychology and philosophy and one of the most scientific religions of the world. Meditation is the general interest of the people and part of Thai Buddhism. Many of famous meditation centers are existing in different parts of Thailand. Beside monks and layman both men and women are engaged in practice of meditation to gain mindfulness, to live in peace and to achieve spiritual power or *nirvāṇa*.

The Buddhist society of Thailand consists of monks, nuns (*Mae Chii*), lay male and female devotees. Monks and lay people live different ways of daily life and have different responsibilities and duties, and enjoy some different kind of happiness. But both are interdependent. According to the *Vinaya* or the discipline, the monks' life is dependent on the lay people for food and other necessities.

Basically the monks get their daily meals on the alms round, but they can go on invitation to the house of the donors or latter may come to the monastery as well. This makes the monk's life bound to lay society and keeps them in daily contact with the people. The monks are exhorted to contemplate again and again on this fact, as the Buddha himself says, "....that my livelihood is bound up with other". So monks will be earnest both in their exertion for own individual perfection and doing for the good of the laity. This latter task of reciprocal nature can be performed by the monks right away on their daily alms round or on subsequent occasion.

The Thai monarchs were patrons of Buddhism. They had been well associated with the religious activities for acquiring religious merit and well acquainted with the rules of the Sangha. Thai kings enter into the monastic life even for a short period for one week or a month. So, Thai Buddhist tradition promulgates virtues and qualities for the king that he observes and possesses. The most important is the Ten Royal Virtues of the kings (Dasarājadhamma) are; *Dāna*—charity, *Śila*—high moral character, *Pariccāga*—self-sacrifice, *Ajjava*—integrity, *Maddava*—gentleness, *Tapa*—austerity, *Akkota*—non-fury, *Ahimsā*—non-violence, *Śānti*—tolerance and *Avirothana*—non deviation from the norm. These virtues are the best-known royal virtues.

Thai Concept of Charity and Practices

Buddhist considers charity as one of the principal themes of religious life. Charity has great importance in Thai social life, believing charity as the best way of leading religious life.

Sangitipariyaya gives an account of eight ways of not giving charity. They are;

(i) Disrespectfully,

(ii) From fear,

(iii) From gratitude,

(iv) In hope of getting something in return in the future,

(v) To follow up the family tradition,

(vi) For fame,

(vii) To be reborn in the heaven,

(viii) To adorn and prepare one's mind for highest good.

The term 'charity' refers not to the material gift but it considers also the mental state of the donors. The merit of a charity increases with its enjoyment i.e., the merit occuring from a gift increases with its use. A person can continue to gain merit for an act of which one is no longer conscious, or for an act performed with unwholesome thought. It has been considered so important that even its fruit can be enjoyed in the future rebirth. If a person could not fully enjoy its result or fruit, he would receive it in the next birth. Charity is considered as one of the lucky things (all ethical).[10] As Buddhology began its course, charity was made one of the parameters, that is, of qualities in which a Buddha must, in previous birth, have perfected himself. We have the well-known stories of the extremes of almsgiving, such as that *King Sivi* who gave away his eyes and *Vassantara* who gave away not only his kingdom, but all the possessions, and even his wife and children. These legends, both of which have a happy ending, are most popular among the Buddhist peasantry. The ethics of the Vassantara story, which is much open to doubt, is discarded in the Millinda. Intoxicating drinks, weapons, poisons, etc. must never be given as gifts. But the best gift of all is the gift of Dhamma.[11] (*sabba dānam dhamma dānam jināti*).

Thai philosophy considers preaching of Dhamma by monks to laity as charity. In Thai philosophy charity means something is to give away. The Dhamma is nothing, but it is truth for liberation that leads to freedom from rebirth. It is the basic of the Buddha.[12] Devout Thais give food offering regularly in the morning, send money contributions on their neighbourhood monasteries, or contribute to some meritorious causes such a building an *Uposatha* hall, or chapel elsewhere. Thai calendars usually show a special day of every week which is known as *Wan Phra*, or the Buddhist holy day, when the pious are often especially active in their merit making. They may take food offering to the monasteries or go to hear sermons and observe meditation.

In Thai social life, merit making (tamboon) has a very important place. Every people acquire it by visiting temples and offerings alms in various ways. The great goal of the Buddhist is to attain Nirvāṇa, much chance to succeed in the foreseeable future. In general manner of willingness for almsgiving, the following considerations are to be kept in mind:

(i) by this merit of almsgiving, may I attain the state of non cankers,

(ii) by this merit of almsgiving, may I attain the extinction of suffering,

(iii) by this merit of almsgiving, may I attain the Paths and Fruit,

(iv) by this merit of almsgiving, may I enter into the state of bliss or

(v) may I transfer this merit of wholesome to all beings.

The more immediate and practical concern of most ordinary Buddhist is to improve themselves and thus get closer to that ultimate state of bliss while going through credits in the heavenly ladder; it improves one's chance in the next life. Thai Buddhists believe that the practice of merit making instills in the individual sense of sacrifice, which directs him towards an act of *generosity* and *loving-kindness*. A person can gain merit by freeing captured birds and fishes, by being charitable to the poor etc. Every king of Thailand sponsors the erection and renovation of *Wats* as a potent, high-level method of making merit.

For a Thai layman, to serve for a period as a Buddhist monk is both a devotional act and an important way to make merit. The period of service might vary from one week to several years. Some men, after joining, remain in the monkhood for life. Others get disrobed and start running their career as professors, teachers, politicians etc. The most common practice is for a man upon reaching the age of 20 to become a monk for three months during Buddhist lent, which coincides with the rainy season.

Conclusion

The concept of charity in Thai Buddhism is entirely based on the theory of karma and rebirth. Thais consider the ultimate goal of life as nothing but *nirvāṇa* which can be achieved through performing good deeds. For Thais, charity is the best way of acquiring merit or *puṇya*. It is performed not only on special occasion but also is a regular feature of Thai life.

The essence of true charity is to give something without expecting something in return for the gift. If a person expects some material benefit to arise from his gift, he is only performing an act of bartering and not charity. The self-reflective motivation in almsgiving remains an issue in the discussion of alms or charity, the benefit of which in the moral sense, is to redound principally upon the giver.

Thai Buddhism emphasizes particularly on merit making. Here charity plays a prominent role. Charity gets reflected in the deeds of Thai laity. It is felt that the merit of charity increases with its enjoyment i.e., the merit accruing from a gift increases with its use.

References

1. The Europa world year book, Europa publication limited, 1999, pp. 34-35.
2. *Ibid.*
3. Political handbook of the world, CSA publication, New York, 1995-96, p. 933.
4. Encyclopedia of Religion, 187 (Vol. I) Almsgiving, p. 214.
5. Daw Mya Tin (tr.), *The Dhammapada* (*Verse and Stories*), Burma: Pitaka Association, Rangoon, pp. 356-359.
6. K. Sri Dhammananda, *What Buddhists Believe*, The corporate Body of the Buddha Education Foundation, Taiwan, 1993, p. 168.
7. K. Sri Dhammanada, *Ibid*, *op.cit.*, p. 160.
8. Phra Rajavaramuni, *Social Dimension of Buddhism in Contemporary Thailand*, Thai Khadi Research Institute, Thammasat University, 1983, p. 35.

9. Phra Rajavaramuni, *Buddhism in Buddhist World*, Mahachulalongkorn Buddhist University, Bangkok, 1990, p. 33.
10. Sutta Nipata, 263.
11. Dhammapada, 554.
12. Sulak Sivaraksa, *Siam in Crisis: A Collection of Article*, Santi Pracha Dhamma Institute, Bangkok, 1990, p. 28.

Bibliography

Aiyappan, A. and Srinivasan P.R., *Story of Buddhism with Special Reference to South India*, The Department of Information and Publicity: Government of Madras, 1960.

Bapat, P.V., *2500 Years of Buddhism*, New Delhi: Patiala House, 1997.

Diwakar, K.R., *Bhagawan Buddha*, Bombay: Chaupatty Press, 1967.

Joshi Lalmani, *Studies in the Buddhistic Culture of India*, Delhi: Motilal Banarsidass, 1967.

Mahachulalongkornrajavidyalaya, *Thai Tipitaka* (Vol. 9), Bangkok: University Press, 1996.

Murty, K. Satchidanand, *Reading in Indian History, Politics, and Philosophy*, London: George Allen & Unwin Ltd., 1967.

Na-Rangsri, Sunthorn, *The Buddhist Concept of Karma & Rebirth*, Bangkok: Mahamakut Press, 1986.

Poonyanubhap, Sujeep, *Thai Tipitaka for people*, Bangkok: Mahamakut Press,1990.

Rajavaramuni, Phra, *Thai Buddhism in Buddhist World*, Bangkok: Mahachulalongkorn Buddhist University Press, 1990.

Phra Rajavaramuni, *Social dimension of Buddhism in contemporary Thailand*, Thai Khadi Research Institute, Bangkok : Thammasat University, 1983.

Roy, M.N., *Science and Philosophy*, India: Ajanta Publication, 1984.

Sarao, K.T.S. (ed.), *A Text Book of the History of Theravada Buddhism*, Delhi: Jayyed Press, 1995.

Thiroux, Jacques P., *Philosophy: Theory and Practice*, New York: Macmillan Publishing Company, 1985.

Upadhyaya. K.N., *Early Buddhism and the Bhagavat Gita,* Delhi: Motilal, 1967.

Chapter 18

Buddhist Art in Thailand

M.C. Subhadradis Diskul

Buddhism probably came into Thailand *via* the two sects, Theravāda (Hīnayāna) and Mahāyāna, at the same time but the former has always been more popular than the latter. From archaeological evidence, the Indian Buddha images discovered in Thailand are of the late Amarāvati style (4th-5th centuries A.D.), Gupta (4th-6th centuries), post-Gupta (6th-8th centuries) and Pāla (8th-12th centuries). They were found in various places, scattered all over the country.

The first historical period of Thailand dates from the 7th to the 11th centuries, that of Dvāravatī, the majority of the population of which were probably of Mon race as a few stone inscription in ancient Mon language dating back to that period have been unearthed. The kingdom of Dvāravatī was presumably situated in the present-day central Thailand and its artistic influence spread far and wide, to northern, north-eastern, eastern and southern parts of the country. Buddha images of this period are mostly carved from limestone. They can be divided into three groups: the first group about the 7th century A.D. showing strong Indian Gupta and post-Gupta influences, with lingering Amarāvatī style; the second from the 8th to the 10th centuries displaying more autochthonous elements such as the symmetry of the body and the monastic dress as well as certain facial characteristics; the third group representing Khmer influences denoting a square face, a cleft on the chin and dates back to the 11th century.

Dvāravatī artists also used terracotta and stucco to decorate architecture. Bronze images are quite few compared to stone ones. As for architecture brick was used for religious structures such as *stūpa, vihāra* and a few *uposatha* (ordination hall). Stūpas are of different forms such as a round one with a square or octagonal base, a solid five square tierred *stūpa* with three niches on each face containing 60 standing terracotta or stucco Buddha images.

The second Buddhist period from the 8th to the 13th centuries A.D. belongs to what is called the Śrīvijaya style developing in southern Thailand. The people of that part professed Mahāyāna Buddhism so the images of Avalokiteśvara Bodhisattva were quite popular. During the early period of this style, the art was heterogeneous. Some specimens would show the southern Indian, the Gupta, post-Gupta and Pāla influences, whereas the others, especially bronzes, would show the Central Javanese style. At the end of the 12th century images of this period especially at Chaiya in the province of Suratthani turned to be homogeneous. Structures resemble those of central Java but some would show the mixture of Khmer, Cham, Indonesian and Dvāravatī influences. Southern Thailand during this period was a place where traders from many countries stopped during their voyage. Buddhist votive tablets were made of clay instead of terracotta or metal like during the Dvāravatī period. The capital of the Śrīvijaya empire is still in dispute whether it was on the island of Sumatra or at Chaiya in southern Thailand.

The third Buddhist period is named Lopburi displaying Khmer influences. During this period both Theravāda and Mahāyāna Buddhism flourished. Stone and bronze Buddha images abound as well as images of Bodhisattva and bronze utensils used for the rites of Mahāyāna Buddhism. Buddha images can be dated after the Khmer styles in Cambodia: those of Baphuon (11th century); Angkor Vat (first half of the 12th century); Bayon (late 12th and early 13th centuries) and typical Lopburi (13th-14th centuries). For architecture there are quite a few built in Mahāyāna Buddhism. The most famous are those of Pimai (early 12th century) at Nakhon Ratchasima (Khorat) and Pra Prang Sam Yod (the Three Towers, early 13th century) at the town of Lopburi.

The Thai people had probably originally lived in south-eastern China. They might have gradually migrated into the present-day Thailand since a long time but they first declared their independence about the middle of the 13th century. Before that period, however, there might be already some small Thai principalities in the extreme northern part of the present-day Thailand. Bronze Buddha images have been found showing some affinities with those of the Pāla school of north-eastern and eastern India. This group of Buddha effigies is classified as early Chiengsaen or Lanna Thai (northern Thailand). Their chronology is not certain. It might vary from the 11th to the 13th century A.D. No architecture dating back with certainty to this period has so far been found. For the second period or late Cheingsaen style there is no chronological problem as both the sculpture and architecture display the influence of Sukhothai art which developed in northern Thailand from about the middle of the 13th century. This late Chiengsaen style is usually attributed to the date from the 15th century onwards. There is, however, one sanctuary outside the town of Chiengmai on the north which still constitutes a problem, Wat Chet Yot. It is built in laterite and follows in style the Mahāvihāra at Bodh Gaya in India. The structure might have been built before the middle of the 15th century whereas the stucco decoration was probably added during that period.

Now we have come down to the best period of Thai art, the Sukhothai style (middle 13th-14th centuries). During this period Theravāda Buddhism of the Singhalese sect became very popular. Though the Sukhothai art flourished only about 150 years, its influence continued over all the successive styles. Buddha images are mostly in bronze and they usually represent the Master in four postures: seated, reclining, standing and walking. The bronze walking Buddha in the round can be regarded as the innovation of Sukhothai artists as before this period the image had existed only in high or bas-relief. The late Sukhothai Buddha statue is rather plump with a round face and four equal fingers. There exists also a mixed group of Buddha effigies displaying characteristics of early Chiengsaen style or from Sri Lanka. During this period glazed ceramics were produced as a chief export and potters fabricated not only domestic utensils but also religious architectural decorations. The lotus-bud *stūpa* can be again reckoned as a Sukhothai innovation. The other types of *stūpa* derived from Sri Lankan, Khmer or northern Thai prototypes. Bronze Buddha images of Sukhothai style probably received also the influence of southern India from Nāgapaṭṭinam.

The other two later styles might be described together: those of U-tong and Ayudhyā. The first one prospered in central Thailand and displays the mixed characteristics of Dvāravatī, Lopburi and Sukhothai arts. The U-tong Buddha images can be divided into 3 groups after their characteristics and their date might extend from the 12th to 15th centuries. Ayudhyā was the capital of Thailand or Siam for about 400 years from the middle of the 14th century. Therefore its art has to be divided into 4 sub-periods. The first one (100 years) continued the U-tong second and third groups. The second sub-period (200 years) shows the Sukhothai influence whereas the third (50 years) displays the Khmer characteristics which might be caused by the subjugation of Cambodia by the Ayudhyan king in the early 17th century. The fourth sub-period (50 years) is typically Thai showing mostly crowned Buddha images. *Stūpa* followed more or less the same trend as Buddha images but the new type, a twelve-sided pagoda, emerged during the third sub-period. Quite a number of Buddhist minor art specimens have remained from the late Ayudhyā period such as small *stūpa* containing the relics of the Buddha, painting in gold on black lacquer book cabinets and mother-of-pearl inlaid door-panels as well as wooden sculptures. Buddhist volive tablets of different types have also been discovered. Mural paintings and illustrated manuscripts representing the life story of the Buddha and various *jātaka* tales have also come to light.

The Bangkok or Ratanakosin period from 1782 A.D. is characterised as eclectic. During the first three reigns there was an attempt to make Bangkok resemble Ayudhyā as much as possible. In the reign of King Rama III (1824-1851) trade with China developed to a great extent and there was also strong Chinese influence in art. In the reign of King Mongkut or Rama IV (1851-1868) western influence began to creep in. Erowned Buddha images were popular in the first three reigns. King Mongkut tried to invent a new style but this was popular only during his reign. From the reign of his son, King Chulalongkorn or Rama V (1868-1910), Buddha images have become more humanized but those imitating former styles like early Chiengsaen or Sukhothai have continued to be popular with the public. Wat or Buddhist monasteries were built in different styles, sometimes mixed together. The famous Marble Temple built by command of King Chulalongkorn is in Thai style with Khmer influence but the material used is white marble from the town of Carrara in Italy. During the Bangkok period Buddhist minor arts also continue to be produced but the workmanship usually declined after the first three reigns. Mural paintings began to show the western influence such as perspective and three dimensions during the fourth reign.

Chapter 19

Buddhism and Chinese Culture

Ren Jiyu

Buddhism that was originated in the Indian subcontinent spread into China along the Silk Route and soon it came to be integrated with the traditional culture and became part of the Chinese tradition. There is not yet unanimous conclusion as to the exact date of the introduction of Buddhism into China. In my opinion, it was first introduced into China in 2 B.C. (the first year of Emperor Ai of the West Han Dynasty). Chinese version of Buddhist Scripture appeared after 70 B.C. and attracted the attention of the upper classes of the society. But the earliest Buddhists are composed of a small number of foreign merchants from the West Region, temples were built in the big cities in the hinterland. They were built merely for the worship of foreign merchants. The Chinese were forbidden to be Buddhist by law.[1]

From the first to the third century (Han to Wei Dynasty), the propagation of Buddhism was confined to the royal families and aristocrats of upper society. There was hardly any detectable influence among the masses. Buddhism became popular in China between the third to the eighth century. At that time, the Indian Buddhist scriptures of various sects were being translated into both Han and Tibetan languages. Up to date, the Han and Tibetan versions of Buddhist scriptures have excelled the whole world in volume as well as in variety. It is not exaggerative to say that China preserves the richest historical sources of the Buddhist culture.

According to the content, the Buddhist culture introduced into China can be classified into the following four categories:

First, books on the elementary knowledge of Buddhism, somewhat like the handbooks of general Buddhist knowledge.

Second, books about the system and norm of monastic life of Buddhist monks.

Third, the biographies and stories of prominent Buddhist leading figures, such as Śākyamuni and his followers.

Fourth, books on the religious theory and practice of Buddhism.

The two former kinds of Buddhist scriptures were current within the Buddhist sangha, while the influences of latter two were far beyond the enclosure of the monastries, they were influenced by the social trends and cultural tradition of their time and vice versa.

The history of Chinese Buddhism manifests the fact that there are some laws in the spread and interexchange of different cultures. There are external and internal conditions for a foreign culture to take root and grow on the land of a new nation. It was in Han Dynasty that Buddhism first spread into hinterland of China. At that time the Chinese society was facing serious crisis. People were desperate and were suffering from poverty and misery because of the stupidity of the emperor and the corruption of the government. Such external conditions were favourable for the spread of religions. In the meantime, China founded her own religion–Taoism. Buddhism was accepted by the people almost with Taoism, and both had great impact on the society. People took advantage of Taoism which was an indigenous religion of China to start an extensive armed uprising–the well-known Huangchin (Yellow Turban) Uprising (A.D. 184-204). Though the uprising was a failure, nevertheless, it shook the rule of the Han Dynasty to its very foundations. As the central government lost its supremacy, the Empire was torn into various principalities for a long time. In the beginning, Buddhism was developing side by side with Taoism. The armed struggle of Taoism greatly alarmed the rulers and they refrained from giving support to it. Hence, Buddhism gained the upper hand and its influence soon surpassed that of Taoism. Since then, Buddhist supremacy has continued for two thousand years. Another reason for the development of Buddhism at high speed was its integration with Chinese tradition by means of which it made itself more acceptable to the Chinese people. When Buddhism was first introduced into China's hinterland, the Chinese royal families and aristocrats who were followers of Huang-Lao's teaching (Huang-ti, the Yellow Emperor, and Lao Tzū's teaching), worshipped Buddha together with Lao Tzū. The emperor built in his palace "a temple for Huang Lao and Buddha" (in A.D. 166). Many ministers were strongly against the Emperor's building the temple. Their reason was Huang-Lao and Buddha were all for non-action (Wu-wei), fond of life, loath of killing, refrain from the lust and the luxuries, while the emperors of Han Dynasty indulged in pleasures and they killed and punished ruthlessly, they thought the emperors were not to be blessed by Huangti, Lao Tzu and Buddha.[2] From the above argument, it can be seen that the Chinese Buddhist adherents regarded Buddha as a god just like Huangti or Lao Tzu and worshipped them together. According to Chinese historical records, Buddha had the ability to teach people how to be immortal and if one succeeded, his body could fly to heaven.[3] It was known that the founder of Buddhism from the very beginning preached *catursatya* (the Four Nobel Truths) and *dvādaśānga pratītyasamutpāda* (The Twelve-linked Chain of Dependent origination) and held that "all things are impermanent and all will be perished." He opposed such legends of spirits as the immortality of souls and the flight of human body to heaven. Chinese Buddhist adherents including certain scholars in Han Dynasty used to look upon Buddhism as a sect of genīī and magic. They said that Buddha was as tall as One Zhang and Six Chi (Chinese measure of length), golden in colour, with a necklace of the light of sun and moon. He was omnipresent and constantly changing without a shape. He could make his body large or small, plunge into the fire without being burnt, walk on the edges of the sword without being harmed. In the mind of the Chinese, Buddha was just like a spirit. Among the intellectual circles, the doctrine of Buddhism was looked upon about the same as the philosophy of Huang-Lao.

The earliest translation of Buddhist scripture in Han language is the *The Sūtra of Fourty-two Sections* which is not able to be checked with the original. Strictly speaking, it is a rewriting rather than a translation. It is quite correct to say that this work is really an expression of the thought in *Yi-ching* (*The Book of Changes*) *Lao Tzu* (*Tao Te Ching*) and *Chuang Tzu*. The Sūtra is not a forgery, though, it reflects Buddhism as understood in the light of *Yi-ching* and Huang-Lao's teaching. *The Sūtra of Fourty Two Sections* as introduced in the light of Huang Lao's teaching is sufficient to prove that it is not a forgery. The influence of the time leaves a trace of Taoist magic and Huang-Lao's teaching in this book, only the theory of retribution was introduced from India, but people in Han Dynasty didn't understand the implications of this theory. According to Buddhism, retribution is a consequence of one's karma, yet in Han Dynasty, the Chinese generally believed that "the offering of sacrifices will bring one happiness, otherwise, there will be calamities".[4] They believed that gods and ghosts could bring good or bad fortune to people. The

Chinese religious tradition also held that the good or evil doing of a person would affect the life of his descendant. Such concept was alien to the theory of karma and it was opposed by Buddhism.

The Buddhist preaching of hell didn't find its way to the Chinese mind in Han Dynasty, the Han people believed one's soul would go to the Tai-mountain after death. So in early Han version of Buddhist scripture, "hell" was translated as "Tai-mountain".

To cater to the interest of the Chinese feudal society, the Chinese translation of the Buddhist scriptures made some additions or deletions. For example, in the *Sūtra of Bhikṣu Nāgasena* (*Milinda–Pañha*), it reads: "These one who attains *nirvāṇa* becomes Non-eternal, otherwise, (These one who) has to go through endless transmigrations becomes Eternal", "One who is fond of giving alms and obedient to one's parents in this life will be rewarded in the next life". The last sentence which appears in the Han version, does not exist in the *Pāli* text. Whereas under the influences of Chinese feudal ethics and tradition of Chinese society, in the Han version of the Buddhist scripture, there are often alterations[5], or omissions[6], of the passages concerning sexual relations in consideration of the feudal ethics and traditions of the Chinese Society.

The philosophy that prevailed in the Wei (220-265) and Jin (Chin 265-424) Dynasties in China was the Hsuen Xue (Chinese metaphysics) which differed from the arts of genii and magical practices in Han Dynasty in the fact that it was more speculative. At the same time, the Buddhist doctrine of *Prajñāpāramitā* was also popular in China. The explanation of "Void" (*Śūnya*) in the system of *Prajñāpāramitā* gave rise to many schools, namely the "Six schools" and "Seven sects".[7] The important Buddhist scriptures which had been translated into Han language one after another before 369 amounted to 1621 consisting of 4180 fascicles. Buddhist monks and scholars at that time interpreted Buddhism in the light of Lao-Chung's doctrine, just as people in Han Dynasty interpreted Buddhism in the light of the art of genii. The doctrine of *Prajñāpāramitā*, which was called Mādhyamika in India, tried to prove the mundane life as an illusion (*māyā*) by means of speculation which denied the real world. It regarded the existence of the material being and spiritual being as illusory, and further it even regarded both beings as *māyā*. The doctrine of this sect had been translated into Han language, though, but was never really understood or accepted by the intellectual circles. Tao An (314-385), an eminent leader of the Buddhists at that time, held that the essential doctrine of *Prajñāpāramitā* was the same as the principle of Original Nothingness in the Hsueu Xue (Chinese metaphysics) of Wei and Jin dynasties, which read, "Nothingness existed before anything came into being, while, 'Void' was the origin of all form" (*The Biography of T'ān Chi,* quoted in *Extract from the Biographies of Eminent monks*). According to Tao An, the thought of Buddhism was equivalent to the thought of Lao Tzu. He held that the main point in Lao Tzu'a thought was nothingness, which was the primary origin of the world, the essential doctrine of *Prajñāpāramitā* was the same. Hui Yuan (374-416), a disciple of Tao An, was a Buddhist leader more influential than Tao An. He had discussions with Kumārajīva (344-413), but he could not understand the essentials of Indian Mādhyamika. As Chinese never had the concept of *Tathatā* (absolute nothingness) in Chinese, *Tathatā* and Original Nothingness are different in meaning. Since the *Tathatā* is understood as Original Nothingness, the counterpart of Tathatā would be understood as Mo-You (every existence). Therefore, the system of *Prajñāpāramitā* thought was naturally fitted into the ideology of Hsueu Xue' which consisted of the categories of Ben-Mo (The Fundamental and the incidental), You-Wu (existant and non-existant, being and non-being), Tsung-hen-su-mo (attaching importance to the fundamental and not neglecting the incidental).

As translation of Buddhist scriptures further developed, *Tathatā* was no longer translated as Ben-Wu and a set of Chinese Buddhist terms was built up, to which Kumarajīva contributed a lot. Some erroneous terms were corrected and translations came closer to the original. However, these praiseworthy can't take the place of correct understanding of Buddhist philosophy in our society. To have a good translation is one thing, but to grasp the idea of the translation is another. These two things are not always identical.

When a culture once spreads to a new region, it takes time for the local culture to absorb it and form a new culture out of it. The process and result of absorbing a foreign culture varied considerably with the different people of the nations, some people having a superior culture and longstanding tradition and some having an inferior culture. If the local culture is inferior to the foreign one, it is apt to be assimilated by the latter. If the local culture is superior and older, as in case of China or India, then the foreign culture will have difficulty in finding its way into the community and taking root there. Buddhism has been introduced into China for nearly two thousand years and the Chinese people have come to regard it as part of their own tradition and not as a foreign culture. Its influence has far exceeded the scope of religion, and it permeates into Chinese philosophy, art, literature, language, dance, music, architecture, medicine and even family and social life. The two cultures mutually absorb each other, permeate into each other; each enriches itself and yet each retains its own distinguished features. The fact proves that the brilliant achievments will result from interexchange of culture and co-existence in peace between the two great nations, China and India for over a long history.

The integration of Buddhism into Chinese tradition has gone through a long period and has achieved brilliant results. As researchers in this field, we have to find out the pattern of its ups and downs in the course of history. We differed from the scholars of past generations in that we are trying to explain the course of change of Buddhism by looking into the effect of social history on Buddhism, not merely within Buddhism itself. Philosophy and religion are reflected in certain degree in the social life and the economic life of the time, though the reflection is sometimes indirect and sometimes zigzag.

With the development of the Chinese society, the study of Buddhism had passed the stage of translation and brief introduction and entered the stage of creative writing. Since the seventh century i.e. Sui and Tang Dynasty, Buddhism had a great leap forward in China, and became an important link of cultural exchange between China and East Asia, whose influences extended to Korea, Japan and other countries. This is beyond the scope of this article, I'd better stop here.

References

1. *Biographies of Eminent monks,* Buddhochinga (*Cho-fotīl-cheng*), Fasci. 10.
2. See *Hou Han Shu* (Annals of the late Han Dynasty) Fasci. last part.
3. *Kuang Hung Ming Chi,* Fasci I, *Mu Tzu on Ignorance.*
4. Wang Ch'ung, *Lun Heng (On Judgement),* Chapter on offering sacrifice.
5. See Nakamura Hajime, *Influence of Confucian Thought on the Chinese Translation of Buddhist Scripture, Studies on World Religion* No. 2, 1982.
6. See Chin yin-ke, *Series of Manuscripts from Chin Ming Kuan.*
7. The Six Schools are Ben-wu (inherently non-existant, or void), Hsin-wu (Nothing exists without the mind), Chi-se (Matter is non substantial), Yuen-hui (Unity of causation), Huan-hua (Manifesting of illusion), and Shi-han (Consciousness within itself). By adding another school Ben-wu-ji (Non-variety), it forms seven sects.

Chapter 20

The Significance of Cultural Values of Buddhism in Modern China

Yu Xintian

Being transmitted into China, Buddhism has deeply melted into the Chinese culture, while having played an active part in China's traditional culture. The more our society is jumping into modern times, the more people always come to understand significance of developing the traditional culture. As the Renaissance anticipated the prelude of the capitalism, and in the great changes of the society in China after the Opium War emerged, Buddhism became typical liberating and mind-saving campaign. Drawing a good deal of enlightenment from Buddhism Renaissance, I shall probe into the significance of cultural values of Buddhism in modern China.

I. An Enlightenment of Modern Buddhism Renaissance

From the second half of the 19th century to the 1920s China witnessed a Buddhism Renaissance. Not only almost all thinkers and reformers of late Qing Dynasty at the beginning of the Republic of China, for instance, Gong Zizhen, Wei Yuan, Kang Youwei, Liang Qichao, Tan Citong, Zhang Taiyan, etc., took great interests in Buddhism, but they also initiated a lot of research institutions and social organizations. After intrusion of the Western powers, the belief in imperial power of the Heavenly Kingdom by the Chinese people was shaken, while the orthodox position of Confucianism was damaged. Along with the influx of guns and commodity goods, Christianity drove straight in China. When the Chinese thinkers sought the road for national liberation, they were also looking for ideological weapon, which can contend with the Western religion and culture. The traditional Chinese culture is mainly composed of Confucianism, Taoism and Buddhism, but Confucianism was only supported by the tiny local gentry and Taoism, which was negative to advocate principle of *wu-wei,* doing nothing, that is nothing against the way, can not be charged with important tasks, then Buddhism being full of spiritual dynamism had become the first choice.

Buddhism became the first choice by the Chinese intellectuals, because its cultural values had potentials to be excavated. First, it explained the reasons for worldly sufferings or miseries of the masses with the Buddhist doctrine, while they were fired with zeal for Great Harmony and Sukhāvati (Pure Land) and ideal for rescuing the common people, Kang Youwei, Liang Qichao and Tan Cidong took Buddhism as their ideal realm and spiritual prop. The Buddhist tradition of standing aloof from the worldly affairs can be easily transformed into the theory of social critique, while designing the new blueprints on the basis of exceeding the defilement and corruption of the worldly affairs. Secondly, the moral doctrine of selflessness and fearlessness must be cultivated to realize the revolutionary ideals. For instance, Buddhist teachings like kind-hearted and merciful thinking of helping people in distress, sacrificing one's own interests for the sake of others, exerting oneself to energetically march, great ambition and fearlessness, all of those could radiate the devotional spirit of the Chinese nation. As Zhang Taiyan thought, the self-devotion like sacrificing oneself, including one's head, eyes, or brains for the sake of others can be realized only by practicing Buddhist teaching "carrying all sentiment beings cross the other river bank" (to the highest stage of *nirvāṇa*, Buddhahood, for the sake not only of individual but of all other sentiment beings. Combing the Western culture of conservation of matter with religious concerning the doctrine of eternal soul, Tan Citong combined the theory of neither being, nor death with that of heart and soul. He chose the sacrifice for reform than having a narrow escape, which confirmed his selfless and fearless spirits with his own blood. Thirdly, to counter the declination and decaying of old etiquette and cardinal guides or constant virtues, he upheld the ideological banner for new world through borrowing Buddhist teachings such as equality of all beings, benevolent liberation etc. so as to match with equality, freedom and universal fraternity or compassion. Liang Qichao pointed out that Buddhism was aimed at the fact that every one will be equal with Buddha. The Qing court should be overthrown because it refused to offer equality to the Han people. As the great heaven and earth are mind-made, every one in the reality can seek independence and realize the individual liberation. It can be seen that the transformed Buddhist thought and belief were, to some extent, given the characteristics of bourgeois political reform with secular, ethical and revolutionary orientations.

So far as the Chinese intellectuals are concerned. Buddhism not only can be used as a means to transform the Chinese society, but it can also serve as a bridge toward the modern learning. The modern transformation of the Chinese learning can be traced to the impact of Western religion and culture, while, on the contrary, the popular philosopher Schopenhauer at the same time was deeply influenced by the Indian philosophy and Buddhist Thought. The intellectuals took interest in Buddhism, because they really wanted to promote the intercourse between the Oriental and Occidental cultures. Liang Qichao was of the opinion that doctrine of Kant's teachings was similar to the Buddhist teachings. Zhang Taiyan was inclined to the Schopenhauer's views of dynamic will rather than the theory of evolution. Liang Shuming argued that culture was the only way of living, when he summarized three cultural patterns i.e., Chinese, Western and Indian patterns, after comparing Henri Bergson's philosophy with the doctrine of the Vijñapatimātratā School. Of course, it is more important that based upon Buddhism, the Chinese philosophers had established their own ideological system which is characteristic of Buddhism. Starting from the Vijñapatimātratā School of Buddhism, Xiong Shili changed his interest to Confucianism and mind science of Lu &Wang. After comparing with Bergson's philosophy and so on, he wrote *The New Cittamātras* which scaled a new height of philosophical thought, while he became a great master of a generation. The philosophy of Vijñapatimātratā School that the most of intellectuals had the greatest esteem for is characteristic of the theory of knowledge in modern philosophy being full of rational mode of thinking, detailed analysis, as well as well-knit logic. It includes the contents of World Outlook, Ontology. Theory of Knowledge, Theory of Truth, Psychology and Ethics, while it deepened the rational mode of thinking of the Chinese people. The philosophy of the Vijñapatimātratā School, to some extent, is the mother of the modern Chinese philosophy. To be different from Confucianism and Taoism, Buddhism was not pounded by the political revolution, and on the contrary it was rejuvenating and developing from the ancient theoretical formation to the modern one. But, due to the new smashing culture movement after the May 4th Movement in 1919, Buddhism began to decline from its climax, because the main ideological stream at that time was to advocate science and democracy which was strongly against religion. For example, Chen Duxu advocated that the science should replace the religion. Cai Yuanpei was in favor of that aesthetic education which may replace religion, and Liang Shuming argued that "the rites could replace religion" and "morality could play the role of religion, while the religious studies were only included in philosophy.

From the rejuvenation of the modern Buddhism in nearly half century we can draw following historical enlightenment.

First, the traditional culture still plays a very positive role in pushing forward the social modernization drive. What counts is that the traditional cultural values must be reformed so as to meet the demands of the time. It will provide food for thought that the idea of renouncing the world must change into the critique and negation of existing social illness, which shall become an active principle of going into society.

Secondly, the transformation of the traditional culture must have an opening-up process and can only be realized through ideological exchanges, debates, tolerance and absorption of different kinds. If there were no Western religion and cultural impacts as strong dynamism, the modernization of Buddhism will be probably not so fast. The new cultural values of the Chinese people being merged with the fruits of Buddhism Western learning and Confucianism have more modernity and universality.

Finally, the rejuvenation of Buddhism had diverted attention of devotees to knowledge-based rational meditation, and kept an eye on the cultural layer of the belief, which took the conclusion of philosophical thinking as a way of living comfort. The philosophical thinking can be looked as a new form of religious belief, but the most of the Chinese devotees did not receive the ultimate concern of religion. This is the result of the fact that Buddhism had played the role of reforming the Chinese society and deep-layer deposit of the Chinese culture. As the national salvation was the most urgent and significant task at that time, the primary thing that the initiators of Buddhism Renaissance thought was world salvation so as to save the nation from distinction. While the aim of mind salvation receded to secondly important position, and the purpose of pondering on ultimate concern was difficult to reach corresponding height.

II. The Significance of the Cultural Values of Buddhism

At present, it will be still necessary to excavate merits of the traditional culture, especially Buddhism so as to promote the cultural progress. First, China's goal of modernization remains to be realized, therefore the arduous task of cultural progress is still lying ahead. China's reform has two goals: one is to fight for the national independence and liberation, which was realized in 1949, another is to build China into a prosperous, rich and civilized nation, for which there will be a long way to traverse. The modernization can only be realized on the basis of cultural progress while introducing foreign advanced science and technology and management experience into China, because progress of the institutional reform must be a process of learning from the civilization fruits. As a matter of fact, these are both aspects of the development progress: If there is no re-cognition of the native culture, there will be no bases of learning or absorption of foreign cultures, and not to mention the success of the modernization drive. Secondly, the rapid development of economic globalization has created unprecedented mutual surging of the world's cultures, and the popular world cultures are being shaped, all nations are reevaluating their own cultures. After the Second World War, especially after the end of the Cold War, along with the raging hurricane of globalization there is flowing floods of capital, commodity goods and people all over the world. However, the information revolution makes it possible for distant geographic areas to know what are happening in the world and to maintain a very close interaction, influencing one another. Cultures have yielded huge impacts to people's habits and psychological thinking. Relying on its powerful economic strength, the Western powers are now practicing a policy of power culture, especially through mass media, they argued that the Western cultural values are universally applicable, which have produced great influences on the young people of the world. But this has also aroused the people's attention of each country to reconsider and re-evaluate their native cultures in a hope to hold a position in the world cultures so as to avoid to lose themselves.

Finally, the mankind is now facing a lot of new challenges, that could hardly be met only by relying upon the Western values, thus, different cultures should perform their own obligations to contribute to the creams of their cultural values. It should be recognized that the Western countries had offered some common-applicable cultural values to the world, such as freedom, democracy, human rights, etc. Though in different cultures exist similar ideological factors, the Western countries had increased them to a new height of modern significance. Like any other cultures, the Western culture, however, has its merits and demerits, while, its demerits could not be compensated by itself. At the turn of the century, all humanity is facing different kinds of new problems, such as population explosion, environmental worsening, chaos caused by frequent wars, a wide gap between the rich and the poor, perishing morality, as well as family disintegration, etc. We are called to overcome them by relying on different cultures, especially the Oriental culture that can provide the distinguished cultural values.

Therefore, at the critical moment of China's reform and opening-up as well as modernization construction, the important agenda of

China's development is to learn and absorb the culture essence of the foreign countries so as to realize the modern transformation of the native cultures and to form new cultural traditions. Buddhism, an indispensable part of China's traditional culture will surely play the un-replaceable role.

China is a super-populous country with poor average resources and low population quality. Although China has made great strides in economic and social construction since its reform and opening-up of last two decades, the road ahead is still overgrown with brambles–a road beset with difficulties.

In order to fulfil the historical mission of uniting the whole nation, it is worthy to advocate and spread the sacrifice spirit and dauntless inspirations in Buddhism. In the course of rapid changes of the Chinese society, the extreme egalitarianism was broken, the income disparity among individuals, the development gaps between the regions have shown a tendency of expansion. If the gaps are widened and led to the disparity between the rich and the poor, those will mean harm to the initiatives of the majority of the people, and harm to healthy development of modernization drive. The value principles concerning "all living creatures being equal" etc., shall restrict the income disparity between the managers and the people. Concrete measures should be designed. Judging by the socialist essence, equality is the crux of its content, the ultimate goal of China's reform and opening-up is to lead to common prosperity. Of course, it is no longer poor extreme egalitarianism, while political and personality equalities and relatively fair distribution of income should be protected.

The above-mentioned are only major points cited, we shall make in-depth research and excavation of the cultural values of Buddhism. At present it is exceptionally necessary to breakthrough the norm of religious practices, which shall be beneficial to the cultivation of spirit of national renovations. The way of human practices falls into the category of indepth structure of culture. Judging from this, although the religious practices belong to ethical cultivation and social reform, may have different scope of human activities and may have common structures including the subject and object engaging activities and their mutual restrictions and mutual actions. These activities can be divided into two ways to attain the goal. One is to take others as the dominant factor in the light of the norms, another is to keep the initiative in our own hands not to follow the old norms. In the traditional Chinese culture, irregular norms of practicing Buddhism were taken in practice, while importance of irregular norms also was stressed theoretically. The theory and practice of Buddhism, especially Zen

Buddhism in China are typical or irregular norms are both contradictory and compensatory to each other. The regular norm has its determinacy that can be easily mastered by the masses, and is suitable to the expansion of the creations. The irregular norm has its uncertainty that can not be easy to master, which is especially applicable to renovation. The invention and creation, institutional reform, adaptation to changing conditions, etc. are all belong to the latter. Both norms have the reasons for their existence, but the attention is paid to the irregular norm today so as to encourage people to be bold in blazing new trails, and to promote the reform and opening-up. Although Buddhism is typical of irregular norm, all kinds of activities beyond the religions can be enlightened or learnt from it. As a matter of fact, those who are engaged in natural sciences or social sciences, after practicing the Zen methods and having great stride in meditation or breaking-through in norms, then they would bring forth new ideas. Before the completion of industrialization China is now facing the abrupt rise of the knowledge-based economy. Therefore, China should combine two steps into one so as to catch up and even surpass the Western countries in a short period. This is an unprecedented challenge for any developing countries because there is no extant experiences to follow. It shall be the crux of victory to be bold in brazing new trails with irregular norms.

III. Promotion of Ultimate Social Concern

One of the experiences of Buddhism rejuvenation in modern times is its failure in promoting the ultimate social concern, and in achieving transcendence. It is not beyond one's comprehension that the more pressing task is to save the country while enlightenment should serve the national salvation. Today, in our cultural progress we should bear in mind this lesson and make the ultimate social concern to be our future object.

By concern, we mean a being, belief or action we can dedicate for, this ultimate concern is meant both a purpose and a process of worship. All that one's personage can tightly control and all things that one is willing to suffer, or even to sacrifice oneself, which can be regarded as ultimate concern, in other words, his "religion". Thus, the powers of human consciousness or unconsciousness shall be focused on the object of his ultimate concern. Religion is the ultimate concern of some people, but not their sole ultimate concern, cause, belief, love, etc., may also become one's ultimate concern. The religious belief is the most ancient and typical ultimate concern of mankind. Those who study ultimate concern but have scanty knowledge of religion are always difficult to catch main ideas. Of course, the ultimate concern we advocate today does not mean people must be converted to Buddhism or some other religions (this is individual's personal freedom), we mean the focus of total social concern is ultimate liberation of man, or humanitarianism.

In China, major part of the population is still enjoying a low living and economic environments. Nearly 70 million people are still living in poverty. Only through modernization the people's living can be improved from the bottom to the top and lay basis for increasing human values. But the progress of modernization has not only increased the living conditions of the vast majority of the people, but also bring new problems and contradiction here. According to an incomplete statistics, there are 80 million people who are flowing between the urban and rural areas. There are more than 10 million laid-off workers in the course of economic restructuring in China, when the rigorous control of the government was greatly decreasing, the original interpersonal relations being totally lax, and the traditional moral norms were not abided by. The aim of reform is to promote the initiative and creativeness of the individuals so as to struggle for a bright future. But, in the course of reform, the adaptation of every individual is different, and different preparations for knowledge and technology will result in the intensification of the social polarization. Thus in the course of modernization drive, stress or ultimate concern will be helpful to government or society's over every individual, especially the weak community and individuals so as to relax the contradictions and pains cropped in the course of rapid social transformation.

In essence, Buddhism is kind of way for extrication, while its ultimate ideal is enlightenment, extrication and attainment of Buddhahood, i.e., *nirvāṇa*—the final escape from the cycle of rebirth.

I shall not dwell on whether one can attain Buddhahood or attainment of *nirvāṇa* or not, but it is beyond doubt that the Buddhist value dogmas are aimed at freeing from all restrictions of the human race. According to Buddhism, the Noble Truth of Suffering in life means the restrictions to the living being forced by the external strength. No matter what this strength is an objective law or an institutional rites established by the people, and no matter what secular social norms or the Buddhist principles of standing aloof from the worldly affairs. Thus, Buddhism itself has a spirit of thorough-going criticism and continuous transcending, it is a thirst for enlightenment and extrication and ideal realm of rest and joy, popularly known form as *nirvāṇa* i.e., freeing from all restriction and *Ātman* (egotistic) realm.

Even if the Buddhist scriptures and ethical conduct (śīla) and mental disciplines will restrict freedom of the man, the real Buddhist teachings would not stubbornly adhere to these scriptures and disciples, while going to a state of complete freedom and independence.

Although Buddhism is in the quest for the freedom, realm in a category of idealism, it will be practical to absorb the transcending and critical spirits of Buddhism in the frame of materialism so as to enhance the spirit to a higher level. If every one has this spirit, there will be a leap in the realization of one's own values. According to Marxism, communism not only means "from each according to needs – the extreme abundance of goods, but also means a community of free beings and complete liberation of man. The two can be interlinked on the later point. Therefore, it is an one-sided approach to only view Buddhism as an ideology of negative escape from reality or as an opium numbing the people by the ruling class. It contains more complicated and rich meanings.

Viewing from the indepth characteristics of the Chinese culture, it is exceptionally important to carry on and promote the individual freedom of Buddhism. The Chinese culture is strongly oriented to secularism and early rationalism. As Liang Shuming pointed out, there will hardly be religious livelihood for particular emphasis. Max Weber criticized China's Confucianism and Taoism, by arguing that they are the root cause of that capitalism was not born in China. To this, the academic community is still at issue. But, he is of the opinion that it is quite reasonable that no one can hold aloof from everything, and the bestowed life style must be furnished with the negative features in essences, and the pursuit for unified "personality" in one's heart of hearts. Though the Confucian tradition, gigmanity trend, patriarchal clerkship in the Chinese culture all have reasons for their existence and may play their positive role, they will, to some extent, limit the personality of a person. After the founding of New China, due to slow development of economy, the rural organizations created by so-called complete revolution could not escape the domain of the original clans. The rigorous control of the planned economy had also limited the development of personal freedom and self-selection. The tradition is characteristic of great inertia. Thus there is not mistaking to develop the creams of the China's Buddhist culture.

After the reform and opening-up the biggest change is the transformation of value conception. When China tried to build itself into a state of market economy and legal system, self-decision of a person and protection of private legal rights were stressed. In the literature of the 15th Congress of the Chinese Communist Party after Senior leader Deng Xiaoping's passing away, it is first time to raise the development of humanitarianism in cultural progress, a milestone for cultivating ultimate social concern, which can be looked as starting point to a more civilized society. It is definitely important to develop economy and improve the material life of the people, but after being abundant in material how will the people live, what they will pursuit shall depend upon the ultimate concern. Now in the coastal regions of China we have already experienced this problem, and it shall be the focus of the whole society in future.

Chapter 21

India in Japanese Writings Through Ages

Saroj Kumar Chaudhuri

I. General Introduction

The accounts of the Chinese monks who travelled to India and the Buddhist literature produced in China were the only sources of information on India for the Japanese, prior to the arrival of the Portuguese in the middle of the sixteenth century. The arrival of the Indian monk *Bodhisena* in the year A.D. 736 provided the Japanese with a chance to learn about India at first hand, but language proved to be a formidable barrier in communicating with him.

Crown Prince Shōtoku's (574-622) commentaries of the *Ho-ke-kyō, Yui-ma-kyō* and *Shō-man-gyō* sūtras, the first literary works of Japan, contained much religious information on India. The Japanese monks studied the accounts of the Chinese travellers to India since early times. Back in the ninth century, the monk Annen (841-?) quoted from Huen Tsang's (602-664) travels in his *Shittanzō*. For instance, the river Sindhu rises from Lake Anavatapta and flows east.[1]

The information on India transmitted by the westerners until the opening of Japan in the middle of the nineteenth century did not generate much popular interest. Even the mission of four Japanese youths sent to the Vatican by a feudal lord of Kyushu in 1582 failed to attract any attention although it actually touched Goa.

II. Indian Geo-Politics

The famous scholar Kitabatake Chikafusa (1292-1354) has given a graphic picture of the Buddhist concept of the universe in his *Jinnō Shōtōki*. He says that according to Buddhist scriptures, there are seven rings of mountains surrounding Mount Sumeru. Beyond these mountains, there are four oceans containing four continents. Each continent has two medium sized landmasses near them. The southern continent is known by the name Jambudvipa. There is a mountain called Anavatapta with a lake on the top at the centre of this continent. The Himalayas are located to the south and Pamir is located to the north of Mt. Anavatapta. North of Pamir is the barbarian country, and south of the Himalayas lies India. China is located to the north-east, and Persia to the north-west. China is a big country, but compared with India, it is insignificantly small. Japan is located inside the sea far away from the above countries.[2]

The famous scholar and statesman Arai Hakuseki (1657-1725) has written about contemporary India in his *Seiyō Kibun* on the basis of information supplied by the Jesuit monk Sidotti. He writes that the ancient land of India is the present day Mughal kingdom. It is a vast country with large population and rich resources. There are frequent military uprisings. Mughals are Muslims. Coast Coromondal is a port city. Bengal is a tributary state located in Eastern India. It produces textiles that the Dutch sell in Japan. The Portuguese are based in Goa, a port in Western India, and control local trade. Malabar is also a Portuguese territory located to the south of Goa.[3]

Another writer to write about modern India is Hirata (1776-1842). He says in his *Indo Zōshi*, that the Mughal kingdom and the region mentioned as India in the Dutch accounts constitute the ancient land of Five Indies. Hirata gives an account of the Mughals as follows. The Mughal kingdom was founded by Tamerlane, a native of Samarkand in the Sakatai county lying on the eastern shores of the Caspian Sea in the land of Tartary. In the beginning he was a brigand, but slowly he grabbed North and Central India, and declared himself the emperor in 1396. After this, he captured Western India and became the ruler of the three regions of India. His capital was Agra. Later on he captured the northern part of South India....The Mughal kingdom is divided into thirty provinces, and the Europeans knew fairly well about the two southernmost provinces of Bengal and Cambay....He mentions that the line roughly joining Cambay in the west and Bengal in the east constitutes the southern limit of the Mughal country.[4]

The Japanese produced the first map of India titled Gotenjikuzu in 1364. It is based on information from Buddhist sources, and shows the travel route of Huen Tsang in red ink.[5] It can be easily imagined that this map lacks authenticity. Hirata has also given a map of India using the same title Gotenjikuzu in his book. Being based on modern cartographic principles, Hirata's map, shown below, is quite authentic, although it shows some legendary places like lake Anavatapta.

Hirata Atsutane's Map of India

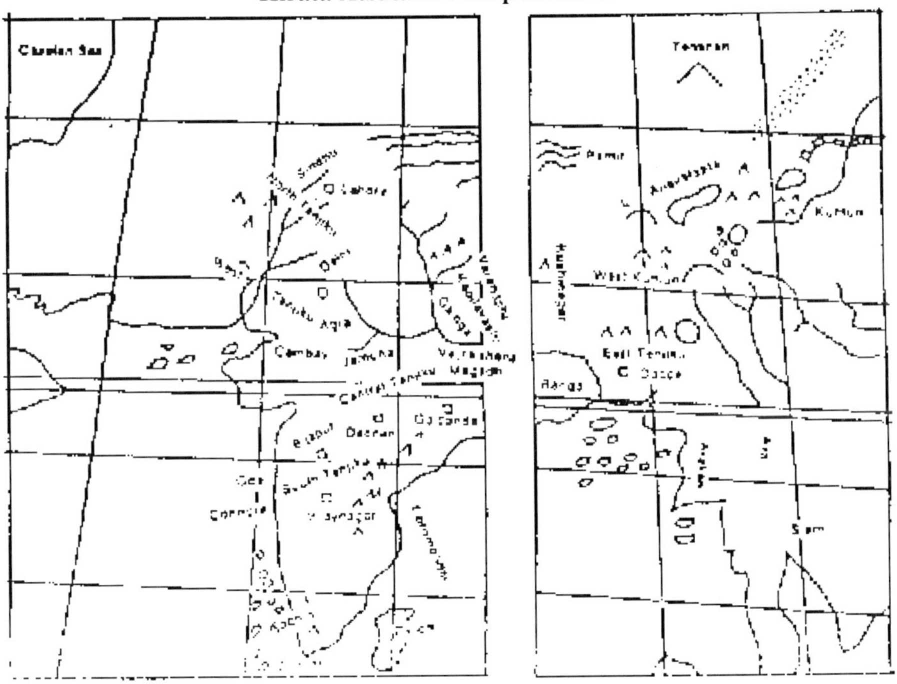

Note:Tenjiku is the name given to India in ancient days

III. Indian Themes in Popular Literature

Konjaku Monogatari, a collection of Japanese Folktales compiled in the twelfth century, has at least three 'stories that can be linked directly to *Pañcantantra*. The story that resembles the *Pañcatantra* version most will be related here. A tortoise wanted to escape from draught-stricken pond with the help of two storks. The storks held a piece of stick in their beaks with the tortoise tightly holding the stick with its mouth. As they flew high in the sky, the tortoise was overwhelmed by the scene below, and asked his friends about the location. As soon as a stork opened his mouth to reply, he fell to the ground and died. In the *Pañcatantra* version, a pair of ganders and not storks are involved. As people below started shouting on seeing them flying, the tortoise opened his mount to ask his friends about noise. As soon as he opened his mouth, he fell to the ground and died.[6]

The sage Riṣyaṣringa is a famous character in *Rāmāyana*. His story appears in major literary works like *Konjaku Monogatari* and *Taiheiki* (fourteenth century), as well as in Noh and Kabuki dramas. In *Ramayana*, the boy ascetic Riṣyaṣringa was seduced by beautiful courtesans and brought to the king's palace to perform a ritual to end prolonged draught. The *Konjaku Monogatari* version introduces Riṣyaṣringa as a sage with supernatural power and a horn on his forehead. He slipped and injured himself while walking on a hilly road on a rainy day. The angry sage withheld rain for twelve years. On a fortune-teller's advice the king sent five hundred beauties to seduce the sage and deprive him of his supernatural power. The beauties accomplished the mission by seducing him. The sage came to the capital carrying a woman on his back. People laughed seeing the funny scene. The angry sage tried to return to the hills flying. Deprived of his supernatural power, he just fell on the ground with a thud.[7]

The following story of the same collection can be linked with the episode of King Ushinar given in *Mahābhārata*. A mother monkey left her two offspring in the care of a lion and went out to collect fruits. Presently the lion started dozing, and a falcon swooped down and carried away the two baby monkeys. Waking up with a start, the lion saw what had happened and begged the falcon to let the little ones go. The falcon refused. The lion finally got the baby monkeys back in exchange for an equal amount of his own flesh. In the *Mahābhārata* story, King Ushinar offered himself to a falcon to save a dove, its natural prey. Here, the gods Indra and Agni disguised themselves as the falcon and the dove in order to test the compassion of the king.[8]

The famous work *Genpei Jōsuiki* carries a story on Aśoka's coronation. Bindusāra's eldest son Sushima was handsome and kind-hearted. The second Aśoka was very ugly, brave and violent in temperament. The king wanted to make Sushima his successor. Suddenly Bindusāra fell sick. At that time, Sushima was away to subdue a rebellion. As the condition of the king worsened, he decided to nominate Sushima as his successor. But Indra came down from the heaven, and put the jewel-studded crown of ten virtues on the head of Aśoka. The shock killed Bindusāra. Aśoka ascended the throne with the assistance of a minister. Hearing this Sushima assembled a large force to punish Aśoka. In the ensuing fight, Sushima and his forces perished in a big fire, Aśoka later became a great emperor ruling over the four seas.[9]

IV. Indian Divinities

IV-1. Lakṣhmī

Lakṣhmī was regarded as an important deity of prosperity in ancient Japan. For instance, the entry in the second official history *Shoku Nihongi* (797) for the New Year Day of the year 749 mentions an edict ordering temples all over the country to hold Kisshō Kekae, a congregation for Lakṣhmī, for forty-nine days, starting with the New Year Day.[10] It was done to ensure prosperity of the nation.

The Kisshō Kekae enhanced the popularity of Lakṣhmī in the society. There are two stories related to her in *Nihon Ryōiki*, the early ninth century collection of folk tales. To relate one here in brief, the goddess responds to the earnest prayer of a poor lady, and saves her from humiliation by bringing delicious food for her guests.[11]

Lakṣhmī was very popular among the aristocrats in the capital. This is attested to by Genji Monogatari, the famous fiction written around 1000, where she has been mentioned as a adorable and impeccable goddess. She was also regarded as the goddess of beauty in Japan. There is a famous shrine named Itsukushima Shrine near Hiroshima. *Itsukushima Honji*, a work of the Kamakura period narrating the story of the origin of this shrine, starts with the episode of the hero's falling in love with a beautiful picture of Lakshmi drawn on a fan, his family heirloom.[12]

As time passed, Lakṣhmī's status declined and Sarasvati replaced her as the goddess of prosperity. Amano Sadakage, a famous essayist, says in this regard in his famous work *Shiojiri* (1733) that Sarasvati is regarded as a goddess of fortune by the Japanese at present. This is not correct. Actually, it is Lakṣhmī who bestows fortune. Sarasvati is the presiding deity of knowledge.[13]

IV-2. Sarasvati

Sarasvati is one of the most popular Hindu deities in Japan. Her most famous shrine is located in Chikubushima Island. *Kōdanshō*, attributed to Ooe no Masafusa (1041-1111), a leading intellectual of his time, records that a famous poet, Miyako no Yoshika (824-879), visited the island in late summer, and composed the following poem to express his feelings.

The Three-Thousand World	Appeared before my eyes,
The twelve causes and effects	Are thoroughly purified in my mind.

It next says that, according to an old legend, the poet composed the first line of the poem, but could not complete the second line. Sarasvati, the presiding deity of the island, told him the second line in a dream.[14]

Heike Monogatari, the famous epic compiled in the thirteenth century, narrates a pilgrimage to the Chikubushima Shrine by Taira no Tsunemasa, an army general and a man of letters, in early summer. The general knelt down before the deity and said: 'Sarasvati, you are a bodhisattva. You are known by several names. You lead people to salvation. I hear that the wishes of those visiting you are fulfilled. This is really a very happy thing'. That night, the general played lute in the sanctuary. The deity was so moved that she appeared in the form of a white dragon and settled on the sleeve of the general.[15]

Sarasvati was also worshipped for defeating one's enemy. *Azuma Kagami*, an official record of events between 1180 and 1266, in the entry dated the fifth day of the fourth month of 1182 states that Minamoto no Yoritomo visited Enoshima on this day. The monk Monkaku established a temple here dedicated to Sarasvati, and worshipped the deity according to tāntric rites for the success of Yoritomo. The main object was to defeat Yoritomo's arch enemy Fujiwara no Hidehira.[16]

The popularity of Sarasvati around this time is also attested to by Noh dramas. For instance, the Noh drama *Chikubushima*, supposed to be a work of the fifteenth century, opens with a scene of pilgrimage to her shrine in the Chikubushima Island by a courtier in spring. On reaching the island, an old man ushers him to the Sarasvati idol. A shrine priest tells him that Sarasvati is a goddess of miracles, and mentions her shrines at Itsukushima and Enoshima in passing. Suddenly the shrine shakes, Sarasvati appears, and introduces herself as the deity of the island. Presently the shrine reverberates with heavenly music, flowers shower from the sky, and Sarasvati starts dancing. After finishing her dance, Sarasvati goes back to the shrine.[17]

IV-3. Brahmā

Brahmā was a minor deity in Japan. He appears only in passing in many major literary works. *Bishamon no Honji*, an anonymous work of the Muromachi period (1336-1575) gives a description of the palace of Brahmā. It is located inside a pine grove near a white beach. It is a jewel-studded palace with gorgeous spires. The ponds are full of blooming lotus. Boats in ponds carry heavenly maidens and holy people accompanied by music and dance. The breeze is full of fragrance.[18]

Hirata Atsutane has discussed Brahmā in some detail in his *Indo Zōshi* (c. 1840). He gives two hypotheses on the creation of human race involving Brahmā. According to one Brahma created four sons, Sanaka, Sanandana, Sanātana, and Sanata-kumāra in ancient times. According to the other, Brahmā created eight divine sons, and they produced the heaven, the earth and everything. They are the fathers of all living beings. Hirata also found that Brahma was the progenitor of the four castes of India. The brahmanas were born from his mouth, the kshatriyas from his arms, the vaishyas from his thighs and the shudras from his feet.[19]

A religious text *Gyō-rin-shō* (1154) of the monk Jōnen gives the following description of Brahmā. He has a white complexion. He has four faces and his hair has a crown-like finish. He has three eyes in each face. He has four hands. In his two right hands, he holds a lotus and a string of beads. He holds a water pot in one left hand. The other left hand makes the auspicious sign of an ascetic. He sits on a goose or on a chariot drawn by seven geese. His mantra is *prajāpatiye svāhā*.[20]

IV-4. Maheśhvara

Hirata Atsutane (1776-1843) found that Maheśhvara was associated with the creation of the living beings. He writes in his *Indo Zōshi* that Maheśhvara created eight women, viz., Diti, Aditi, Soraba (Surabhi), Vinata, Kapila, Mato (Muni), Ira and Kato (Kadru). Aditi gave birth to gods, Diti to asuras, Surabhi to snakes, Vinata to birds, Kapila to four legged animals, Muni to human beings, Ira to crops, and Kadru to crawlers and insects. It is needless to say that this is a modified version of the famous Indian legend of creation of living beings through the daughters of Dakśa.[21]

IV-5. Mārichi

Kaku-zen-shō (1217) narrates the following story of Marichi, a deity not known much in India. The *asura* king Vimalachitra was born in Jambudvipa. He had a beautiful daughter named Śachi, and her father thought of betrothing her to another *asura* king Rāhula. Indra was enchanted by the beauty of Śachi and abducted her to his Trayastrimsas heaven. On Indra's order, Viśvakarmā built the City of Sudarśana along with a palace with ten thousand rooms in seven days of the human world. Indra covered it with a net called indrajāla, and hid Śachi inside this palace. Coming to know about it, Vimalachitra attacked Indra's palace with his allies. As fighting went on, the *asuras* got the upper hand and reached Indra's palace. Seeing this, the Sun and the Moon emitted pure light and illuminated the pupils of the *asura* kings. Rāhula stretched his hands and was about to catch the Sun and the Moon, when Mārichi appeared as a three-year old child and confused the *asura* king by hiding the palaces of the Sun and the Moon. The *asuras* were finally defeated.[22]

V. Sanskrit in Japan

Sanskritic studies in Japan started with the monk Kūkai, the founder of the Tāntric Shingon Sect. Sanskrit was known as Shittan (a corruption of Siddham), the script in which the language was written in the Far East. Urging his disciples to learn Siddham, he said in his *Bonji Shittan Jimo narabini Shakugi* that one attains Buddha-wisdom by reading and writing the Brāhmī letters. They are at the root of all teachings and knowledge.[23] He introduced the Siddham letters along with their esoteric meanings in this work.

V-1. Siddham Ligatures and Compounds

The monk Annen (841-?) gives us a detailed picture of Siddham as it was known in Japan during his time in his exhaustive work *Shittanzō*. He has discussed the modified forms the letters assume, using terms like *hanji*, half-letter, for consonantal ligatures, and *manji*, full-letter, for compounds. He cites the word siddham to explain half-letter and full-letter. The compound ddha is composed of da and dha. 'Annen says that when da is not added on the top of dha, the letter dha is a half-letter. When da is added to dha, a full-letter is obtained. This suggests that a half-letter meant a consonantal ligature and a full-letter meant a compound letter.[24]

V-2. Alphabetic Behaviour of Siddham Consonant Letters

The Siddham letters possess the dual property of syllable and alphabet. The *halanta* sign is often added to a consonant letter to show specifically that it a pure consonant. For instance, ka + *halanta* sign→ /k/. Annen has discussed the *halanta* sign in detail. He uses the term *hanji* for consonantal ligature and the term *hanon* for *halanta*. He cites the word dharma and says that the letter ra coming on the top of the letter ma is *hanon*. What Annen wanted to say is that the letter ra behaves like the pure consonant /r/ here.[25]

The alphabetic behaviour of Siddham consonant letters attracted the attention of other Siddham scholars also. One is Myōkaku (1054-?). He found an explanation in *Dai-nichi-kyō-gi-shaku* of the Chinese monk Ichigyō (683-787). It says that the letters ka and short a make the sound ka. Without this short a it is not possible to produce the sound ka. It is a compound sound. Myōkaku then says that the sound of the letter ka is *kua*. If *a* is eliminated, it immediately becomes *ku*. It is obvious that Myōkaku wanted to express /k/ with this *ku*. This innovation of using the u-vocalic form to express the single consonants is continuing even today.[26]

V-3. Inflection

Annen has given some information on Sanskrit grammar. About declension, he writes that *subanta* has eight declined forms. They are *nirdeśa, upadeśana, kartrikaraṇa, sampradādike, apādāttih, svamibhavadih, samnidhanadi* and *amantrana*. He gives the words in Siddham script along with their Chinese transcriptions. He next continues that these have singular, dual, and plural forms. Thus, there are twenty-four inflected forms in all. Again, there are masculine, feminine, and neuter gender forms. Each of these has twenty-four forms. This makes a grand total of ninety-six forms. He illustrates his point with the Sanskrit words *bhabhana, puruṣa, bhagavata,* and *buddha*.[27]

V-4. Properties of Sounds

Annen's list of *Varṇamālas* collected from diverse sources shows that the Sanskrit categorisation of the plosive consonants into velars, palatals, retroflexes, dentals, and labials was known. But it was not standardised as in India. For instance *ta, tha, da, dha,* and *na* have been mentioned as gutturals in one case and dentals in another. This trend continued in Japan also.[28]

The unvoiced-voiced classification was also known. The twenty-five plosive consonants are arranged in five rows with five letters in each row. Annen says that the first two letters in each row constitute the *jūsei* sound, the next two the *dosei* sound, and the last one the *hijūdosei* sound. These three terms can be identified positively as unvoiced, voiced, and nasal sounds respectively. For the unvoiced and voiced sounds, Annen has used the terms *seion* and *dakuon* in the context of Chinese. For the unaspirated and aspirated sounds he used the terms *kei* and *chō*. These concepts attracted much attention among latter-day scholars in Japan. One of the earliest Japanese writers to address the problem of the two sets of terms for the unvoiced and voiced sounds is Myōkaku (A.D. 1054-?). After quoting Annen, Myōkaku says in his *Shittan Taitei* that *jūsei* is *seion* and *dosei* is *dakuon*. He also gives examples that the letters *ga, gha, ja, jha,* hard *da* and *dha,* soft *da* and *dha, ba,* and *bha* are *dakuon*. Here, he has added the note *chō* with the aspirated letters *gha, jha,* hard *dha,* soft *dha,* and *bha*. Perhaps the best exposition on this point has been given by the monk Jiun (A.D. 1718-1804). The following table given in his *Jōjū Kichijōgi* explains the concept in a very lucid manner.[29]

Properties of Siddham Letters Given by Jiun

	pa	ta	ṭa	ca	ka	*kei* 軽 (unaspirated)
sei 清						*jūsei* 柔声 (Unvoiced)
(unvoiced)	pha	tha	ṭha	cha	kha	*chō* 重 (aspirated)
	ba	da	ḍa	ja	ga	*kei* (unaspirated)
daku 濁						*dosei* 怒声 (voiced)
(voiced)	bha	dha	ḍha	jha	gha	*chō* (aspirated)
	ma	na	ṇa	ña	ṅa	*bisei* 鼻声 (nasal)
						hijū hido 非柔非怒 (nasal)
	shin	*kō*	*zetsu*	*shi*	*ga*	
	脣	喉	舌	歯	牙	
	labial	guttural	lingual	dental	velar	

VI. Sanskrit and Japanese Linguistic Studies

VI-1. Origin of the Kana Characters

The Japanese started borrowing the script from China from around the fifth or sixth century of the Christian era, and by the ninth century they evolved two kana syllabaries, katakana and hiragana, to write their language.

There was much speculation about the origin of the kana characters during the Edo period (1603-1868). An eminent scholar Arai Hakuseki (1657-1725) writes in his *Dōbun Tsūkō* (1715) by taking a cue from the consonantal ligatures of Brāhmī letters, the katakana characters were formed by omitting parts of the Chinese characters and then pronouncing these truncated characters according to their original readings. The word *kata* has a meaning similar to the consonantal ligature of Siddham.[30]

There is one kana character of non-Chinese origin. It is the kana *n*. This is a non-native Japanese sound that appeared under the impact of large-scale borrowings from Chinese. Arai Hakuseki says that both the katakana and the hiragana *n* were obtained by modifying the Siddham *candrabindu* sign.[31]

{*Candrabindu* → (katakana *n*), (hiragana *n*)}

VI-2. Arrangement of the Kana Characters

A very important question in the process of evolution of the kana characters is the number of sounds involved in Japanese. Arai Hakuseki writes that the monk Kūkai analysed the sounds involved in Japanese on the basis of Siddham and found that there were forty-seven sounds.[32] Once an idea of the number of kana characters was obtained, the question of their arrangement cropped up. The Japanese designed a number of arrangements, of which the one used in school textbooks is the Gojūonzu or the fifty sound chart. This is based on the model of Siddham *Varṇamāla*. The voiced kana characters are excluded in this chart.

VI-3. Diacritical Sign for Voicing

The voiced kana characters are basically the same as their unvoiced counterparts. The only difference is that they have a diacritical voicing sign, called *dakuten*, constituted by two elongated dots added on the top right-hand side. For instance, the unvoiced kana character *ka* turns into voiced *ga* with the addition of the voicing sign. (*ka* → *ga*).

In earliest works like *Kojiki* (712), the unvoiced sounds were rendered with unvoiced Chinese characters, and the voiced sounds with voiced Chinese characters. This distinction broke down completely during the ninth century. This coincided with the time when the Japanese started writing their language using the kana characters. The voiced sounds were written with the unvoiced kana characters, and a literate Japanese of the period could say easily whether a kana character in a passage was unvoiced or voiced from the context.

The need for specifying the voiced sounds arose from the necessity to pronounce the *mantras* correctly. The translators of sūtras, by and large, left the *mantras* in their original Siddham script, but added Chinese transcriptions to assist the recitation. With the founding of the tāntric sects in the beginning of the ninth century, emphasis shifted to correct pronunciation of the *mantras*. For the Japanese monks, the Chinese transcriptions of the Siddham letters were good guide indeed, but the breakdown of unvoiced-voiced distinction created a serious problem. Since the *mantras* were totally foreign to the Japanese, specifying the voiced sounds in the transcriptions became an urgent necessity to ensure correct pronunciation. This forced the monks to add voicing pronunciation notes to the transcriptions.

One of the earliest texts recording the diacritical sign for voicing is a copy of *Kon-gō-chō-ren-ge-bu-shin-nen-ju-gi-ki*. This text carries many *mantras* written in Siddham script along with their Chinese transcriptions. In the copy concerned, a Japanese monk added the voicing diacritical sign to the Chinese transcriptions of the *mantras* around A.D. 889. The voicing diacritical sign told the readers that the readings should be in voiced form. The diacritical sign used here has the shape of the water radical, which happens to be the radical of the character *daku* of *dakuten*, meaning voicing sign also. The voicing diacritical sign in this text appears only with the transcriptions of *mantras* and nowhere else.[33]

VI-4. Phonetic Changes

The Japanese words, especially verbs, undergo phonetic changes called *onbin* under certain circumstances. The monk Myōkaku mentioned above used these to explain phonetic changes in Sanskrit words. He was the first Japanese to record the *onbin* phenomenon. For instance, *kakite* → *kaite*, *kirite* → *kitte*, and so on. An attempt to classify these changes was made by Motoori Norinaga (1730-1801), the foremost scholar of his time. It will be seen in the second example cited above that /t/ is duplicated. Since the Japanese kana characters have the CV pattern, where C is a consonant or nothing and V is a vowel, there was no way to express the first isolated /t/. Myōkaku used the kana character *tsu* to express such single consonants. Motoori was very much familiar with the Siddham phonetic theories that played an important role in the development of Japanese linguistic studies. He says that knowledge of Siddham is a must for those who want to study the science of phonetics. Motoori reasoned that when a consonant is duplicated, say */kk/*, */tt/*, */pp/*, etc., the first consonant of the two is not a character. Hence it is not correct to use the kana *tsu*, a character, to express a single consonant. So he decided to use the *visarga* sign, which was used by the Siddham scholars to express the entering tone endings */-k/*, */-t/*, and */-p/* in the Chinese characters. Despite his reputation, his innovation was not accepted.[34]

VI-5. Keichū's New Japanese Characters

Keichū (1640-1701) proposed a new form of script for writing Japanese in his *Waji Seiranshō* written around 1693. He designed his script on the basis of Siddham. The concept he described can be summed up as follows. In Siddham writing, the vowels are modified into signs when they are added to the consonants....Take for instance the letter *ka*. When *i* is added to it, it becomes *ki*, and when *u* is added it becomes *ku*....New characters can be formed in the same manner for other kana syllables also.[35]

Keichū designed his kana characters on the Siddham principle of forming vocalic combinations of the consonants. In Siddham, all the vowels combine with the consonants, except for the first vowel, the short *a*. Instead of adding the vowels as such to the consonants, they are modified into signs in such combinations. In China, these vocalic signs were called *ten*, as against the term *ji* used for the vowel letters. In his proposed kana syllabary, Keichū selected five Chinese characters for the five vowels *a, i, u, e,* and *o,* and nine Chinese characters for the nine consonant kana syllables *ka, sa, ta, na, fa, ma, ya, ra,* and *wa*. Next, he modified the four *i, u, e, o* vowel characters into signs by eliminating a part of the four characters following the Siddham principle. The vocalic signs proposed by Keichū are shown below.

Keichū next added these signs to the nine Chinese characters to get the other kana characters. For example, in Siddham the letter *ki* is obtained by adding the vocalic i-sign to the consonant *ka*. Keichū designed the kana *ki* exactly in the same way by adding the vocalic sign for the vowel *i* to the kana *ka*. Keichū designed fifty kana characters in this way and arranged them in the form of a Gojūonzu. After compiling the chart, Keichū writes that he prepared the chart on the basis of Siddham. The kana table proposed by Keichū is shown below.[36]

Vocalic signs of Keichū: 以 → 人 for *i*, 宇 → 于 for *u*, 江 → 工 for *e*, 遠 → 袁 for *o*

Keichū's Gojūonzu of his new kana characters

和・ wa	良・ ra	也・ ya	末・ ma	波・ fa	奈・ na	太・ ta	左・ sa	加・ ka	安・ a
[illegible] i	[illegible] ri	[illegible] i	[illegible] mi	[illegible] fi	[illegible] ni	[illegible] chi	[illegible] shi	[illegible] ki	以・ i 人
[illegible] u	[illegible] ru	[illegible] yu	[illegible] mu	[illegible] fu	[illegible] nu	[illegible] tsu	[illegible] su	[illegible] ku	宇・ u 于
[illegible] e	[illegible] re	[illegible] e	[illegible] me	[illegible] fe	[illegible] ne	[illegible] te	[illegible] se	[illegible] ke	江・ e 工
[illegible] wo	[illegible] ro	[illegible] yo	[illegible] mo	[illegible] fo	[illegible] no	[illegible] to	[illegible] so	[illegible] ko	遠・ o 袁

References

1. Annen 安然, *Shittanzō* 悉曇蔵, Taishō Shinshū Daizōkyō 大正新修大蔵経, V. 84, p. 371M

2. Kitabatake Chikafusa 北畠親房, *Jinnō Shōtōki* 神皇正統記, Nagahara Keiji et al 永原慶二他 tr., Nihonn no Meicho 日本の名著 V. 9, *Ennin・Kitabatake Chikafusa* 円仁・北畠親房, Chūō Kōronsha 中央公論社, Tokyo, 1971, pp. 341-42.)

3. Arai Hakuseki 新井白石, *Shintei Seiyō Kibun* 新訂西洋記聞, Miyazaki Michio 宮崎道生 ed., Tōyō Bunko 東洋文庫 V. 113, Heibonsha 平凡社, Tokyo, 1970, pp. 48-49.)

4. Hirata, Atsutane 平田篤胤, *Indo Zōshi* 印度蔵志, Inoue, Yorikuni 井上頼囯 and Maeno, Sadayuki 前野忠行, eds., Hirata Atsutane Zenshū Kiseikai 平田篤胤全集期成会, Hōbunkan 法文館, Tokyo, 1917, pp. 22 T 12-13, 19 T 2-12, 19T 15-20, 19 T 18-19.

5. Ōgata, Kōhei 大形孝平編, ed., *Nihon to Indo* 日本とインド, Sanseido 三省堂, Tokyo, 1978, p. 13

6. Arthur W Ryder tr., *The Panchatantra*, "Shell-Neck, Slim, and Grim", Jaico Publishing House, Bombay, 1962, pp. 127-129; Nagazumi, Yasuaki 永積安明 et al., trans. *Konjaku Monogatari* 今昔物語 V. 5, Story No. 24, Heibonsha 平凡社, Tokyo, 1989.

7. *Konjaku Monogatari* 今昔物語, V. 1, Iwanami Koten Bungaku Taikei 岩波古典文学大系, Iwanami Shoten 岩波書店, 1959, pp. 348-352.

8. Ibid., V. 5, Story No. 14; Sinha, Kaliprasanna, trans. *Mahabharata* Pt. 2, Vanaparva, Chapter 131, Saksarata Prakashan, Calcutta, 1974, pp. 135-137.

9. *Genpei Jōsuiki* 源平盛衰記, V. 2, Geirinsha 芸林舎, Kamakura City, 1975, pp. 30-31.

10. Aoki, Kazuo 青木和夫 et al., eds. *Shoku Nihongi* 続日本紀 V. 3, Shin Nihon Koten Bungaku Taikei 新日本古典文学大系 14, Iwanami Shoten 岩波書店, Tokyo, 1992, p. 61.

11. Harada Toshiaki 原田敏明 et al. tr., *Nihōn Ryoiki* 日本霊異記, Chū 中, Story No. 14, Tōyō Bunko 東洋文庫 V. 97, Heibonsha 平凡社, Tokyo, 1982, pp. 100-101.

12. *Genji Monogatari* 源氏物語 V. 1, Iwanami Koten Bungaku Taikei 岩波古典文学大系 V. 14, Iwanami Shoten 岩波書店, Tokyo, 1958, p. 81; Waley, Arthur, trans. *Genji Monogatari* V. 1, Charles E. Tuttle Company, Tokyo, 1993, p. 34; *Itsukushima Honji* 厳島本地, Zoku Gunshoruijū 続群書類従 V. 3(2), Heibonsha 平凡社, Tokyo, 1976, p. 553T.

13. Amano, Sadakage 天野信景, *Shiojiri* 塩尻 V. 2, Nihon Zuihitsu Taisei 日本随筆大成 3-14, Yoshikawa Kōbunkan 吉川弘文館, Tokyo, 1977, p. 447.

14. Gotō, Akio 後藤昭雄 et al., ed. *Kōdanshō*, *Chūgaishō*, *Fukego* 江談抄, 中外抄, 富家語, Shin Nihon Koten Bungaku Taikei 新日本古典文学大系 32, Iwanami Shoten 岩波書店, Tokyo, 1997, p. 121.

15. Ichiko, Teiji 市古貞次, trans. *Heike Monogatari* 平家物語 V. 2, Shinpen Nihon Koten Bungaku Zenshū 新編日本古典文学全集 30, Shōgakkan 小学館, Tokyo, 1979, pp. 44-46.

16. Nagahara, Keiji 永原慶二, ed. *Zenyaku Azuma Kagami* 全訳吾妻鏡 V. 1, Shinjinbitsu Ōraisha 新人物往来社, Tokyo, 1976, p. 122.

17. Koyama, Hiroshi 小山弘志 et al., trans. *Chikubushima* 竹生島, *Yōkyokushū* 謡曲集 V. 1; Shinpen Nihon Koten Bungaku Zenshū 新編日本古典文学全集 33, Shōgakkan 小学館, Tokyo, 1963, pp. 88-96.

18. Ichiko, Teiji 市古貞次 et al., eds *Bishamon no Honji* 毘沙門の本地, Muromachi Monogatarishū 室町物語集 V. 2, Iwanami Shoten 岩波書店, Tokyo, 1992, pp. 145, 189-91.

19. Hirata, pp. 10 T20-B7, 4 B15-16, 40 T8-11, 13 T20-B1.

20. Jōnen 静然, *Gyō-rin-shō* 行林抄, Taishō Shinshū Daizōkyō 大正新修大蔵経 V. 76, Tokyo, pp. 410M, 409T.

21. Hirata, p. 4 B9-14.

22. Daihōrin Sensho 大法輪選書, ed., *Bukkyō to Kamigami* 仏教と神々, Daihōrinkaku 大法輪閣, Tokyo, 1991, pp. 205-07.

23. Kūkai 空海, *Bonji Shittan Jimo narabini Shakugi* 空海著梵字悉曇字母并釈義, Taishō Shinshū Daizōkyō 大正新修大蔵経, V. 84, p. 362T.

24. Annen, p. 390B.

25. Ibid., p. 405M.

26. Myōkaku 明覚, *Shittan Yōketsu* 悉曇要訣, Taishō Shinshū Daizōkyō 大正新修大蔵経, V. 84, p. 527M-B.

27. Annen, pp. 384B - 385T.

28. Ibid., pp. 408T, 415B.

29. Ibid., p. 384T, 382T, 382B; Mabuchi Kazuo 馬渕和夫, *Nihon Ingakushi no Kenkyū* 日本韻学史の研究, Pt. 1, Rinsen Shoten 臨川書店, Kyoto, 1984, p. 408; Jiun 慈雲, *Jōjū Kichijōgi* 成就吉祥儀, Jiun Sonja Zenshū 慈雲尊者全集, V. 9(1), Shibunkaku 思文閣, Kyoto, 1974, p. 137.

30. Arai, Hakuseki 新井白石, *Dōbun Tsūkō* 同文通考, Kokugogaku Taikei 国語学大系, V. 5, Kokusho Kankōkai 国書刊行会, Tokyo, 1975, p. 160B, 166T.

    For instance, the syllable イ (*i*) came from the of the character 伊 with the same pronunciation.

31. Ibid.ō, pp. 171.

32. Ibid., p. 162B.

33. Tsukishima Hiroshi 築島裕, *Kokugo no Rekishi* 国語の歴史, Tokyo Daigaku Shuppankai 東京大学出版会, Tokyo, 1992, pp. 52-57.

    Other voicing sign innovations have also been discussed here.

34. Myōkaku, pp. 529T – M, p. 509M; Motoori, Norinaga 本居宣長, *Kanji Sanonkō* 漢字三音考, Kokugogaku Taikei 国語学大系, V. 3, Kokusho Kankōkai 国書刊行会, Tokyo, 1975, pp. 89-90.

35. Keichū 契沖, *Waji Seiranshō* 和字正濫鈔, Keichū Zenshū 契沖全集, V. 10, Iwanami Shoten 岩波書店, Tokyo, pp. 117 - 18, 1973.

36. Ibid., pp. 117 – 20.

Chapter 22

Buddhism and National Culture in Korea

Rhi, Ki-Yong

I. General Aspect

Buddhism has had a very important influence on the Korean national culture for more than 1600 years. At the time of the introduction of Buddhism from China to the Korean peninsula, the three kingdoms occupied the territory: kingdom of Koguryō in the North, kingdom of Paeckche in the South-West and the kingdom of Silla in the South-East. Koguryō introduced Buddhism in 372 A.D., Paeckche in 384 and Shilla adopted Buddhism in 527 as her official religion. The rulers of Koguryō and Paeckche accepted Buddhism without hesitation considering it a powerful means for the protection of their kingdoms and royal families. But the Silla royal court was split and serious efforts were required to get the unanimous agreement for the adoption of Buddhism among the aristocrats. The agreement was arrived at after the extraordinary event of a martyr, the death and miracle of young Yi-cha-don. Legend says that at the moment Yi-cha-don's neck was cut, white milk spouted from his neck instead of red blood under the rainfall of heavenly flowers and celestial music. For centuries the three kingdoms were in a struggle for hegemony of the territory. At last in 668, Silla defeated the two others and inaugurated the first unified nation state which existed until 917 or about two and half centuries.

The Buddhism of the Silla dynasty during the 7, 8, 9 centuries attained its peak in various ways. Mahāyāna Buddhist thought was studied and widely spread among the leading personalities. There were very scholarly monks such as Won-Kwang, Cha-Jang, Won-Hyo and Ui-Sang and so on. There were also kings and ministers as well as generals who were deeply aware of the Bodhisattva ideals. Most of them in their youth were members of the Hwarangdo groups of young elites who endeavoured to train themselves spiritually and physically for patriotic and altruistic service. So to speak, it was the age of the Hwarang (Flower Boys), who were the builders of a new nation deeply inspired by the Bodhisattva ideal. They had brought about the unification of three small kingdoms into one nation and it was these same elites who realized the brilliant, lofty, artistic creations and philosophical ideas. They believed firmly that their country was forever the Land of Buddha. They gave the country, mountains, capital, kings and royal family members the same names as those of Gotama Buddha's country, family and ideals. There was for example Queen Śrīmalādevī and her relatives' names were used; the word which designates the capital "So-Ra-Bol" (Seoul) came from the name of an Indian town Sāvatthi (Śravasti in Skt.). There was also Mt. Gṛdhrakuṭa (the Peak of Holy Eagle) and Mt. Vajra (the Diamond Mt. as indicated in the Avatamsakasūtra). A Buddhist historian of 14th century recorded that there was the firm belief of Shilla people on the existence of a rock on which the Buddha Kāśyapa sat for the meditation. Besides that the names of kings and the names of their reigns clearly demonstrated their ideals and goals. For all of these reasons we can presume the hidden merits of the spiritual leaders were enormously great. The most illustrious of those was Won-Hyo. Later we will specifically deal with this personality.

The glory and the light of Silla was fading gradually during its last century and finally disappeared under the rise of another sun. It was in 918. A general from a local town, Wang-Kon, took the majestic power to begin the reign of his family, the Koryo dynasty for some four and a half centuries.

Wang-Kon, the founder of new dynasty took for his dynasty the name of Koryo (an abbreviation of Kogurya), the name of Shilla's former rival kingdom. Koryo literally means "lofty and beautiful". Wang-Kon too was a fervent Buddhist who proclaimed his reign would be based upon the grace of the Lord Buddha. But his Buddhist faith was quite different from that of the Silla kings who stressed the Bodhisattva ideal. His mind was thoroughly imbued with faith in divination based on topography and in magic effects of various rites of tāntric character. Since then for the whole period of Koryo, magic rituals of the royal family and ruling clans became more and more increased. This tendency was certainly assisted through the infiltration of native Shamanistic superstitions which became so easy because of the theoretical gap these people had. Apparently the kingdom of Koryo was a perfect Buddhist kingdom. No single day was passed without any Buddhistic ritual events. The situation was very similar to the

Mediaeval Europe. The monks could interfere very often in political affairs playing bad roles and the temples became for some time the escapees' sanctuaries and agitation places. The Buddhism of Koryo was no longer a Mahāyānic Bodhisattva Buddhism which in principle emphasizes altruistic moral deeds and self purification of the mind.

The attempt to redress this kind of aberration was made by illustrious renovators such as Ui-Chon and Chi-Nul. Ui-Chon (1055-1101) urged his fellow monks of Koryo to be conscious of necessity of learning, as well as of meditation. For the same purpose he introduced the doctrine of T'ien-Tai from China and also undertook the total collection of Buddhist scriptures in Chinese translation, aiming at a wide diffusion of the righteous Dharma of Buddha. It was he who took the initiative to carve on the woodplates the whole Tripiṭaka. On the other hand, Chi-Nul (1158-1210) lived during the period in which the military clan of Choe seized power and ruled for sixty-four years. Chi-Nul was practically the founder of a new Zen movement. He organized a meditation group at Mt. Song-gwang-san; there he emphasized the equal importance of Zen meditation and philosophical learning. Chi-Nul's efforts were welcomed and supported by Choe's clan who understood at least the bad effect of blind devotion filled with esoteric elements. Since 1275 A.D. the Koryo royal court entered into the hands of Mongolian Emperors who were ruling the mainland China. The characteristics of their Buddhism was, as is already well known, very Shamanistic and tāntric. The Buddhism of Koryo, under this influence, became more and more Shamanistic and tāntric and finally it could not resist the violent attack from the newly introduced Neo-Confucian scholar-aristocrats.

During the Yi dynasty Buddhism became the object of disgrace after it lost all its privileges. The dark age for Buddhism began in 1392. The new era was that of Neo-Confucianism; and its chauvinistic character was widely known. Buddhism was oppressed with the political power and the philosophical despotism introduced in the peninsula, which still deeply affects Korean mentality even today. It is well-known fact that partial attachment to any particular dogma is never praised in *Buddha śāsana*. There were the monks who attempted to harmonize the ideals of two religions. For example take the case of Hamho-Kihwa (1376-1433) who wrote essays on the subject. But it was not easy to convince stubborn dogmatists. If the Buddhism of that period could survive without completely dying, it was because on the one hand there were the devotional members of royal family who still expected the graces of Lord Buddha and Bodhisattvas for their tragedic misfortunes brought on by the power struggle and on the other hand thanks to the strenuous efforts of monks to preserve the tradition of Buddha Dharma. After a few decades of time in which all the possibilities of ordination in the monkhood was extirpated, a rare chance came in the middle of 16th century to disseminate the new seeds for the future revival of Buddhism. A fervent mother princess who took the regency of her young king reintroduced the official examination system for monkhood and this reestablished the succession of lineage for the later monks of Korea. As the result of this event two remarkable masters were born: Chongho-Hyu-Jong (1524-1604), Buyong-Yonggwan (1485-1571). All the monks of Yi dynasty were the direct discendants of these two. Even today this traditional lineage of monkhood is respected as something very important following the custom of Chinese Zen sect.

Principally Buddhism of Yi dynasty was Zen Buddhism which pretends to be the legitimate heir of the 6th Patriarch, Chinese master Huei-Neng through the intermediate of Thaego-Bowu (monk of Koryo, 1301-1382) and Lintsi-Yihiuan (died in 866 or 867), which is still a matter of controversy today.

The most remarkable contribution made by the Buddhists for the kingdom and society of Yi dynasty Choson was their active, voluntary participation in the military operations against the invaders of Japan and Manchuria and their successful efforts for the protection of the homeland. We might say that this is contrary to the Buddhist ideal of *ahiṁsā*, non-violence, but also one might understand that it was an unavoidable Dharma to them to realize in such an extraordinary situation. No one could efficiently mobilize collective force including the royal armed force, to save the mother country and its people. It seems to us, the Buddhists of today, very ironical to see that most neglected, alienated people of one epoch were the most indispensable people who made a truly precious contribution to the same epoch. This was the first ordeal to overcome for the Yi dynasty monks after Buddhist rehabilitation since the end of 16th century until the middle of 17th century. Inspite of such an extraordinary contribution, the treatment of Confucian dogmatists toward Buddhist monks was never ameliorated. Thus, the spiritual and cultural standard of monks who followed these general monks in later periods, for about three centuries, could not recover their wounded hearts. During these lapses of time Catholicism was introduced in 1685 and one century later Protestantism followed.

In 1910, on the eve of Japanese military occupation, a prophetic poet-monk Han-yong-woon began to talk about the necessity and the tasks of modernization for traditional Korean Buddhism. Today people of Korea generally take it for granted, but at that time his cry went unheeded. Inside, sleep was deep, outside circumstances were too dull. And the land and people with all of its long history and culture fell into the hands of Japanese colonial masters; since then Korean Buddhism was to follow inevitably the intention of those who wanted to Japanize the Korean tradition. One of the effects of this was the apparition of the system of married monkhood which still provokes in Korean Bhikkhus strong animosity.

We are now witnessing the post-war period under the strong pressure of Western civilization, which demands the real awakening of Buddhists who are expected to play a greater role for the genuine prosperity of future of mankind. Now with this vision, I would like to look back on our traditions picking up only one example, the essence and value of Won-Hyo's thought.

II. The Essence and Value of Won-Hyo's Thought

Won-Hyo (literally means "Primordial Dawn") was born in 617 in Silla. It was about one hundred years after the death of Won-Kwang ("Perfect Light"), the pioneer of Buddhist philosophy who, for the first time in Korean history, embodied the philosophies of Laotse, Chuangtse and Confucius in the light of Saddharma-puṇḍarīka's Ekayāna (One Vehicle) insight. Won-Hyo, even though he could not meet him directly in person, seems to be profoundly influenced by his writings which emphasized mainly the Bodhisattva ideal. Won-Kwang was the one who gave the guidelines to the Hwarang, Flower Boys, the elite groups of Silla youth. Won-Hyo also passed his boyhood in this group, keeping in mind the "Secular Pañcasīla", Won-Kwang had already dictated. It was a kind of situation ethics, a version of Bodhisattvasīla for the particular people in that particular situation. He taught them to observe the following five principles: (1) Be selective when you are obliged to kill any living being, (2) Be faithful and honest to your masters, (3) Be kind and merciful toward your parents, (4) Be confidential to your friends and (5) Do not retreat at the battlefield.

In his twenties Won-Hyo entered into the traditional Saṁgha and gradually gained the reputation as one of the most learned monks. At the age of 52 he could see Silla's unification of the three kingdoms, for which his contribution as the nation-wide spiritual guru was generally admitted. He wrote during his 70 years of life about 82 titles which comprise 282 kiuans (volumes in Chinese style), mostly the commentaries on Mahāyāna scriptures. They were the commentaries on Avatamsaka, Saddharmapuṇḍarīka, Mahāparinirvāṇa, Laṅkāvatāra, Sandhinirmocana, Prajñāpāramitā, Vajrasamādhi, Suvarṇaprabhāsottamarāja, Sukhāvatīvyūha, Vimalakīrtinirdeśa, Śrīmālādevīsimhanāda, Mahāyānasaṁgrahabhāṣya, Mahāyānottaratantraśāstra, Yogācāryabhūmīśāstra, Mahāyānasraddhotpādaśāstra, Madhyāntavibhāga and so on. It is written in his biography that he had no definite teacher, that is to say he was a liberal creative thinker. Seemingly he had in his mind several examples as his idealistic model. For instance the figures like Seng-Chao (Chinese, 374-414) or Che-Kong (Chinese, 5c.) existed whose liberalism was quite akin to Laotse and Chuangtse. It appears that he was not following blindly patterns, which seemed to him probably too indulgent. He was rigid at the same time as he was free. He was free to speculate on Dharma, he was demanding of himself to fulfil his responsibility. Around the age of 44, he gave up his Srāvaka-hood, and entered family life as a common person in order to work in a common secular way in society. He himself wanted to live the genuine life of a Bodhisattva dropping off all the elements of vain decoration.

When he was studying Dharma, his basic concern was the problem of Yon-Gi (pratītyasamutpāda, interdependent co-origination) which is forever the structure of the universe. According to him, Yon-Gi is not only the principle of human affairs but also the principle of the whole universe, the *Dharmadhātu*, exactly like Avatamsakasūtra's teaching. It is a well-known fact among Korean people that Won-Hyo was the proponent of peace, of unity. The word most frequently used by him and which became later his own surname given by a king of Koryo was *Hwa-Jaeng, Peaceful Integration through Harmonization of Disputes.* Won-Hyo believed with conviction that the *Dharmadhātu* is One and the dharmas are nothing but one *Dharmadhātu*. Saying this he meant that someone who has the clear insight realize that all the apparent phenomenon of this universe are nothing but the Yon-Gi, "mutually dependent co-origination harmoniously integrated without any conflict", in Korean expression Bopkye-Muae-Yongi. To Won-Hyo, this was the *Dharmakāya*, the Essential Body of Buddha. "Faith" for him was his conviction to this ultimate reality. To explain this ultimate reality, he cites often the famous expression of Avatamsaka: One is all, all is one; one in all, all in one. One in Korean language is "Hana", from which derives the word "Hana-Nim", the God; Nim being the postfix which means "lord" Hananim is the personification of the abstract concept. It is a personal presumption that Won-Hyo, for his extraordinary erudition could not fail to notice the wonderful remarks on the meaning of *Ātman*, one of fourfold *guṇas* of

Mahāparinirvāṇa *sūtra* (*Nitya, Sukha, Ātman, Vimala*), The *sūtra* says that *Ātman* is *Maheśvara*. This *Maheśvara* was often translated as "Great Freedom" or "Great Self-Existence" in the Chinese Tripiṭaka. If we combine these two, exactly we will arrive at the conclusion: Hana, One or Oneness means the Great Freedom, the Great Self-Existence, that is *the Process Harmoniously Integrated Without any Conflict,* the Bopkye-Muae-Yongi.

Won-Hyo was keenly aware of the tragic conflicts in secular human society. He even lived in a society fighting among small three Kingdoms. He was completely different than the calm Zen masters who retired in the deep mountain sides far away from the secular villages and towns. He was attacked from various sides by those who were envious or jealous. In his biography, the historian wrote that Won-Hyo was the enemy of ten thousand people. Won-Hyo did not escape from such surroundings and he did not blame the society. On the contrary, he had a completely different view with regard to the people of his surroundings and he saw the need to work among them and for them, to explain the Dharma which shows the way to attain the ultimate reality, Oneness, Hana. So he created a double objective to realize: to return everybody's scattered mind into the depth, the pure harmonious peaceful comprehensive One-mindness and to do altruistic service to all living beings (*sattva*). The two, undeniably converge to form the same goal, that is to realize a society of harmonious integration without any conflict where nobody is alienated not only by men but also by the nature. It is not to say that every human individual is destined to be the same in capacities and to have the same right to obtain the same merits. All the success and failure only depend upon the "in" (Korean word to express *hetu*, the cause one makes by oneself in principle) and "yon" (*pratyaya*, the different ties or relationship, which are also to be made by oneself).

He looked at the world or the universe including human society as a huge scale *Saṅgha* (Community), which is essentially destined to be the process of "harmoniously integrated interrelationship", but actually which shows the disintegrated aspects caused by the selfish minds of living beings (*sattva*). He saw as the most fundamental reason the unawareness of the reality by men who by consequence could not understand the original, primordial Oneness of the different dharmas. And he never thought that any particular definite religion or philosophy can pretend to be unique and of absolute value. In his essay on Saddharmapuṇḍarīka, he clearly declares that one can find the truth everywhere, in everything, in everyone. He firmly believed that every living being derives from the "seeds of Buddhahood (perfect image of human integration)", the *Tathāgatagarbha*.

Consequently his moral conception could not be any formalistic, clerical and fugitive one. The kings and ministers of Shilla, once young Flower Boys, indeed proved, by their concrete works, how Won-Hyo's influence was great for them.

Won-Hyo too loved, like the other Flower Boys (Hwarang), the Bodhisattva Maitreya, the Future Buddha, who was believed to be residing in the *Tuṣita* Heaven. This was often represented as the symbol of *Maitrī* (Mercifulness). It seems to us his faith in Heaven was not real but symbolical, since his conception of the *dhātu* (realm) was not ontological but epistemological. His emphasis was always put on the *samādhi*, spiritual concentration or rather the spiritual concentration which accomplishes *Advaita* between the subject and the object. Practice of this kind of *samādhi* would be realized everywhere and everytime. The Bodhisattva Maitreya was the symbol of this *samādhi* from which only the truly altruistic virtues were derived. So to speak, Won-Hyo's Buddhism was surpassing even this category of Buddhism in order to become a more universal principle of life.

During the whole history of Korea, sometimes the ideal of Won-Hyo was not well appreciated, but as we have already seen it was just like the sunshine which was hidden for those who had blind eyes, shining forever its universal light for everybody and every time. He was really a wonderful fruit that was grown on the Korean soil after the dissemination of the Indian grain. I personally hope as one of his unfitting disciples that once again this fruit-grain could grow and flourish in order to illuminate this dark age of selfish materialism.

Chapter 23

A Brief History of Vietnamese Buddhism

Thích Minh Châu

Vietnamese Buddhism has a long history of more than 2000 years. Its origin dates back to the 3rd century B.C., when numerous Buddhist missions were sent abroad by Emperor Asoka to disseminate Lord Buddha's teachings in such distant countries beyond the borders of India as those in Africa, West and Central Asia as well as South-East Asia including Malaysia, Burma, Thailand, Laos, Cambodia and North Vietnam, which was known then as Giao Châu (modern Bac Ninh province).

Vietnamese Buddhism can be roughly divided into 4 periods:

1. From its beginning in ancient times to the 10th century AD.,
2. Its Golden Age from the 11th century to the 14th century,
3. Its decline in the 15th century and its restoration in later centuries,
4. Contemporary Vietnamese Buddhism and its activities in the present situation.

I.Vietnamese Buddhism from Ancient Times to the 10th Century

It is believed that among the three Buddhist centres of ancient China (Lo Yang, Ring Ch'eng and Luy Lâu), Luy Lâu centre in Giao Châu (South China) was then the first to be founded under the Han Dynasty (around the early part of the first century AD). Luy Lâu, the capital of Giao Châu, which was then a Chinese vassal, was on the main trade route between India and China; therefore undoubtedly it became a favourable and prosperous resort for Indian pioneer missionaries to stay and preach the Buddha's teachings before continuing their journey to the North.

The Order of Giao Châu monks was founded before Buddhism spread to other places. From the evidence of historical records under the Latter Eastern Han Dynasty, we may conclude that Luy Lâu was the first to adopt the new faith from Indian monks who gradually found their way to the North, i.e., South China and the Yangtse River Valley, and then to Lo Yang, the capital of China, where the two other Buddhist centres were successively founded. According to the documents recorded in THIỀN UYỂN TẬP ANH (an Anthology of the Most Talented Figures in Ch'an Park), our most ancient Buddhist literary collection, Master K'ang Seng Hui, a monk of Sogdiana origin was the first Buddhist Master at Luy Lâu Centre. He was born in Giao Châu, where he was received into the Order of Monks afterwards. He became the most famous monk scholar who translated a large number of Buddhist Canonical books into Chinese (Han characters) and later he visited Nanking, where he built the first pagoda and preached the Dhamma. Besides Master K'ang Seng Hui, there were many famous Indian monk scholars such as Mahajivaka, Kalaruci (Tche Kiang Liang) and a Chinese scholar Mao Pa (Mui Tsu), who immigrated to Giao Châu and studied Buddhism under Indian monks there. At that time, there were about 20 pagodas with at least 15 translations of Buddhist Text Books and 500 monks at Luy Lâu center. "The Buddha's Sutta in 42 Sections" which appeared at Giao Châu in the 2nd century AD, is believed to be the first selection of Suttas translated into Chinese at Luy Lâu.

Therefore, one of the characteristics of Vietnamese Buddhism in ancient times is that it had been introduced by Indian missionaries into Giao Châu long before it spread to China. The literary evidence in the above translation proved that in its very beginning, Vietnamese Buddhism adopted the fundamentals of Orthodox Buddhism from Indian monks and in later centuries with the development of Buddhism in China, it received another trend of Buddhist thought, the Mahāyāna doctrine, especially Chinese Ch'an Buddhism.

Another salient feature of Vietnamese Buddhism is that it has been closely connected with national life and Buddhist monks have made their active contribution to the construction and protection of their country. The best learned class of society Vietnamese monks practised their religion side by side with common people and were on friendly terms with members of other religions such as Taoism, Confucianism. A large number of Ch'an Masters were great Confucianist scholars who, besides their religious duty, played an important part in social life. They might have made use of favourable conditions of Chinese Buddhism under the Sui (in the 6th century AD) and the T'ang dynasties (in the 7th and 8th centuries) in order to develop Vietnamese Buddhism and further a national movement for liberation from Chinese yoke.

The first period of Đại Việt's independence began with King Lý-Nam-Đế, who highly honoured Buddhism and used to consult Buddhist monks and follow their advice on religious and worldly affairs in protecting the young nation against foreign invasions. Finally came the glorious victory at Bạch Đằng River in 930, which opened a new page of Đại Việt history.

II. The Period of National Independence from the 11th Century to the 14th Century: The Golden Age of Vietnamese Buddhism

The 10th century marked a new era of both the independence of Đại Việt nation and the prosperity of Vietnamese Buddhism. Many Buddhist monks were engaged in politics under the Đinh (968-980), the Former Lê (980-1009), the Lý (1010-1225) and the Trần (1225-1400) Dynasties. Some were appointed both "State Counsellors and National Teachers" such as Ch'an Masters Khuông Việt, Pháp Thuận, Viên Chung and above all, Ch'an Master Vạn Hạnh, who made his great contribution to the enthroning of King Lý-Thái-Tổ, the founder of the Lý reign, and was later granted the title "Sangha President".

As a monk of great talent, he devoted himself to the teaching of the Dhamma and the construction of the kingdom; yet, he remained aloof from worldly life. His philosophical attitude was beautifully expressed in his serene and noble utterance before his death: (Our personal existence is like a lightning flash that passes into nothingness. All plants prosper in Spring and wither in Autumn. Despite all the ups and downs of fortune, we feel no fear, for these are mere dewdrops on the grasstips).

The prosperity of Vietnamese Buddhism reached its height under the Lý and the Trần Dynasties during 4 centuries, King Lý-Thái-Tổ and his successors were devout Buddhist supporters and patrons who officially recognized Buddhism as state religion and ruled righteously in accordance with the TEN DUTIES of a king (Dasarājadhamma). They showed their great compassion and tolerance towards their people, even criminals, prisoners and foreign enemies or rebels. By order of the kings, thousands of pagodas and stupas were built all around the country, among which One-Pillar Pagoda (in Hà Nội) was the most famous. Some of the kings resigned their power after a time of reigning, and became Ch'an Masters such as Lý-Thái-Tổ, Lý Thánh Tôn, Lý Anh Tôn, Lý Cao Tôn, Trần Thái Tôn, and in particular, King Trần Nhân Tôn, a great Buddhist scholar who, after his two victories over the Mongols (Yuang Meng), abdicated and became the founder of the Trúc Lâm (Bamboo Grove) at Mount Yên Tử. It was the first Vietnamese Ch'an Sect that had ever been founded and the king was consecrated as the first Patriarch of Trúc Lâm Ch'an sect of VietNam, the others being Vinitaruci (an Indian monk), Wu Yan T'ung (a Chinese), and Tsao T'ang (a Chinese). It was under his leadership that the three Ch'an sects (Vinitaruci, Wu Yan T'ung-Speechless Understanding, and Tsao T'ang-Hermitage) were unified into one Vietnamese Ch'an Sect.

During the Golden Age, Vietnamese Buddhist thought, literature and architecture were best developed in poetry, in prose and in various works of arts. Above all, the achievement of engraving Buddhist scriptures, which lasted 24 years (1295-1319) at Quỳnh Lâm Pagoda under the auspices of King Trần Anh Tôn was the most influential one. The great task was carried out by Master Pháp Loa, the second Patriarch of the Trúc Lâm Ch'an Sect, alongside hundreds of monks and lay followers, making over 5000 engravings of Buddhist Scriptures including those composed by the Trúc Lâm Sect. Master Pháp Loa made his best contribution to the growth of over 15,000 monks in more than 200 Trúc Lâm monasteries then. Next to Pháp Loa was Huyền Quang, thus forming the Trinity of Trúc Lâm Patriarchs, the symbol of the Buddhist Golden Age. Master Huyền Quang, a great monk scholar and poet, led a secluded life at Mount Côn Sơn, teaching the Dhamma, practising Ch'an meditation, and composing poems after 20 years of serving the Court.

What is essential of Trúc Lâm Ch'an Buddhism is that it lays the emphasis on the mental cultivation whatever condition one may live. It is a mind-oriented training for every Buddhist, whether he is a monk or a lay follower. This way of practising the Dhamma is best expressed in a hymn entitled "Cư Trần Lạc Đạo" (Taking Delight in Religion While Dwelling in the World) composed by King Trần Nhân Tôn, Trúc Lâm First Patriarch, who concluded the hymn with the following reputable verse:

(Let's take delight in religion in whatever condition we may live.

Let's eat when hungry and sleep when tired.

Within ourselves lies the gem, so let's give up searching elsewhere.

When our mind is detached from the surroundings, there is no more question of concentration).

Another interesting feature of Lý-Trần Buddhism is its trend of blending Buddhism with Taoism and Confucianism. This growing tendency of combining the three religions together in a harmonious way resulted in producing experts in the three branches of learning. Many of them were Ch'an Masters, kings and court mandarins who played a very active role as leaders in several struggles against the Sung's army and later the Mongols' invasions. In peace-time as well as in war time, these Buddhists made their great effort to bring welfare and happiness to their nation. In the period of unprecedented prosperity of Vietnamese Buddhism, both Taoism and Confucianism were also well-developed and very popular with all social classes.

III. The Decline of Buddhism in the 15th Century and its Restoration in Later Centuries

By the end of the Trần Dynasty, as Confucianist scholars gained their monopoly at court, Buddhism gradually lost its influence especially after the invasion of the Ming in 1414, Đại Việt became a Chinese vassal again, and the Ming rulers oppressed Vietnamese Buddhists by confiscating most of Buddhist text books in Đại Việt, then sending them to Chin-Lang and destroying a large number of pagodas. Moreover, numerous talented monks were sent to China in exile. All that lay in the policy of assimilating the Vietnamese into the Chinese and spreading Confucianism as the only dominating doctrine while keeping Buddhism and Taoism under strict control.

After a ten-year fight against the Ming, finally came the victory won by Lê Lợi, the national hero who founded the Latter Lê. But Buddhism was in unfavourable condition then: By King Lê Thái Tổ's order, Buddhist monks had to pass an examination or they had to return to secular life. Confucianism had a great influence on the king and especially on the intellectuals of the time since it was the best way leading to power and glory at Court. What remained fortunate was that Buddhism had been so deeply rooted in all classes of people that they constantly kept their faith alive in hard times by building pagodas, temples and reprinting Buddhist Scriptures despite Confucianist scholars' strong opposition and the kings' exclusive order.

In the 16th century and during the Trịnh-Nguyễn Conflict lasting about 300 years, the Trịnh and Nguyễn Lords tried to restore Buddhism in order to win people's heart. Many of them were devout Buddhists who decreed the building or renovating of lots of well-known pagodas or stupas such as Thiên Mụ Pagoda in Huế (buy Lord Nguyễn Hoàng's decree in 1601), Thiên Thể (Bảo Giác) Pagoda, An Tôn (Từ Đàm) Pagoda... In the 17th century, a number of Chinese monks came to Vietnam founded such Ch'an sects as Lin Chi and T'sao Tung Sect. They were warmly received by the Trịnh who, at the same time, encouraged the restoration of Trúc Lâm Ch'an sect.

One of the brilliant torch-lights of Vietnamese Buddhist Sangha in North Vietnam (Đành Ngoài) was Ch'an Master Chân Nguyên, who was conferred the title ȘSangha President¿ by king Lê Dụ Tông. The Master and his excellent disciples Như Hiền, Như Trung made their great effort to restore the Trúc Lâm Ch'an Sect tradition and reprint numerous literary works composed by Trúc Lâm Patriarchs. Another outstanding figure was Ch'an Master Hương Hải, who preached the Dhamma at Nguyệt Đường monastery to thousands of disciples. Some of them became very famous and were later appointed Sangha Presidents.

In the South (Đàng Trong), the Nguyễn Lords heartily welcomed numerous Ch'an Masters from China. They founded the Lin Chi Sect and the T'sao Tung Sect and built pagodas in many provinces while the territory extended southwards. Besides, Vietnamese Ch'an Masters tried their best to restore Vietnamese Buddhism; among them, Ch'an Master Liễu Quán was considered the leader of the Buddhist restoration. He preached the Dhamma in many provinces and was highly esteemed by the Nguyễn. He belonged to the Lin Chi Sect, but his teaching was coloured by Vietnamese way of thinking since he tried to remodel the religion imported from China, making it completely Vietnamese and lively in such aspects as rites and hymns or poems. His chief disciples continued to spread this way of teaching throughout the South and the influence of this Ch'an Sect could be found even in the Buddhist Restoration in the 20th century.

From the beginning of the French colonialists' domination over Vietnam, the condition of Buddhism was obviously worse. Under the Nguyễn Dynasty, Buddhism got violent opposition from courtiers who were Confucianist scholars while it was neglected by most of the kings who were not zealous Buddhist supporters. In addition, as a time-honoured religion, Buddhism was confronted with many difficulties from the colonialist government.

IV. Contemporary Vietnamese Buddhism and its Activities at Home and Abroad

Under the influence of Chinese Buddhist Restoration in 1920, there was a movement for the Restoration of Vietnamese Buddhism headed by Master Khánh Hòa and many Buddhist associations were established in South VN, central VN and North VN from 1931 to 1934. The Buddhist Reformation received great approval from Buddhists especially the intellectuals in all over the country, but it was interrupted by World War II.

In 1948, the United VN Buddhist Association came into being and it resumed its activities in Hà Nội. Many Buddhist magazines and Vietnamese translations of Buddhist books were issued then. In Huế, the Most Venerable Elder Giác Tiên and Doctor Lê Đình Thám, a lay Buddhist scholar, founded a Buddhist Institute at Trúc Lâm Pagoda, then "The Buddhist Association of An Nam" at Từ Quang Pagoda and two Buddhist schools for monks and nuns. It was Dr. Lê Đình Thám who made his best contribution to the Buddhist Restoration by disseminating the Buddha's teachings in Vietnamese, founding various Buddhist youth organisations and translating the Suramgama Sūtra into Vietnamese. He was, in fact, the spirit of the Buddhist Restoration then.

In 1951, a National Buddhist Conference held in Hue aimed at unifying all Buddhist Associations and re-organising the Sangha's activities. Besides, it approved the participation of Vietnamese Buddhists in the World Fellowship of Buddhists (WFB) founded in Colombo in 1950.

From 1954, after the division of VN into two regions by Geneva Agreement, Vietnamese Buddhists in the South suffered from the religious discrimination and restrictions imposed by the Diệm Regime until the day when its oppression grew stronger and the non-violent Buddhist demonstrations broke out all over the country, the Bodhisattva Thích Quảng Đức's self-sacrifice (by burning himself alive for the cause of religion) followed by those of other Buddhist martyrs paved the way for the overthrow of the Diệm Regime in 1963. In 1975, after the Liberation Day of the South, there was a movement led by the Most Venerable Thích Trí Thủ to unify all Vietnamese Buddhist sects and organisations and then the VN Buddhist Sangha was founded in 1981. The VN Buddhist Sangha headed by the Most Venerable Dhamma Patriarch Thích Đức Nhuận approved an action program for national cooperation and harmony among all Buddhist sects, disseminating the Dhamma at its best so as to make known its special features, establishing a system of monastic education and promoting friendship among world Buddhist organisations for peace on earth.

In 1981, the Institute of Higher Buddhist Studies was established in Hà Nội, and in 1984, another one in Hồ Chí Minh City. Their purpose is to train a new generation of well-qualified monks and nuns so that they can effectively serve the VN Buddhist Sangha in various activities. The monk and nun students are instructed in both canonical and non-canonical subjects include the Doctrines of three main Buddhist schools: the Theravāda (Orthodox Buddhism), the Sarvāstivāda (the Theory of the Pan-Realists) and the Mahāyāna (Developing Buddhism). Graduate students can continue their studies at home or abroad in order to become researchers at the VN Buddhist Research Institute founded in 1989.

The VN Buddhist Research Institute as a new field of activity of the VN Buddhist Sangha undertakes the important responsibility of elucidating the Buddha's teachings, emphasising creativeness in the Dhamma dissemination in accordance with the social and scientific progress of our time. Moreover, it tries its best to widen world Buddhist activities and promote exchanges of Vietnamese Buddhist culture with those of other countries.

The leadership of the VN Buddhist Research Institute consists of the Most Venerable Elder Thích Thiện Siêu as Vice Rector in charge of the Department of Vietnamese Buddhism and the Venerable Dr. Thích Thiện Châu (at Trúc Lâm Pagoda, France) as Vice Rector in charge of the Department of world Buddhism.

In addition, there are other Departments such as The Department of Buddhist Specialties, The Department of Monastic Education, and above all, The Department of Translating and Publishing the Tipitaka (The Buddhist Canon) into Vietnamese. The great task of translating The Tipitaka from Pali, English and Chinese into Vietnamese, and publishing the Vietnamese Tipitaka has been under way since 1991. It will take about 2 decades to fulfil the assignment.

As far as world activities are concerned, the VN Buddhist Sangha's (VBS) delegations attended the 6th and 7th ABCP general conferences and the Most Venerable Dr. Thích Minh Châu was elected Vice President of the ABCP Leadership and President of the VN ABCP National centre. In 1984, the VBS delegation attended the Round-Table Conference in New Delhi and in particular, the VBS and the ABCP National Centre hosted the Conference of the ABCP Executive Council and the International Secretariat in Hà Nội in 1985. In 1986, the International Year of Peace, two seminars on the theme "Buddhism and Peace" were held in Hà Nội and Hồ Chí Minh City. In recent years, many VBS delegations have attended religious seminars or conferences held in different countries such as India, Sri Lanka, Japan, Australia, Rome, France, Taiwan...

Conclusion

Throughout twenty centuries in the long history of VN, Vietnamese Buddhism has been closely linked with the survival of the nation, whether in its rise and fall. Since the early days of its introduction, the mind of Vietnamese Buddhists has been so well imbued with the Buddha's teachings about love, tolerance and sympathetic understanding that Vietnamese Buddhism has been able to co-exist in peace with other religions for over 2000 years. On the one hand, generations of Vietnamese monks and nuns and lay followers, unknown or well known, have somehow participated in making it a unique Vietnamese religion coloured with Vietnamese ways and customs. On the other hand, Vietnamese Buddhism has had a great influence on Vietnamese literature, art, music, architecture and Buddhism, so to speak, has become a part of Vietnamese life.

Chapter 24

The Advent of Buddhism in Vietnam

Nguyễn Xuân Vinh

Introduction

Like most South and South-East Asian countries, Vietnam had welcomed Buddhism at a very early time. Buddhism was introduced into the country over a period of several centuries. It is difficult, however, to determine exactly its date. Scholars have put forth many historical documents relating to it. This article is an attempt to make a survey on the advent of Buddhism in Vietnam through possible historical sources.

Geographically, Giao Châu (Chiao-chou) or Giao Chỉ (Chiao-chih), present-day Vietnam, was situated on the Indo-Chinese peninsula. It was bordered not only by southern countries, such as Phù Nam, Chân Lạp, Chăm Ba (Campa), which had an influence of Indian culture and language (Sanskrit),[1] but also by China on its northern frontier. So, Giao Châu had occupied combination of both the most ancient civilizations of Asia: Indian and Chinese, and had thus been appreciably influenced by these two cultures. Moreover, Giao Châu had got the way direct to India by the sea route; hence it was subject to influences of Indian civilization earlier than Chinese, even though in ancient time it had been for many centuries a province of the Chinese empire.[2] Although Vietnam was under the Chinese domination over 1000 years, which had thereby much influenced its language and culture, Vietnamese Buddhism has still maintained some words as *Bụt (Buddha)*, *Thiền (Dhyāna)*, etc. that came from Sanskrit, instead of *Fo* and *Ch'an* of China respectively. It is said that "Giao Châu ('intersectant region') had been the intersection of the religious movements of India (Brahmanism, Buddhism), China (Confucianism, Taoism), and the aboriginal country (Đông Sơn with Copper-Drum, Lạch Trường with Ancient Tomb, etc.). All had domiciled together in an attempt to adapt and integrate so that they all would have been merged into a Vietnamese religion."[3]

From the background above, Vietnamese Buddhism must have had a distinctive position at its beginning. Then, when and how was the arrival of Buddhism into Vietnam? Who were the first missionaries there? And which doctrines were prevailing at that time? These are necessary to be brought out for investigating the religion at the beginning of it. The following are some investigative views in which the scholars and historians are interested.

Vietnamese Buddhism After the Propagation of Aśoka Abroad

a) We do know that after the Third Council of Buddhism (in the 3rd century BC), Emperor Aśoka carried his message of Buddhism far beyond the limits of his empire, and his missions permanently determined the religious history of a large part of the world. One of his missions, led by Uttara and Sona, was sent to Suvaṇṇabhūmi, the gold-bearing land. It is supposed whether this land might have been South-East Asia, that is to say, including Giao Chỉ at that time?[4] This question has been proposed by scholars with some relevant data.

According to *Ch'ien Han Shu, Hou Han Shu*, archeological data, and several early sources, the ports of Vietnam were bustling with trade during the first centuries A.D.[5] Indian traders and even merchants from the Roman Empire were already making the trip by sea to the ports in Giao Châu (Tonkin). Accordingly, such ports must have come into existence beforehand. At the same time, we also know that Aśoka had made use of the channels of communication, both commercial and diplomatic, that had existed from the time of Chandragupta, to convey the treasures of Buddhism abroad in all directions. Besides this, during the period when Aśoka invaded Kāliṇga on the eastern coast, number of monks and laymen in order to save their life immigrated to overseas countries by sea routes. With the various above mentioned motives, Indian Buddhists might have arrived in Giao Châu at that period.

b) Significantly, many Chinese and Vietnamese historical documents conduce to interesting similarities for the date of Vietnamese Buddhism in this period. The earlier historical works, regrettably, have been lost, and the existing texts were compiled very lately, over thousand years after. However, more auspicious than this, the better part of the earlier material is of China being helpful to our research (from ca. the late 4th century A.D. on).

Hu Shih, a great Chinese historian, holds that Buddhism had arrived in Giao Châu very early, perhaps c. 400-500 years before the existence

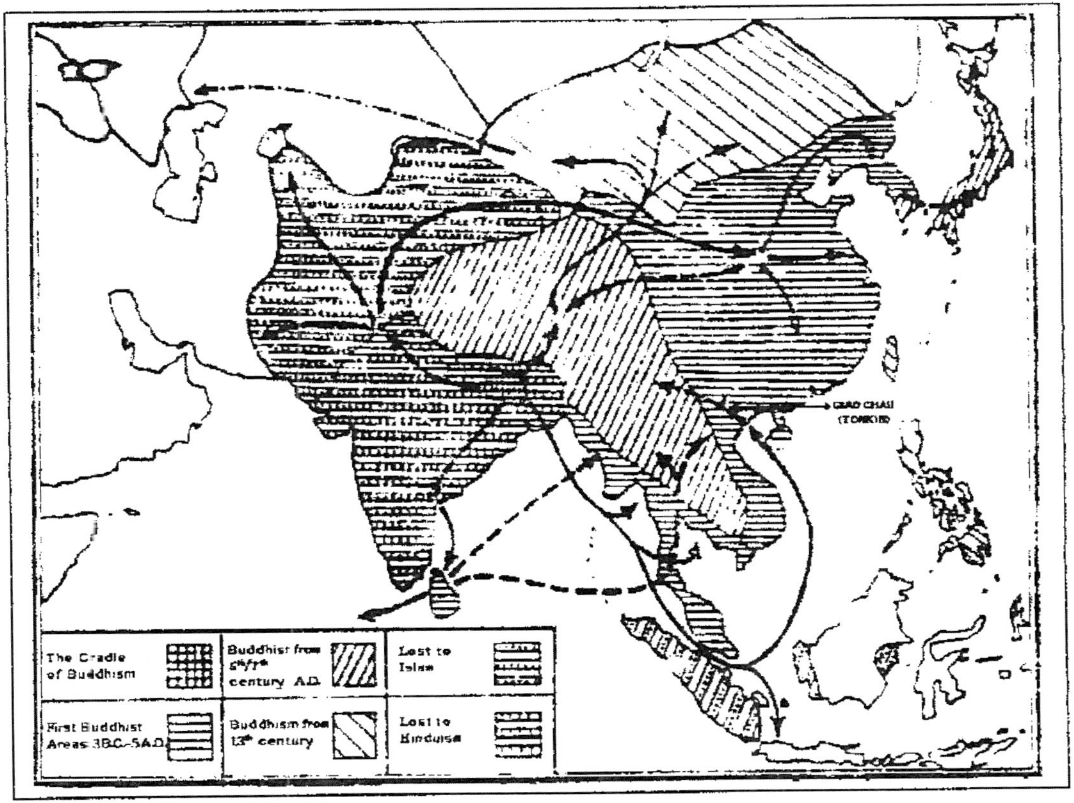
GIAO CHAU
(TONKIN)
The Cradle of Buddhism
Buddhist from 6th/7th century A.D.
Lost to Islam
First Buddhist Areas 3B.C.-5A.D.
Buddhism from 13th century
Lost to Hinduism

of *Mou-tzu li-huo lun* at the end of the second century A.D.[6] An early historical text of Vietnamese Buddhism, *Thiền Uyển Tập Anh Ngữ Lục (Anthology of the Zen Garden)* (the early 14th century), mentions the date of Buddhist introduction into Vietnam by means of the conversation, which was repeated in Vietnam by National Preceptor Thông Biện to Empress Dowager Ỷ Lan (1096), between T'an Ch'ien (a Chinese bonze, 542-607) and Chinese Emperor Wen: "The area of Giao Châu has long been in communication with India. Early on, when the Buddha-Dharma came to China and still had not been established, yet in Luy Lâu more than twenty precious temples were built, more than five hundred monks were ordained, and fifteen volumes of scriptures were translated. Thus Buddhism had entered Giao Châu before it reached Chiang-tung."[7]

However, such a conversation does not make us identify the date of the introduction of Buddhism into Chiang-tung, but it suggests some early time for the advent of the religion in Giao Châu. In his *The History of Vietnamese Buddhism,*[8] Prof. Lê Mạnh Thát, a modern Vietnamese historian, finds several pieces of valuable historical data, and then he pieces together the date of Buddhist introduction into Giao Châu. The story "Nhất Dạ Trạch" in *Lĩnh Nam Trích Quái (The Strange Stories of Lĩnh Nam)* (the late 14th century), another early text, is considered as the crucial foundation for his argument. It may be rendered as follows:

> "...Đồng Tử and his wife, Tiên Dung, had established their business and had their commercial exchanges with trading foreigners, who had honestly regarded the couple as their proprietors. One day, a great businessman told Tiên Dung, "You should invest a bar of gold in precious goods so as to get ten in next year." The couple consulted together and agreed with that suggestion. Then Đồng Tử went out to sea with some foreign traders. Offshore, there was a mountain called Quỳnh Viên on which a hut was situated. When their vessel landed there to get fresh water, Đồng Tử called on the hut and met there a young bonze, named Phật Quang (*Buddhaprabhā?*). This bonze taught Buddhist doctrine to Đồng Tử. Then Đồng Tử decided to stay behind and gave all his gold to the traders to get goods, and request them to pick him up on their return. When Đồng Tử took leave of his master to go home, the bonze granted him a stick and a hat, saying "They were talismans." Once back to his native country, Đồng Tử communicated the doctrine to his wife. Thereafter, the couple gave up their occupations as traders and went forth to look for some teacher to learn the Dharma."[9]

According to Thát's investigation, the details in the story should have been historical events. The first formation of Vietnamese Buddhism could include Đồng Tử and Tiên Dung as the first Vietnamese Buddhists, Phật Quang as the first monk, and the doctrine of power and capacity.[10] Determining the date and place that Đồng Tử's conversion took place is really complicated, but he seeks to determine them by means of the relevant documents.[11] The place of the conversion, in the story, was on the mount of Quỳnh Viên, which is today suggestively located on Mt. Nam Giới in the South of the Sót estuary.[12] And the date should be under the reign of Hùng Nghi Vương, i.e., ca. 3rd–2nd centuries BC.[13] In conclusion for the story, he writes, "the mentioning of existence of pagodas and towers relating to Aśoka' time in Vietnam is considered to be the earliest information that should have implied the mission of Sona sent by Aśoka. Therefore, it is not gratuitous that Đồng Tử's conversion into Buddhism by monk Phật Quang was recorded in *Lĩnh Nam Trích Quái.*"[14] With several events that occurred around, before and after the Common Era, Thát's argument comes for the date of the advent of Vietnamese Buddhism in the 2nd century BC.[15]

In finding pagodas and towers relating to Emperor Aśoka in Vietnam, we may consider a quotation that is said to be in *Giao Châu Kĩ (Records of Giao Châu)* by Lưu Hán Ký, in Chin Dynasty 360-420, "Nê-Lê Citadel is situated in Dinh An District, in the south-east direction seven *li* distant from the river, which there still exist tower and hall founded by Aśoka. The woodmen call it Kim Tương"[16] Claude Madrolle, a member of *BEFEO*, bases himself on such documents in drawing attention to the fact that there was an Aśoka tower at Nê-Lê Citadel in Giao Chỉ, present-day Đồ Sơn in Hai Phòng City (North Vietnam).[17] For him, *Nê-Lê* (in Chinese) means "black mud", and hence it is located at some land of black mud in Hai Phòng. However, this reason is not admitted by Lê Mạnh Thát because the word "black mud" is to be *Lê-Nê* (*Li-ni*), not *Nê-Lê* in Chinese grammar.[18] According to Lê Mạnh Thát, *Nê-Lê* is the transliteration of *naraka* in Sanskrit, meaning *hell*. And in Tam Đảo District today, there exists a pagoda named Tây Thiên, also called Địa Ngục Pagoda (*Địa Ngục* means *Hell*). He supposes whether the former Nê-Lê Citadel could be Địa Ngục Pagoda in Tam Đảo today. This appears to be reasonable, but we still expect a certain archeological conclusion for it.

So far we cannot determine whether the mission of Sona and Uttara had arrived in Giao Châu. On the basis of above mentioned circumstances in Giao Châu as well as of the movement spreading Buddhism abroad at that time, however, Buddhism could have been introduced into Giao Châu during the second and first centuries BC. And the form of Buddhism now was that of incipient one with the doctrines that were orally transmitted.[19] It is easier to be aware of this when the appearance of *Mou-tzu li-huo lun* has proved the existence of Buddhism so long before, as Hu Shih said.

Luy Lâu (Tonkin) Center with the Appearances of Mou-tzu and K'ang Seng-hui

a) As glanced over earlier, Luy Lâu or Tonkin was the important seaport of Giao Châu, where foreign merchants resorted to for their trade, which served as the link of the two ancient civilizations, Indian and Chinese, by sea route. We can know further about it through the following description by Yü Ying-shih, "The prosperity of Chiao-chih (Tonkin) as a seaport during the Later Han particularly deserves attention. Chiao-chih was known especially for the production of such curiosities as pearls, ivory, tortoise shell, incense, and so forth, from which its immense wealth derived.... It is also highly significant that toward the end of the Later Han period when the famous Shih Hsien (136-226) was Governor of Chiao-chih, the streets of Tonkin were filled with barbarian merchants. All these facts can be properly comprehended only against the commercial background of Chiao-chih at that time. I can think of no better explanation than overseas trade that can account at the same time for both the prosperity of Chiao-chih and the frequent presence of foreigners there."[20]

It is also written by K. Ch'en that "there were at least three centers of Buddhism during the Han Dynasty: P'eng-ch'eng, or the Lower Yang-tze region in east China, Lo-yang, and Tonkin in south China (now in Vietnam). The Tonkin (Luy Lâu) center was primarily started by monks arriving by sea. One can only guess how and when the P'eng-ch'eng center was started. Hu Shih has suggested that there might have been some links between the south and east China centers. He thought it was possible for some monks to have made the trip overland from Tonkin to Wu-chou in Kwangsi, thence to Canton, then northward over the mountains into the lower Yangtze Valley. Han records mention some sea voyages between the Yangtze River and Tonkin, which would have provided another avenue for monks to get to the north."[21]

Thus, Tonkin or Luy Lâu was an important Buddhist center of Giao Châu. It is said by Nguyễn Lang that Luy Lâu center was established in the early first century A.D. by Indian traders and bonzes for their worship. When Buddhism had developed there, it gradually became a Buddhist center of culture and education.[22] It was at Luy Lâu that such personalities as Mou-tzu and K'ang Seng-hui matured in the practice of their faith. Significantly, *Li-huo lun* by Mou-tzu was written there and known as one of the earliest Buddhist texts of both Vietnam and China. This text provides a lot of invaluable information relating to the history of penetration and development of early Vietnamese Buddhism.

b) We know that *Mou-tzu li-huo lun* (*Mou-tzu on the Settling of Doubts*) is preserved in a Buddhist collection entitled *Hung-ming-chi* (*Collected Essays on Buddhism*) [*Taishō* 2102, compiled by Seng-yu probably between 515 and 518]. The Preface of it is filled with detailed historical data so that the scholars like Paul Pelliot, Hu Shih, etc. date the total text at the end of the second century.[23]

Mou-tzu or Mou-pa, Yung as an alias, was of Han ethnic origin, born around 165 at Ts'ang Wu in China. About 178, he led his mother to Giao Châu and immigrated there, then converted to Buddhism. Having worked at Luy Lâu he in 198 A.D. wrote *Li-huo lun* that contributed to defending Buddhism against attacks from followers of Confucianism and Taoism.

However, a great deal of controversy and discussion about the date and authenticity of the text has arisen among scholars. A series of studies that were done during the first half of the twentieth century have resulted in a great evaluation on the text by various historians and scholars such as Liang Ch'i-ch'ao, Henrri Maspero, Tokiwa Daijō, P. Pelliot, Chou Shu-chia, Hu Shih, Matsumoto Bunzaro, Yü Chia-hsi, and Fukui Kōjun.[24] Of them, Liang Ch'i-ch'ao, Tokiwa Daijo and Matsumoto Bunzaro contend *Mou-tzu li-huo lun* as a spurious work composed at a later period of time. Fukui Kōjun, however, having done a careful investigation based on most of the pros and cons of the preceding theories and opinions, especially having investigated the data claimed by Maspéro, Pelliot, Chou Shu-chia, Hu Shih and Yü Chia-hsi, comes to conclusion in favor of its authenticity.[25] Even so, Fukui still leaves some apparent gaps, such as some information being in the text that is found in the versions translated at later periods, by which the date of *Li-huo lun* is to have been placed around the middle of the third century, when Mou-tzu would have been quite an old man. Among modern scholars on the side of the text's authenticity and its author, however, there are two views put forward below to resolve this.

Firstly, according to K. Ch'en and Nguyễn Lang,[26] all scholars' viewpoints are right in some instances and wrong in others. Instead of adopting the view that the entire work was compiled at one time, either at the end of the Han Dynasty or during the fifth century, it is more reasonable to presume that the earliest parts of the text very likely were composed during the end of the Han Dynasty, but there were also later accretions. That is, these scholars agree that *Li-huo lun* was written by Mou-tzu at the end of the second century A.D., yet its contents would have been modified or supplemented somewhat afterward.

Secondly, as Hu Shih's view, however, Lê Mạnh Thát also dates the entire treatise at the end of the second century. Along the lines of Lê Mạnh Thát's investigation, the arguments of Tokiwa, Matsumoto and Liang Ch'i-chao, who endeavored to date the text around the third or the fifth century, were unstable and have been overcome by the justifications of Pelliot, Chou Shu Chia, and Fukui.[27] But there exists one problem that the body of the text contains passages that, for the critics, are strikingly similar to portions of the later translations, especially *Liu-tu chi-ching* in the third century.[28] As regards this, Lê Mạnh Thát leads the problem to an interesting debate that *Liu-tu chi-ching* translated by K'ang Seng-hui into Chinese was neither from a Sanskrit text[29] nor composed by him as some scholars said,[30] but from a Vietnamese one, probably one of the fifteen texts mentioned by T'an Chien.[31] This means that this text had prevailed during Mou-tzu's time, and later on, K'ang Seng-hui translated it into a Chinese text.[32] This scholar contends that the circulation of Buddhist scriptures had for certain arisen in Giao Châu during the second century A.D. and Luy Lâu was well-known Buddhist center, so that the data in the *Li-huo lun* as well as the figure of Mou-tzu are authentic and conceivable.

Thus, Giao Châu's Buddhism had taken shape under an outstanding organized form. Buddhist monks must have been present, for it is found in the *Li-huo lun* (Section XIX) that monks "shave their heads, wear red robes, eat only once a day, shut off their six senses, and cutting themselves off from the world."[33] And Buddhist scriptures were said to be "so many" there. Besides, we also find even a passage such that "The monks are addicted to their wine and spirits. Some support wives and children. They buy cheap and sell at an excessive profit. All they do is trick and cheat people" (Section XVI).[34] All these prove that Buddhism had been overwhelming in the land over a long period of time. As a matter of fact, *Mou-tzu li-huo lun* and the historical events of Vietnamese Buddhism, as far as we know, would have just represented the historically transitional stage of the religion in Giao Châu because soon after that K'ang Seng-hui then inherited a complete educational system and became an eminent monk in the history of early Chinese and Vietnamese Buddhism.

c) K'ang Seng-hui's biography and his activities are recorded fairly and completely in Chinese texts. He has gained an admirable position during the early phase of the Buddhist history in China. Writing the preface to *Ch'u san-tsang chi-chi* (*Collection of Records concerning the Tripiṭaka*) (*Taishō* 2145, 1a), Seng-yu regards K'ang Seng-hui as one of the two personalities, An Shih-kao and K'ang Seng-hui, who have made the foundation for Buddhist Studies of China.

According to *Kao seng chuan*[35] (*The Stories of Eminent Monks*), K'ang Seng-hui was born early in the third century in Giao Chỉ, near present-day Hanoi. His father, a Sogdian merchant, had come to Giao Chỉ and settled in this important commercial town after having lived in India for generations.

K'ang Seng-hui became an orphan when he was in his early teens. After his parents' death he joined the Sangha. This fact again proves the existence of an organized Buddhist order in Giao Chỉ at the beginning of the third century. K'ang Seng-hui certainly knew Sanskrit, and he excelled in his great knowledge of *Tripiṭaka*. Besides, he had also widely read in the Six (Confucian) Classics, and was well-versed in astronomy, diagrams and apocrypha.

In 247, K'ang Seng-hui arrived in China and spread Buddhism at Chienyeh. Especially, he persuaded and converted Emperor Sun Ch'üan to Buddhism, who after that built for him the first Buddhist monastery at the Southern capital, the Chien-ch'u ssu. So, Buddhism at Chienyeh became flourishing. Besides the biography of K'ang Seng-hui mentioned by Hui-chiao in *Kao-seng chuan*, we could also know him through such writings as the preface to the *An-pan shou-i ching* and that to the *Fa-ching ching* as well as his translations of *Liu-tu chi-ching*, *Chiu tsa-p'i-yü ching*, etc.[36] K'ang Seng-hui's Buddhism is known to have formed a continuation of the Northern school of An Shih-kao and An Hsýan with its stress upon *dhyāna*.

It is through K'ang Seng-hui's biography and writings that we may know the Vietnamese Buddhist situation during the first half of the third century, in which he was born and grown up, in which he enjoyed an outstanding and complete education that made him great and eminent in the history of spreading Buddhism in China. His two prefaces mentioned above have manifested his deep and strong attachment to Giao Chỉ: "I was born late. I had just known how to bear firewood when both my parents died. The three masters all passed away. Looking contemplatively into the sky and clouds, I was full of dolefulness for nobody to inquire, looking round with speechlessness and moved to tears reticently."[37]

The three masters here were required to preside over the ceremony of admission to the *Sangha*, i.e., *upādhyāya, karmadāna* and *Ācārya*. Vietnam's influence on K'ang Seng-hui can be found in the context by itself. His masters and their teachings must have made a deep impact on his knowledge and thinking, for many glosses are headed by the words "the master says." Unfortunately, we do not know who his masters were. But through such expression of K'ang Seng-hui, they might have represented the style of Giao Chỉ's Buddhism at that time. This style was, on the one hand, based on the practical methods of meditation like that of An Shih-kao's meditation, and on the other hand, on explanation of doctrine and thought by means of the stories of fable and legend.[38] Thus it was the combination of ideal and practice, of thinking and living. This doctrinal thought could be manifested in K'ang Seng-hui's translations and writings. It is at Giao Chỉ that made him mature as such. This also indicates that Vietnamese Buddhism became perfect during the third century A.D.

It has been said that K'ang Seng-hui was the founder of *Thiền* (*dhyāna or zen*) of Vietnamese Buddhism. Rather, it is due to K'ang Seng-hui that we can distinguish how Vietnamese meditation was during the time of the third century. In his preface to the *An-pan shou-i ching* (*Taishō* 602, p. 163abc), he explained the *An-pan* meditation (*Hināyāna*) of An Shih-kao corresponding with *Mahāyāna* viewpoint, which is found in the *Aṣṭasāhasrikā-prajñāpāramitā* and the *Vimalakīrtisūtra*. In fact, *Mahāyāna* Buddhism existed in Vietnam during the third century, when the *sūtra* of *Fa-hua san-mei ching (Saddharma-puṇḍarīkasūtra)* was translated at Giao Châu in 255-256 by Kalyānaśiva (Chih Chiang-li-ang-chueh), and the meaning of the text was verified by Đạo Thanh, a Vietnamese monk, contemporary with K'eng Seng-hui.[39] The word "*san-mei*", meaning *samādhi* or concentration, was put on such the title of the text and this shows the importance of *dhyāna* in this period. And *Thiền* or Vietnamese meditation has been then coming on.

Conclusion

The events brought out above would direct us to conclusion that the process of penetration and development of Vietnamese Buddhism had lasted for several centuries. This process may be divided into three periods as follows: the first, as folk cult (introduced by Indian traders at the 2nd and 1st BC), the second, Buddhism current with unwritten scriptures (before the time of Mou-tzu), and the third, Vietnamese Buddhism with the historical evidences of the texts and the organized *Saṅgha* (198-247 A.D.). On the basis of the literary evidences as mentioned above, the date of advent of Buddhism in Vietnam must be placed in 198 A.D. The fact we have examined about K'ang Seng-hui is to prove the existence of *Mou-tzu li-huo lun*, which had arisen shortly before, that is to say, 198 A.D. In actual fact, it is very reluctant to assert the historical date of Vietnamese Buddhism by reason of the emergence of *Li-huo lun* as such. Damien Keown seems to be prudent to write, "The history of Buddhism in the territory now covered by the country of Vietnam dates back at least to the 2nd century CE, when it was transmitted southward from China to the area then known as Chiao-chou.... Stories dating from this period show the presence of monastic Buddhism, and present tales of scripture-chanting, the erection of images, and the miraculous intervention of monks with little comment, which indicates that such things were common enough for the reader to need no explanation."[40]

References

1. According to archaeological evidence in Champa (present-day Nha Trang), the inscription of Võ Canh was written in Sanskrit in the 2nd centuty A.D. Thus it may be estimated that this language had been used long before [Cf. L.M. Thát, *Lich sử Phật giáo Việt Nam (The History of Vietnamese Buddhism)* (Thu□n Hóa, 1999), p. 24 f; see also L. Finot, "Outlines of the History of Buddhism in Indo-China", in *Buddha and the Spread of Buddhism in India and Abroad*, compiled by Mahendra and P. Mittal (Originals, 2002), p. 322].
2. *Ch' ien Han Shu* writes that Vietnamese King, *Triệu Đà* (207 BC), brought tribute in person to King Han Wen (179 BC) with a couple of peacocks. Peacock came from India, named *mayūra* (in Sanskrit); Cf. Nguyễn Đăng Thục, *Lịch sử Tư tưởng Việt Nam (History of Vietnamese Thought)* (Publishers of Hochiminh City, 1992). vol. II, 125 f.
3. Cf. Nguyễn Đăng Thục, *op. cit.*, vol. III, 332.
4. See L.M. Thát, *op. cit.*, p. 35. But we may also read in *The Encyclopedia of Religion*, vol. I, 468 (New York: Macmillan, 1987) that "Burmese Buddhists still look up to the missionary monks Sona and Uttara as the apostles of Burma, but there is no evidence, archeological or otherwise, of their activities there."
5. Kenneth Ch'en, *Buddhism in China* (Princeton 1964), p. 42; L.M. Thát, *op. cit.*, vol. I, 24; Yü Ying-shih also portrays the commercial importance of Chiao-chih as follows: "During the decades from Wang Mang's time to the early years of the Later Han, in which relations between China and the Western Religions were generally interrupted. Sino-Indian overseas silk trade probably became more flourishing as a result of the cutting off of the overland trade route. During this period, there seems to have been even some increase of Chinese silk in the Roman market, which, it is believed, was due to the more frequent use of the sea route by the Indian intermediary. It may further be conjectured that the growth of the overseas silk trade between the east and the west resulted partially also from the fact that both sides found it is beyond doubt that in Later Han times Sino-Indian economic intercourse often resorted to the sea route.... In Later Han times, overseas trade seems to have gained much progress. In this respect, both Jih-nan (Annam) and Chiao-chih played a very important role by serving as a link of intercourse between China and the various maritime countries" (Yü Ying-shih, *Trade and Expansion in Han China* (Berkeley, 1967), p. 175 f).

* The chart is drawn from *The Buddhist Handbook* by John Snelling (London, 1987), p. 122.

6. G.E. Sargent, *The intellectual Atmosphere in Linh Nan at the Time of the Introduction of Buddhism*, University of Hongkong, 1964 (Cf. Nguyễn Đăng Thục, *Lịch sử Tư tưởng Việt Nam* (Publishers of Hochiminh City, 1992), vol. II, 124).
7. Cf. Cuong Tu Nguyen, *Zen in Medieval Vietnam*, p. 129. The original quote is leaf 20b7-9).
8. The Vietnamese title: *Lich sử Phật giáo Việt Nam* (Thuận Hóa, 1999), vol. I, 11-35.
9. L.M. Thát, *op. cit.*, vol. I, 20.
10. *Ibid.*, p. 70. However, in *The History of Vietnamese Thought* (vol. II, 102) Nguyễn Đăng Thục argues that, with certain legends, the atmosphere of cult in Giao Châu around the period of the first century A.D., which has been regarded to be of Buddhism, was in reality not Buddhism but Brahmanism, or somehow some Buddhist form of local totem or genie cult, because the bonze Kṣudra, of Brahmin clan, was said to have likely performed yogic magic, practiced one-leg standing, abstained from food for several days, stayed at foot of a tree or in cave, or did wanderings, etc. See also L. Finot, "Outlines of the History of Buddhism in Indo-China", in *Buddha and the Spread of Buddhism in India and Abroad*, compiled by Mahendra and P. Mittal (Originals, 2002), p. 322.
11. First, he asserts that *Lĩnh Nam Trích Quái* could not have been a collection of legends, but a historical text, by which its two later variant versions was compiled, as well that its contents are found to be consistent with that of the other literary texts such as *Liu-tu chi-ching* (*Taishō* 152) and *Chiu tsa-pi-yü ching* (*Taishō* 206). Next, he finds out the place-name of Quỳnh Viên from the separate sources of the l4th century A.D. when it had been called as ancient Quỳnh Viên with its location. As far as we know, these data would be the new finds that are under consideration anyhow (Cf. L.M. Thát, *op. cit.*, pp. 15-17).
12. *Ibid.*, pp. 20-21.
13. *Ibid.*, pp. 24-26.
14. *Ibid.*, p. 35.
15. Trúc Viên Pagoda had been under the period of Lữ Gia, c. 110 BC; Lady Bat Nan, a heroine, had joined in the Buddhist order in 43 A.D. when defeated by Mã Viện; about 100 A.D., some Buddhist community could traditionally planted Uất Kim Hương (tulips), after that, it was used to make the medicinal wine (L.M. Thát, *op. cit.*, pp. 26-28).
16. The original extract is (Cf L.M. Thát, *op.cit.*, p. 30).
17. C. Madrolle, "Le Tonkin Ancien." *Bulletin de l'Ecole française d'Extrême-Orient XXXVII* (1937), pp. 263-332.
18. L.M. Thát, *op. cit.*, p. 31.
19. According to Hu Shih, a number of Buddhist texts prevailing during the Late Han are not found because Buddhism at the beginning was spread within the peoples who had not been sinicized yet and its scriptures were just transmitted orally (Cf. G.E. Sargent, University of Hongkong, 1964; Cf. Nguyễn Đăng Thục, *Lịch sử Tư tưởng Việt Nam* (1992), vol. II, 124-125).
20. Yü Ying-shih, *Trade and Expansion in Han China* (Berkeley: University of California Press, 1967), pp. 175-87.
21. Kenneth Ch'en, *Buddhism in China* (Princeton 1964), p. 40.

22. Nguyễn Lang, *Việt Nam Phật giáo Sử luận* (*A Historical Survey of Vietnamese Buddhism*), vol. I, 23-24.

23. In a letter to Chou Shu-chia, Hu Shih remarks, "This text which was at the time of Han-Wei (172-220 A.D.). can be considered to be a good piece of writing... Its Preface has had apparently historical proof, so then the whole *Li huo lun* would have been an evidently historical source worthy of belief.

24. Liang Ch'i-ch'ao, "Mou tzu li-huo lun", in *Fo-hsüeh yen-chiu shih-pa pien* (part II), pp. 234-238; Tokiwa Daijō, "Kanmin guhosetsu no kenkyu", *Tōyō Kyōkai Chōsabu X* (1911), 1-49, and see also in *Shina ni okeru Bukkyō to Jūkyō dōkyō* (Tokyo: Tōyō bunko ronsō 1937), pp. 89-100. H. Maspèro, "Le songe et l'ambassade de l'empereur Ming: Etude critique des sources," *Bulletin de l'Ecole française d Extréme-Orient X* (1910), pp. 95-130; P. Pelliot, "Meou-tseu ou les doutes levès," *T'oung Pao XIX* (1920), pp. 255-286; His Shih, "yü Chou Shu-chia lun Mou-tzu shu." in *Lun-hsüeh chin-chu*, vol. I, 151-154: Yü Chia-hsi "Mou-tzu li-huo lun chien t'ao, in *Yen-ching hsüeh-pao XX* (1936), pp. 1-23.

25. Fukui Kōjun, "Dōkyō no kisoteki kenkyū" *Fuikui Kōjun chosaku shū* (Tokyo: 1952), pp. 332-436.

26. K. Ch'en, pp. 37-38; Nguyễn Lang, pp. 60-61.

27. L.M. Thát, *op. cit.*, pp. 178-192.

28. In his study c. 1959 (*Buddhist Conquest of China*, pp. 13-15). E. Zürcher collected the problems of anachronisms from his predecessors so as to refuse authenticity of *Mou-tzu li-huo lun* with four reasons. (1) The most evidently insoluble obstacle, with which the scholars would so far meet, is the mention of the *Vessantara-jātaka* (in section XV) that is contained in the *Liu-tu chi-ching,* translated by K'ang Seng-hui around the period of 247 and 280. Besides, the three others, which, as drawn by Zýrcher (p. 14), are (2) the "*Sūtra in Forty-two Chapters*", (3) the date of Khotanese Buddhism, and (4) the mention of "the enormous size of Buddhist scriptures", which derived from the *Pañcaviṃśahasrikā*, translated by Dharmaraksa ca 286 A.D., are obscure because there exist some separate evidence-sources for the dates of their existence before the time of *Li-huo lun*. In response respectively, (1) under consideration is the existence of the *Vessantara-jātaka*, with which we are going to deal in the context above. But the rest three should be done with a cursory discussion here. First, (2) it is known that the "Sūtra in Forty-two Chapters" had been running popularly during the 2nd century A.D. so that it was quoted in Hsiang K'ai's memorial of 166 A.D. Secondly, (3) the introduction of Khotanese Buddhism was very early, with the vague time of its advent, but we are reported that, "the king of Khotan is said to have converted Kashgar to Buddhism in about 100 CE" (Cf. *The Encyclopedia of Religion*, M. Eliade (ed. in Chief), Macmillan 1987, vol. II, 402). And thirdly, (4) it is observable that any Buddhist literati could not have been unaware of "the enormous size of Buddhist scriptures," even although they would have not yet been translated into Chinese. In addition, J.P. Keenan would be correct to say, "It cites Buddhist sources only infrequently and does not evince any doctrinal sophistication. Perhaps only the existence of a large number of scriptures was known and not their doctrinal content" (See John P. Keenan (1997). *How Master Mou Removes Our Doubts*, p. 76). Generally speaking, the extraction of these three problems thus seems to be not strongly convincible.

29. It is found that in *Liu-tu chi-ching* (*Taishō* 152) several elements could not have sprung from India, such as contempt for Coficianism (Sūtra 49, p. 28a22-24), the custom of burial (Sūtra 68, p. 36c3-14), and so forth.

30. T'ang Yung-T'ung, *Han Wei liang-chin Nan-pei ch'ao fo-chiao shih* (Shanghai 1938),

p. 101; Cf. L.M. Thát, *op. cit.*, pp. 47-50.

31. Cf. L.M. Thát, *op. cit.*, p. 200; see also Nguyễn Lang, p. 39.

32. For his investigation, there were at least three texts current in Giao Châu during the time of Mou tzu, i.e., *Liu-tu chi-ching* (*Taishō* 152), *Tsa pi-yü ching* (*Taishō* 205), and *Chiu tsa pi-yü ching* (*Taishō* 206). There remain some constructions of Vietnamese grammar, for instance, *"Buddha-statue"*: *(Taishō* 205, p. 510a5) (Vietnamese) instead of in Chinese; *"tree-deity"*: (*Taishō* 152, p. 22c12) (Vietnamese) instead of in Chinese; *"in heart"* (*Taishō* 152, p. 21b27 or p. 40b5, and so on) (Vietnamese) instead of or in Chinese, etc.

33. See John P. Keenan, *How Master Mou Removes our Doubts* (Sri Satguru Publications, 1997), p. 119.

34. *Ibid.,* p. 110.

35. *Taishō* 2059, 325 a-326b.

36. *Kao-seng chuan* by Hui-chiao, *Taishō* 2059, 325a-326b; the two Prefaces by K'ang Seng-hui in *Ch'u san-tsang chi-chi* (*Taishō* 2145) compiled by Seng-yu are "An-pan shou-i ching hsü" (43abc) and "Fa-ching ching hsü" (46bc), which are preserved as well in *Taishō* 602, p. 163abc and in *Taishō* 322, p. 15a respectively; *Liu-tu chi-ching*, *Taishō* 152, lb-52b; *Chiu tsa-p'i-yü ching*, *Taishō* 206, 510b-522b.

37. *Taishō* 602, p. 163b29-c2 (also *Taishō* 2145, p. 43b24-26, compiled by Seng-yu), we read... **Some words may be missing from here.**

38. *Liu-tu chi-ching* (*Taishō* 152) and *Chiu tsa-pi-yü ching* (*Taishō* 206) are the collections of tales and legends (*jātaka*), several stories of which are similar to the ancient legends of Vietnam. For instance, the legend of the *Hundred Eggs*, which relates the origin of Vietnamese people and so on, is maintained in *Liu-tu chi-ching* (p. 14a26-14c18) (See, L.M.Thát, *op. cit.*, pp. 308-309, and p. 315).

39. L.M. Thát, pp. 383-6. We have information about the *Fa-hua san-mei ching* including its translator, commentator as well as location where the Chinese version took shape by way of *Li-tai san-pao chi* V, (*Taishō* 2034, p. 56c19-24), yet its body text has lost. The remark on Vietnamese meditation above would be regarded out of no more than the title of text.

40. Damien Keown, *Dictionary of Buddhism* (Oxford University Press 2003), p. 326.

References

1. Ch'en, Kenneth, *Buddhism in China*, Princeton, 1964.

2. Cuong Tu Nguyen, *Zen Medieval Vietnam, A study and translation of the Thiền Uyển Tập Anh*, Honolulu: University of Hawaii Press, 1997.

3. Damien Keown, *Dictionary of Buddhism*, Oxford University Press, 2003.

4. Eliade, M. (ed. in chief), *The Encyclopedia of Religion*: I, 468. New York and London: Macmillan, 1987.

5. Finot, L. "Outlines of the History of Buddhism in Indo-China", in Mahendra and P. Mittal (eds.) *Buddha and the Spread of Buddhism in India and Abroad*, Delhi: Originals, 2002.

6. Fukui Kōjun (1952) "Dōkyō no kisoteki kenkyū" (Basic Research on Taoism), in *Fukui Kōjun chosaku shū (A Collection of the Works of Fuikui Kōjun)*, Tokyo: Hōzōkan.

7. Galen Eugene Sargent. *The Intellectual Atmosphere in Ling Nam at the Time of Introduction of Buddhism*, University Hongkong, 1964.

8. Keenan, John P. *How Master Mou Removes our Doubts*, Delhi: Sri Satguru

Publications, 1997.

9. Lê Hữu Mục (trans. with introduction), *Lĩnh Nam Chích Quái (A Collection of Strange Stories of Lĩnh Nam)*, Saigon, 1961.
10. Lê Mạnh Thát, *Lịch sử Phật giáo Việt Nam (The History of Vietnamese Buddhism)*, Vol. I, Thuận Hóa Publishers, 1999.
11. *Nghiên cứu về Thiền Uyển Tập Anh Ngữ Lục (A Study of the Anthology of the Zen Garden)*, Hochiminh City Publishers, 1999.
12. Madrolle, C. "Le Tonkin Ancien", *Bulletin de 1'Ecole française d'Extrême-Orient XXXVII*, Hanoi, 1937.
13. Mật Thể, *T. Việt Nam Phật giáo Sử Lược (The Historical Brief of Vietnamese Buddhism)*. Minh Đức Publishers, 1943.
14. Minh Chi, H.V. Tấn, N.T. Thu. *Buddhism in Vietnam*. Thế Giới Publishers, 1999.
15. Nguyễn Đăng Thục. *Lịch sử Tư tưởng Việt Nam (History of Vietnamese Thought)* Vols. II-III, Hochiminh City Publishers, 1992.
16. Nguyễn Lang, *Việt Nam Phật giáo Sử Luận (The Historical Survey of Vietnamese Buddhism)* (4th Ed.), Vol. I, Hanoi: Văn Học Publishing House, 1994.
17. Takakusu, J. and Watanabe, K. (Eds.) *Taishō issaikyō (Taishō)*, 55 Vols., Tokyo, 1924-1929.
18. T'ang Yung-t'ung, *Han Wei liang-Chin nan-pei ch'ao fo-chiao shih*, 2 vols., Shanghai, 1938.
19. Trần Văn Giáp, "Le Bouddhisme en Annam dés origines au XIII siécle," *Bulletin de l'Ecole française d'Extrême-Orient XXXII* (1932): 191-286. Translated into Vietnamese by Tuệ Sĩ as *"Phật giáo Việt Nam, Từ khởi nguyên đến thế kỷ XIII"*, Saigon, 1968.
20. Yü Ying-shih, *Trade and Expansion in Han China*, Berkeley: University of California Press, 1967.
21. Zürcher, E, *The Buddhist Conquest of China*, Leiden: Brill, 1972.

Chapter 25
A Glimpse at Buddhism in Vietnam
Rev. Thich Tam Duc

Many times in the history of mankind, things have happened that can only be put in the category of *wonderful phenomena*. Such phenomena have fascinated both historians and scientists. The story of Vietnamese struggle and liberation is a phenomenon as such. Vietnamese victory and independence after one thousand years from foreign yoke, after having defeated the powerful empires such as China, Mongolia, France, the USA, especially its crushing defeat of the Mongols in 1258, 1285, 1287-1288 is seen nothing short of a wonder. This phenomenon defies explanation. It may be pointed out that in term of material aspect, Vietnam was hardly a match for these mighty and ruthless empires. So, one has to look else where for an explanation.

Buddhism originated in India over 2500 years ago and has spread throughout the world following its founder's instructions: *Let not two of you go in one and the same direction*. Hence, keeping the spirit of peace, friendship, toleration, compassion and no-self this faith traveled to various nooks and corners of the world as a messenger of peace and for the welfare and happiness of the manifold. This very nature of Buddhism has given it so much versatility that it adapted itself to the different environs wherever it went. *Zen, Ch'an* or meditation is one such example of its characteristic adaptability.

In the Buddha's times, *Zen* was regarded as *the one sole way* not only for the overcoming of sorrow and grief but also for realizing the ultimate goal of *nirvāṇa*. Great advantages are to be expected from practising it. It is depicted through rich and elaborate images and concepts. *Zen*, however, did not become an independent sect until the arrival of *Bodhidharma* from India to China. He is regarded as the First Patriarch of the Chinese *Ch'an* sect. But from the 6th Patriarch, *Hui-neng* (d. 713) onwards, with the spirit of *freeing ourselves* in the philosophy of the *Vajracchedikā-sūtra* (Diamond sūtra) *Zen* sect was also a typical Chinese character of its own. From now onwards, the Chinese with a practical mind accepted *Zen* as the essence of Buddhism which they could understand and practise. This made *Zen* extremely popular in the Chinese society at that time. Meanwhile, three *Zen* Masters from China traveled to Vietnam. It is here, they founded three *Zen* sects bearing their names, respectively:

1. *Vinītaruci*, an Indian (d. 594),
2. *Vo-Ngon-Thong*, a Chinese (d. 826), and
3. *Thao-Duong*, a Chinese (d. around 1100).

Buddhism, especially Mahāyāna, from India arrived in Vietnam around the 1st century A.D., by sea and land routes, in the context of this nation incessantly struggling for its liberation from Chinese yoke.

I. The Situation of Vietnam during the Advent of Buddhism

Before 179 BC, i.e., before the time of the Chinese domination, Vietnam had two names *Van-lang* (before 208 BC) and *Au-lac* (208 BC – 179 BC) respectively. *Van-lang* covered the furtile area of the *Hong, Ma* and *Ca* rivers in what now are a part of *Kwang-si*, *Kwang-tung* in China, north[1] and north of central Vietnam. In 207 BC *Trieu-Da*, a Chinese posed as a Viet chiefdom, invaded two prefectures, *Tuong* and *Qua-lam*, a part of the Viets' territory, making *Nan-yueh* kingdom. Not long after that *Trieu-Da* was defeated by Han troops in 111 BC. During the Han Vietnam was divided into two commanderies: (i) *Giao-chi* in what now include a part of *Kwang-si*, *Kwang-tung* in China and north Vietnam, and (ii) *Cuu-chan* in what now is north of central Vietnam. This southernmost extension of Chinese Empire was designated by the *Trieu* and Han dynasties as *Nan-yueh* (South Viet) and by the Tang dynasty (618-906) as *An-nam* (Pacifying the south), or, in the current speech of the people living there, *Nam-viet* and *An-nam* respectively. *Giao-chi* had a population of 746,237 people and *Cuu-chan* 166,013; so, Vietnam had a population of 912,250 at the time.

The early inhabitants in Vietnam included the ethnic groups of Indonesian and southern Asian belonging to the Mongoloid in the south which was formed in a long process of race-mixture between the Australoid and Mongoloid in which the latter step by step prevailed. According to the Chinese archives in the fourth and third centuries BC, i.e., at the end of the *Hung-vuong* dynasty the inhabitants in Vietnam composed of *Lac-Viet* and *Tay-au* ethnic groups which were incorporated into the realm of *Nan-yueh (Nam-Viet)*, one of the heterogeneous *Yueh kingdoms (Bach-Viet)* lying south of the Yangtze river and the purely Chinese kingdoms to the north of it.

The beginning of the Viets' civilization probably dates back to approximately 4,000 years ago. At that time the tribes of *Phung-nguyen*, the cradle of the Viets in the basin of the *Hong* river, who had known how to grow wet rice, raise cattle, fish, make pottery and metals laid the material and spiritual foundations of the *Hung-vuong* times. The most startling discovery occurred at *Phung-nguyen* in *Phu-tho* province of north Vietnam in 1959. Subsequent excavations in the area – *Phu-tho, Ha-tay* and *Vinh-phu* provinces – revealed the existence of an extensive culture, today encompassing more than twenty sites, which range from late Neolithic to bronze, iron in objects and date. The study of this *Phung-nguyen* culture complex, so called after the type-site of that name, has had far-reaching effects, throwing new light on the continuity of traditions in decoration, pottery, bronze, and stone goods in north Vietnam sites from *Phung-nguyen* to *Dong-son*, and it has also demonstrated the further extension of *Phung-nguyen* culture complex links into the center, especially *Sa-huynh*, the south, particularly at *Long-khanh* sites, and into maritime south-east Asia.

The discovery of *Phung-nguyen* complex, intimately linked with the *Hung-vuong* and their *Van-Lang* kingdom, enables one to arrange the chronology of the archaeological sites in Vietnam and to state, for the first time with solid material proofs, that the pre-3rd century BC is pre-*Nam Viet* (207-111 BC) history of the region. The discovery of the *Phung-nguyen* culture and its development into what is usually called *Dong-son* (traditionally 4th – 3rd BC) also argues strongly against Heine Gilderm's supposition that *Yunnan* was the cradle of the civilization and that the Vietnamese manifestations were its last phase.[2]

Civilization of the Viets was that of villages. Villages, the solid units of the Viets, were places where all their customs and habits, cultural life, were carefully preserved. During the Imperial domination the authorities just reached down to district but not to village administrations. Villages still remained the independent areas of the Viets.

The speech of the early Vietnamese inhabitants in the area is matter of some uncertainty. Some scholars considered Vietnamese to be a mere dialect of Chinese. Others considered it developed from a *Mon-Khmer* or *Thai* language. *Nguyen-Van-Huyen* (1944), Minister of Education in the Democratic Republic of Vietnam, who considers that Vietnamese belongs to the Austroasiatic family languages, has been strongly influenced by Chinese, Malay and Aryan languages and in its modern form is a very complex mixture of various kinds of speech. Apart from its being a tonal language, Vietnamese is characterized as "monosyllabic."

The evolution of Vietnamese language and writing can be chronological summarized as follows:

1. Under the Chinese colonialism (111 BC–938 AD)

   a) Two languages: Vietnamese and Chinese

   b) One writing system: Chinese

2. Under the monarchical independence (938–1651)

   a) Two languages: Vietnamese and Chinese

   b) Two writing systems: Chinese (Sino-Vietnamese) and ideographic Vietnamese (Nom)

3. Under the monarchical independence and Catholic separatism (1651–1861)

   a) Two languages: Vietnamese and Chinese

   b) Three writing systems: Chinese (Sino-Vietnamese), ideographic Vietnamese (Nom) and Romanized Vietnamese.

4. Under the French colonialism (1861–1945)

   a) Three languages: Vietnamese, Chinese and French

   b) Four writing systems: Chinese (Sino-Vietnamese), ideographic Vietnamese (Nom), Romanized Vietnamese (*Quoc ngu*) and French.

5. Under the national independence (1945–present)

   a) One language: Vietnamese

   b) One writing system: *Quoc ngu*

Under the times of Chinese invasion there have been resistance and uprisings of the Viets, typical are as follows:

i. In 218 BC the *Ch'in* troops invaded *Bach-Viet*. Then the Viets rose up against the enemy in the years from 214 BC–208 BC; finally, they defeated the *Ch'in* troops. This was the first victory of the Viets over the Chinese.

ii. 179 BC *An-Duong-Vuong*, the leader of *Au-Lac*, fell into a trap of *Trieu-Da* and was defeated by him. In 111 BC the Han China defeated the *Trieu* opening the period of domination over the Viets for more than one thousand years.

iii. 39 AD two Viet women, surnamed *Trung*, members of an aristocratic family, led a revolt against the Imperial governor and drove the Chinese out. Their triumph was short-lived three years and they both committed suicide when their troops were defeated.

iv. During the 2nd century A.D. there were a lot of the Viets' armed movements against the Chinese authorities.

v. In 248 A.D. the leader was young woman, *Trieu-Au*, who wore golden armor and led her forces mounted on an elephant. Defeated, she committed suicide at the age of 23.

vi. From the 3rd till early in the 6th century A.D. the political separation force from the Chinese colonial rule increased with a number of the Viets' uprisings.

vii. The Former *Ly* and *Trieu* dynasties (546–603): In 542, *Ly-Bi* led a revolt against the Imperial Governor successfully. He, the first Vietnamese, ascended the throne himself defying the Chinese permission and naming the state *Van-Xuan* (Ten Thousand Springs). He gave instruction to build the Buddhist temple *Khai-Quoc* (The Opening of the State). He was supported by the Buddhist circles. Successors after *Ly-Bi* were *Ly-Thien-Bao, Trieu-Quang-Phuc* and *Ly-Phat-Tu*.

viii. 603-905, during these three centuries the Viets rose up continuously everywhere but were defeated because: (i) the *Tang* was still strong, and (ii) the survival of the independent feudal chiefs was an objection to the national unity.

ix. In the early 10th century the liberal *Tang* China collapsed. Taking the advantage of the confusion the Viets made several efforts to shake off Chinese rule. 931, *Duong-Dinh-Nghe*, one landlord, defeated the Imperial troops and liberated the country. However, in 937, he was killed by one of his feudal low-ranking generals named *Kieu-Cong-Tien*, who being protested by people, called the Chinese for help. But *Kieu-Cong-Tien* was killed by *Ngo-Quyen*, a national hero and son-in-law of *Duong-Dinh-Nghe*, before the Chinese troops entered Vietnam. Then, in 938, with a decisive victory over the Chinese on the *Bach-Dang* river, *Ngo-Quyen* established a national entity which, except for a brief period from 1407 to 1427, maintained its independence until 1883.

II. The Advent of Buddhism in Vietnam: Time & Routes

Buddhism came to Vietnam from two directions: (i) southernly, from India, and (ii) northernly, from China.

1) Buddhism coming to Vietnam from India

In the early centuries A.D. one important centre of Buddhism, *Luy-lau*, was formed in *Giao-chau* or *Giao-chi* what is now northern Vietnam. The advent of Buddhism in Vietnam for the first time was perhaps originated from Mahāyāna Buddhism in India. Some archaeological and textual sources throw light on the way how Buddhism came to Vietnam. First of all, there have been maritime and land routes connecting India-Vietnam-China.

As early as between 300 BC and 300 A.D., the south-east Asian chiefdoms particularly those in coastal areas, were increasingly exposed to direct contact with Indian merchants and Chinese emissaries or armies. Historically, the Indian subcontinent during this period witnessed the rise of empires and their subsequent fragmentation into competing kingdoms. During the ensuing millennium, small polities centered on royal dynasties developed, within which ritual and ceremony lay in the hands of the senior of four social groups: Brāhmaṇas (priests), Kṣatriyas (nobles), Vaiśyas (originally a person settled on the land) and Śudras (serfs). The critical role of the Brāhmaṇas regarding kingship lay in their prerogative over the rites of consecration, but they also fulfilled advisory function and acted as ministers. Their privileged status was marked by exemption from taxes, and by gifts or donations from those seeking merit. Sanskrit evolved into local languages, but was retained by the Brāhmaṇas as the language of ritual and the sacred texts. The Brāhmaṇas, who inherited their special status, administered the Hindu religion.

However, Hinduism was not alone in attracting devotees. Buddhism arose during the 5th century BC by Gautama the Buddha, who taught in the Vernacular Pali in order to reach the masses to whom Sanskrit was the esoteric liturgical language of the Brāhmaṇa. Neither religion was mutually exclusive, and their co-existence was accepted.

Under the reign of the Mauryan Empire from c 321 BC agriculture and both local and International trade were encouraged, since the collection of state revenues turned on their success. By 150 BC the Mauryan Empire was in decline and fragmented into regional kingdoms, a situation which prevailed until the emergence of the Kuṣānas in north India and the Sātavāhanas in the Deccan (1st century BC–3rd century A.D.). The fall of the Mauryan Empire did not inhibit trade. Indian merchants employed the prevailing winds to travel in both easterly and westerly directions. The latter was concerned with the Iranian and Gracco-Roman worlds. The Romans were interested in silks, pepper, pearls, ivory and textiles, while for their part the Indians took glass, copper, tin, lead, orpiment, wine, antimony and gold coins. The physical embodiment of this exchange system has been revealed by Wheeler's excavations at Arikamedu (Wheeler 1955). And then, how about the easterly direction? The seasonal wind pattern across the Bay of Bengal reflects the regular rise and ebb of the monsoon, and maritime technology was well equipped to cope with the necessary distances. Their boats were large enough to handle at least 200 tons of cargo. It was at Tāmralipti (Tamluk on the mouths of the Ganges) that the Chinese pilgrims *Fa-hsien*, in the early 5th century, and *I-Ching*, late in the 7th century, embarked on their return from India to China. It was also at Tāmralipti that merchants starting from Benares or Champa, in the valley of the Ganges, took to the sea in the direction of Suvannabhumi, the land of gold, from the time of the composition of the Jātakas (Samkha Jataka, No. 442; Mahājanaka Jātaka, No. 539).

To avoid the long way along the shores of Bengal and around through the strait of Malacca voyagers from southern India made use of the 10-degree channel between Andaman and Nicobar or, farther south, the channel between Nicobar and the headland of Achin to land on the narrowness of the isthmus of Kra, or the peninsula near Takauapa, Kadah of the Malaya peninsula. The archaeological research has uncovered ancient objects at these latter two sites.[3] From these sites travelers took the short trans-peninsular routes to reach the eastern coast of the Malaya peninsula, these routes have been revealed by archaeological research,[4] and then continue by sea routes to *Funan* (Cambodia), *Champa* (Central Vietnam), *Tonking* (North Vietnam) or *Canton* in south China.

Besides, in farther north, there was a route connecting India and China through Assam, upper Burma, and *Yunnan*. There is clear evidence that this route was used from the beginning of the 2nd century A.D.[5] and its use probably dates back to the 2nd century BC. By this route Indian influence, after affecting upper Burma, reached *Nanchao* (China).[6] And then, there was the connection between *Yunnan* and *Giao-chau*, though the route to Vietnam, today the line of the railway built in the early years of the 20th century A.D. by the French, was not easy nor much traveling in antiquity. The Hong river seems to afford the obvious and natural line between *Yunnan* and Vietnam. On the role of Indian ports Poussin writes: "All the eastern ports of India up to Tamralipti (Tamluk) contributed to this Indian expansion but the south played the great role."[7]

The Indian vessels visited south-east Asia to exchange trade goods. They almost certainly reached south-east Asia before the end of the lst millennium BC, it is probable that interest in the area intensified after the Emperor Vespasian, who succeeded in 69 A.D., prohibited the export of gold coinage from the Roman Empire. The seasonal pattern of the prevailing wind, in which north-east winds dominated between November and May, and south-west winds from May to November, meant that landfall in south-east Asia lasted for some months. Among their passengers were numbered Hindu Brāhmaṇs and Buddhist monks. Naturally, following trading affair is cultural expansion which resulted in the Indianized kingdom in the Indo-chinese peninsula and in the islands of Indonesia. But the oldest archaeological remains these routes have left us are not necessarily evidence of the first civilizing wave. It is probable a *piori*, that priests who consecrated the first Brāhmaṇic or Buddhist sanctuaries and the scholars who composed the first Sanskrit inscription were preceded by seamen, traders, or immigrants – founders of the 1st Indian settlements. These settlements, in turn, were not always entirely new creations; in many cases (*Oc-eo* in south Vietnam, *Cho-dinh*, *Mi-son* in central Vietnam, Kuala Selinsing in Perak, Sampaga in Celebes, etc.), they were built on Neolithic sites that the seamen from India had frequented perhaps from time immemorial. Coedes writes: "The relations between Indian proper and Father India date back to the pre-historic times."[8]

Meanwhile, in China, during the western Han, the oriental international trade has already developed. Trade goods and Han envoys, by the land routes, reached such countries as *O-ton* (north-west India), *Dai-uyen* (Fergan), *Khang-cu* (Sogdiane), *Dai-nhuc-chi* (north India the area of the Indoscythes), *Dai-ha* (Bactriane), *An-tuc* (Iran) and *Than-doc* (Hindu, i.e., India). Maritime routes were also busy in the center of *Quang-zhou* and China sea. Many Chinese merchants arrived in Vietnam. Due to its favorable place and owing lots of tropical products *Giao-chau* became an important place on the maritime route between China and South-east Asian countries. One paragraph in *Tien-han-thu*[9] goes like this:

> "From *Tu-van*, *Hop-pho* (China), *Nhat-nam* (central Vietnam) one sails to *Do-nguyen* (Malaya) for five months. And, it takes four months for one to sail from *Do-nguyen* to *Ap-lo-mot* (Myanmar coast); then, twenty days from *Ap-lo-mot* to Sam-ly (?). Next, ten days by land route from *Sam-ly* to *Phu-cam-do-lo* (Pagan of Myanmar). Lastly, one sails for more than two months to reach *Hoang-chi* (Kancipura or Conjeveram of south India). That region is very large, thickly populated and having abundant strange things. From *Han-wu-di's* times up to now China has been sent tributes. The Eunuch Mandarin and his attendants went sailing buying jewels, precious stones, strange things and carrying gold, silk with them. When reaching each kingdom they have been given food and accompanied by local people.

The barbarian boats bring merchandise profiting the exchange... Voyageurs were killed by pirates and suffered from big waves; drowned; and survivors must spend several years for reaching home. From *Hoang-chi* one sails for around eight months to *Bi-tong* (Pisang in Malayasia), and two months to *Nhatnam*. In the south of *Hoang-chi* is *Di-trinh-bat* (?) kingdom. Messengers of the Han reached there, then returned back home."[10]

Furthermore, during the mid-Eastern Han, the northern trans-Asian trade route with the west was cut off by intervening states, a situation which fostered interest in a southern maritime route. In the late Han an embassy from the Roman Emperor Marcus Aurchin Antonius arrived at the Chinese court (166). In any case they certainly came by sea, and a few years later, in 222, an official envoy from the Roman Empire was received at the southern court of Wu, one of the Three kingdoms between which the Han Empire had been divided. He too came by sea, and the court of Wu proposed to send back with him by the same route, their own envoy.

Again, monk *Dam-Thien* answered the Sui Emperor Wen-di (603-617):

"The region of *Giao-chau* has routes connected to *Thien-truc* (India). By the time Buddhism (in China) did not yet become popular in *Giang-dong*, the region (of *Giao-chau*) had had already more than twenty stupas in *Luy-lau*, five hundred monks and fifteen translated sutras. So, Buddhism was introduced into Vietnam before into our state. At that time such monks as *Marajivaka*, *Khuong-Tang-Hoi*, *Chi-Cuong-Luong*, *Mau-Bac*, etc. have stayed there already."[11]

Again, *Khuong-Tang-Hoi* whose parents were the Sogdianes (central Asia) migrating to *Giao-chau* and doing business, in the early third century A.D. (200-247) was ordained in *Giao-chau*, became a well known ch'an master and was good in Sanskrit, Chinese. He translated some sūtras from Sanskrit to Chinese, for example, *Aṣṭasāhasrikā* which was one of the most ancient sūtras of Mahāyāna Buddhism. After that he arrived in *Kien-nghiep* (*Nanking*) for propagation and was considered as the first Buddhist monk preaching meditation there.

Last, the *Tam-Quoc-Chi*[12] recording the story of *Si-Nhiep* mentioned a letter by *Vien-Huy* sent to *Tuan-Huc* in 207 A.D., which praised *Si-Nhiep* for ruling *Giao-chau* peacefully for more than twenty years and "when going or coming he was accompanied with solemn ritual including plenty of horse-carriages, brass brand, scores of the Ho[13] burning incense...".

All the historical factors mentioned above prove that there appeared a fairly developed form of Mahāyāna Buddhism in *Luy-lau* (present north Vietnam) in the late 2nd century A.D. coming directly from India. And, it may be accepted that simple forms of Buddhist beliefs must be spread there earlier by Indian seamen and traders, at least in the1st century A.D.

2) Buddhism Coming to Vietnam from China

In the late first century BC Buddhism had been introduced into China by Indian missionary monks by the land route across central Asia, and the Hindukush from north west India, a route which had been opened up by the armies of the Chinese Emperor *Han-wu-ti* in the first century BC. Buddhism was officially recognized and received court patronage early in the 1st century A.D. and there after slowly gained headway.

In the 1st and 2nd century A.D. Buddhism was considered as a religion of the occult arts, not really differing from the occultism of the *Yi-yang* school or of the later Taoist religion, and the Buddha was regarded as a disciple of *Lao-tzu*, Buddhist sūtras as a foreign variant of *Tao-Te-Ching*. By late Han times two different trends had already developed in Buddhism. One was the *Dhyāna* school based on the translations of *An-Shih-Kao* and was Hīnayāna in nature. Opposed to this was the *Prajñā* school based on the translations of *Chih Ch'an* and inclined toward Mahāyāna in spirit. Beginning with the mid-3rd century A.D. this school became the dominant teaching within Buddhism in the south.

From the mid-3rd to 5th century A.D., an increasing number of Buddhist texts were translated, Buddhism was regarded as similar to philosophy of Taoism or *Chuang-Tzu*. Buddhist writings were interpreted with ideas taken from philosophical Taoism. As a result, there existed a synthesis of Indo-Buddhism with Taoism, leading to the foundation of a Chinese form of Buddhism. However, Chinese Buddhism always tried to establish doctrines for its own so that the Buddhist schools were no longer Indian systems introduced into China, but were really schools of Chinese Buddhism. Such schools were *Tien-t'ai* whose founder was *Chi-K'ai* (538-597 A.D.), *Hua-yen* whose founder *Fa-shun* (557-640 A.D.), Pure Land whose founder *Tan-lan* (476-542 A.D.) but mainly Shan-Tao (613-681 A.D.), and Ch'an whose founder was *Boddhidharma* (378-528 or 536 A.D.). It is, in fact, until this period the Buddhist faith spread in China, throughout the country from the north to the south. It is also under the *T'ang* dynasty, which played an important role in the flowering of the different Chinese schools of Buddhism that appealed more to the mind than to the heart of the Chinese.

For 250 years the *T'ang* rule in Vietnam was unchallenged, and this long period during which the country was under Chinese government when that government had never been so highly organized before, and the reigning dynasty fostered what is perhaps the finest age of Chinese culture, made a deep impression on the Viets. It is from this period onwards, Chinese *Ch'an* schools spreading to Vietnam were *Vinītaruci* (580-1213 A.D.), *Vo-Ngon-Thong* (820-1221 A.D.), *Thao-Duong* (1069-1205 A.D.), and some others. However, when Vietnam was independent she showed no desire to repudiate the cultural heritage which she had required during the *T'ang*. Also, Vietnamese Buddhism tended to create an independent Buddhism from Chinese Buddhism. This occurred under the *Tran* dynasty with the birth of the *Truc-Lam ch'an* school.

So, it can be said that Buddhism was introduced into Vietnam directly from India by sea route in the early centuries A.D. However, in course of time this direction of introduction changed. The Chinese monks from the north step by step replaced the role of Indians in propagation of Buddhism in Vietnam.

3) The Situation of Buddhism in Vietnam in the Early Two Centuries A.D.

a) Religious Beliefs and Learning of Giao-chau People:

Before the advent of Han and Indian civilization into Vietnam the ancient Viets who based on the material culture, i.e., cultivation of irrigated rice, domestication of cattle and buffalo, rudimentary use of metals, knowledge of navigation, with a social organization resulting from the requirements of irrigated agriculture have had the forms of primitive religious beliefs.

> "They believed in animism and worshipped such gods as sun, soil, mountain, river... and reproductive organs or copulation with ceremonies for good crops and fertility."[14]

They worshipped and deified their ancestors and heroes of the nation. The decoration on the bronze finds of *Dong-son* culture can give us some information about the Viets' spiritual life at that time. The stars on drums have been regarded as evidence of a sin cult; and between the stars' rays are symbols of sexual organs of both male and female representing the fertility.

Some bronze drums decorated with frogs (or toads) are constantly linked with rain, water leading to an old-age conception: "Toad is Heaven's uncle," and more especially with the deities of tumultuous waters (dragon) stirred up by a storm. A drum represents thunder for it makes the same sound and stimulates its energy. Pledge of prosperity for the land and its inhabitants, it embodies the voice and the energy of a deity who presides over the fruitfulness of nature. The people, when burying their drums, wish to bring the thunder into contact with the underground waters and to ensure that this quickening water, animated by the thunder, remains in their earth. On the other hand, the association of the themes drum-thunder-underground waters-beneficial rain sheds light on certain scenes of ceremonies linked to the fertility of the earth and to agricultural labour.

A number of sculptures of birds on the *Dong-son* bronze drums perhaps give the evidence of bird-worship. That is why the ancient Viets called themselves "Dragon's sons and Fairies' nephews." Here Fairies identify with birds.

The function of bronze drum is also used at Lunar New-Year, rice rituals, marriage and funeral ceremonies; all of which are fertility situations and for venerating their ancestors.

On the lids of *Dong-thinh* jars at burial sites are copulating figures perhaps suggesting rebirth and fertility, or fecundity and fruitfulness. Special are the hollowed-out log (canoe) burials from the important site of *Viet-khe* suggesting the boat of the dead.

The Viets also had mythologies and cosmological dualism in which are contrast between mountain and sea, the winged race and the aquatic race, people of the heights and those of the coasts, etc. Mythologies are handed down to the present day such as: (i) *Au-co* gave birth of one hundred eggs which hatched into fifty boys who later followed their mother going down to the sea and fifty girls who followed their father going up to the mountain, and (ii) *Son-tinh* (the god of mountain) and *Thuy-tinh* (the god of water). In a competition between the two gods for marrying a beautiful girl *Thuy-tinh* was defeated; he later on stirred and raised huge waves to kill the opponent. However, *Son-tinh* raised the mountain higher than the level of water *Thuy-tinh* did. Finally, *Thuy-tinh* accepted the failure.

Until early in the 1st century A.D. customs and morals of the Viets were much different from civilization of the Hans. A letter of *Hoai-nam-vuong Luu-An* sending to Han Emperor *Wu-di* writes:

> "The Viets shave their head, tattoo their body, they cannot be administered by Chinese law... not following the Chinese calendar."[15]

The Han historians also said:

"The people of *Giao-chi* do not know the ethics of father and son (for both swimming at the same river), they only follow sexual indulgence not knowing the ethics of husband and wife (free marriage after knowing each other at seasoning rituals), etc."[18]

At that time the Viets had no system of writing though they had a fairly high cultural life. Its distinctive feature was oral culture developing in the forms of mythical tales, legends, folk-songs and proverbs. The life of peasants still remained limiting to the boundary of the village.

In the 1st century A.D. two Imperial Governors *Tich-Quang* in *Giao-chi* and *Nham-Dien* in *Cuu-chan* imposed the Chinese way of life on the customs and morals of the Viets: "From marriage, making caps and shoes, styles of clothes to agricultural technique; all of which must imitate the Chinese patterns. Both of them opened schools teaching the Chinese Confucian politeness and uprightness."[17]

Under the Chinese domination Confucianism and Sinology step by step developed and played a considerable role in the late 2nd century A.D. Sinological scripts conveyed the ideas not only of Confucianism and Taoism but also of Buddhism in *Giao-chau*. However, Confucianism which was essential for the low-ranking officials serving the imperial authority was never flourished in *Giao-chau*.

In addition to Confucianism, from late in the 2nd century A.D. onwards the Chinese magical Taoism spread to Vietnam and comingled with the temples and old-age religious beliefs of the Viets. The Vietnamese primitive images of *Lac-Long-Quan, Chu-Dong-Tu, Tan-Vien, Son-Tinh, Phu-Dong Thien-Vuong*... were gradually Taoized.

b) The Initial Contact and Adaptation of Buddhism in Vietnam During the Early Centuries A.D.

Unlike Buddhism in China, Buddhism in Vietnam spread more easily because its activities were not only in accordance with the religious beliefs of the common people but also full of interest to the upper class and literati.

In the 1st A.D., during the initial contact Indian traders and Buddhist monks accidentally or intentionally carried with them the simple religious activities; for example, saying prayers to *Dipankara* Buddha and Bodhisattva *Avalokitesvara* for their safety and salvation particularly on boats across heavy seas, taking refuge in *Buddha-Dhamma-Sangha*, observing precepts, donating for merits in both this and next life, etc. Such simple religious activities were in accordance with the religious beliefs of the common people in Vietnam particularly during the Chinese cruel domination. The *Tam Cam*, one of the most ancient legends, which the Viets liked best, was handed down from generation to generation; it conveyed a content in which *But* (Buddha) living around people and possessing magic always helped the good-natured while the evil were always harmed by *Troi* (Heaven) staying in the sky. The legend obviously contains the Buddhist theory of cause and effect. The simple Buddhist beliefs were also suitable to the local peasants who asserted that souls still remained after the death of physical bodies as well as suitable to their realization of the circulation of vegetation.

However, in the 2nd century A.D., in *Giao-chau* started the foundation of Buddhist *sangha*, translation of Buddhist Sanskrit *sūtras*, building Buddhist *stūpas* and temples, and composing Buddhist texts, for example, the *Ly-hoac-luan* was composed by *Mau-Tu*. It is this book which gave information about the situation of Buddhism in Vietnam during the early centuries A.D. Kenneth K. S. Ch'en writes:

> "The first point we learn from the preface of *Mou-tzu* is that, in addition to the Buddhist centers in east China and *Loyang*, there existed a flourishing Buddhist community in south China during the Han dynasty. The origins and early development of this community are shrouded in mystery we do know that Indian traders were already making the trip by sea to ports in China during the Han dynasty. Even merchants from the Roman Empire appear to have participated in this trade, for in 166 an individual who claimed to be an envoy of the Roman ruler An-tun (Marcus Arelius Antonius) arrived in China by sea. Among the Indian traders undoubtedly were Buddhist converts. Buddhist monks must have been present also, for we find them described in *Mou-tzu* as shaving their heads, wearing saffron-colored robes, eating a meal per day, controlling the six senses, leaving the household life and abandoning their wives and children. *K'ang-Seng-Hui*, who arrived in *Nanking* in 247, was said to have been descended from a Sogdian family who had moved to *Tonkin* for commercial reasons after having lived in India for a number of generations."[18]

The *Ly-hoac-luan* aroused a lot of controversies over date and authenticity. However, according to Kenneth K.S. Ch'en: "It is more reasonable to suppose that the treatise, as we have it now, was in proccss of composition for a long time. The earliest parts of the text very likely were composed during the end of the Han dynasty,"[19] and Pal

Pelliot and *Hu-Shid* dated the *Ly-hoac-luan* at the end of the 2nd century A.D.[20]

The *Ly-hoac-luan* (Treatise for removing doubtfulness), which composes of thirty seven pairs of questions and answers, is important not only for their information about Buddhism in Vietnam it gives but also for the distinction it enjoys as the first treatise on Buddhism to be written by a Chinese convert. By protecting Buddhism and criticizing the ideas and practices of native cults, superstitions or arguments of the opponents, the text may be said to highlight the superiority of Buddhism to Confucianism and Taoism at the time. At the end of the text the hearers after listening to the author's explanation about Buddhism requested to be taken refuge in him.

One important thing in the text, in the background of Chinese rule, *Mau-Tu*, a representative of Buddhism in Vietnam dared to refuse the sense of self-respect of the Chinese, especially the Confucians, that China is the center of Heaven-and-Earth and all other countries are barbarians. In the pairs No. 1, 2 and 14 he said that not China but India was the center of Heaven-and-Earth and had peaceful nature, hence, the Buddha was born there. In addition, in the pairs No. 11, 12 he justified the habits and customs of Buddhist monks in Vietnam. For these reasons, it can be said that Buddhism in Vietnam even during the early centuries A.D. did present its independence from Chinese culture, indirectly affirmed its political role in supporting the natives' uprisings against the Chinese.

The text not only converted the upper class but also met the religious belief need of the people with definition about the supernatural power Buddha, "Buddha is awakened, endowed with supernatural powers without limit, untouched by fire, weapons, impurities, bad luck, able to fly in the air and illuminating when sitting."[21]

The *Ly-hoac-luan* appeared in the late 2nd century A.D. in which the "Sūtra in 42 sections" was mentioned. Thus the latter must appear in the early 2nd century A.D. and it was translated in *Luy-lau*, a spring-board for Buddhism reaching China. Notably, on the list of the earliest Chinese sūtras, *Tong-ly-chung-kinh-muc-luc*, compiled by *Tao-An* in 347 A.D., there were no the *Ly-hoac-luan* and *Sutra in 42 Sections*. According to *Tao-An*, all the earliest Chinese sūtras were translated in *Loyang*. *Tao-An* was a Chinese staying in Loyang and knowing well the circulation of Buddhist sūtras in the north; but, he did not hear about the *Sūtra in 42 Sections*. This fact proves that this sūtra was not generated in the north. Paul Pelliot says this sūtra was perhaps generated in the south of the Yangtze river,[22] i.e., *Luy-lau*. Of course, it is very reasonable for some authors to think that the most ancient translated text in China is the *Sūtra in 42 Sections* in the 2nd century A.D. because at that time *Luy-lau* was a Buddhist center under the Chinese domination.

So, in *Giao-chau*, during the times of *Mau-Tu* and *Khuong-Tang-Hoi* from the late 2nd to early 3rd century A.D. there were at least 15 *sūtras* circulated, 500 Buddhist monks and 20 *stūpas* erected. And, the contents of the *Sūtra in 42 Sections* mainly aimed at the monkhood rather than the laity life.

III. A Brief Account of Buddhism in Vietnam

At first, Buddhism was accepted as a *savior* by the Viets, who wished a supernatural Buddha (*Amitābha*) to save their spirits and nation. But, it all appeared to have been of no use. Day by day the Viets realized that only their own power could save them. That is the reason why *Zen* later on played a decisive role on Buddhism in Vietnam. No doubt that the first Buddhist pagoda *KHAI-QUOC* (The Opening of the State) was built in the time of the short-lived successful resistance (545-603) led by Ly-*Ban*.

A trend of supernatural Buddhism (extrovert) was turned into a trend of political Buddhist Zen (introvert). This explains the political tendency inter-twined with the spirit of non-attachment and self-reliance of Vietnamese Zen Masters from the *Vinītaruci* to *Truc-Lam* Zen sect, manifesting a very close tie between the discipline of *Zen* Masters and the protection of their fatherland. Not only politics but also many others were the spheres that Buddhism had the contribution to this nation. And here, we should not miss *True-Lam*, a particular Vietnamese *Zen sect*, an effort for an independent ideology.

Early in the 13th century, three sects—*Vinītaruci*, *Vo-Ngon-Thong* and *Thao-Duong* gradually united together. The *Tran dynasty* (1225-1400), based upon the achievements of the former dynasty (*Ly*) in uniting and keeping the stability of the state continued to insist on the national independence and on the need of an independent and united ideology with the purpose of: (1) escaping the impacts of exotic ideology, (2) uniting the power to the central government, and (3) maintaining the social order.

In the process of struggle and assimilation between the exotic religions from the early centuries A.D. till the *Ly* dynasty, Buddhism in Vietnam had predominance over Confucianism, Taoism and indigenous religious beliefs. At that time, besides *Zen* sects there were others such as Pure Land, Tantrism. However, with its non-attachment spirit *Zen* sect could conciliate other thoughts and religious beliefs. The *Tran* dynasty selected *Zen* as the leading ideology, and the contemporary *Zen* sects affected by Chinese were being adapted in response to the above-mentioned purpose. Accordingly, King *Tran-Nhan-Tong* (1258-1308), having yielded his throne to his son did launch a Vietnamese Buddhist movement nationwide under the guidance of *Truc-Lam Zen* sect. This sect flourished for a short time, till the middle of the 14th century then declined. For losing the favor of kings the *Truc-Lam* in particular and Buddhism in Vietnam in general withdrew to hide itself in the rural areas or mountains, stopping playing its important political role till late in the 16th century.

After the *Tran* dynasty, Vietnam spent a period of instability and civil war till 1802 when king *Gia-Long* started the *Nguyen* dynasty, uniting again the territory. Unfortunately not for long after that, Vietnam again suffered the ruthless invasions by the French (1864-1954) and the U.S. (1954-1975). Responding to these foreign invasions Buddhism in Vietnam re-exercised its patriotism. Robe was also armour. However, early in the 20th century there started a renaissance of Buddhist studies till now.

The history of Buddhism in Vietnam has always been linked with the survival of the nation whether in its rise or fall, and it has left plenty of Buddhist legacy on the present Vietnamese society. However, some of the Viets do not recognize the active role of Buddhism in Vietnam as a politico-socio-philosophical-cultural-religious entity of the nation. For instance, Prof. *Dang-Thai-Mai*, a famous Vietnamese scholar, quoted and commented a two-line verse by a Vietnamese *Zen* Master under the *Ly* dynasty as follows:

"As young one ought to nurture a great ambition,

not to follow the way of *Tathāgata*.

A Buddhist monk did not follow the way of the *Śākyamuni-Buddha*. How is that?"

Furthermore, some historical books in present Vietnam are written on either history of Vietnam or history of Vietnamese Buddhism, but not on the combination of the two. As a result, readers hardly recognize the history of Vietnamese Buddhism as an inseparable component of the Vietnamese history. But many questions relating to the Vietnamese history would not be clear if one did not understand the history of Buddhism in Vietnam with all its aspects.

As history is a witness, right from the beginning, that is, as early as the early centuries A.D. Buddhism has survived in Vietnam alongside Confucianism and Taoism. But from the 10th to 14th century, for about five centuries, *Zen* became a decisive ideology of Buddhism and of the state, especially under the *Ly* (1010-1225) and *Tran* (1225-1400) dynasties. During this period, Buddhism was a state religion, a king was also a *Zen* Master, and this period was the golden age of the Vietnamese Buddhist and Feudal State histories. Conversely, from the 15th to 19th centuries Confucianism replaced Buddhism in its vanguard role. However, Confucianism failed to do much for the fatherland. Now, the situation has changed again in Vietnam. Both Confucianism and Taoism are hardly there, whereas Buddhism flourishing in its full length with many traditions. Theravāda and Mahāyāna, survive as a religion which is followed by the majority of the Vietnamese people.

References

1. Phan-huy-Le et. al., *Lich-su Vietnam*, I, Hanoi, 1991, p. 100.
2. R.B. Smith and W. Watson, *Early South-east Asia*, New York, 1979.
3. Wales, "Archaeological Researches on Ancient India Colonization in Malaya," JMBRAS, XIII, 1, 1940.
4. Jean Y. Cleys. "L'archeologic du Siam," BEFEO, XXXI, p. 378.
5. Paul Pelliot, "Deux itineraries du Chine in Inde, a la fin du VII siecle," BEFEO, IV, pp. 142-43.
6. *Ibid*, pp. 154ff; "L'origine du nom de Chine," pp. 733-34.
7. Louis de la Vallee Poussin, *Dynasties et histoire de L' inde*, Vol. 6, Paris, 1935, p.193.
8. G. Coedes, *The Indianized States of South-east Asia*, trans. Susan Brown Cowing, Hawai, 1968, p. 14.
9. History of the former Han in China.
10. Phan-huy-Le, *et. al.*, pp. 164-66.
11. *Thien Uyen Tap Anh*, trans. Ngo-Duc-Tho and Nguyen-Thuy-Nga, Ha Noi, 1993, pp. 91-92.
12. History of the Three China kingdoms during the third century A.D.
13. Referring to the Indians and Central Asian Buddhist monks.
14. Phan-huy-Le, *et. al.*, *op. cit.*, p. 107.
15. *Ibid.*, p. 250.
16. *Ibid.*
17. *Ibid.*, p. 171.
18. Kenneth K. As. Ch'en, *Buddhism in China*, Princeton, 1964, p. 38.
19. *Ibid.*, p. 37.
20. *Ibid.*
21. Tang-Huu, *Hoang-Minh- Tap*, Chinese *Tripitaka*, I, p. 2a7-13.
22. Nguyen-Lang, *Viet Nam Phat Giao Su Luoc,* I, Saigon, 1974, p. 57.

Chapter 26

A General Survey of Buddhist Thought in Vietnam

Bhikkhuni Gioi Huong

Vietnam is located in the center of the South-east Asia, in the Eastern-coast of the Indo-china peninsulas. Vietnam's position is curved in the figure of the letter 'S'. Mainland territory of 330,991 sq. km with a coastline 3,260 km and its inland border measures 3,730 km. Northern side of it, China is situated. Laos and Cambodia are in the west. The East Sea and Pacific Ocean is in the South-east. Out of 78.685.800 million population, number of Buddhists at present is around 70%.[1] Vietnamese latitude arises from 8.30^0 to 23.22^0.

I. The Beginning of Buddhism in Vietnam

A general survey of Buddhist history, will enable us to realize how the system of Buddhist thought developed in Vietnam. That is to say, from the early period when Buddhism was introduced into Vietnam, it had the shade of *Mahāyāna* ideas. Khuong-Tang-Hoi (251 A.D.) was well-versed in Sanskrit and Chinese. He translated the text of Six *Pāramitās* (*Luc Do Tap Kinh*, 9 volumes)[2], *Ṣaṭpāramitā sannipāta, Ne-hoan Pham-boi, Aṣṭasāhasrikā*... Dao-Thanh who cooperated with Chi-Cuong-Luong in translating the whole text *Saddharma Puṇḍarīka* for the first time in 225 A.D. under the title *Phap-hoa Tam-muoi Kinh*[3]... Khuong-Tang-Hoi's ancestors lived in India. His father migrated to Giao-Chi (ancient name of Vietnam) to trade and settled there. His mother was Vietnamese. At that time, Vietnam was like the intersection between India and China. People could make a trip either walking, or by boat from India to China or vice versa, in doing so they must cross Vietnam. Hence, Vietnam was a popular place visited or stopped by many Indian Buddhist missionary monks or foreign business people. From this, Buddhism from India came to Vietnam probably in the first century A.D.[4] But there is also one source that reveals:

"Back to 3rd century BC, after King Asoka organized the Third Council – a Conference to Collect the Dharma – at Pataliputra, India, he sent nine Buddhist monk delegates overseas. The monks went from Afghanistan to the Mediterranean to teach Dharma. One of these, lead by Sona and Uttara went to Burma and then Indo-china, including Viet Nam. Now, in Haiphong (60 miles north-east of Hanoi) there is a memorial tower to commemorate King Asoka that was built by local Vietnamese Buddhists at that time to express their gratitude to King Asoka. From that evidence, we may come up with conclusion that Buddhism came to Vietnam as early as 300 years BC, even before China".[5]

Vietnam developed as a major Buddhist center in the region commonly known as the Luy-Lau centre, (now Bac-Ninh, Hanoi), the capital of Giao-Chi by the end of the second century and a number of *Mahāyāna sūtras* and the *Āgamas* were translated into Chinese scripts at this centre. Si-Nhiep (Vietnamese), who was governor of Giao-Chi toward the end of the Han dynasty (187-226), is revered in later Vietnamese annals as a shaper of Giao-Chi culture and promoter of Confucian values[6].

In the 1st century A.D., accidentally or intentionally in the initial contact Indian traders and Buddhist monks carried with them the simple religious activities; for example, saying prayers to *Dīpankara* Buddha and Bodhisattva *Avalokiteśvara* for their safety and salvation particularly on boats across heavy seas, taking refuge in *Buddha-Dhamma-Saṅgha*, observing precepts, donating for merits in both this and next life, etc. Such simple religious activities were in accordance with the religious beliefs of the common people in Vietnam particularly during the Chinese cruel domination. The *Tam cam*, one of the most ancient legends, conveyed the content in which *But* (Buddha) living around people and possessing magic always helped the good-natured. The legend obviously shows the Buddhist theory of cause and effect. The simple Buddhist beliefs were also suitable to the local peasants who asserted that souls still remained after the death of physical bodies as well as suitable to their realization of the circulation of vegetation. In Vietnamese folk literature, *But* (Buddha) is present in the daily life of Vietnamese people. His presence is always timely, right in place and fit for each situation to help effectively each individual or community to have sufficient power and energy to protect their life and hold peacefulness and happiness for themselves. Where there is *But*, there is blissfulness.

The Ly-hoac-luan was composed by Mau-Tu, gave information about the situation of Buddhism in Vietnam during the early centuries A.D., Giao-chau started the foundation Budddhist *saṅgha*, translation of Buddhist Sanskrit sūtras, building Buddhist *stūpas*, temples, and composing Buddhist texts, as Kenneth K.S.Ch'en writes:

"The first point we learn from the preface of Mou-tzu is that, in addition to the Buddhist centers in east China and Loyang, there existed a flourishing Buddhist community in south China during the Han dynasty. The origins and early development of this community are shrouded in mystery we do know that Indian traders were already making the trip by sea to ports in China during the Han dynasty. Even merchants from the Roman Empire appear to have participated in this trade, for in 166 an individual who claimed to be an envoy of the Roman ruler An-tun (Marcus Aurelius Antonius) arrived in China by sea. Among the Indian traders undoubtedly were Buddhist converts. Buddhist monks must have been present also, for we find them described in Mou-tzu as shaving their heads, wearing safiron-colored robes, eating one meal a day, controlling the six senses, leaving the household life and abandoning their wives and children. K'ang-Seng-Hui, who arrived in Nanking in 247, was said to have been descended from a Sogdian family who had moved to Tonkin for commercial reasons after having lived in India for a number of generations"[7].

Buddhism in Vietnam seemed to have the shade of supernatural powers by Buddhist monks in Giao-Chau (Vietnam) and their Buddhist activities would determine the features of Buddhism in Vietnam from the 3rd to 5th century A.D.

The conception of a supernatural power Buddha met the religious needs of the Vietnamese people at that time. Simultaneously, the conception reflected the Vietnamese people's dream of power for fighting against Chinese aggression. In such a condition, the belief in supernatural power of Buddhism had good chance to develop in the next centuries. *Ly-Hoac-Luan* wrote that: "Buddha is a wakened, endowed with supernatural powers without limit, untouched by fire, weapons, impurities, bad luck, able to fly in the air and illuminating when sitting"[8]. Or in 247 A.D., Khuong Tang Hoi performed the magic of Buddha's relics, king Ngo-Ton-Quyen admired him very much and had a stūpa erected for worshipping the relics. The name of the stūpa was Kien-so (the First Pagoda). After that, Buddhism flourished in Giang-Dong (China).

According to the text *Thien Uyen Tap Anh*[9], monk Thong-Bien quoted monk Dam-Thien's words that as soon as Buddhism reached

China, there had been such monks as Khau-Da-La, Ma-Ha-Ky-Vuc, Khuong-Tang-Hoi, Chi-Cuong-Luong and Mau-Tu in Giao-chau already. *Cao-tang-truyen* mentioned that there are only three biographies of monks who had some certain relations to Buddhism in Giao-chau in the 4th century A.D. They are Vu-Phap-Lan. Vu-Dao-Thuy and Ma-Ha-Ky-Vuc and in *Co chau phap van phat ban hanh ngu luc* wrote Khau-da-la and Man-Nuong which all showed the such unusual magic activities as persuading tigers, crossing river without boat, knowing the past lives, standing on one leg reciting sūtras for unbroken seven days... which proved that was embodiment of the concept of the supernatural power Buddhism.[10] This tendency becomes clearer when Ma-ha-ky-vuc appeared.

The above facts prove the shade of *Mahāyāna* ideas and supernatural power Buddhism in Vietnam in the early centuries A.D.

II. Three Thien Schools

The way of *thien*[11] established by Hue-Nang (sixth patriarch of *Ch'an* in China) is referred to by historians as the new *thien* because of its emphasis on complete and sudden enlightenment, its iconoclastic attitude toward the Buddhas, Bodhisattvas, and its disregard for literature, rituals. From the 6th century A.D. onwards Medieval Buddhism in Vietnam continued developing with the advent of alien Buddhist *thien* masters, i.e., Vinītarūci (an indian, 594), Vo-Ngon-Thong (a Chinese, 826) and Thao-Duong (a Chinese, 1069) who were founders of three *Thien* schools under their names respectively in Vietnam.

1. The Vinītaruci School

Co Chau Phap Van Phat Ban Hanh Ngu Luc (XIV century) wrote: "Between the Eastern Jin (317-419) and the Dajjan era (569-582) there was a monk named Vinītaruci, originally from Western India, who, by his journeys through many countries, knew that Buddhism already existed in this country (i.e., Giao-chau). He came to dwell at Phap van temple. Here, he established a sect, admitted students and spread the dharma. Because of this, the Buddha-dharma flourished in Vietnam and became prosperous."[12]

The Genealogy of the Vinītaruci *thien* school was inclusive of 19 successive generations. Vinītaruci translated Tong-tri and Tuong-dau tinh-xa *sūtras*. Tong-tri is a *sūtra* of Tāntrism. The *Tāntrist* practice is a close co-ordination between the manipulation of *mudrā, dhāraṇi* and *yoga*. According to *Mantrayāna*, the Buddha had no secret fist, which he demonstrated by his own hand, and was preaching the truth perpetually, but the listeners had no ear to hear and no mind to understand... Through the prescribed mantra ritual, we can realize the perfect communion between the Buddha and the aspirant, thus attaining the result of the 'Buddha-in-me, I-in-Buddha'; hence, the theory of *Buddhahood* as attainable in this corporeal life.[13]

In the circle of Buddhist *thien*, the mind-sign was a symbol of the important transmission between master and pupil, hence the pupil gains the truth under the master's initiation. Vinītaruci was quietly deeply affected by the third patriarch Tang-Xan. This affection was clearly displayed in Vinītaruci's words to Phap-Hien, his pupil, before death:

"The mind-sign of the Buddhas does not deceive us at all, the mind-sign is as full as space, neither lack nor abundance, neither going nor coming, neither gain nor loss, neither unity nor diversity, neither permanence nor annihilation, neither production nor extinction..."[14]

2. The Vo-Ngon-Thong School

Vo-Ngon-Thong was born in Kwang-chow, China, surnamed Trinh, ordained a monk at the Song-lam pagoda in Vu-chau. He was taciturn and yet intelligent; for that reason, one called him Vo-Ngon-Thong. In the 15th year of Nguyen-hoa title of the Tang dynasty (820) Vo-Ngon-Thong left Kwang-chow for Vietnam and stayed at the Kien-so pagoda at Phu-dong village, Tien-du district, Bac-ninh province.[15] Apart from the two light meals everyday, he spent much time for meditation without saying a word. For long nobody paid attention to him except Lap-Duc, the Abbot of the pagoda, who having seen his extraordinary manners took care of him carefully. For this contact, Lap-duc received the mind-sign from Vo-Ngon-Thong who, after that, changed Lap-duc's name into Cam-Thanh. Vo-Ngon-Thong died in 826 and stayed at the Kien-so pagoda for 6 years.[16]

The Vo-Ngo-Thong school was influenced by the southern *thien* school in China founded by the 6th Patriarch Hue-Nang who used the *Vajracchedikā Prajñāpāramitā Sūtra* as a basis to his teachings. The Vo-Ngon-Thong school considered the *Prajñapāramitā* literature as the basis which advocated the sudden enlightenment, mind ground and non attachment to realization.

In Ly dynasty, Dinh-Huong (1050), the 7th generation, was a well-known elderly person though he was not a monk. He had many disciples and left a verse as follows:

"Things have no region of reality by origin,
The region of reality is the true sect (or teaching).
But the true sect (or teaching) is illusory
Being is illusory, then, non-being is void."[17]

A *thien* person attaining the enlightenment realizes that all things which are conditioned have no separate reality (*svabhāva*) of their own. No separate reality (*nis-svabhāvatva*). There is no the dual concepts such as gain/loss, right/wrong, being/non-being, *saṁsāra-nibbāna*... and according to the *Mādhyamika* school, it is synonymous with devoid (*śūnyatā*). Hence, all things are equal and void.

The Vo-Ngon-Thong school was handed down for four centuries from the early 9th century A.D. to the early 13th century A.D. This affection was manifested in the way of presenting the history of *thien*; in the advocation of sudden enlightenment and non-attachment to obtaining the truth; in the way of organizing the *thien* monasteries, in the use of a device for the sudden enlightenment (the direct and instant one) and poetry images; besides, it was influenced by Tantrism and Pure land doctrine.

One day, Vo-Ngon-Thong came to Bach-Truong for learning. One monk asked Vo-Ngon-Thong: "Which *Mahāyāna dharma* can help us obtain the truth instantly?" Bach-Truong answered: "If the Ground of Mind was not put a cover on, the sunshine of wisdom would naturally come out". Vo-Ngon-Thong suddenly obtained the truth after hearing it.[18]

Nam-Tuyen asked Trieu-Chau (IX century) about the purpose of Bodhidharma coming to China, Trieu-Chau also used his finger to point at the garden nearby and said: "Look at the Tung tree." It means to realize the true nature of vision through the concrete image of reality of Tung tree.

One day, king Ly-Thai-Tong went to the mountain to visit Thien-Lao (1037) belonging to the 7th generation.

- King asked: "How long have you been here?"
- Thien-lao replied: "Living at the present moment. Who cares the past time".
- King: "What do you do here?"
- Thien-lao: "The bluish green bamboo and yellow flowers are in the garden. Under the moonlight white clouds become clear".
- King: "Then, please tell me the meaning of it".
- Thien-lao: "It is inconvenient for us to speak further".

Thien Uyen Tap Anh also recorded Tinh-Luc (1175) who attained the enlightenment by repeating the Buddha's name. He taught his pupils that they should not seek enlightenment from outside and should use the method of repeating the Buddha's name through mind and speech to extirpate the evil *karmas*.

Thien-Pure Land practice later became important element in Vietnamese Buddhism. There are some Vinītaruci and Vo-Ngon-Thong masters engaged in society particularly in politics in imperial palace but still maintained their own independent spiritual activities.

3. The Thao-Duong School

According to An Nam Chi Luoc[19], Thao-duong (a Chinese) followed his master and stayed in Champa. When Champa was invaded (in 1069 by Vietnamese troops led by King Ly-Thai-Tong).[20] Thao-duong was captured and used as a servant for a Tang-luc, that is, the Chief monk in the royal court. One day, when the Tang-luc went outside and left on the desk a text he was composing, Thao-duong unexpectedly entered the room correcting mistakes in the text. On going back to his room the Tang-luc was very surprised and informed this event to the king who after that conferred Imperial Preceptor on him. He died in the cross-legged posture[21].

Mai-Tho-Truyen[22] writes in *Buddhism in Vietnam:* "In 1069, to be precise, a significant event occurred. At that time, the country was at war with the kingdom of Champa, a turbulent neighbour, whose frequent incursions into Vietnamese territory caused great alarm. The Emperor returned from an expedition against Champa with a number of prisoners of war, among them the Chinese monk Thao-duong, who had been temporarily in Champa teaching the unified Thien-Pure Land practice with fellow Chinese Buddhists. On Ly-Thanh-Ton's return to the palace he assigned Thao-duong to assist Vietnam's Royal Head Monk (Tang-luc); one day when this monk was out on a visit, according to historical sources, Thao-duong took his Ngu-Luc, a record of the teachings of great Buddhist bronzes, and made corrections in the text. After Ly-Thanh-Ton heard of this, he sent for the prisoner to test his understanding of Buddhism. Thao-duong explained the teachings of numerous Buddhist texts and answered questions with penetrating insight, thoroughly convincing the king of his extraordinary abilities. Then, learning of Thao-duong background of study with the Chinese master Tuyet-dau Minh-Giac (980-1052) and of his teaching activities in Champa at the time of his capture, King Ly-Thanh-Ton admitted him to the Vietnamese *Saṅgha* with the title of National Teacher, and placed him in charge of teaching *Thien* practice and Buddhist philosophy in the royal palace; thereafter Thao-duong stayed at Khai-Quoc temple in the capital city of Thang-Long (now Hanoi). With Ly Thanh Ton as his earnest supporter, the master's fame spread quickly to the surrounding countryside; hearing of his residence at Khai-Quoc, Dharma-seekers journeyed from both China and Vietnam to benefit from his teachings.

As some maters of Vo-Ngon-Thong, Thao-duong also advocated the unified practice of Thien-Pure Land methods for attaining enlightenment. Heinrich Dumoulin writes in *A History of Zen Buddhism*:

"It seems especially surprising in view of the basic difference in structure between the two movements. But here too the embedding of Zen in Buddhist piety—a piety which Zen may surpass in mystical enlightenment but can never fully deny—becomes evident. Moreover, there is a remarkable psychological similarity between the rhythmic repetition of the Buddha name in the so-called nien-fo (chanting the Buddha name) and the intensive practice of the koan."[23]

Therefore, Ven. Thien An[24] noted here that: "Thao-duong's philosophy is "one purpose through different methods" or "same destination but different directions." 'Different methods' refers to the Buddhist practices of meditation, contemplation, and chanting the Buddha name. 'One purpose' is to go in one direction with one aim and for one purpose that is, to keep the mind at all times on its goal, inner-realization of the Pure Land. According to Thao-duong's philosophy, meditation, contemplation, and Buddha's-name-recitation are all ways within the one practice of Buddhism for stripping mind of attachment to desire, thus eliminating self-clinging which obscures the Dharma-eye, preventing attainment of *nirvāṇa* and arrival at the other shore, the Pure Land. For achieving this aim Thao-duong clearly indicates that Buddha's-name-recitation supplemented with the four types of outlook[25] is both an easy and an efficacious practice.

Because of Ly-Thanh-Ton's dedication in realizing the Bodhisattva ideal and his insight acquired through continual practice of both meditation and recitation, Thao-duong transmitted the seal-of-mind to him, thus establishing the king as the first patriarch of the Thao-duong *Thien* school. Ly-Nhan-Ton (reigned 1072-1127), Ly-Than-Ton (reigned 1128-1138), Ly-Anh-Ton (reigned 1138-1175), and Ly-Cao-Ton (reigned 1176-1210), the four successive monarchs who brought the prosperous Ly dynasty to a close, all emulated Ly-Thanh-Ton in their patronage and study of Buddhism. They often sent distinguished masters to teach *thien* and Buddhist doctrine in the sovereign of empire, honored them with the positions of national teachers, and sought their advice regarding administration of internal and foreign affairs. Among these later Buddhist kings, Ly-Anh-Ton and Ly-Cao-Ton were most achieved in their religious life, receiving the seal-of-mind and transfer of patriarchal authority in the tradition of Thao-duong *Thien*.

In Buddhism the Vinītarūci, Vo-Ngon-Thong, and Thao-duong *Thien* sects, predominated during the Ly dynasty because of the liberal support and spontaneous interest of the Ly dynasties and their officials whose practiced the Buddhist way.

Hence, Buddhism developed from a national religion to a nationalist religion from the Dinh (969-981) to Tran (1225-1400) dynasties before merging with aspects of Taoist and Confucian beliefs characteristic of the unification of the three religions following the decline of Buddhist influence in the Late Tran dynasty. The beginning of Buddhism as the national religion of the Vietnamese can be placed as early as the Dinh-Bo-Linh established a Vietnamese *Saṅgha* and initiated the practice of appointing eminent monks to serve as royal advisors on political, religious, and domestic matters.

After that, from the early of the 13th century A.D., three *thien* schools of Vinītarūci, Vo-Ngon-Thong and Thao-Duong gradually united together. Ven. Thuong-Chieu can be considered as the first monk combining these three *thien* schools and as a hyphen of Vietnamese Buddhism between the Ly and Tran dynasties. In other words, although the three Vietnamese *thien* schools were founded in different times but almost ended in the beginning of the Tran dynasty and gave up their positions to converge on a new united Buddhist movement which had a close relationships to customs and morals, society and especially politics to struggle for the independence and happiness of the nation. The apogee of this movement was the founding of the Truc-Lam *thien* school (Bamboo grove) whose founder was king Tran-Nhan-Tong (1258-1308).

Earlier, the Ly laid the foundations of a united Dai-Viet with resounding victories—destroying the Sung and pacifying the Chams—and held fast its territory. Having had independence on politics, economy and military, Dai-Viet must seek for its own independence on ideology. King Ly-Thanh-Tong saw it. The king wanted to build an ideology based on the Thao-Duong *thien* school, and the One-pillar pagoda[26] is a typical remaining vestige. However, the effort of the Ly king was not perfectly successful. The Tran continued to hold fast the national independence and was also aware of the need of an independent and united ideology on purposes of (i) escaping the impacts of exotic ideology, (ii) uniting power to the central government, and (iii) maintaining social order and its throne.[27]

In terms of religious ideology in Vietnam and in the process of struggle and assimilation between such exotic religions as Buddhism, Confucianism, Taoism and indigenous religious beliefs from the early centuries until the Ly, Buddhism was predominant. In Vietnamese Buddhism, besides *thien* schools there were other schools such as Pure Land, Tantrism… However, with its non-attachment spirit *thien* school could conciliate other thoughts or religious beliefs. The Tran selected *Thien* school as the leading ideology.

Thien Uyen Tap Anh was compiled in Vietnam around the third decade of the fourteenth century. It is a collection of biographies of well-known *Thien* monks in Vietnam from the sixth to the thirteenth century, presented in the form of the transmission of three *Thien* lineages or schools (Vinītarūci, Vo-Ngon-Thong and Thao-Duong) and their absolute aim is to guide *thien* practioners obtain the truth of Thusness (Buddhahood) inside them, no looking outside.

Thien master Thuong-Chieu (?-1203) of Luc-To temple,[28] Dich-Bang, Thien-Duc Prefecture, hailed from Phu-ninh village. One day, a monk asked: "What is the Truth Body (*Dharmakāya*) that pervades all?" Thuong-Chieu said: "Just as one pore contains the whole Realm of Ultimate Reality (*Dharmadhātu*), so do all pores. You should know that there is not the smallest place anywhere in Mind or in space where there is no Buddha-body. Why so? Because the Truth Body manifests itself in the Emanation Body (*nirmāṇakāya*) which attains perfect enlightenment (*samyaksambodhi*), there is no place that the Truth Body does not reach. Thus, you should know that the *Tathāgata*, through the sovereign power of mind without origination or revolution, turns the wheel of truth (*Dharmacakra*). The *Tathāgata* knows that all phenomena are not originated, so he uses the three *dharmas* to teach annihilation. The *Tathāgata* knows that all phenomena are free from false views, so he dwells in the realm separate from desire—but not its annihilation-to turn the Wheel of Truth. The *Tathāgata* also enters the realm of the emptiness of all phenomena; therefore without reply in words, he turns the Wheel of truth. The *Tathāgata* knows that all phenomena are ineffable, so he dwells in the ultimate peace to turn the Wheel of Truth. The *Tathāgata* knows that all phenomena are originally *nirvāṇa*. This is called formless true nature, inexhaustible true nature, unborn, undestroyed; selfless true identity, where nothing is not self, true nature without sentient beings, where nothing is not sentient beings, true nature without '*Boddhisattvas*', without the Realm of Ultimate Reality (*Dharmadhātu*), without 'emptiness' – nature where there is no "achieving perfect enlightenment".[29]

Thien master Cuu-chi of Dien-linh temple on Mount Long-Doi, one day as he was reading, he signed and said: 'Both Confucius and Mozi were attached to being. Both Zhuangzi and Laozi were attached to non-being. The conventional classics are not the teaching of liberation. Only the Buddhist teaching approves neither being not non-being and completely comprehends birth and death. One must maintain discipline and advance energetically, and seek the seal of approval from enlightened teachers'. So, he abandoned conventional studies and went to call on the Elder Dinh-Huong of Cam Ung temple on Mount Ba-Son to receive ordination.

One day, while he was asking for instruction, Dinh-Huong asked him: 'What is the ultimate truth?' Cuu-Chi said: 'I do not know'. Dinh-Huong said: 'I already give you the ultimate truth'. As Cuu Chi hesitated trying to think what to say, Dinh-Huong said 'You've missed it'. At these words, Cuu-Chi discovered the gist (of the Buddhist message). Accordingly, Dinh-Huong named him Cuu-Chi (which means 'Investigating the Gist').

During the Chuong-Thanh-Gia-Khanh era (1059-1065), when he was about to depart from the world, Cuu-Chi called together his disciples and said: "All Buddhist teachings originally come from your own inherent nature. The true nature of all phenomena originally comes from your mind. Mind and phenomena are one Thusness: fundamentally there is nothing else. All defilements that bind you are empty. Misdeeds and merits, right and wrong are all illusions. There is nothing but cause and effect, in the realm of karma, do not differentiate: If you do you will not find freedom. You see all phenomena, but without any objects of knowing. You know that all phenomena have dependent origination (*pratīyasamutpāda*) as their basis. You see that all phenomena have true reality as their source. Even amidst defilement, you understand that the world is like a magical apparition. You clearly comprehend that the true identity of sentient beings is the One Reality. There is no other reality. You do not abandon the karmic realm: You use the proper skillful means to show the uncreated Dharma in the realm of the created, but without differentiating and without the marks of creation. This is because desire is ended, self is forgotten and conceptual elaborations (*prapañca*) are abandoned."[30]

Therefore, *Thien Uyen Tap Anh* reveals us that Vietnamese Buddhist history is a continuation of the development of the Chinese *Thien* tradition and centering on *Thien* masters enlightenment experiences – it contains relatively few references to Buddhist philosophy in which, the *Tāthagatagarbha* doctrine of the identity of the essence of mind with Thusness (*Buddhahood*) approving that all sentient beings are originally possessed of this pure mind.

III. The Truc-Lam Thien School

Vietnam did not gain political independence from Chinese hegemony until the tenth century.[31] After four centuries Vietnam formed its independence from China, the Vietnamese ruling dynasties constantly engaged distinguished monks to assist them in religious, political, and literary affairs. During this period, Buddhism was able to establish itself as an important factor in politics and culture.

The kings of the Ly dynasty (1010-1225) went on to get aid from Buddhism, and in return they propagated Buddhism at large prospect. While the Dinh and (Former) Le had been short-lived empires that rose and fell in political uproar over three generations, the Ly dynasty lived for two centuries. The Ly had more time to establish a system of rule and an official world vision and under the Ly the relationship between the court and Buddhism became more formal and organized way.

In Ly dynasty, the eminent Buddhist monks were Ven. Van-Hanh and Ven. Man-Giac who had long impact on the following Vietnamese Buddhist generations.

Thien master Man-Giac, a respected and popular monk whose disciples including the Emperor and the Empress, wrote:

When spring goes, the hundred flowers wither
when spring comes, the hundred flowers blossom
One thing after another, lives passed before our eyes
Old age comes from above
Don't think that all flowers fall as spring ends
In the courtyard last night a plum branch bloomed.[32]

This poem is very wonderful, pictorial and colorful in which Ven. Man Giac refers to the flow of natural events as emblematic of ultimate realty. Once we realize that the phenomenal world is impermanent, we will experience no fear at any change of unstable world.

Ven. Van-hanh composed one of the famous poems that:

The body is like a lightning, it's there and then it's not
Its like myriad plants and trees—fresh in the spring but fading in autumn
Trust in your destiny, unafraid of ups or downs

Because ups and downs are (as evanescent) as drop of dew on the blade of grass.[33]

This poem also carries a very simple idea and easy to understand the face of the impermanence of the phenomenal world. Before passing away, he taught his disciples the last lesson: Don't be afraid of the constantly changing of the phenomenal world. Yourself are as a drop of morning dew. At present, it's bright under the sunrise as a diamond, but next it will disappear into the air. That is the nature of yourself and all.

The Tran dynasty (1225-1400) also made serious efforts to legitimize its dynastic power. The official examination system encouraged well-born men to become familiar with Confucian ideas of statecraft and channeled members of the royal clan and other powerful clans into the service of the central power. The Mongol invasions[34] early in the Tran period caused a national emergency that helped solidify the role of the Tran kings as the leaders of the nation.

Within Vietnamese Buddhism, *Thien* learning also became more established in this period with the arrival of Chinese *Ch'an* monks and literature.

For the Tran rulers, Buddhism represented the most profound soteriological aspect of the Three Religions (Buddhism, Taoism and Confucianism), whereas Confucianism was more effective and appropriate for worldly affairs.[35] Most of the Tran kings lived out this worldview in their own careers: After abdicating the throne to become "retired emperors" they would withdraw to Mount Yen Tu to practice Buddhism and become spiritual leaders of their people.[36]

Under the Tran dynasties, Buddhism was a sincere imitation of the idealistic version of the 'new' Buddhism—the Chinese 'Patriarchal Ch'an' that had been showing its way into Vietnam since the Ly dynasty. The Truc-Lam (Bamboo Grove) *Thien* school, a genuinely Vietnamese Buddhist school was founded by Tran-Nhan-Tong (1258-1308), the third king of the Tran dynasty. The Truc-Lam School was short-lived,[37] but it signified the first serious accomplishment to create a *Thien* school in medieval Vietnam. After defeating the Mongols, King Tran-Nhan-Tong established a united and independent Buddhist ideology nationwide, which was the Truc-Lam *thien* school bearing Vietnamese characteristics, only one and replacing the then three foreign *thien* schools (Vinītaruci, Vo-Ngon-Thong and Thao-Duong).

From the early centuries A.D. until late in the fourteenth century A.D. Vietnamese Buddhism gradually played a significant role in the victorious career of the nation. In its contribution, *Thien* of Vietnamese Buddhism under the Tran Dynasty is the most symbolic.

The founder of the Truc-Lam *thien* school is Tran-Nhan-Tong, but in fact the school is founded with the contributions of *thien* masters Tran-Thai-Tong and Tue-Trung-Thuong-Si. Tran Thai Tong is the first king founding the Tran dynasty. Like Hui-neng, the sixth ch'an patriarch in China, Tran-Thai-Tong attains enlightenment from the line one should use ones's mind in such a way that it will be free from any attachment in the *Vajracchedikā Prajñā-pāramitā Sūtra*. Tue-Trung-Thuong-Si is considered by the contemporary as Vimalakīrti Bodhisattva in Vietnam, and is Tran-Nhan-Tong's master.

The Truc-lam *thien* school advocated various methods of self-cultivation such as repentance, repeating the name of a Buddha, observing commandments, sitting meditation, studying sūtras.

- On repentance, Tran-Thai-Tong says:

"That which help people go to and fro on the rivers and roads are boats and vehicles; that which wash away taints from body and mind are repentance rites... Due to the Buddha's supernatural power and one's devotion, every evil karma accumulated in hundreds of thousands of *kalpas* can be all removed only in a day or moment...".[38]

Meditation and studying sūtras together is a specific feature of the Truc-lam *thien* school when compared to Hui-neng's *ch'an* in China, which advocates to realize the Thusness (*Buddhahood*) not paying attention to words and sūtras. This is illustrated in a verse of Tran-Nhan-Tong's:

> "Living peacefully with the imperturble heart among the quiet scenery,
>
> A cool wind blew to the shadow of a pine tree.
>
> Under the tree are a meditation cushion and sūtra,
>
> Two words leisured-life are much more valuable than gold."[39]

It is no care whatever forms you are, turn back inside yourself contemplating your real nature, essence of mind (*Buddhahood*), do not look for anywhere else; Believe your capacity. That is the essential point of meditation. Tran-Thai-Tong says:

"No matter you are monks or laymen, the thing is to realize the essence of mind."[40]

One day, Tran-Nhan-Tong asked Tue-Trung-Thuong-Si about the guiding principle of meditation. Tue-Trung-Thuong-Si answered:

"Turn back inside yourself to realize your origin, certainly nowhere else."[41]

The Truc-Lam *thien* school also had the attitude of entering the world-serving both the individual emancipation and the welfare of society. The advice of Imperial Preceptor Dao-Vien, whom king Tran-Thai-Tong met on the Yen-Tu mountain, is considered as a lodestar for a Buddhist politician:

"As a king, he must regard his people's wish and heart as his. Now, the whole people want to take Your Majesty back to the capital, how could You refuse? Except that Your Majesty should not neglect studying Buddhist sūtras." King Tran-Thai-Tong said: "We received the Buddha's teachings from saints and sages. Now, there is no reason why we do not regard the duty of the saints and sages as ours."[42]

Tue-trung-Thuong-si, Tran-Nhan-Tong's master said: "Mixing with the secular life mingling our radiance in the worldly life."[43] King Tran-Nhan-Tong traveled throughout the country advised people to practice Thap-thien ... Followers of the Truc-Lam *thien* school did not advocate secluding themselves from the world since 'There is no Buddha in the mountain'; they did not call upon the followers to leave home for a secluded life on the mountain. They accepted the forms of both Buddhist priests and lay Buddhists. According to them, the individual must serve society with Buddhist spirit.

They did not call upon people to abandon the secular life but only advise people to practise continence... The Truc-Lam *thien* school relied on the non-attachment (*śūnya*) of Nāgārjuna which manifested tolerance, freedom, equality, democracy, national independence in the cultural, social and political life of the country.

Ten centuries passed, the *Mahāyāna* ideal had still developed and reached its zennith by *Thien* masters in Tran dynasty (1225-1400) such as Tran-Thai-Tong, Tran-Nhan-Tong, Tue-Trung-Thuong-Si... *Mahāyāna* Buddhism formed out the nature of Vietnamese Buddhism and made Buddhism to be the Buddhism of Vietnamese people which is agreed with Vietnamese characters, especially Tran-Nhan-Tong who created *Thien* school of Truc-Lam which was the first and unique *Thien* school in the history of country. Truc-Lam *Thien* school of Vietnam was considered as the mature form of Vietnamese Buddhist Thoughts which was cultivated for almost three centuries from Ly to Tran dynasty.

During Tran dynasty of two centuries, Vietnamese people as well as Vietnamese Buddhists enjoyed the golden time of Buddhism in Vietnamese Buddhism history. In this historical era, the country's intellectual class was mainly consisting of Buddhist monks. Buddhism was then regarded as the official religion dominating court affairs. It was preached broadly among the population and it enjoyed a profound influence on people's daily life. Its influence also left marks in various areas of traditional literature and architecture and many pagodas and temples were built during this time.

IV. Buddhism in the Contemporary

Buddhism was spread in the South by King Nguyen-Phuc-Chu (1691-1725). He was enthroned at the age of seventeen and was a strong devout Buddhist more than any of his predecessors. With the help of Ven. Dai-San (Chinese), King Nguyen-Phuc-Chu opened a Grand Bikkhus Ordained in Hue (1695), which had more than 1,400 Vietnamese monks attended. It was a big ordain in Vietnamese Buddhist history, especially in South of Vietnam. He also built or upgraded many pagodas. He and his predecessors had best effort to propagate Buddhism and made it to become the state religion in his kingdom for over one century. Nguyen-Hoang also was considered as a pioneer of a movement that Vietnam's history call 'Southern Forward Campaign' that aimed at expanding Vietnam territory to the South. After that he found a Southern kingdom named Great Vietnam (Dai Viet) and claimed independence from the North that led to a war between two lineages, the 'Trinh-Nguyen Civil War' in Vietnamese history that prolonged more than two centuries.

Since 1858, Vietnam had been endured the French colonist for almost a century. There were many movements attempted to liberate the country. Finally, what we called 'The First Vietnam War' (the war between Vietnam and France) ended in 1954. The Geneva Accord divided Vietnam into two countries, which put the North under Communists control and the South to the nationalists, which was led by Bao-Dai, the last emperor of Vietnam. Prime minister Ngo-Dinh-Diem (a Catholic) later overthrew Bao-Dai to become the head of state.

President Diem applied the same discrimination policy of the French and persecution against Buddhism. Vietnamese Buddhists had no choice but to stand up to condemn the killings and struggle for the religious freedom. On June 11, the Most Venerable Thich Quang-Duc was self-immolated on a busy intersection of Saigon to protest. His last words, a respectful plea to Diem, asking the president to show 'charity and compassion' to all religions.

On November 1, 1963 the regime of President Ngo-Dinh-Diem was brought down and opened a new chapter to Buddhism in Vietnam. A Buddhist Conference was held in Saigon on December 31, 1963 with the birth of 'Unified Vietnamese Buddhist Church' (UVBC), the organization to represent the Buddhism in Vietnam at that time.[44]

In 1975, Communist North took over the whole country, North and South united as one. In 1981, a new Buddhist organization: Vietnamese Buddhist *Saṅgha* (GHPGVN) was found and represented the Vietnamese Buddhist interests of the whole country. More than 20 years after Vietnamese has gained peace and independence, Buddhism day-by-day has settled and developed. According to the report of Vietnamese Buddhist *Saṅgha* in 3-1-2000 about Vietnamese Buddhist Activities in 1999,[45] some figures are given as follows:

Total of *Mahāyāna*, Khmer *Theravāda*, Kinh *Theravāda* and *Mendicant* (local sect) priests and their pagodas are as the following table under:

	Mahāyāna	**Theravāda**
Mendicant	**Total**	
Priests	21.606	7.793(Khmer) 401(Kinh)
2045	31.845	
Pagodas	12.799	469
516		
Temples	357	
14.554		
Chanting Halls	413	

Besides, Vietnam Buddhist *Saṅgha* has three Institutes of Buddhist studies in North, Centre and South of Vietnam, three Higher Buddhist schools in HCM city, Baria-Vungtau and Cantho and 28 schools of Basic Buddhist studies. After having graduated in Vietnam, hundreds of monks and nuns are able to continue opening the religious as well as secular educations in foreign countries such as India, China, Taiwan, Japan, America, Australia ... by scholarship or their self-supporting finance.

V. Buddhist Sects in Vietnam

Another feature which is different from other Buddhist countries in the world is that in Vietnam in modern time has existed the three sects; *Mahāyāna* (Northern Tradition), *Theravāda* (Southern Tradition) and *Mendicant Saṅgha* which all composed out what we called Buddhism in Vietnam. As we know, Buddhism in Japan, China, Taiwan, Vietnam and Korea...are almost belong to *Mahāyāna*, Srilanka, Thailand, Burma, Lao, Cambodia, Myanmar and India... are almost belong to *Theravāda*. Majority of Vietnamese Buddhists are *Mahāyāna* from the early period of Buddhism introduced into Vietnam, it had the shade of *Mahāyāna* ideas and Vietnamese Buddhism has been greatly influenced by the development of *Mahāyāna* Buddhism in

China with the dominant traditions of *Thien*, Pure Land and Tantra as we mentioned above. But besides that *Theravāda* and *Mendicant* sects have also well recognized in Vietnam especially since 20th–21st centuries.

According to Andrew Skilton in *A Concise History of Buddhism,*[46] the southern part of the present Vietnam was originally occupied by the Champa (Cham) and the Cambodian (Khmer) people who followed both a syncretic Saiva–*Mahāyāna* Buddhism and *Theravāda* Buddhism, although Champa probably had a *Theravāda* presence from as early as the 3rd century CE, whilst Cambodia received the *Theravāda* as late as the 12th century. The Vietnamese started to conquer and absorbed the land in the 15th century, and the current shape of the country was finalized in the 18th century. From that time onward, the dominant Vietnam followed the *Mahāyāna* tradition whilst the ethnic Cambodian practiced the *Theravāda* tradition, and both traditions peacefully co-existed.

There were a number of movements in Vietnam for the revival and development of Buddhist activities in the 1920s and 1930s. Parallel with the re-organisation of *Mahāyāna* establishments, an arousing interest in Theravādin *thien* and also in Buddhist materials based on the Pāli Canon, specially *Nikāya-Āgama* literature and in *Abhidhamma* studies also arose. Among the volunteers who brought *Theravāda* Buddhism to Vietnam was Le-Van-Giang who was born in the South, received higher education in Hanoi, and after graduation, was sent to Cambodia, to work for the French government.[47] Later, he ordained and took the *Dhamma* name of Ho-Tong (*Vansarakkhita*).

Venerable Ho-Tong with a group of Vietnamese Venerables Thien-Luat, Buu-Chon, Kim-Quang, Gioi-Nghiem, Tinh-Su, Toi-Thang, Giac-Quang, An-Lam… started teaching the *Buddha Dhamma* in Vietnamese language. Ven. Ho-Tong also translated many Buddhist materials from the Pāli Canon and *Theravāda* became part of Vietnamese Buddhist activity in the country.[48]

The Vietnam *Mendicant Saṅgha* was founded in 1946 by Master Minh-Dang-Quang[49], who was born at Vinh-Long in 1923. Since his passes away[50] in 1954, his disciples have continued spreading his teachings, which nowadays has spread from the South to the Central Vietnam. Since 1966, the *Saṅgha* of this group has officially recognized and known as The Congregation of Vietnam *Mendicant Saṅgha*.[51]

The doctrine of the Vietnam *Mendicant Saṅgha* is consistent selection of elements from the *Mahāyāna* and *Theravāda* after they had undergone some refinements and adjustment so as to keep them in accordance with the pivotal ideas of the founder and with the Southern Vietnamese mind which was shown by Master Minh-Dang-Quang and written in the 'Chon-Ly' (The Truth). Monks and nuns wear yellow robes and walk for alms rounds[52] resembling the *Theravāda* and follow a vegetarian diet and there is an Order of Nuns (*Bhikkhunis*). They observe 348 rules[53] of *Dharmaguptaka Vinaya* like the *Mahāyāna*. In the *Theravāda* tradition in Vietnam, there is no Order of Nuns, even now there are only four first *Bhikkhunis* who were recently ordained at the Ordination Ceremony organized on 3rd and 4th March 2002 in Sri Lanka. *Bhikkhunīs* who belong to the *Theravāda* tradition, observe 311 rules.[54]

Different from the other two former traditions, *Mendicant Saṅgha* daily chants the suttas which were translated into the Vietnamese language. In *Theravāda*, they chant in the *Pāli* language, and in *Mahāyāna* they chant in the Chinese language with Vietnamese pronunciations. However, nowadays some of *Mahāyāna* pagodas have started to translate their sūtras in Vietnamese and chanting in Vietnamese language. *Mendicant Saṅgha* study both *Nikāya suttas* and *Mahāyāna sūtras*. Their practicing methods are similar to other traditions, namely, practicing *sīla-samatha-prajñā*, but for meditation, they practice *Tathāgata*[55] (*samatha* and *vipassanā*) like *Theravāda* while *Mahāyāna* follows Patriarchal meditation, Truc-Lam thien school, Thien-Pure Land...

VI. Practical Method

To discuss about the practice methods of Buddhists in Vietnam mention can be to the cultivating of *Thien*, Pure Land and Tantric schools... through the three sects: *Mahāyāna, Theravāda* and *Mendicant*. It also depends on the time, dynasties, circumstances, these elements seem to appear in diversity and particular. However, among them *Thien* still is the main Buddhist method and has influenced almost Buddhist activities in Vietnam since a long time.

Nowadays, there are many eminent masters in *thien* and Pure Land schools in Vietnam. In the limit of this essay, the author would like to introduce two well-known *thien* masters.

First of all, Ven. Thanh-Tu was born in 1924, Can-Tho. In 1949, he became a novice at Phat-Quang pagoda. One night, he dropped tears while he was reading the *Śūraṅgamasamādhisūtra* to the page in which Buddha showed Ven. Anan the way how to realize the Buddha-nature by nature of vision and hear. From that, he was interested to follow the method of meditation. In 1968, he enlightened the nature of *rūpa-śūnyatā* and comprehended the deep meaning of *Mahāyāna sūtras*.[56] He has started spreading the method of meditation and revived the Truc-Lam *thien* school of King Tran-Nhan-Tong in modern time. He has given hundreds of *thien* lectures in Vietnam and abroad and founded many famous *Thien* Institutes in and outside of Vietnam among them as Chan-Khong (Vung-tau), Thuong-Chieu, Linh-Chieu (Dong-Nai), Truc-Lam (Da-lat)... The number of his disciples (both monks, nuns and laymen) in and out of Vietnam is up to thousands. He also translated lot of *Mahāyāna sūtras*, *śastras* and composed many valuable *thien* books and poems. Among them, the poem *Life in my Vision*[57] which may be in the forms of instructional verse or an expression of the spiritual understanding, experience and attitudes toward human life always optimist and positive, not to pay attention at any the impermanence or permanence, poor or rich, failure or success ...He also advocated as master Bach-Truong's standpoint "Day without a labor, a day without food". Therefore, how nice it is! Almost of his *Thien* pagodas located in the green villages, on the high mountains ...in which his *thien* pupils everyday go to field to plant vegetable, rice, to plough, to cut wood...in the spirit of optimist and positive *thien*.

Another Vietnamese famous *Thien* master is Ven. Nhat-Hanh who is now living in France. He has written lot of *Thien* books in Vietnamese and English. He is well-known in the world by giving valuable *Thien* lectures to Vietnamese and foreigners. In 1982, he founded Plum Village, a Buddhist monastery for monks and nuns and a practice center for lay people in France. During the course of the year, Plum Village welcomes thousands of retreatants from all over the world. Due to its rapid expansion in recent years, the community is now comprised of seven hamlets. Upper Hamlet, Middle Hamlet, West Hamlet and Lower Hamlet, located south east of Sainte Foy la Grande; New Hamlet, Gatehouse New Hamlet and Hillside New Hamlet, located just west of Duras.[58]

Ven. Thanh-Tu and Ven. Nhat-Hanh are the big names among other eminent masters in modern Vietnamese history, Buddhist history as well as Buddhist thought.

In short, in the first century A.D. Buddhism came into existence in Vietnam. Buddhism is popular religion in Vietnam until now. If the time is the measure of truth, then with the length of that history, Buddhism confirmed true value of its on this country. In the fields such as society, culture, politics, especially thought, Buddhism directly or indirectly contributes to form the ideal of living and activity for Vietnamese people. The root sense of philosophical ideas are the Dependent-Origination (*Paticcasamuppada*), Four-Noble-Truth (*Ariya saccas*) and Eightfold-Path (*Atthangika-magga*) ... which are considered to be the basic philosophy in *Mahāyāna, Theravāda* and *Mendicant* sects. *Thien* is no attachment to everything and no tie to any form, therefore we may practice *Thien* everywhere whether we are working, eating, talking, laboring...and at anytime we want. If we hope to gain peace, then Vietnamese *Thien* may offer us a living method. Therefore, *Thien* method even Patriarchal meditation, Truc-Lam *thien* school or Tathāgata (*samathā* and *vipassanā*) pre-dominated over others. Although the rituals and traditions of the three Vietnamese *Mahāyāna*, *Theravāda* and *Mendicant* sects are different, they all practice the *dhamma* and perfect the function of the Buddha's message to train themselves and spread the *Dharma* to bring all human beings to calmness, eternity and welfare. Three sects have made a lot of efforts to develop Vietnamese Buddhism as well as Vietnamese society.

References

1. See Website: http://www.Vietnamtourism.com
2. Lich Su Phat Giao Vietnam, Le Manh That, Hoc Vien Phat giao Vietnam tai Hue, 1999, Chuong V. See Website: http://www.Buddhismtoday.com
3. B. Nanjio, A Catalogue of the Chinese Translations of the Buddhist Tripitaka, Delhi, 1989, p. 390 (no. 22).
4. Nguyen Lang, Vietnam Phat giao Su luan, vol. I, (*A Critical History of Buddhism in Vietnam*), 1973. However, there are some source stated that Buddhism came to Giao Chi as early as second cent CE. See Nguyen Duy Hinh "Three Legends and Early Buddhism in Vietnam", Vietnam Forum 13, 1990, 10-23.
5. Introduction to Buddhism in Vietnam & Vietnamese Zen, Tam Ha Le Cong Da in Website: http://www. Buddhismtoday.com
6. Viet Dien U linh Tap (21-22) (Potent Spirits of the Viet Realm), various editions. See Chan Hing-Ho ed. Also see Keith Weller Taylor, The Birth of Vietnam, Berkeley and Los Angeles: University of California Press, 1983, pp. 70-74.
7. Kennth K. S. Ch'en, Buddhism in China, Princeton, 1964, p. 38.
8. Tang-huu, Hoang-minh-tap, Chinese Tripitaka. I, p. 2a7-13.
9. Zen in Medieval Vietnam: A Study and Translation of Thien Uyen Tap Anh, Cuong Tu Nguyen, Hawai: Kuroda Institute, 1997.
10. Luc do tap kinh, Khuong Tang Hoi, fasc. 7, fol. 39b16-23.
11. Meditation i.e., Thien (in Vietnam), Ch'an (in China) and Zen (in Japan).
12. Quoted from Zen in Medieval Vietnam: A Study and Translation of Thien Uyen Tap Anh, Cuong Tu Nguyen, Hawai: Kuroda Institude, 1997, p. 38.
13. Junjiro Takakusu, The Essentials of Buddhist Philosophy, Delhi, 1975. p. 155.
14. Nguyen Lang, Vietnam Phat giao Su luan, I, Saigon, 1974, p. 116.
15. Tran van Giap, Lich su Phat giao Vietnam tu Khoi dau cho den The ky thu XIII (A History of Vietnamese Buddhism from the beginning to the 13th century A.D.), trans. Tue sy, Saigon, 1968, pp. 119-120.
16. Nguyen Lang, Vietnam Phat giao Su luan, I, Saigon, 1974, p. 155-6.

17. Uy Ban Khoa Hoc Xa Hoi Vietnam—Vien Van hoc, TVLT, I, HN, 1977, p. 345.
18. Nguyen Lang, Vietnam Phat giao Su luan, I, Saigon, 1974, p. 154.
19. An Nam Chi Luoc (A Short History of An Nam), Le Tac, vol. 15, p. 7.
20. Nguyen Lang, Vietnam Phat giao Su luan, I, Sai gon, 1974, p. 187.
21. An Nam Chi nguyen (The Original An Nam), vol. 3, p. 209.
22. Mai-Tho-Truyen, Buddhism in Vietnam. p. 42 in Ven. Thien An, Thao Duong Zen School (The Zen-Pure land and Modern Vietnamese Buddhism). See on Website: http://www.Buddhismtoday.com
23. Heinrich Dumoulin, A History of Zen Buddhism. p. 125. Quoted in Ven. Thien An, Thao Duong Zen School (The Zen-Pure land and Modern Vietnamese Buddhism). See on Website: http://www.Buddhismtoday.com
24. Ven. Thien An, Thao Duong Zen School (The Zen-Pure land and Modern Vietnamese Buddhism). See on Website: http://www.Buddhismtoday.com
25. This is Lin-chi technique in the form of the four types of outlook within a practice traditionally ascribed to the Pure Land school, the recitation of the name of Buddha Amitabha, a form of mantra practice leading to single hearted concentration through which the other-Power finds a channel of expression. Within the workings of the recitation of the name of Buddha Amitabha, the four distinctions are self-acting or self-perpetuating in the sense that an outside agent, such as a Thien master, does not apply them. They arise of their own through the "power of the other" which may actually result from concentrated belief and complete faith in the efficacy of the practice. The four distinctions, listed below as formulated by Lin-chi. are central to his methodology of self-realization:
    1. Eliminating subject, leaving object;
    2. Eliminating object, leaving subject;
    3. Eliminating both, leaving neither;
    4. Eliminating neither, leaving both.
26. Now it is still located in Hanoi capital and considered the important historical monument in Vietnamese Buddhist.
27. Nguyen Xuan Kinh, Thien of Vietnamese Buddhism under the Tran dynasty; Thesis of Ph.D., Delhi University, 1996, pp. 130-1.
28. According to the Dai Nam Thong Nhat Chi (28:72) "Bac Ninh province, section on Temples and shrines", Luc to temple was identical with Truong Lieu temple. The Su Ky record that Master Van Hanh was the abbot of that temple. When he died Emperor Ly Thai To himself came to pay homage and had an altar erected to pray for his salvation He also assigned men as temple attendants to look after worship services the whole year. According to this, we have on the one hand Truong Lieu temple at Tieu Son, Yen Phong district, on the other hand, it is said in this biography that Luc To temple was at Dich Bang village, Thien Duc prefecture, now Dinh Bang village, Tu Son prefecture. Thus, Luc To temple and Truong Lieu temple could not be identical.
29. Avatamsakasūtra, T 10.275b17-276a6.
30. Zen in Medieval Vietnam (A Study and Translation of the Thien Uyen Tap Anh), Cuong Tu Nguyen, 1997, Honolulu: Kuroda Institude, 123-5.

31. Keith Weller Taylor, The Birth of Vietnam, Berkeley and Los Angeles: University of California Press, 1983.
32. Zen in Medieval Vietnam: A Study and Translation of Thien Uyen Tap Anh, Cuong Tu Nguyen, Hawai: Kuroda Institude, 1997, p. 132.
33. *Ibid.*, p. 60.
34. Le Thanh Khoi, Histoire du Vietnam: Des origines ao, 1858, Paris: Sudestasie, 1987, p. 182-192.
35. Toan Thu, Ban Ky, 5:332.
36. Ke Dang Luoc Luc 5a2-7a10.
37. Ke Dang Luoc Luc, 11a3-4.
38. Tran Thai Tong, Khoa Hu Luc, trans. Thich Thanh Kiem, HCM, 1992, p. 56.
39. Uy Ban Khoa Hoc Xa Hoi Vietnam, Vien Van Hoc, TVLT, I, HN, 1977, p. 545.
40. Tran Thai Tong, Khoa Hu Luc, trans. Thich Thanh Kiem, HCM, 1992, p. 27.
41. Uy Ban Khoa Hoc Xa Hoi Vietnam, Vien Van Hoc, TVLT, I, HN, 1977, p. 546.
42. Uy Ban Khoa Hoc Xa Hoi, Vien Van Hoc, Tho Van Ly Tran, Vol. II, 1989, p. 27-8.
43. Tue Trung Thuong Si, Ngu Luc, trans. Truc Thien, Saigon, 1969, p. 172.
44. Tam Ha Le Cong Da, Introduction to Buddhism in Vietnam and Vietnamese Zen; See on website: http://www.Buddhismtoday.com
45. Bao cao Tong Ket Cong tac Phat Su nam 1999 cun GHPGVN, ngay 3-1-2000, trang 4-22.
46. Andrew Skilton, 1994. A Concise History of Buddhism. Website: http://www.Buddhismtoday.com.
47. Le Minh Qui, 1981. Hoa Thuong Ho-Tong (Biography of Maha Thera Ho-Tong). See Website: http://www.Buddhismtoday.com and http://www.Buddhasasana.com
48. *Theravāda* Buddhism in Vietnam, Binh An son. See Website: http://www.Buddhasasana.com
49. See Han On, Minh Dang Quang Phap Giao (The Dhamma of Minh Dang Quang), Binh Dinh, 1960, p. 25.
50. Master Minh Dang Quang was caught by Tran Van Soai (Nam Lua), in Can Tho, on the way he went from Sadec to Vinh Long and to Can Tho on 1st February 1954. (See Han On, The Dhamma of Minh Dang Quang, p. 40f.).
51. Quoted by Thich Giac Tri, Su Hinh Thanh va Phat trien cua He Phai Khat Si (The formation and development of the Vietnam Mendicant Saṅgha), Hoc Vien PGVN, 2001, p. 26.
52. Since 1975, Vietnam society has developed, with the government policy; they no longer live their life traveling but have to live at registered places.
53. See Ann Heinnann, Rules or Nuns according to The Dharmaguptakavinaya, vol. II. And see Thich Giac Nhien, Luat Nghi Khat Si (Rules and monastic principles of Vietnam Mendicant Saṅgha) MDQ Monastery, 1965, pp. 174-199.
54. See William Pmitt (ed), K.R. Norman (tr): The *Pātimokkha*, p. 113ff.
55. Thich Giac Nhien, Luat Nghi Khat Si (Rules and monastic principles of Vietnam Mendicant Saṅgha) MDQ Monastery, 1965, pp. 109-118.

56. http://www.thuongchieu.org
57. Cuoc doi qua mat toi, Hoa Thuong Thanh Tu, Thien Vien Chan Khong, Thang 6, 1984.
58. http://www.langmai.org.

Chapter 27

Theravada Buddhism in Vietnam

Binh Anson

Buddhism came to Vietnam in the first century CE.[1] By the end of the second century, Vietnam developed a major Buddhist centre in the region, commonly known as the Luy-La^u centre, now in the Ba('c-Ninh province, north of the present Hanoi city. Luy-La^u was the capital of Giao-Chi?, former name of Vietnam, and was a popular place visited by many Indian Buddhist missionary monks on their way to China, following the sea route from the Indian sub-continent by Indian traders. A number of Mahāyāna sutras and the Āgamas were translated into Chinese scripts at that centre, including the sūtra of *Forty Two Chapters,* the *Anapanasati,* the *Vessantara-jataka,* the *Milinda-panha,* etc.

In the next 18 centuries, due to geographical proximity with China and despite being annexed twice by the Chinese, the two countries shared many common features of cultural, philosophical and religious heritage. Vietnamese Buddhism has been greatly influenced by the development of Mahāyāna Buddhism in China, with the dominant traditions of Ch'an/Zen, Pure Land, and Tantra.

The southern part of the present Vietnam was originally occupied by the Champa (Cham) and the Cambodian (Khmer) people who followed both a syncretic Saiva-Mahāyāna Buddhism and Theravāda Buddhism,[2] although Champa probably had a Theravāda presence from as early as the 3rd century CE, whilst Cambodia received the Theravāda as late as the 12th century. The Vietnamese started to conquer and absorbed the land in the 15th century, and the current shape of the country was finalised in the 18th century. From that time onward, the dominant Viet followed the Mahāyāna tradition whilst the ethnic Cambodian practiced the Theravāda tradition, and both traditions peacefully co-existed.

In the 1920s and 1930s, there were a number of movements in Vietnam for the revival and modernisation of Buddhist activities. Together with the re-organisation of Mahāyāna establishments, there developed a growing interest in Theravādin meditation and also in Buddhist materials based on the Pali Canon. These were then available in French. Among the pioneers who brought Theravāda Buddhism to the ethnic Viet was a young veterinary doctor named Le Van Giang. He was born in the South, received higher education in Hanoi, and after graduation, was sent to Phnom Penh, Cambodia, to work for the French government.[3]

During that time, he developed a growing interest in Buddhism. He started to study and practice the Pure Land and Tāntric ways but was not satisfied. By chance, he met the Vice Sangharāja of the Cambodian Sangha and was recommended a book on the Noble Eightfold Path written in French. He was struck by the clear message in the book, and decided to try out the Theravāda way. He learnt meditation on the breath *(Ānapānasati)* from a Cambodian monk at the Unalom Temple in Phnom Penh and achieved deep samadhi states. He continued the practice and after a few years, he decided to ordain and took the Dhamma name of Ho^.-To^ng (*Vansarakkhita).*

In 1940, upon an invitation by a group of lay Buddhists led by Mr. Nguyen Van Hieu, a close friend, he went back to Vietnam and helped to establish the first Theravāda temple for Vietnamese Buddhists, at Go' Du+a, Thu? Ddu+'c (now a district of Saigon). The temple was named Buu-Quang *(Ratana Ramsyarama*). Later, the Cambodian Sangharāja, Venerable Chuon Nath, together with 30 Cambodian bhikkhus established the *Sima* boundary at this temple[4]. The temple was destroyed by French troops in 1947, and was rebuilt in 1951.

Here at Buu-Quang temple, together with a group of Vietnamese bhikkhus, who had received training in Cambodia, such as Venerables Thie^.n-Lua^.t, Bu+?u-Cho+n, Kim-Quang, Gio+'i-Nghie^m, Ti.nh-Su+., To^'i-Tha('ng, Gia'c-Quang, A^'n-La^m, Venerable Ho^.-To^ng started teaching the Buddha Dhamma in Vietnamese language. He also translated many Buddhist materials from the Pāli Canon, and Theravāda became part of Vietnamese Buddhist activity in the country.

In 1949-1950, Venerable Ho^.-To^ng together with Mr Nguyen Van Hieu and supporters built a new temple in Saigon, named Ky'-Vie^n Tu+. *(Jetavana Vihāra).* This temple became the centre of Theravāda activities in Vietnam, which continued to attract increasing interest among the Vietnamese Buddhists. In 1957, the Vietnamese Theravāda Buddhist Sangha Congregation (Gia'o Ho^.i Ta(ng Gia' Nguye^n Thu?y

Vie^.t Nam) was formally established and recognised by the government, and the Theravāda Sangha elected Venerable Ho^.-To^ng as its first President, or Sangharāja.

During that time, Dhamma activities were further strengthened by the presence of Venerable Nārada from Sri Lanka. Venerable Nārada had first came to Vietnam in the 1930s and brought with him Bodhi tree saplings which he planted in many places throughout the country. During his subsequent visits in the 1950s and 1960s, he attracted a large number of Buddhists to the Theravāda tradition, one of whom was the popular translator, Mr Pha.m Kim Kha'nh who took the Dhamma name of Sunanda. Mr Kha'nh translated many books of Venerable Nārada, including *The Buddha and His Teachings, Buddhism in a Nutshell, Satipatthāna Sutta, The Dhammapada, A Manual of Abhidhamma, etc.* [5]. Mr Kha'nh, now in his 80s, lives in the USA and is still active in translating Dhamma books of well-known meditation teachers from Thailand, Burma and Sri Lanka.

From Saigon, the Theravada movement spread to other provinces, and soon, a number of Theravāda temples for ethnic Viet Buddhists were established in many areas in the South and Central parts of Vietnam. As at 1997, there were 64 Theravāda temples throughout the country, of which 19 were located in Saigon and its viccinity[6]. Beside Buu-Quang and Ky-Vien temples, other well-known temples are Bu+?u-Long, Gia'c-Quang, Tam-Ba?o (Da'-Na(~ng), Thie^'n-La^m and Huye^'n-Kho^ng (Hue^'), and the large Sakyamuni Buddha Monument (Thi'ch-Ca Pha^.t Dda'i) in Vu~ng Ta~u.

In the 1960s and 1970s, a number of Vietnamese bhikkhus were sent overseas for further training, mostly in Thailand and some in Sri Lanka and India. Recently, this programme has been resumed and about 20 bhikkhus and nuns are receiving training in Burma.

Historically, there has been a close relationship between the Cambodian and the Vietnamese bhikkhus. In fact, in 1979, after the Khmer Rouge were driven out of Phnom Penh, a group of Vietnamese bhikkhus led by Venerables Bu+?u-Cho+n and Gio+'i-Nghie^m came to that city to re-ordain seven Cambodian monks, and thus re-established the Cambodian Sangha which had been destroyed by the Khmer Rouge when they were in control[7].

Dhamma literature in the Vietnamese language comes from two main sources: the Pāli Canon and the Chinese *Āgamas,* together with a large collection of Mahāyāna texts. Since 1980s, there has been an ongoing programme to publish these materials by scholar monks of both Mahāyāna and Theravāda traditions. So far, 27 volumes of the first 4 *Nikayas,* translated by Venerable Minh-Cha^u, and the 4 *Āgamas,* translated by Venerables Tri'-Ti.nh, Thie^.n-Sie^u and Thanh-Tu+', have been produced. Work is under way to translate and publish the 5th Nikāya. In addition, a complete set of the *Abhidhamma,* translated by Venerable Ti.nh-Su+., has been printed, together with the *Dhammapada,* the *Milinda-Pañha,* the *Visudhi-Magga*, the *Abhidhammatthasangaha* and many other works.

In summary, although Buddhism in Vietnam is predominantly of the Mahāyāna form, the Theravāda tradition is well recognised and is experiencing a growing interest especially in the practice of meditation, in Nikāya-Āgama literature and in Abhidhamma studies.

References

1. Nguye^~n Lang, 1973. Vie^.t Nam Pha^.t Gia'o Su+? Lua^.n, vol 1 *(A Critical History of Buddhism in Vietnam).*
2. Andrew Skilton, 1994. *A Concise History of Buddhism.*
3. Le Minh Qui, 1981. Ho'a Thu+o+.ng Ho^.-To^ng *(Biography of Maha Thera Ho^.-To^ng).*
4. Nguyen Van Hieu, 1971. Co^ng Ta'c Xa^y Du+.ng Pha^.t Gia'o Nguye^n Thu?y ta.i Vie^.t Nam *(On The Work of Establishing Theravada Buddhism in Vietnam).*
5. Pham Kim Khanh, 1991. *Narada Maha Thera.*
6. Giac-Ngo Weekly, no. 63, 14-06-1997.
7. Thi'ch Ddo^'ng Bo^?n, 1996. Tie^?u Su+? Danh Ta(ng Vie^.t Nam *(Biography of Famous Vietnamese Monks).*

Chapter 28

Thao - Duong Zen School:

The Zen-Pure Land Union and Modern Vietnamese Buddhism

Ven. Thich Thien An

(Note: The Vietnamese names in this essay are written with the VIQR-VietNet convention)

Before considering the Zen-Pure Land union as introduced to Vietnam through the Tha?o - Ddu+o+'ng school, let us survey the Vietnamese Buddhist scene from the Ddinh (969-981) to Tra^'n (1225-1400) dynasties when Buddhism developed from a national religion to a nationalist religion before merging with aspects of Taoist and Confucian beliefs characteristic of the unification of the three religions following the decline of Buddhist influence in the Late Tra^'n dynasty. The beginning of Buddhism as the national religion of the Vietnamese can be placed as early as the Ddinh- Bo^.-Li~nh established a Vietnamese Sangha and initiated the practice of appointing eminent monks to serve as royal advisors on political, religious, and domestic matters. The Early Le^ dynasty (981-1009) continued this policy in addition to providing Vietnam's Buddhist heritage with a firm basis for development by obtaining from China the complete Chinese Tripiṭaka, the collection of Buddhist sacred texts. During this period of growth and assimilation, Buddhism adjusted itself to local practices, absorbing diverse areas of belief in the comprehensive goal of enlightenment for all sentient beings. The teachings of the Buddha flourished in the land and with the coming of the Ly' dynasty (1010-1225), the Vo^- Ngo^n-Tho^ng sect was particularly prosperous; the first two kings, Ly'-Tha'i-To^? (ruled 1010-1028), a former disciple of Ty'-Ni-Dda- Lu+u-Chi master Ven. Va.n-Ha.nh, and Ly'-Tha'i-To^n (ruled 1028- 1045), a student of Ven. Thie^'n-La~o, a famous master of the Vo^- Ngo^n-Tho^ng Zen sect, continued the practice begun by Ddinh- Bo^.-Li~nh of appointing learned monks to advisory positions in the government, thus providing a basis for the merging of religious and national interests characteristic of the Early Tra^'n dynasty.

The first real propagation of a Buddhist sect occurred under the third king of Ly', Ly'-Tha'nh-To^n (ruled 1054-1072), Dharma-successor to Ven. Tha?o-Ddu+o+'ng. As first patriarch of the Tha?o-Ddu+o+'ng sect, Ly'-Tha'nh-To^n was instrumental in establishing the teachings of his master in Vietnam and in providing a suitable ecology for the growth of Tha?o- Ddu+o+'ng Zen. The four successive monarchs of the Ly' were likewise earnest Buddhist patrons; among them Ly'-Anh-To^n (ruled 1138-1175) and Ly'-Cao- To^n (ruled 1176-1210) received the seal-of-mind (V. Ta^m-a^'n, J. Shin-in) in the Tha?o-Ddu+o+'ng tradition. With emphasis on the merging of loving-kindness (S. *karuṇā*) and insight (S. *prajñā*), the Tha?o-Ddu+o+'ng sect provided the background material from which the first monarch of the Tra^'n dynasty, Tra^'n-Tha'i-To^n, constructed his all-encompassing philosophy of humanism, which was to weave an important pattern in the Zen of the Tru'c-La^m sect founded by Tra^'n-Nha^n-To^n in the thirteenth century.

The interval separating King Ly'-Cao-To^n's abdication to accept the seal-of-mind within the patriarchial tradition of the Tha?o-Ddu+o+'ng school from King Tra^'n-Nha^n-To^n's resignation to become a monk and founder of the Tru'c-La^m school was marked by three significant events acting as a catalyst phasing the religion of the Ly' dynasty into the national religion, the comingling of nationalism and religion of the Tra^'n dynasty. These events-the Mongol invasions of 1257, 1285 and 1287-led to a reassessment of national character, inner conviction, and ethnic aim culminating in the founding of the Tru'c-La^m Zen sect. Thus we may say of the Tra^'n dynasty, in contradistinction to the Ly' dynasty, that Buddhism adapted itself to the nationalist tendencies of the Vietnamese which were then finding their full expression under the stimulus to reevaluation provided by the Mongolian threat of foreign domination; during the Ly' dynasty, however, with which we are concerned in this chapter, Buddhism captivated the Vietnamese to such extent as to make the teaching of Śākyamuni the one belief of the entire country. The Tha?o-Ddu+o+'ng school, with its practical methods suitable for all to follow in everyday life, opened the way by which Buddhism penetrated the heart of the nation and over the years transformed and directed the energies of the Vietnamese towards the Pure Land.

Speaking of the circumstances leading to the introduction of Tha?o-Ddu+o+'ng Zen during King Ly'-Tha'nh-To^n's reign (1054-1072), Mai-Tho.-Truye^'n writes in his 'Buddhism in Vietnam' (p. 42): "In 1069, to be precise, a significant event occurred. At that time the country was at war with the kingdom of Champa, a turbulent neighbor, whose frequent incursions into Vietnamese territory caused great alarm. The Emperor returned from an expedition against Champa with a number of prisoners of war, among them was the Chinese monk Tha?-Ddu+o+'ng (C. Ts'ao-tang), who had been temporarily in Champa teaching the unified Zen-Pure Land practice with fellow Chinese Buddhists. On Ly'-Tha'nh-To^n's return to the palace he assigned Tha?o-Ddu+o+'ng to assist Vietnam's Royal Head Monk (V. Ta(ng-Iu.c); one day when this monk was out on a visit, according to historical sources, Tha?o- Ddu+o+'ng took his Ngu+ ~-Lu.c, a record of the teachings of great Buddhist bronzes, and made corrections in the text. After Ly'- Tha'nh-To^n heard of this he sent for the prisoner to test his understanding of Buddhism. Tha?o-Ddu+o+'ng explained the teachings of numerous Buddhist texts and answered questions with penetrating insight, thoroughly convincing the king of his extraordinary abilities. Then, learning of Tha?o-Ddu+o+'ng's background of study with the Chinese master Tuye^'t-Dda^.u Minh-Gia'c (C. Hsueh-t'ou Ming-chueh, 980-1052) and of his teaching activities in Champa at the time of his capture, King Ly'- Tha'nh-To^n admitted him to the Vietnamese Sangha with the title Quo^'c-Su+ (C. Kuo-shih, J. Kokushi), or National Teacher, and placed him in charge of teaching Zen practice and Buddhist philosophy in the royal palace; thereafter Tha?o-Ddu+o+'ng stayed at Khai-Quo^'c temple in the capital city of Tha(ng-Long (now Hanoi). With Ly'-Tha'nh-To^n as his earnest supporter, the master's fame spread quickly to the surrounding countryside; hearing of his residence at Khai-Quo^'c, Dharma-seekers journeyed from both China and Vietnam to benefit from his teachings.

Tha?o-Ddu+o+'ng, one of seventeen Dharma-successors to Tuye^'t- Dda^.u Minh-Gia'c, advocated the unified practice of Zen and Pure Land methods for attaining enlightenment. The combined teachings, known as the doctrine of Ch'an-ching I-chih (Thie^'n Ti.nh Nha^'t Tri'), were accepted and widely cultivated during the development of Sung (To^'ng) dynasty syncretism, a movement grounded in the late T'ang (Ddu+o+'ng) dynasty when leaders of different Buddhist schools found it profitable to join together with their fellow Buddhists in soliciting the favor of the imperial court. Emphasis shifted to the harmonious elements under-lying all Buddhist teachings, and, through the interchange of doctrine and practice, the traditional boundaries once separating various sects merged with one another as Chinese Buddhism found a new mode of expression in the philosophy of syncretism. The union of Zen meditation and Pure Land avocation, a lasting result of Sung syncretism, may, at first glance, as Heinrich Dumoulin writes in '*A History of Zen Buddhism*' (p.125), "seem especially surprising in view of the basic difference in structure between the two movements. But here too the embedding of Zen in Buddhist piety-a piety which Zen may surpass in mystical enlightenment but can never fully deny-becomes evident. Moreover, there is a remarkable psychological similarity between the rhythmic repetition of the Buddha name in the so-called nien-fo (Jap. Nembutsu) and the intensive practice of the koan."

The similar goal of meditation and of Buddha's-name-recitation, or mantra as devotional invocation designed to produce a certain state of mind, and their connection in the history of Buddhist propagation in China, goes back to the early days of the introduction of the Dharma. As Buddhism developed in China, by the time of the sixth patriarch Hui-ne^ng (J. Eno, 638-713), looking into one's own nature to perceive the Buddha was tantamount to perfecting the mind to reach the Pure Land. Due to the growth in popularity of Pure Land teachings, questioners seeking to understand the nature of faith in Amitābha and the essence of his Western Heaven frequently approached the patriarch soliciting his opinion. His remarks, as recorded in the Altar Sūtra (trans. Lu K'uan Yu, pp. 40-41), present an outlook supported by most enlightened monks within the Ch'an tradition. According to Hui-ne^ng:

> "The deluded man repeats the Buddha's name to seek rebirth in the (Western) Paradise but the enlightened man purifies his own mind (instead). This is why the Buddha said that purification of mind is simultaneous with purification of the Buddha land. The ignorant man who does not know clearly about his own nature and ignores the Pure Land which is within himself, looks to the east and the west. For the enlightened man, the position in which he may find himself makes no difference. This is why the Buddha said that happiness existed anywhere one might happen to be. If your mind is entirely right, the West(ern) Paradise is near at hand. If your mind is wrong, it will be very difficult to reach it by (merely) repeating the Buddha's name...If thought after thought and without interruption you perceive your own nature, and if you are constantly impartial and straightforward, you will arrive there in a snap of the fingers and will behold Amitābha Buddha. If you practice the ten good virtues, there

will be no need for you to be reborn there. If you do not get rid of the ten evils, which Buddha will come and receive you? If you are awakened to the instantaneous doctrine of the uncreate, you will perceive the Western Paradise in an instant (*kṣaṇa*). If you are not awakened to it and if you (only) repeat the Buddha's name to be reborn there, the distance being so great how can you go there?"

Hui-ne^ng's teachings provided a basis for the subsequent union of Zen and Pure Land traditions-a union producing a co-operant methodology drawn from the source of knowledge and inspiration cultivated by each school. One of Hui-ne^ng's chief disciples, Nan-yueh Huai-jang (Nam Nha.c Hoa'i Nhu+o+.ng, J. Nangaku Ejo, d.744), did in fact suggest the recitation of Buddha's name to augment Zen meditation. The important compiler of the basic rules for monastic living, Pai-chang Huai-hai (Ba' Tru+o+.ng Hoa'i Ha?i, J. Hyakujo Ekai, 720-814), a student of Ma-tsu Tao-i (Ma~ To^? Dda.o Nha^'t, J. Baso Doitsu, D. 788), the famed disciple of Nan-yueh Huai-jang, included in his twenty monastic principles the method of Buddha's-name-recitation. Contemporaneous with Pai- chang, a school of practice developed by Hsuan-shih in Szechwan, claiming descendance from the fifth patriarch Hung-je^n (J. Gunin, 601-675), advocated meditation on the recitation of Buddha's name. So we see that between Zen and Pure Land Buddhism, as Heinrich Dumoulin writes in 'The Development of Chinese Zen' (pp. 36-37), "connecting links had existed for a long time. The Nembutsu, the devout invocation of Amidā Buddha's name, was practiced by many important adherents of Zen, as for instance Hoji, the Fourth Patriarch of the branch line of Gozu Zen, by Eno's disciple Nangaku Ejo, and others.... Yomyo Enju of the Hogen Sect, one of the greatest syncretists of Chinese Buddhism, declared himself emphatically in favor of combining the Nembutsu and Zen (zenjo icchi). While one who limited himself to Zen practice alone reached the goal only with difficulty, he who combined Zen with the Nembutsu was certain to attain enlightenment."

This basic attitude stressing the ease and sureness with which enlightenment may be won by the practice of both meditation and Buddha's-name-recitation comes through clearly in the teachings of Tha?o-Ddu+o+'ng as presented to his disciples in his famous 'Warning Statement', a summary of his essential views containing the most central doctrines of Zen-Pure Land union. In the poem below introducing his 'Warning Statement', Tha?o-Ddu+o+'ng emphasizes giving rise to a psychological disposition of mind such that the teachings of Buddhism may bring about their effect. Thus in order to enter the unchanging realm of *nirvāṇa*, we prepare for this attainment by realizing the world of *samsāra* as though-construction, knowing the body as the production of our mind working through *karmic* causes, and experiencing the ceaseless change and unsatisfactoriness of life conditioned by birth and death. Unless consciousness be set free from these bindings, the force of illusion continues to control the content of our mind and shape the aspects of our being. Knowing the power of the *samsāric* current holding us within its confines, keeping us from purifying our mind of illusion-creating thought-construction veiling the nature of reality, Buddha in his compassion comes to teach the doctrine of liberation from suffering and the means whereby this may be attained.

Warning Statement

Regard the world has an air-flower, Unreal.

See the body as though a vision, Without basis.

All the things change and are not dependable.

Unless you seek the path of purification.

You live in illusion for many lives.

Knowing this, Buddha came to the world in compassion, using the Way to teach us how to vanquish suffering, how to cut off desire, release birth and death, and enter *nirvāṇa's* unchanging abode.

Before continuing with Tha?o-Ddu+o+'ng's 'Warning Statement', we may note briefly that his understanding of Buddha's appearance in the world is upheld by most followers of the Mahāyāna, and as detailed in the Lotus Sūtra (S. Saddharmapunḍarika Sūtra), its applicability extends to influence a large area of basic Mahāyāna belief. Essentially the Lotus Sūtra regards Buddha's appearance in this *sahaloka*, our world of birth and death, as the natural outcome of compassion working through wisdom resulting in fitness of action, or skillful means (phu+o+ng tie^.n, S. *upāya*, C. fang-pien, J. hoben), the inherent way of all Tathāgatas who neither come nor go but abide in thusness (S. *tathātva*). As stated in the Lotus Sūtra (pp. 76- 77): "He, the Tathāgata... who has reached the highest perfection in the knowledge of skillful means, who is most merciful, long- suffering, benevolent, compassionate... appears in this triple world... in order to deliver from affection, hatred, and delusion the beings subject to birth, old age, disease, death...."

Thus with the appearance of a Buddha, practice of the Dharma becomes possible. Acknowledging the variety of available methods, Tha?o-Ddu+o+'ng condenses them as follows:

"Though you may practice Buddhism in many ways, in summary there are three main methods: meditation, contemplation, and Buddha's-name-recitation. The method of meditation has no definite way to follow and is therefore a difficult practice. If you do not have an enlightened master or a capable mind, you may stop midway in your progress or remain mistaken for your entire life. Contemplation is a very subtle method; without a good teacher or prajñā wisdom, complete enlightenment is hard to attain. Buddha's- name-recitation [V. Nie^.m-Pha^.t] is a quick and easy method. In all the ages past both intelligent and dull, both men and women have been able to practice Nie^.m-Pha^.t. Nobody makes a mistake with this method because of the applicability of the four types of outlook [V. Tu+' Lie^.u-gia?n]. Putting worries aside, you may therefore proceed with a decisive heart."

According to Pure Land tradition as formulated by the Chinese patriarch T'an- luan (J. Donran, 476-542), Nāgārjuna first distinguished between difficult and easy practice in his Daśabhūmivibhāṣā Śāstra (Tha^.p tru. Ti' Ba' Sa Lua^.n, C. Shih- chu P'i-p'o-sha Lun, J. Fujubibasharon), section five "On Easy Practice," in which he writes that a practitioner wishing to quickly reach the stage of no-turning-back should keep the Buddha's name ever before his mind. In Tha?o-Ddu+o+'ng's threefold classification, meditation and contemplation, the ways of the Holy Path schools in contradistinction to the Pure Land path, come under the heading of difficult practices, while the Nie^^.m-Pha^.t, or way of recitation, is considered the easy way to Buddhahood.

Before discussing Tu+' Lie^.u-gia?n, the four types of outlook formulated by the founder of the Lin-chi (J. Rinzai) sect in China, and their relation to Buddha's-name-recitation (V. Nie^.m-Pha^.t), we may note here that as regards the practice of Buddhism, Tha?o-Ddu+o+'ng's philosophy is one of Ddo^'ng-quy nhi thu'-ddo^' a Vietnamese expression meaning "one purpose through different methods" or "same destination but different directions." Thu'- ddo^' refers to the Buddhist practices of meditation, contemplation, and Nie^.m-Pha^.t. Ddo^'ng-quy is to go in one direction with one aim and for one purpose, that is, to keep the mind at all times on its goal, inner-realization of the Pure Land. According to Tha?o-Ddu+o+'ng's philosophy, meditation, contemplation, and Nie^.m- Pha^.-are all ways within the one practice of Buddhism for stripping mind of attachment to desire, thus eliminating self- clinging which obscures the Dharma-eye, preventing attainment of *nirvāṇa* and arrival at the other shore, the Pure Land. For achieving this aim Tha?o-Ddu+o+'ng clearly indicates that Buddha's-name-recitation (V. Nie^.m-Pha^.t) supplemented with the four types of outlook (V. Tu+' Lie^.u-gia?n) is both an easy and an efficacious practice.

As we turn to the topic of Tu+' Lie^.u-gia?n (C. ssu-liao-chien, J. shi ryoken), we begin to see the results of combined Zen-Pure Land methods; that is, the operation of Lin-chi (J. Rinzai) techniques in the form of the four types of outlook within a practice traditionally ascribed to the Pure Land school, the Nie^.m-Pha^.t (C. Nien-fo, J. Nembutsu), or recitation of the name of Buddha Amitābha, a form of mantra practice leading to single-hearted concentration through which the other-power finds a channel of expression. Within the workings of Nie^.m-Pha^.t the four distinctions are self-acting or self-perpetuating in the sense that an outside agent, such as a Zen master, does not apply them. They arise of their own through the "power of the other," which may actually result from concentrated belief and complete faith in the efficacy of the practice. The four distinctions, listed below are as formulated by Lin-chi, are central to his methodology of self-realization:

eliminating subject, leaving object
eliminating object, leaving subject
eliminating both, leaving neither
eliminating neither, leaving both

Regarding the applicability of the four distinctions from a more general viewpoint, "eliminate" can be looked upon as a form of emptying; the four distinctions themselves can then quite readily be seen as relating to the first four types of emptiness, or negation, comprising the twenty, sometimes eighteen, styles of emptiness outlined in the Great Perfection of Wisdom Sūtra (S. Mahāprajñāpāramitā Sūtra, C. Ta-pan-jo Po-lo-mi-to Ching, J. Daihannyaharamittakyo): emptiness of subject, emptiness of object, emptiness of both subject and object, and emptiness of emptiness. In Zen methodology, depending on the astuteness of the master, the particular level or experience of attainment of the student, and the aptness of circumstance, one sometimes empties the subject of itself, sometimes the object. Sometimes one empties both subject and object, sometimes neither, thereby leaving emptiness void of that emptiness. The third patriarch of Zen Se^ng-ts'an (J. Sosan), writing on this subject in his "On Having No Doubt in Mind" (Ti'n Ta^m Minh, trans. Suzuki, Manual, p. 78), declares:

"The two exist because of the One,
But hold not even to this One;
When a mind is not disturbed,
The ten thousand things offer no offense.
No offense offered, and no ten thousand things;
No disturbance going, and no mind set up to work:
The Subject is quieted when the object ceases,
The object ceases when the subject is quieted.

The object is an object for the subject,
The subject is a subject for the object:
Know that the relativity of the two
Rests ultimately on one Emptiness."

Within this one emptiness, according to Tha?o-Ddu+o+'ng,

"Nie^.m-Pha^.t is to keep your mind on the six syllables Nam-mo^ A-Di-Dda' Pha^.t and not let it move and jump freely about. While practicing Nie^.m-Pha^.t the eyes look at the image of Buddha, the mouth recites the Buddha's name, and the ears hear the chanting sounds. When you feel heavy and frustrated, try harder and keep on without losing a single second. A quiet mind naturally returns."

With these instructions on Buddha's-name-recitation, Tha?o-Ddu+o+'ng introduces Pure Land meditation as cultivated in China where it drew increasingly for doctrinal support from the teachings of the Dharma-ending-age, when, because of accumulated evil karma, men would be able to attain enlightenment only through reliance on Amitabha Buddha's compassionate vow to save all suffering beings. Holmes Welch remarks of this attitude in The Practice of Chinese Buddhism (pp. 89 90):

> "Since we are living in the age of the decay of the Dharma, it is difficult... to reach *nirvāṇa* here through our own efforts. Therefore most Buddhists in China prefer to get the help of Amitābha by reciting his name (nien-fo). That is, they repeat the words 'homage to the Buddha Amitābha' (na-mo O-mi-t'o-fo) in the belief that if they do so wholeheartedly they will be reborn in the Western Paradise. 'Wholeheartedly' means making their minds 'whole and still' (i-hsin pu-Iuan, nha^'t ta^m ba^'t loa.n), so that nothing is there but Amitābha. He is in their mouths (as they recite his name), in their ears (as they listen to

the recitation), and in their minds (as they visualize him). This is called 'perfect concentration in reciting Buddha's name' (nien-fo san-mei, nie^.m Pha^.t tam muo^.i). It corresponds to a degree of enlightenment achieved in the meditation hall."

In Zen-Pure Land practice in Vietnam, as in China, both hua-t'ou (thoa.i dda^'u, J. wato), which are similar in function to the koan exercise, and Nie^.m-Pha^.t may be pursued. Describing the actual Chinese practice, identical in many aspects with Vietnamese ways, Holmes Welch notes, again from his 'Practice of Chinese Buddhism' (pp. 398-399):

"Many monastries carried on the joint practice of Ch'an and Pure Land (ch'an-ching shuang-hsin, thie^'n ti.nh song ha'nh). This usually meant that they had both a meditation hall and a hall for reciting the buddha's name. But there was also a special form of joint practice in one hall.... There seem to have been eight periods of work a day... and each period was divided into circumambulation and sitting. While the inmates circumambulated, they recited Buddha's name aloud. While they sat, they either worked on a Ch'an hua-t'ou or employed 'Buddha's name meditation' (nien-fo kuan, nie^.m Pha^.t qua'n). The latter included different techniques for people at different stages of proficiency. Beginners used the technique termed 'reciting Buddha's name while meditating on the buddha image' (kuan-hsiang nien-fo). That is, they would fix their eyes on the image in the hall. Those further advanced would attempt to visualize the form of Amitābha with their mind's eye. This was termed 'reciting Buddha's name while meditating on the mental image of the Buddha' (kuan-hslng nien-fo). Those furthest advanced strove to avoid having any Buddha to visualize or any ego to do the visualizing. This was termed 'reciting Buddha's name while meditating on the quintessence of the Buddha' (shih-hsiang nien-fo). Explanations were given of both Ch'an and Pure Land methods.

Abiding of mind in the Pure Land results from continued practice of these three gradations of method. According to Tha?o-Ddu+o+'ng:

"If you continue to practice Nie^.m-Pha^.t, your mind will stay in the Pure Land; your heart will join with Amitābha Buddha. Without walking a step the Pure Land appears in front of you; without waiting for a future life the blessings of the Western Heaven are yours. Why do you tarry in this short, impermanent life of birth, old age, sickness, and death, rather than reaching for an unlimited life of permanency, joyfulness, substantiality, and purity? Is this not happier?"

In this section of his 'Warning Statement' Tha?o-Ddu+o+'ng presents the form which Pure Land doctrine assumed under practical interpretation of the Chinese mind. Originally based on the Larger Sukhāvativyūha Sūtra and related at least in aim with the cult of Maitreya, Pure Land tradition as developed in China evolved from the idea of a Pure Land in the West where one seeks entrance by various practices as noted in the Larger Sukhāvativyūha Sūtra (C. Ta-wu Liang-shou Ching, J. Daimuyrojukyo), the Smaller Sukhāvativyūha Sūtra (C. O-mi-t'o Ching, J. Amidakyo), and the Amitāyurdhyāna Sūtra (C. Kuan-wu Liang-shou Ching, J. Kammuryojukyo), to the identification of the Chinese character for "land" or "realm" with the meaning of "mind"; hence in the process of Zen-Pure Land union, the Pure Land came to mean the realm of Pure Mind. Speaking of this transformation of Pure Land doctrine, Hajime Nakamura notes in '*Ways of Thinking of Eastern Peoples*' (pp. 253-254) that the authority of the Vimalakirtīnīrdeśa Sūtra which teaches "the pure mind is identical with the Pure Land" provided support for the growth of "a mind-only doctrine" resulting in the dictum that "the Pure Land of the pure mind exists in all parts of the world." As a development of Sung dynasty syncretism, "the Chinese Buddhists exclusively followed this pure-mind view, and after the Ming dynasty, no contradiction was felt in practicing simultaneously sitting and the Pure Land practice."

The Chinese, with their emphasis on the practical value of belief, its demonstrable validity in the everyday world, gradually shifted the distant or non-too-distant Pure Land of the Sukhāvativyūha Sūtra to the immediate presence-of-mind, a shift creating a rich field of cultivation for Chinese Buddhists by providing a basis from which the practices of both common man and monk could grow. Thus when pressed for an explanation of the combination of seemingly contradictory methodologies in the Zen-Pure Land union, "many enlightened Chinese Buddhists," as Reginald Johnston writes in his '*Buddhist China*' (p. 93), "will declare that the Ch'an and Ching-t'u teachings are not really inconsistent with one another, but that the Ch'an doctrines are to the educated Buddhist what the Amidist doctrines are to the ignorant." Shifting the Pure Land from the beyond to the here-and-now, the beyond within, resulted in recognition of the potentiality of all beings to attain an enlightened state of mind in this very life. The Chinese, like the Vietnamese, were not overly interested in preparing for something in the distant future which might or might not come about. With a practical bent of mind already steeped in the this-wordly traditions of Confucianism, they sought the substantiation of belief through its efficacy in daily life.

In closing his 'Warning Statement' with the *gāthā* below, Tha?o-Ddu+o+'ng emphasizes awakening to the original mind of Ch'an, one's own true abode, which is none other than the Pure Realm, the real native land.

"Three worlds like the burning house,
Eight merit-giving-waters refresh and purify;
To leave this suffering world,
Direct your mind towards Pure Land.

Six syllables Nam-mo^ A-Di-Dda'-Pha^.t form the links
Returning mind's natural, unmoving condition;
Amitābha Buddha dwells not in seclusion;
The wise man wakes to this realization.

84,000 wonderous Buddha-shpaes
Derive no form outside of mind;
Don't hesitate or wait!
The Pure Land's truly your native land."

Tha?o-Ddu+o+'ng's verse contains principles and teachings recognized by almost all Buddhist sects, and here we might do well to dwell momentarily on the background tradition from which he draws his gatha. The three worlds or realms (tam gio+'i, S. traidhātuka or trailokya) with which he opens his gāthā refer in Buddhism's cosmology of mind to the world of sensuous desire (du.c gio+'i, S. kāmadhātu) including the six heavens of desire, the human world, and the hells where existence is characterized by desires deriving from six and appetite; the world of form (sa('c gio+'i, S. rūpadhātu) inclusive of the four dhyāna heavens and located above kāmadhātu; and the formless world (vo^ sa('c gio+'i, S. arūpadhātu) of pure spirit comprising the four attainments beyond form (S. arāpyasamāpatti). All such realms are generally considered indications of various states of consciousness; according to the Lankāvatāra Sūtra (pp. 145,75), for example, "The triple world is no more than thought-construction (prajñapti), there is no reality in its self-nature." And, "The being and nonbeing of things subject to causation have no reality; the triple world owes its existence to the Mind put into confusion by reason of habit-energy."

Thus in the authoritative text of early Zen Buddhism the triple world appears as none other than mind disturbed by the permeating and dwelling nature of *vāsanā*, or "habit-energy" (C. hsi-chi) according to Chinese translation; as put concisely in the Avatamsaka Sūtra (C. Hua-yen Ching, J. Kegonkyo): "The three worlds are only Mind." (S. Svacittamātram traidhātukam). That mind is the foundation of both *samsāra* and *nirvāṇa*, and that samsāra is but the obscured function of mind confused by habit-energy (S. vāsanā) and solidified by wrong views (S. vikalpa, C. fe^n-pieh, J. fumbetsu), while *nirvaṇā* is mind's original nature undisturbed by the structural elements of *samsāra*, the nature of which is like a house eternally devoured by flames, is a basic outlook of Mahāyāna Buddhists symbolized in part through the parable of the burning house contained in the Lotus Sūtra. Tha?o-Ddu+o+'ng's *gāthā* contrasts the burning house of *samsāra* with *nirvāṇa's* Pure Land where eight waters of good qualities extinguish the flames of the passions. To pass beyond the misery of the triple world Tha?o- Ddu+o+'ng teaches in accordance with the Larger Sukhāvativyūha Sūtra, and as provided for in the sixteen meditations comprising the Amitāyurdhyāna Sūtra, to form a firm thought of the Pure Land in order to lead mind to its realization.

The desire to see the Pure Land, made possible by the grace or power of Buddha's vows (S. praṇidhāna, adhis-thāna), but initiated in action by the stirring of self-nature in search of its own fulfillment, is one of the deepest perceptions of human consciousness, and one in which the other-power of Buddha's compassion to save us and the self-power of our own determination to attain enlightenment merge in the One Mind of neither self nor other, the fourth outlook of Lin-chi's distinctions (V. Tu+' Lie^.u- gia?n). As presented in the Amitāyurdhyāna Sūtra (p. 169), by the power of Buddha and his vows we may see the Pure Land, but only if we direct our mind to that realm and make it "our only aim, with concentrated thought, to get a perception of the western quarter." And so in Tha?o-Ddu+o+'ng's *gāthā* he points out "to leave *samsāra* behind, send your thought to Pure Land."

The concentration of mind necessary to achieve this aim in Tha?o-Ddu+o+'ng's school is accomplished through the efficacy of *mantra* meditation, or concentration on the name of Amitābha Buddha, which, as taught in the Amitāyurdhyāna Sūtra, is the way to sever the bonds of samsāra and, as Tha?o-Ddu+o+'ng says, "return mind to its original, unmoving condition." In the Smaller Sukhāvativyūha Sūtra (p. 99), meditation on the name of Amitābha is held up as the way even to the exclusion of the performance of good deeds. No stock of merit amassed in this life leads to birth in; the Pure Land, in contradistinction to the teaching of the Larger Sukhāvativyūha Sūtra (p.15), but rather,

> "whatever son or daughter of a family shall hear the name of the blessed Amitāyus, the Tathāgata, and having heard it, shall keep it in mind...then that Amitāyus, the Tathāgata, surrounded by an assembly of disciples and followed by a host of Bodhisattvas, will stand before them at the hour of death, and they will depart this life with tranquil minds. After their death they will be born in the world Sukhāvati, in the Buddha country of the same Amitāyus, the Tathāgata."

That Amitābha Buddha does not dwell in seclusion as Tha?o-Ddu+o+'ng teaches in his *gāthā* is indicated in the Amitāyurdhyāna Sūtra which provides for this realization through various visualization exercises leading to the clear perception that 84,000 shapes of Buddha have no substance outside of mind; the three Pure Land practices of visualizing the form of Amitābha Buddha while meditating on the essence of the name likewise lead to an undeniable experience of the emptiness of all form as perceived by mind-that is, its emptiness apart from the content or substrate of mind. As stated in the Amitāyurdhyāna Sūtra (pp. 177-178):

> "When you have perceived this, you should next perceive Buddha himself. Do you ask how? Every Buddha Tathāgata is one whose (spiritual) body is the principle of nature (Dharma-dhātu-kāya), so that he may enter into the mind of any beings. Consequently, when you have perceived Buddha, it is indeed that mind of yours that possesses those thirty-two signs of perfection and eighty minor marks of excellence (which you see in Buddha). In fine, it is your mind that becomes Buddha, nay, it is your mind that is indeed Buddha. The ocean of true and universal knowledge of all the Buddhas derives its source from one's own mind and thought. Therefore you should apply your thought with an undivided attention to a careful meditation on that Buddha Tathāgata, Arhat, the Holy and Fully Enlightened One."

And, as put concisely in Lu K'uan Yu's translation of this same sūtra (p. 93): "When the mind is set on thinking of (that) Buddha, it is identical...because Mind realizes Buddhahood; Mind is Buddha...." "Therefore," says Tha?o-Ddu+o+'ng, "what are you waiting for? This Pure Land-you've been there before."

We find in Tha?o-Ddu+o+'ng's 'Warning Statement' a unification of the practices of the Zen and Pure Land schools of Buddhism and a fusing of the concepts of self-power and other-power which, up to the time of the Sung dynasty, had served to distinguish meditation as the way of self-power and Buddha's-name-recitation as the way of other-power, an outlook preserved today in Japanese Buddhism in contrast to Chinese and Vietnamese Buddhism. Approaching the subject of self-power and other-power in terms of *prajñā* and *karuṇā*, the foundations supporting Mahāyāna Buddhist practices, D.T. Suzuki writes in '*The Essence of Buddhism*' (pp. 46,76):

> "There are two pillars supporting the great edifice of Buddhism: the Daichi (tai-chi), *Mahāprajñā*, the Great Wisdom, and the Daihi (tai-pei), *Mahākaruṇā*, the Great Compassion. The Wisdom flows from the Compassion and the Compassion from the Wisdom, for the two are in fact one, though from the human point of view we have to speak of them as two....In Japanese Buddhism, Zen represents the *Prajñā* phase of the Mahāyāna, and the Pure Land school claims the *Karuṇā*."

In Vietnamese Buddhism, with its emphasis on syncretism, these two pillars are one in practice; the *prajñā* phase of Zen and the *karuṇā* aspect of the Pure Land, joined in the Zen-Pure Land union originally introduced to the country by Tha?o-Ddu+o+'ng, support the framework of modern Vietnamese Buddhism. Though appearing somewhat antithetical, Zen and Pure Land Dharma- doors ultimately open on the same goal; approached from this standpoint, various fluctuations in methodology are of small concern, for as Holmes Welch notes in '*The Practice of Chinese Buddhism*' (pp. 399-400):

> "Regardless of contradictory details, the main principles of the joint practice of Ch'an and Pure Land seem clear enough. In both sects the goal was to reduce attachment to ego. The Pure Land method of "no stirrings in the whole mind" (i-hsin pu luan) did not differ essentially from the Ch'an method of "meditating to the point of perfect concentration" (ch'an-ting). Pure Land speaks of getting the help of another, that is, Amitābha, to reach the Western Paradise, while Ch'an asserts that one must depend on oneself to reach enlightenment. But, as the abbot of Chin Shan remarked, "Who is going to help you stop your whole mind from stirring? You have to do it yourself." A lay informant said he had been told by Hsu-yun that "all the buddhas in every universe, past, present, and future, preach the same dharma. There is no real difference between

> the methods advocated by Śākyamuni and Amitābha...." The methods of the two sects are connected in many ways. For example, the hua-t'ou most often used in orthodox Ch'an meditation halls directly involved Pure Land practice, for how could one ask "Who is this reciting buddha's name?" unless one had been reciting it?...Many monks told me that they regarded Ch'an and Pure Land as complements essential to one another. "Pure Land without Ch'an cannot be depended upon (k'ao-pu-chu). Ch'an without Pure Land has no 'principle' (mei-yu chu)."

Even the distinctions "Ch'an" and "Pure Land" vanish in Vietnamese Buddhism where all ways are Buddha-ways and are one in the communal quest of enlightenment through Thie^'n-Ti.nh Nha^'t-tri' (C. Ch'an-ching I-chih, J. Zenjo itchi), the unification of meditation and recitation. In the Vietnamese view, if we practice Nie^.m-Pha^.t with mouth calling Buddha's name, eyes seeing Buddha's form, ears hearing Nam-mo^ A-Di-Dda'-Pha^.t until the Pure Land appears in front of us and if we realize 84,000 wondrous Buddha-shapes are not outside of mind, then what real difference is there with the Zen aim of meditating until Mind, Buddha, and sentient beings are not three separate things or until realizing one is all, all things are one, *samsāra* is *nirvāṇa*, and passions are Bodhi? The fusion of Zen and Pure Land systems, of no-mind and one-mind in the Tha?o-Ddu+o+'ng school, is the significant junction of the loving-kindness (S. *karuṇā*) and wisdom (S. *prajñā*) of Buddha and his teachings. According to Vietnamese Buddhists, when *karuṇā* (V. Tu+'-bi) and *prajñā* (V. Tri'-hue^.) are united there is no difference between Zen and Pure Land, between self-power and other-power; instead there is oneness and togetherness within the *Karuṇā-Prajñā* Mind which is indeed the meeting place of all sects in Buddhism. This unified philosophy of Tha?o-Ddu+o+'ng was keenly attuned to the character and aspirations of the Vietnamese people; having inherited the various teachings of Buddhism, Taoism, and Confucianism with their accompanying cultural traditions, the Vietnamese ever sought to consolidate these traditions into a spiritual rationale or ethical mean consonant with their own cultural background and indigenous beliefs. Since Tha?o-Ddu+o+'ng's philosophy of syncretism was so suited to this purpose, dignitaries of high position, kings, and officials of the imperial court, as well as the Vietnamese people, accepted it with their earnest heart. King Ly'-Tha'nh-To^n, as mentioned previously, when once aware of Tha?o-Ddu+o+'ng's position as a distinguished Chinese Zen master, gave him his full support, openly praising his philosophy and concept of practice. As Tha?o-Ddu+o+'ng's first disciple the king was instrumental in creating and spreading the doctrine of this third Zen school in Vietnam; Ly'-Tha'nh-To^n was not just a Buddhist patron in word, but in deed as well. Many instances of his kindness and benevolence are recorded in Vietnamese history, and stories such as the ones below are familiar to Vietnamese Buddhists.

According to historical sources King Ly'-Tha'nh-To^n was a most sincere Buddhist, incomparable in devotion and compassion. During the winter months his thoughts often dwelt on the suffering of the prisoners and poor people. Calling his attendant one bitter-cold day the king lamented, "Here I am in the palace-warm clothes and shelter-yet still I feel cold. What of those in our prison cells who don't have enough to eat or enough to wear? How they must suffer from cold and hunger! And what of those suspects who have yet to be questioned. Are we to assume them guilty and treat them like criminals? They could suffer unjustly merely waiting for interrogation which would be most pitiful. Surely we must do something about all this." The king then ordered sufficient clothing, bedding, and food for all prisoners and suspects being detained by the state.

A second frequently related incident concerns the time Ly'-Tha'nh-To^n's daughter Princess Ddo^.ng-Thie^n attended a Thie^n- Kha'nh court session over which the king presided. After issuing his judgment on a particular case before the court he turned to his board of jurors and said, "Today my daughter is here, Princess Ddo^.ng-Thie^n. Though I love my peoples as I love my daughter, when they break laws they must be punished. Nonetheless I feel deeply for them; from now on we must mitigate every penalty."

Due to Ly'-Tha·nh-To^n's dedication in realizing the Bodhisattva ideal and his insight acquired through continual practice of both meditation and recitation, Tha?o-Ddu+o+'ng transmitted the seal-of-mind (V. Ta^m-a^'n, J. Shin-in) to him, thus establishing the king as the first patriarch of the Tha?o-Ddu+o+'ng Zen school. Ly'-Nha^n-To^n (ruled 1072-1127), Ly'-Tha^'n-To^n (ruled 1128-1138), Ly'-Anh-To^n (ruled 1138-1175), and Ly'-Cao-To^n (ruled 1176- 1210), the four successive monarchs who brought the prosperous Ly' dynasty to a close, all emulated Ly'-Tha'nh-To^n in their patronage and study of Buddhism. They frequently arranged for esteemed masters to teach meditation and Buddhist doctrine in the imperial palace, honored them with the positions of national teachers, and sought their advice concerning administration of internal and foreign affairs. Among these later Buddhist kings, Ly'-Anh-To^n and Ly'-Cao-To^n were most successful in their religious life, receiving the seal-of-mind and transfer of patriarchal authority in the tradition of Tha?o-Ddu+o+'ng Zen.

Following Ly'-Tha^'n-To^n's death, Ly'-Anh-To^n (Prince Thie^n-To^., ruled 1138-1175) succeeded to the throne, where he studied meditation and recitation with Ven. Kho^ng-Lo^., sixth patriarch in the second generation of the Tha?o- Ddu+o+'ng school, from whom he received the seal-of-mind. Ly'-Anh-To^n supported other Buddhist sects as well as his own; during his reign Buddhism prospered in the country under many enlightened monks such as Venerables Tri'-Thuye^'n, Am-Tri', Ba?o-Gia'm, and Vie^n- Tho^ng. In 1144, though his own disposition of mind lay with the Tha?o-Ddu+o+'ng teachings, Ly'-Anh-To^n chose to name Ven. Vie^n-Tho^ng, a famed master of the Ty'-Ni-Dda-Lu+u-Chi Zen sect, as national teacher. The king ever urged people to expand their educational horizons by becoming aware of their diverse cultural background and the significance of the teachings of the three religions; in 1169 in order to stimulate study he opened an examination based on the doctrines of Buddhism, Taoism, and Confucianism as a means of selecting government officials. Speaking of these educational reforms and noting commercial advancements made during Ly'-Anh-To^n's reign, Professor Howard Sosis writes in his "Introductory Notes on the Meditation Sects of Buddhism in Ancient Vietnam" (p. 19, n.188): "Under the rule of this Emperor commercial relations were made with China, Java, and Thailand in precious metal and jewels, elephants for warfare, rhinoceros horns, silk and brocades.... This ruler was also to open schools in religious instruction in the three major religions in the land: Buddhism, Confucianism, and Taoism."

The last monarch of the Ly' dynasty, Ly'-Anh-To^n's son Prince Long-Ca'n (ruled as King Ly'-Cao-To^n 1176-1210), inherited the throne at the age of three, but national affairs ran well due to the guidance of mandarin supervisor To^-Hie^'n-Tha'nh. As Prince Long-Ca'n grew older he evinced the same earnestness in pursuing Buddhist studies as did preceding kings of Ly'; he practiced meditation and recitation with Ven. Tru+o+ng-Tam-Ta.ng of the fourth generation of the Tha?o-Ddu+o+'ng sect and upon receiving his master's seal-of-mind became the sixteenth patriarch in Tha?o- Ddu+o+'ng tradition. After coming of age and assuming actual control of the government, he received the name of King Ly'-Cao- To^n; in this position he continued his father's work, propagating Buddhism in the country and sincerely practicing both Zen and Nie^.m-Pha^.t. Ly'-Cao-To^n belonged to the fifth and last generation of the Tha?o-Ddu+o+'ng school. Subsequent history does not mention the names and biographies of any other successors.

Generally speaking, Buddhism, especially the Ty'-Ni-Dda-Lu+u-Chi, Vo^-Ngo^n- Tho^ng, and Tha?o-Ddu+o+'ng Zen sects, flourished during the Ly' dynasty due to the generous support and sincere interest of the Ly' monarchs and their officials whose practice of the Buddhist way influenced the people to join their hearts and minds with the teaching of Buddha. The Tha?o-Ddu+o+'ng sect, having a number of kings among its patriarchs, was most prosperous during this period of Vietnamese history and, as we see from the following lineage of the school, various eminent monks and outstanding laymen as well as these monarchs contributed to the extension of Tha?o-Ddu+o+'ng tradition through five generations and eighteen patriarchs, spanning the years from Ly'-Tha'nh-To^n (1054) to Ly'-Cao-To^n (1210).

Lineage of the Tha?o-Ddu+o+'ng Zen School

Founding Patriarch: Ven. Tha?o-Ddu+o+'ng (d. eleventh century)

First Generation:

1. King Ly'Tha'nh-To^n (ruled1054-1072)
2. Ven. Ba'-Nha~
3. Laymana Ngo^-Xa'

Second Generation:

4. Prince Ngo^-I'ch
5. Ven. Thie^.u-Minh or Hoa'ng-Minh
6. Vven. Kho^ng-Lo^.
7. Ven. Ddi.nh-Gia'c or Gia'c-Ha?i

Third Generation:

8. Layman Ddo^~-Vu~
9. Ven. Pha.m-Am
10. King Ly'-Anh-To^n (ruled 1138-1175)
11. Ven. Ddo^~-Ddo^

Fourth Generation:

12. Ven. Tru+o+ng-am-Ta.ng
13. Ven. Cha^n-Huye^'n
14. Layman Ddo^~-Thu+o+'ng

Fifth Generation:

15. Ven. Ha?i-Ti.nh

16. King Ly'-Cao-To^n (ruled 1176-1210)

17. Layman Nguye^ ~ n-Thu + 'c

18. Layman Pha.m-Phy.ng-Ngu + .

Taken from Thich Thien An, 1975. "*Buddhism & Zen in Vietnam, in relation to the Development of Buddhism in Asia*", Chapter 4, published by Charles E. Tuttle, ISBN 0-8048 1144-X, edited by Carol Smith. (Sincere thanks to Anh Minh Quang, BuddhistI@aol.com , who kindly posted this article to the vn-buddhism@saigon.com mailing list on 4 January 1998).

Chapter 29

Buddhism and Indian Literature

Prabhakar Machwe

'Buddhism and Indian Literature' could be the subject of an entire book. But I confine myself to a few salient authors and works in Indian languages and works written by Indians, in English. My paper is mainly informative and not an evaluation of such vast material.

I begin with Rabindranath Tagore's famous words in 1934, quoted by Tan Yun Shan in the appendix of *Twenty Years of the Visva-Bharati Cheena Bhavan;* addressing 'My friends in China', Tagore said:

> "The truth that we received when your pilgrims came to us in India, and ours to you, that is not lost even now. What a great pilgrimage was that! What a great time in history! It is our duty today to revive the heroic spirit of that pilgrimage, following the ancient path which is not merely a geographical one but the great historical one that was built across the different barriers of race differences and differences of language and tradition, reaching the spiritual home where man is, in the bonds of love and co-operation!"

The same spirit is echoed in the work *Japanese Buddhism,* in *Essays in Zen Buddhism* by D.T. Suzuki (p. 348):

"When the East as a unity is made to confront the West, Buddhism supplies the bond".

Buddha was the first revolutionary and rationalist, believer in equality of man and one whose message of compassion attracted kings and commoners, throughout India and beyond its geographical boundaries. As a philosopher he is *par excellence.* He was the first existentialist. He was not a world-and-life-negationist, a mendicant and escapist; on the contrary after a long tortuous process of penance for six years and forty-nine days, he attained *Sambodhi*. Karl Jaspers wrote in *Way to Wisdom* (p. 100): "The spiritual process took place between 800 and 200 B.C. . . .It was then that the man with whom we live today came into being. . .In India, it was the age of the Upanishads and of the Buddha; in China, all philosophical trends were developed". The influence of Buddha was very extensive, as the Nagarjunakonda inscription refers to fraternities of monks who converted Kashmir, Gandhara, China, Tosali, Aparanta, Vanga, Varanasi, Yavana, Damila and islands of Sri Lanka. How literary men all over the world came under his spell is a remarkable story. Rainer Maria Rilke, the German poet wrote two sonnets on him. Edwin Arnold's *Light of Asia* based on Aśvaghośa's *Buddha-Carita* became a minor classic. Colin Wilson mentions in the *Outsider* (p. 58) that Strindberg regained his sanity through study of Buddhist texts. Herman Hesse's *Siddhartha* made him Nobel Laureate. Heideggar has written on Nāgārjuna. Amongst foreign scholars, Rhys Davids, Kern, Kotz, Keitz, Ward and Coomaraswamy's works are available in English for scholars and laymen.

I had also the proud privilege of helping in setting up an All-India Book Exhibition, arranged in 1956, in 2500th year of the *Parinirvāṇa* of Buddha. The exhibition was attended by Pandit Jawaharlal Nehru, Dr. S. Radhakrishnan, Sri C.D Deshmukh, Sardar Panikkar, Humayun Kabir and Maulana Azad. Amongst the foreign dignitories who visited it were the late Bandaranayake whom Nehru himself had invited. The Panchen Lama and Dalai visited it. This Exhibition contained under each Indian language section, a sizeable number of books on or about Buddha. The Sahitya Akademi had taken up Dharmanand Kosambi's Marathi minor classic *Bhagwan Buddha* for translation in all Indian languages. It was published in half-a-dozen languages. I personally knew Dharmanand Kosambi and in his last days in Sevagram, he gave me a manuscript of his Marathi play on Buddha's life to be translated in Hindi. I also came in close contact with Mahapandit Rahul Sankrityayan. The Sahitya Akademi awarded a posthumous award to Acharya Narendradeva for his *Bauddha Darśana Sangraha* in Hindi. I visited Sri Lanka in 1963 and lectured in two universities on 'Buddhism and Existentialism'. Three years ago I visited Japan and saw Figi Guruji's Nichiren Centre and also Zen monasteries. Thus, my involvement with Buddhism is as early as my first M.A. in philosophy in 1937. Now I present a specimen of the information I have collected on this subject and which may not be readily available in English, for further supplementation by scholars. Buddhism has directly influenced some philosophers and historians and literary artists; others are translators and commentators as well as research-oriented persons. I am aware that all works by them cannot be compressed in one paper.

Dr. Nagaraja, the Jain monk, in his *Agama and Tripitaka* (Vol. 2), a learned work on languages in Hindi, has devoted eighty pages to Pali Buddhist literature and forty pages to Ashokan edicts in Brahmi. There are different etymologies of the term Pāli. It occurs for the first time in the fourth century A.D. in *Visuddhi-magga* and *Atthakathā*. Buddhaghośa equated Pāli with *Tripiṭaka*. *Dipavamsa* was written in the fourth century earlier, wherein Pāli meant Buddha's vacanas. *Chulavamsa* also corroborated the same meaning. Pandit Vidhushekhar Bhattacharya equates it with *Pankti* or line. Jagdish Kassap has found three discrepancies in such an etymology. He thinks Pali originated from *Pariyāya*. Bhikkhu Siddharth thinks it is from path. Dr. Maxwelser gives patali as the root. Bhandarkar and Vaketnagal think the word is from Prākṛt. Rajwade thinks the origin may be from Prakata. Bharatsingh Upadhyaya suggested Praleyaka. The old Buddhist dictionary *Abhidhāna-Dipikā* has given a probable etymology as Tanti. If one word Pāli is open to so many meanings, how many interpretations would there be, of the Buddhist texts, which were carried from land to land and across the seas, to different language-speaking people?

As with the medium that is language, so with the mode of writing or the script. In *Lalitavistara* there are 64 scripts mentioned, in which Brāhmī is the first one, in which Ashokan edicts are found. Many of the scripts were named after areas, provinces or castes speaking those languages, some names are descriptive and give some idea of the way characters were written, some are based on mythological names. In *Suttapiṭaka,* in *Dīgha Nikāya,* in *Solakkhandha Sutta, Brahmajāla Sutta* mentions *Akkahatika,* letters written in the sky, or on the back of a person, to be recognized by others. In Buddhist Jātakas there are several references to pens, books, schools, writings, writers, writing material made of wood, bamboo, leaf, goldleaf, wooden boards etc.

It has been a thousand years saga from Buddhist literature to its translation and transmission to modern Indian languages. I shall deal with the latter, one by one.

Assamese

The earliest Assamese compositions are 47 *Dohas* or *Padas* composed by 84 Buddhist Siddhas. These *Caryāpādas* influenced *Dehabicharer Geet.* Achintyayogi Minanath is Machchendra (Viṣṇu is worshipped by Nepalis as Avalokiteśvara) who wrote three texts on Tantricism.

In Assamese, the works on or about Buddha are more recent. Dr. Birinchi Kumar Barua wrote *Bauddha Dharma Aru Sahitya;* Nataraj Barua *Buddha Paricaya;* Kshetradhar Borgohain *Asamat Bauddhadharma;* Pragnananda Mahasthabir *Mahābarga*; Pandit Dharmadhar Sthabir *Dharmapada*; Bhikshu Silabhadra *Digghanikāya,* Srimat Nandabamsha Mahasthabir wrote eight books in which *Siddhārtha Carita* and *Buddha Carita* are in poetry. Dr. Benimadhav Barua had edited *Prākrit Dharmapada.*

In 1961 "Assam Research Society for Buddhistic Studies" was formed – the president was Haliram Deka, Chief Justice, and Gangapada Chaudhury was the secretary. This Society published one booklet *The Buddhist Relics in Assam,* written by G.P. Chaudhury. Chakreshwar Bhattacharya translated Dharmanand Kosambi's *Bhagwana Buddha* in Assamese, for the Sahitya Akademi.

I remember one irreverent Assamese poem by Nabakanta Barua called *Bodhidrumar Prārthanā,* in which a poor peasant shivering in cold is waiting for a branch of the dry tree to fall and become fuel for his fire. This was translated in English and published in 'Indian Literature'.

Bengali

Earliest Bengali text is *caryācaryā viniścaya* (A.D. 950) found in Nepal Royal Library, containing poems of 24 Buddhist Siddhas. They contain Śunyavāda and Vijñanavāda philosophy. The Sahajiyā cult is similar to 'Madhyama' path of Buddhists.

There is a tradition of great Buddhist scholars in Bengal who wrote on the Buddhist texts and lore both in Bengali and in English.

I shall first list twelve good works of outstanding value:

1. Ajay Mitra: *Outline of Early Buddhism* – a historical survey of Buddhology, Buddhist schools and Sanghas, mainly based on the study of pre-Gupta inscriptions (1965).
2. A.C. Banerji: *Buddhism in India and Abroad* (1973).
3. Bimal Charan Law: *Buddhist Conception of Spirits* (1923).
4. N. Ganguli: *The Buddha and His Message* (1955).
5. Nalinaksha Dutta: *Early Monastic Buddhism* (1971).
6. Satkari Mukherji: *Buddhist Philosophy of Universal Flux* (1935).
7. Sujit Kumar Mukhopadhyay: *Outline of Principal Methods of Meditation* (Tr. from Chinese, 1972).
8. Sukumar Dutta: *Buddhist Monks and Monasteries of India* (1962).

9. P. K. Bhattacharya: *Marxism and Buddhism: Problem of Emancipation* (1976).
10. Bidhushekhar Bhattacharya: *Pātimokkha* (1935).
11. Shashidhar Barua: *Thergāthā* (in Bengali) (1974).
12. Gokuldas De: *Significance and Importance of Jātakas* (Special reference to Bharhut, 1951).

Buddha featured in biographical, poetical, philosophical works in Bengali, even in plays, from the last part of the nineteenth century. The primary source was Sir Edwin Arnold's *The Light of Asia,* based on the Mahāyāna Sanskrit work *Lalitavistara.*

In 1887, Girish Chandra Ghosh wrote a play *Buddhadeva-Carita,* based on Arnold. Nabin Chandra Sen's poetical work *Amitābha* (1895) followed. The first scientific work on Buddhism in Bengali was Satyendranath Tagore's *Bauddhadharma,* published in 1901. Inspired by his elder brother Satyendranath Tagore and by Rajendralal Mitra's work Rabindranath wrote a number of poems and plays like *Natir Pūjā, Candālikā* and *Mālinī.*

There is a humorous story about Swami Vivekananda in U.S.A. Attracted by his saffron turban, an American asked in the peculiar pronunciation: "Are you a 'budist'" (Buddhist). Swamiji replied instantaneously, "No, I am a florist". Swami Vivekananda was attracted to Buddha's '*Lokahita*' (welfare of the mankind). Vivekananda recorded that he had 'vision' of Buddha.

Satish Chandra Vidyabhushan wrote a book *Buddhadeva* and studied Pāli extensively. Haraprasad Shastri discovered in Nepal a portion of Aśvaghośa's *Buddha Carita,* which was not in Cowell's translation, published from Oxford in 1893. Haraprasad Shastri's *Saundarānanda* was published by the Asiatic Society in 1910. His other work was published in 1916—*Hajar Bachcharer Purana Bangla Bhashay Bouddha Gan O Doha.* This was a landmark in tracing the earliest specimen of Bengali language and literature. There is also a good work published on Buddhist Literature in Bangladesh, in Bengali, which I saw in Dhaka.

Dr. Sukumar Sen mentions in his *History of Bengali Literature* that "Bankimchandra was influenced more by Hindu rituals and Rabindranath Tagore took inspiration from Upanishads and Buddha". In Sudhanshu Vimal Barua's thesis *Rabindranath O Bauddha Sanskriti* there is ample documentation of this kind. There are stray poems on Buddha and passages influenced by Buddhist lore in the writings of Premendra Mitra, Jibanananda Das, Bishnu Dey and Sudhindranath

Dutta. But in prose the most remarkable work was the novel *Shashanka* by the archeologist Dr. Rakhaldas Bandyopadhyaya. Plays on Buddhist period are written by D.L. Roy. Sujātā, Mahendra and Sanghamitra have attracted many creative writers.

Gujarati

Buddhist philosophy was studied in ancient times at the universities like Valabhi in Gujarat. In a third century B.C. Ashokan edict, found at Junagarh, in the Girnar foothills, it is stated that Buddhism was propagated in that part of India. Many ruins of old Buddhist Vihāras are still found there. On medieval Gujarati literature, the influence of Jainism was more; not much literature was written on Buddha or Buddhist themes.

In modern period, attraction towards Buddha was seen in the new renaissance. Kavi Narsinghrai Divetia was very much influenced by Sir Edwin Arnold's *The Light of Asia*. He composed lyrics and poems on that, which were published in a book-form in 1934 as *Buddha-Carita*. This work, particularly the portion on *Mahābhiniśkramaṇa* has been very much appreciated in Gujarat.

In 1920 Mahatma Gandhi founded Gujarat Vidyapeeth, where a department was established to study ancient history and culture, called *Purātattva-Mandira*. Dhammanand Kosambi was invited to do research work in that Institute. Pandit Sukhalalji was already there. Kosambi wrote and published through the Vidyapeeth, works like *Buddhalīlā, Buddha-Carita, Bhagwana Buddhānā* 50 *Dharmasamvādo* (from *Majhim-nikāya*), *Dharma-cakrapravartana* (based on Ashokan edicts), etc.

Kavi 'Sundaram' was one of the students of the Vidyapeeth. He wrote his famous poem *Buddhanā Cakṣu*. It was also appreciated as a masterpiece in Gujarati poetry. Umashankar Joshi, in his *Prācīna,* has written two long dialogues on Buddhist themes—*Bāla Rāhula* and *Aśanka*. They are both based on Jātaka tales. Umashankar Joshi later wrote a verse-play *Nimantraṇa* based on *Ambapāli*. He also wrote a poem *Einstein ane Buddha*. Poet Sunderji Betai has written a *Khaṇḍa Kāvya* called *Sulocanā locanadāna,* based on *Therigāthā*. There is also a Gujarati novel entitled *Ambapālī*. Poet Ramnarain Pathak 'Shesh' has written a good poem entitled *Buddhanu Nirvāṇa*. Kavi Nanhalal wrote a play on *Sanghamitrā*.

Jātaka tales have been translated in Gujarati by Dr. Harivallabha Bhayani. Its first edition was titled *Jātaka Kathāo,* the second is called *Kamalanātantu*. Mukul Kalarthi wrote on *Avadāna* stories *Dasa pāramitāoni suvārtā*. *Dhammapada* is translated in Gujarati in several forms, two are in verse. Gandhian philosopher Kishorilal Mashruwala wrote *Buddha and Mahāvīra* Dr. Nagin H. Shah has written *Buddha-Dsaśana.* Pandit Dalsukh Malvania is a famous Gujarati Buddhist scholar.

Hindi

If one only sees the bibliographies attached to two theses in Hindi, there are at least a hundred works in this language concerning Buddha's life and teachings; philosophy and art, and critical and creative works based on or influenced by Buddhism. Not that all these works are outstanding, but there is formidable amount of information and new material in them, which needs scrutiny and towards which our scholars have not yet devoted full attention.

1. *Hindi Sant-Sahityapar Bauddhadharma ka prabhava* Dr. Vidyavati Malavika (1966)
2. *Madhyakālīna Hindi Sāhitya para Bauddha Dharma kā Prabhāva* by Dr. Sarala Trigunyata (1963)

In medieval literature the concept of Śiva as *Yogi* influenced Buddhist and Jaina devotional literature. In *Sādhanamālā,* Buddha as *Padmanṛtteśvara* is a later form of Śiva. In Ellora's Kailaśa temple there is a Bodhi-tree on the top of the Śiva icon. In Chamba the king Ajayapal got Brahmā, Varuna, Śiva and Buddha sculpted as deities. In Khajuraho, Kokkal's Vaidyanatha temple has an inscription in which Brahmā, Jina, Buddha and Vāmana are all called forms of Śiva.

The earliest Hindi literature by Siddhas is of Tantric Buddhism. Kanhapa refers to Jalandarpa. Darikpa writes

Kinto Bhanto Kinto Tanto Kinto Jhāna Bakhāne sui Bauddha Rupa Hai Kaliyugare Śivu Rahi.

(What is the use Speech, Tantra or Jnana; in Kaliyuga Śiva is the same as Buddha).

In Kabir, Namdev, Dadu and other Nirguna poets one finds many similarities and traces of Buddhist philosophy. For example in *Samyutta -Nikāya* (34, 1, 3, 6) the passage occurs: "O Bhikkhus, everything is burning? What is burning? The eye is burning? The form is burning? The knowledge by sight is burning. Joy, pleasure, indifference, pain all are burning. By what are they burning? By attachment, by hate, by love, by old age, sickness, death, and *dukkha*, it is burning". ...Kabir says –

Dekhahu Yah Tan Jarat Hai

Ghaḍi, Pahar, Mile, Baire Bhai Jarat Hai

(Look, this body is burning—every minute, every hour while meeting or hating, it is burning).

The Buddhist stand of not relying on one Holy book is repeatedly preached by Kabir. So the castelessness.

Bamhan—chhatri na sur baisva

Mughal pathan na sayyad sesava

Adijyoti nahi gaur—ganesava

Brahma—bisnu—mahes na sesava

Das kabir le aye sandesava

Sar sabda gahi chalo vahi desva

These lines remind one of *Panditavaggo* in *Dhammapada*.

Though the influence of Vaiṣṇavism was more seminal in the Hindi area, in modern times interest in Buddhism was revived when Acharya Ramchandra Shukla translated *The Light of Asia* by Arnold as *Buddha Carita* in 1922, in Avadhi, and also the Bengali novel *Śaśanka*. In later years great scholars and writers like Mahapandita Rahula Sankityayana, Bhadanta Ananda Kausalyayan, Bhikhu Jagadish Kassap, Shanti Bhikkhu, Acharya Narendra Deva, Bharatsingh Upadhyaya and many others have enriched research and commentary on Buddhism. The most monumental work was of Rahula Sankityayana who resuscicated Asanga and Vasubandhu's original texts through Tibetan sources.

In creative writing Maithilisharan Gupta, wrote a *Khaṇḍa-Kāvya Yaśodharā* (1934), and Anup Sharma *Siddhārtha* (1937). S.H. Vatsyayana Agyeya's *Asādhya Vinā* is based on a Buddhist *Jātaka* tale. So is his play *Uttara-Kalinga* on a Buddhist theme. There are many novels based on the Buddhist period like *Divya* and *Amita* by Yashpal, *Ambapāli* by Rambriksha Benipuri, *Bhagwana Buddha* by Seth Govindadas, *Koṇārka* by J.C. Mathur, some one act plays by Udaishankar Bhatt and Ram Kumar Varma are also well known. Mohan Rakesh wrote a play *'Laharon ke Rajahansa'* (1963) based on Aśvaghośa's *Saundarānanda*.

Bachchan wrote '*Buddha aur Nācaghara*'. Nagarjun, a modern Maithili-Hindi poet is very much influenced by Buddha's Śunyavāda and nihilism. Bhadanta Kausalyayan has translated *Jātaka* tales in several volumes. Nagendranath Upadhyaya wrote a work on Tantric Buddhism and literature. There are many writers and scholars who are now taking to Buddhist philosophy very seriously. Some are interested in Zen too. New Hindi poetry of Agyeya and others has Zen overtones.

Kannada

In Kannada books influenced by Buddhist thought are the following:

1. *Kisa Gotami,* a play by K. Shivaram Karant—best known of his works.
2. Shri G.P. Rajarathnam translated several *Jātaka* tales into Kannada for children, published in several small books.
3. The Mahabodhi Society, Bangalore, is doing a translation of *Tripitaka* in Kannada. They have already published a translation of the *Dhammapada.*
4. K.V. Putappa has written a play, *Jalagara,* which can be said to have been influenced by Buddhism. It is about converting lower class of people into a higher class.
5. The Bangalore University has published a book, *Murthi Shilpa,* by Prof. S.K. Ramchandra Rao, where sections are devoted to Buddhist art-history.
6. Two books written by Prof. S.K. Ramachandra Rao are *Boddiya Belakanalli* and *Pali Sahitya,* both published by Kavyalaya of Mysore. The first deals with the Buddhist philosophy of 'Entering the Light of Bodhi'.
7. An article by the same Professor appeared in three parts in Jeevana magazine on the biographical sketch of Sariputta and *Moggalana.* Another article in the same magazine by the same author was a description of Buddha's homecoming, entitled *Tavurunalli Tathagatha.*
8. *Aśvaghośan Buddhacarita* (Tr. of Buddhacarita) by S.V. Parameshwara Bhatta
9. *Buddhande Chinte*—Satyamurti
10. *Buddhan Kategalu*—Jog
11. *Buddha*—Venkataramayya
12. *Buddha Mantu Basava*—Kumaraswamy
13. *Buddhadeva*—Venkatayya
14. *Buddha Ja Takagalu*—Sali Ramachandra Rao

Biographies of Buddha by Gangadharan, H.V. Shrirangaraju, G.S. Siddhilingayya and Narasayya arc also important. G.P. Rajaratnam started a 'Śākya Sāhitya Mandapa', which planned to translate Buddhist literature in Kannada, but for last four years after the passing away of the founder this Mandapa is not active.

Kashmiri

In ancient Kashmir there was trade-traffic and cultural exchange between Central Asia. In the Kashmir museum there are Kushan *terra-cota* and evidence of the influence of Buddhist art through Kashmir upto Bamiyan and Tajikstan. Kashmir was an important centre of Mahāyāna Buddhism and some traces of the influence of Buddhist philosophy are found in *Lalla Vakhani,* the earliest recorded mystic writings of the poetess Lalla Dyed. Before the Christian era there were small principalities in the southern part of Central Asia from Khotan to Lebnar which were centres of Buddhist thought and religion. Very little is left in the form of literary evidence. *Mahāyāna Prakāśa* by Shitikanth has Kashmiri Tantric Shaivistic base. But modern Kashmiri has hardly any Buddhist work. Dogri has some writers who have read Buddhism and like it.

Marathi

Old Marathi literature had hardly any Buddhist influence, though Maharashtra has some of the most memorable Buddhist cave-sculptures and frescoes. Some people opine that Vithoba (the Marathi deity Vitthal) is in fact a reincarnation of Viṣṇu in Buddha form. Jnaneshwar wrote—"*Jo Khandavaya ghavo ghali/ki lavani jayane keli/dogha ekachi sauli/Vrukshu de jaisa*" (One who axes the tree in parts and one who plants it, both get equally, the shade of the tree) and this seems to have Buddhist philosophical influence. Many other saint-poets advocate compassion (*karuṇā*) of Buddha and *jīvadayā* of the Vaiṣṇavas.

Buddha and Buddhism did not figure much in medieval Marathi literature. Only after the spread of English education and in late nineteenth century renaissance, does one come across the interest in Buddha being revived. Sane Guruji wrote a book on Buddha for children. Buddha's phenomenalism was attacked by Tilak and Ahitagni Rajwade. But modern philosophers again wrote about his logic and ethics, like Dr. Surendra Barlinge and Bhawani Shankar Niyogi. The recent issue of Paramarsha has two long articles on Buddha. There is a translation by V.D. Gokhale of Otto Rozenberg's lecture on Buddhism in Far East, in 1919, in St. Petersberg—and of G.R. Joshi's 'God and Brahma in Tripiṭaka'. One of the most modern poems, on 'Buddha in Bombay slums' was by Mangesh Padgaonkar in the special number on Buddha of Sadhana.

Valchand Hirachand Shah wrote a historical novel 'Aśoka'. Gangadhar Ramchandra Mogre (1858-1915) translated *Light of Asia* as '*Buddhajanma*', but it was incomplete. Vasudev Govind Apte (1817-1930) wrote *Aśoka Caritra* and *Bauddhaparva,* Justice M.G. Ranade wrote its introduction. *Bhagwana Buddha* was a play written by Snehalata Pagar in the forties. Savarkar opposed Buddhism in his play *Sanyasta Khadga*. Durga Bhagavat translated the *Jātakas*, and Tagore's 'Buddha' in Marathi. Great scholars of Buddhism like Dharmanand Kosambi, Gune, P.L. Vaidya, V.V. Gokhale, P. V. Bapat, C.V. Joshi and B.R. Ambedkar were from Maharashtra. Some neo-Buddhist Dalit writers have done great service in the revival of Buddhist thought.

Malayalam

In *A History of Malayalam Literature* by Krishna Chaitanya, there are only three references to Buddhist lore. Edisseri in his poem *The Buddha, Leopard and I,* paints a worker hastening home with the rice anxiously awaited by his hungry children, takes a short-cut through a forest, and is attacked by a leopard. But he manages to kill it by hurling at it an old stone image of Buddha that lay nearby. The worker feels regret that he had to use the Buddha image for this act of violence; but he feels no guilt.

In another poet's work, Buddha's discourse is memorable:

"Heed not the scriptures that violate the truth
Of man and his moral law; not the words of men
who stand to gain by interpreting them wrong.
For the ignorant crowd, Yesterday's error
Hardens into today's tradition, tomorrow's law.
It is in love that the world takes its birth,
Love nurses it to growth."

These lines are from Kumaran Ashan (1873-1924) who wrote this famous narrative poem *Cāṇḍāla-Bhikṣuki* (1922) based on Buddhist lore.

N.V. Krishna Warrier also wrote an *Attakathā* named *Buddha-caritam*. Balamani Amma reminds in one of her poems that from motherhood a woman reaches the motherhood of god and of all creation.

That day you'll become the mother of the world
When its creator becomes the infant you fondle.

Krishna Chaitanya sees the echoes of the *Jātaka* narrative on Siddhārtha's renunciation, that Buddha wanted to take his son Rāhula with him, but could not bring himself to do it because the mother's hand lay protectingly over the child. After many years, he rediscovered the profound meaning of that protecting gesture of the mother's hand even in sleep. So Buddha said, "As a mother protects her only son, so let everyone cultivate a boundless compassion towards all that has life."

Oriya

Buddhism influenced Orissa from earliest times and continued up to 17th century. Tepussa and Bhellika were the two earliest disciples of Buddha and both were from Utkala. So Aśoka's change of heart happened in Kalinga war. Kalinga was the original home of Pāli according to Oldenberg, Kern, Bhandarkar and Nalinaksha Dutta. Bhaursaila in Puri was the centre of Buddhist logic. Tosali and later Ratnagiri in Cuttack district became the Buddhist Yoga centre. From Dantapura and Punyagiri, by the seventh century, Buddhism spread all over.

Buddhists believe that Buddha's tooth is inside the Jagannatha icon. Saraladasa in his *Mahābhārata* (14th century) writes that Jagannatha was Buddha's incarnation at Puri. In Puri temple there is a Buddha-idol. From an old Tibetan text *Pag-Sam-Jon-Jhang, Tantra-Yāna* was first developed at Uddiyan (Orissa). This *Tantra Yāna* had three forms: *Vajrayāna*, *Kalacakrayāna*, *Sahajayāna*. Dr. S. Dasgupta in his *Introduction to Tantrik Buddhism* has described '*kāla*' as *Dharmadhātu*, and it considers human body as a universe in miniature. Both *Vajra* and *Kāla* are indebted to *Vijñānavāda*. *Sahajayāna* introduces the element of sex-energy and believes not in inhibiting or suppressing it, but describes *Ānanda, Paramānanda, Viramānanda* and *Sahajānanda* (or *Mahāsukha*) as four stages of Yoga. Saraha, (*Sādhanamālā*) Nāgārjuna (*Guhyasamājatantra*), Sabaripa (*Caryācarya*) Lui-pa (*prefaced yoginikula*) Vajraghanta, Kambala (author of *Kambala Gītikā* 810 to 850 A.D.) and Padmavajra (Guhyasiddhi) authored six works on *Heruk-Sādhana* and *Hevajratantra,* Anangavajre (author of *Prejnokāya-Viniścaya Siddhi!*) Indrabhuti (author of 23 works including *Jñāna-siddhi*), Lakshmi Karā, a poetess; Udaivajra (author of *Advayasiddhi*) were the Tantrik writers. Chaitanyadas said Buddha is greater than Kṛṣṇa, in medieval Oriya literature.

Shudramuni Saraladasa wrote *Oriyā Mahābhārata* in the 15th century. In this work he has invoked Buddha. From 15th to 19th century there is no reference to Buddha in Oriya. Later, the following works are significant:

1. An essay in *Sāhitya Prasanga*. Buddhadeva-Madhusudan Rao (1853-1912)
2. Fakir Mohan Senapati–*Bauddhavatara Kavya* (1843-1920).
3. *BUDDHA DEVA*–Dr. Karunakar kar (Poetry).
4. *BUDDHA* (Drama)–Dr. Mayadhar Mansinha (1951).
5. *Jataka Galpa*–Utkal University Publication.
6. *Jataka Galpa*–Shridhar Mahapatra.
7. *Śramaṇa Ānananda Aru Śanti* (Poetry)–Radhamohan Gadnayaka.
8. *Candra o Campa* (Novel)–Vamacharan mitra.
9. *Mahānirvana* (stories)–Surendra Mahanti.
10. *Odishare Bauddha–Dharma*-Banshidhar Mohanti.
11. *Mahamanava Buddha*–Brajkishore Sahu.
12. *Buddham Śaranam Gachchami*–Krishna Chandra Bhuinya.
13. *Buddhadeva–Raja Jalandhar Dev* (19th century work now not available).
14. *Gautama Buddha*–Radhakrishna Sahu.
15. *Gautama Buddha*–Janaki Ballabh Patnaik (Biography).
16. *Buddhism in Orissa*–D. Litt. Thesis in English by Dr. Navinchandra Sahu.

Punjabi

In Guru Nanak's *Bāni* there are references to '*Tathāgat Jñānakhaṇḍa Kā Nivāsi'*, or *Kete Sidh Budh Nath, Akhahi isar akhahi siddh akaahi kete kite budh.*

No reliance on mere book knowledge was emphasised both by Buddha and Guru Nanak. There are very few comparative studies of Buddhism and Sikh philosophy.

In modern literature excepting stray poems or references in prose to Buddha's biography or *Jātaka* stories, there is not much of an influence of this monastic order in Punjabi literature.

Sanskrit and other Literature

Vast amount of Buddhist literature in hybrid and pure Sanskrit can be a subject of an entire huge book. I shall not touch here that aspect of historical value, about which so much has been written authoritatively by experts, as in Baldeva Upadhyaya's *Bauddha–Darśana-Mīmānsā* in Hindi, P.V. Bapat's 2500 *years of Buddhism* (which I translated in Hindi), Har Dayal's work on

Bodhisattva Doctrine in Buddhist Sanskrit literature; G.K. Nariman's *Literary History of Sanskrit Buddhism* (Taraporewala, 1920) and many other reference works.

To give two examples. Bidhushekhar Bhattacharya edited *pratimokṣa* (both for *Bhikshus*, and *Bhikshunis*); it was printed in Russia in 1869, with an introduction in Russian by Minayeff; W. Pachau made a comparative study of *pātimokṣa* in Chinese, Tibetan, Sanskrit and Pali texts. Similarly, in Hindi, the text was published by Bhikkhu Jagdish Kasyap and *Sanskrit*-Marathi by Chintamani Vaijnath Rajwade. *Dhammapada* has several editions: Dhammanand Kosambi's in Gujarati, Rahul's in Hindi, C. Kunjan Raja's and Dr. S. Radhakrishnan's in English; N.K. Bhagawant's in Marathi. Harihararananda published a sanskrit translation and commentary of Dharmapada from Hoogley in 1905. There is an *Abhanga Dharmapade* in Marathi by S.B. Warnekar. There is a *Bauddha Sanskrit Kāvya Samīkṣā* in Sanskrit published from Benaras Hindu University in 1976.

Pandita Kshama Rao has written a *Kāvya* on Buddha. A remarkable work by Prof. V. Subramaniam entitled *Aspects of Buddhist Culture* (with four dance-dramas) takes up four characters from Buddhist lore like Sujata, Sanghamitra, Ambapali, Yashodhara as base. There is an interesting chapter on 'Buddhist dilemmas inherited by Hinduism.' Commenting on how Gaudapada acknowledges his debt to Buddha in Māṇḍukya-Kārikā in the invocatory verses, the author traces the conflict between Saivism and Vaishnavism as the tussle between intellect and emotion, purity versus flexibility. In Tamil, it was Ahattinai versus Atrupaddai. The author mentions 'vegetarian and non-vegetarian mother-goddesses in Gujarat' as symbols of Prakritic and Sanskritic modes.

Sindhi

In Sindhi, there is not much work done on Buddha except the following three books—

1. *Porab Sandesh*—Translation of Edwin Arnold's *Light of Asia* by Dewandas Kishnan 'AZAD'.
2. *Bhagwan Buddha* (1956)—Translation of Dhammanand Kosambi's work by Narain Das Ratanmal Malkani.
3. *Siddhartha* (1955)—Translation of Herman Hesse's novel by Ishardas Wadhumal Raisinghani.

Tamil

In the third century A.D. an epic named *Manimekhlai* was composed by the Buddhist monk Chittalai Chattanar. It has 30 cantos and 2000 lines. It deals with the sacrifice and service to the people done by the Buddhist nun Manimekhala. She was the daughter of Kovalan and his dancing paramour. This epic describes north Indian cities like Ujjain, Kalinga, Gandhar, Champa, Magadha and so on.

Sri Shankaran translated *Mahavamsham,* the Sinhalese work of Buddhist history in Tamil in 1962. A novel on Buddha's life and philosophy was written in 1956, by P. Ramaswami entitled *Bodhimadhavam.* Mayile Chini. Venkatasami wrote, in 1940, a research work on Buddhism in Tamil–*Bauddhayum tamilum.* It gives illustrations from old Tamil texts influenced by Buddhism. Srikrishna Dutta Bhatt's Hindi publication from Sarva-Seva-Sangh, Benaras, was translated in Tamil in 1965, and used for neo-literates, entitled Bauddham. 'In the footsteps of Buddha' was the work by Shivapada Sundaram, published of 1956, entitled *Buddhar AdichchuvaYYil.* It contains accounts of author's travels to Buddhist places of interest. There are several small and big tracts and books on Buddhist religion, Buddhist lore, translation of *Dharmapadan* and Jataka Tales.

In a meeting of the International Union of Academies held in Sweden, in summer 1961, which I had attended, there was a proposal on Encyclopedia of Buddhism, initiated from Ceylon as its place of birth. To my great surprise there was no Indian in its Advisory Board. I suggested many names. But what happened to my suggestion later, I do not know. Dr. Malalsekhara was one of the editors, and I think Gunatilake was another. But the common bond between Srilanka and Tamilnadu was Buddha. Subramanya Bharati wrote a poem on him. Later references to Buddha's compassion are in many forms and images. But no outstanding work on Buddha is available in modern Tamil creative writing.

Telugu

So also with Telugu. In spite of Nagarjunakonda, founded by Nagarjuna (Madhyamika, 4th century, from Krishna district) and Dharmakirti (Logician of Tirumalai according to Scherbatsky) who were both from Andhra, very little interest in Buddha is seen. They went to Takshashila and developed Buddhist logic. There is not much to be found in old Telugu literature on Buddha or Buddhist themes, in medieval ages. In the renaissance, Vireshalingam Pantulu had referred to Buddha in his reformistic writings. In the 20th Century Kavidvaya tirupati Venkata Kavulu has written an epic called *Buddha-charitam.* Narla Venkateshwar Rao wrote a book on Buddhism in Andhra Pradesh, in 1956. There is some reference to these ancient ties in Suravaram Pratap Reddy's *Andhrula Sanghik Charitami.* But Telugu has not very many books on Buddhist themes in modern creative writing. In Dr. C. Narayan Reddy's *Vishvambhara*—Buddha features with Ashoka.

Urdu

In Urdu, I came across in the history of literature one play named *Buddha Dev* by Bishambhar Sahai 'Vyakul'. There may be stray short stories or essays on Buddhist period or philosophy but this literature did not seem to be influenced by Buddhist thought in any extensive form. Though Urdu poetry has many images of flux and transitoriness of life, the inevitability of death and moments of 'Angst', they are not due to Buddha's philosophy but stem from Arabo-Persian cultural links. The despair of a desert and the ecstasy of an Omar Khayyam do create a tension which is very close to *Sabba Sankhara Anichcha* (All impressions are fleeting). "All is void, all is a vale of tears", Urdu has this tragic under-current in its poetic master-pieces; but Ghalib or 'Jigar' had probably never read Buddha; 'Firaq' and 'Faiz' did.

Conclusion

After this flying survey of Indian literatures, wherein only a hundred works by good authors in Indian languages are spot-lighted, which were about Buddha or influenced by Buddhist thought, I shall give some general observations in conclusion. In creative writings in English by Indians, one sonnet by Sarojini Naidu on *Buddha sitting on a Lotus*, and Harindra Nath Chattopadhyaya's *Siddhartha* are the only two references.

All modern Indian languages, in their early period, from tenth to sixteenth centuries, had devotional or Bhakti poetry, mostly based on Shaiva or Vaishnava themes. Orthodox Hindu psyche, borrowed from Sanskrit epics like the Ramayana, Mahabharata, Bhagavatam and so on. There was no place for Buddha in all this theocentric literary creation. There were non-conformists or heretics like Kabir or Tukaram, Dadu or Nanak, Basava or Vemana, Akho or Bhim Bhoi, Lalan Fakir or Lalla Dyed and some Sufies too, but they wrote against hide-bound ritualism, Brahmanical or Mullah priest-craft and hypocrisy, and the cruelty and callousness of caste-ridden discrimination between man-and-man. But after Ashvaghosh, there is hardly any Buddhist poet of note in Sanskrit or other Indian languages, in medieval period. After the rise of Brahmanism, Buddhism left Indian shores. It became the religion of Indian export value. It travelled beyond Himalayas, beyond the seas. Except *Nagananda,* there is hardly any Sanskrit Buddhist play. Some Sanskrit farces made fun of Buddhist monks, juxtaposing them against a prostitute (*Bhagavadujjakiyam*) or showings a scene where a Buddhist monk with his medicine rejuvinates a woman declared dead. But for such weird and oblique references, which are exceptional; Jayadev alone referred to Buddhavatara in his Ashtapadi. That is all!

It was in the nineteenth century that Buddha was again remembered, by our intellectuals and creative writers, via Edwin Arnold and Rhys Davids; thanks to Pali studies and archeological surveys of Amaravati, Taxila, Sanchi, Shravasti and Sarnath. Buddha was suddenly placed *on par* with Christ; and as he was pre-Christ and a contemporary of Pythagorus and Heraclitus in Greece, he was used by our revivalists as a good rebuff to the West, which came to us on a 'Civilizing' mission. This created antithetical attitudes: angry orthodox Brahmins put all the blame on the weak-kneed and non-violent Jains and Buddhists (read the writings of Savarkar or Satwalekar in Marathi or Laxminarain Mishra in Hindi) who did not resist 'foreign' aggression. Some went to the extent of suggesting that Buddha permitted Kisa Gotami to admit nuns in his fold, and so as soon as women were considered equal with men, the downfall of Manu's mansion was hastened.

If one studied carefully the cultural history of our country, as reflected through regional literatures, one will see that in the eastern region where Assamese was exposed to Mongolian influence (Garo) tribals also worship Yab-Yung, as Dr. Banikant Kakati observes in *Mother-Goddess Worship in Assam*); Biharis were close to Nepali and Newari moreas on the border; and Orissa and Bengal were under the influence of Vajrayāna and Tantrayāna, there was greater permissiveness towards intercaste marriages, and lesser rigidity in caste-compartmentalization. Attitude towards women also became liberal. So in Bihar and Bengal the so-called lower castes also joined the mainstream of the nationalist movement of Gandhi. The Scheduled tribes and castes did not stand aloof: Birsa Munda or Matangi Hazra, Jagjivan Ram or Jaipal Singh, Karpuri Thakur or Bhola Paswan did not become secessionists. The same cannot be said of the leaders of the untouchables in the South, West or extreme North of India. Ramaswami Naicker, or B.R. Ambedkar, or a Ladakhi Buddhist or a Vishal Punjab leader is not exactly in the same mood. They find in non-Hindu sects and beliefs a safe religious armour, or an identity-shelter, or the satisfaction of their crippled altar-ego. The Dalit Panthers in Maharashtra embraced neo-Buddhism, and become ultraleftists. All the secessionist activists seem to cling to some such fanatic ideology which is anti-orthodoxy. If it is of Indian origin all the better. Literary evidence shows that Buddha and Marx seemed to be very close to the heart of many a young revolutionary materialists in India, 'Vishwa-

Vani', a Hindi monthly, published in the thirties from Allahabad, and edited by Bishambharnath Pandey (the present Governor of Orissa) had published a special number on Buddhism, wherein Bhadant Ananda Kausalyayan had written an article *Buddha aur Marx*. I have a book in Marathi, published by PPH Bombay called *Buddha ani Marx* with articles by many Marathi Communists and neo-Buddhists. P.K. Bhattacharya's work on *Buddhism and Marxism* published from Calcutta in 1976, is mentioned earlier. It is worth studying whether Buddhism can cement the 'ethnic' differences amongst small groups, which are trying to crop up with the sole aim of challenging the unity of India, I hope that unity of India is not merely a 'mental construct', Buddha leads to 'Dharma' and 'Sangha'. Let us hope our writers and artists preach again his message of universal brotherhood and peace, *Metti* and *Karuna* to have a better future of our country and mankind. Let us start a new *Onāmāīdḥam!* (the first alphabet taught to children, a corrupt *form of 'Om Namah Siddham'*)!

Chapter 30

Alex Wayman's The Buddhist "Not this, Not this" – An Appraisal

G.C. Nayak

Prof. Alex Wayman is a well-known name amongst Buddhist scholars, who does not need any introduction in the Buddhist circle. I shall be discussing in the sequal his learned paper, 'The Buddhist "Not this, Not this"'[1], for I find it not only interesting but also significant in more than one way.

In the above paper, Wayman has drawn our attention to and thrown light on certain aspects of the Buddhist position which is extremely relevant to a proper understanding of the same. He has brought in the question of gap in experience and communication in what are well-known as "mystical experiences". He has very rightly pointed out that W. James in his classic *Varieties of Religious experience* points to the mystical state as being especially characterized by ineffability and noetic quality and that the Indian teachers had long ago evolved an indirect method of teaching these exceptional states through 'neti' 'neti', through a sort of negative method. To add to this observation of Wayman, one may say that the Buddhist doctrine of apoha also points to some such negative method of understanding even the ordinary states and expression. Wayman is at the same time aware of the contrary view, as expressed by philosophers like A. J. Ayer, according to which the state of mystical intuition is not a genuinely cognitive state.

While I agree to a large extent the way Wayman has characterized the Indian thought, I have however certain reservations about the use of what I would regard to be a blanket term, 'mystical', to all possible exceptional states, on the one hand, and also about the emphasis on such states in the Indian thought in preference to reason. I would plead in favour of a more discriminative understanding of the Indian thought, especially of the Buddhist one, *vis-à-vis* those that are designated as mysticism in the West. The whole of Indian thought, including that of the Buddhist, cannot be reduced to some sort of mysticism, by any stretch of imagination, although at places similarity of approach cannot be ruled out of course.

The second point which I would like to make is regarding Wayman's remark in respect of the term '*Śūnyatā*'. "When early Buddhist authors used this Sanskrit term, which was translated into both Chinese and Tibetan as 'emptiness'", says Wayman, "they intended this basic meaning. Hence, it is proper to translate the terms into English as 'emptiness', 'voidness', or 'vacuity'. This is not to deny the connotation of an unexpressed factor, hinted at by negation of the expressible, just as a mystery is suggested by a deserted village". Now the above characterization by Wayman that points to only two possibilities, one of 'emptiness' smacking of nihilism on the one hand and a sort of mysticism of the inexpressible on the other, is somewhat inadequate, to say the least, as far as *Śūnyatā* is concerned. First of all, it is indeed not *Śūnyatā* in its literal sense nor is it sheer mysticism of a sort.

Emptiness does give us an insight into the nature of *Śūnyatā*, it is true, only if it is not allowed to boil down to sheer nihilism. His Holiness the Dalai Lama has rightly grasped the spirit of Emptiness when he points out, "Emptiness should be understood in terms of the interdependent nature of reality: It is by virtue of their dependent origination that things are devoid of independent existence".[2] *Śūnyatā* then is the same as *pratītyasamutpāda*. That this *pratītyasamutpāda* which really is the pivotal, the central doctrine of Buddhism, from whatever angle one may look at it, does not in itself connote any sort of nihilism or mysticism, should be amply clear to any impartial student of Buddhist philosophy. Nāgārjuna's famous *Kārikā*, "*Yah pratītyasamutpāda Śūnyatāṃ Pracakṣmahe*" and the other one, viz. "*Śunyamiti na vaktavyaṃ aśūnyamiti vā bhavet*" are extremely relevant for the proper understanding of what *Śūnyatā* really means, which is certainly not nihilistic, nor mystical either. Not that Wayman was not aware of these subtle nuances of Nāgārjuna. Even if wayman favours the translation of *Śūnyatā* as voidness, he clearly points out that "voidness here is the great principle of efficiency" and candidly admits that "Nāgārjuna is difficult to understand, and his primary stress on "voidness" may well have contributed to a one-sided appreciation of this doctrine". Moreover, Wayman's reference to the *Madhyānta-Vibhaṇga* is quite relevant in this context, which, as he has rightly pointed out, teaches that liberation is achieved by eliminating the duality of subject and object. "According to the commentary", says Wayman, "the middle path means avoiding the extremes of only voideness or only non-voidness".[3] So middle path, as I see it, cannot be reduced to void in its literal sense in the Buddhist context.

The third point is regarding the reference to the 'neti' (not-this) of the *Bṛhadāraṇyaka Upaniṣad* given by wayman as the celebrated source of the negative method. This is no doubt true, so far as it goes, but I wonder if there is anything corresponding to *Ātman* here in the context of Buddhism, especially in the context of the *Śūnyatā* theory, although negative methodology in some way or the other is relevant to the Buddhist framework especially in the framework of *Śūnyatā*.

The fourth point to which I would like to draw the attention of the learned scholars is regarding the middle path and whether this in itself represents and leads to a realisation of "not this, not this". As per Wayman's understanding, Buddhism in its beginning, the path, as well as the goal, represents "not this, not this". In the beginning, it is worth pointing out, the Buddha adopted a middle path, avoiding two extremes of life of indulgence and that of self-mortification, it is true, but I fail to grasp in what sense it could represent a sort of 'neti' 'neti' as it is originally conceived in the *Bṛhadāraṇyaka*. Similar is the case with *nirvāṇa*, the end, the goal, the *summum bonum*. Here the negative method of understanding is quite relevant of course, but it is not the same as a sort of realization of the Ātman through 'neti' 'neti', for there is a definite trend in Buddhism to go beyond ontological claim of all sorts in the context of *nirvāṇa*. In *Śūnyatā* doctrine, the climax of the same is reached by pointing to *nirvāṇa* as '*sarvakalpanā kṣaya*' or '*niravaśeṣa kalpnākṣaya*' in the words of Candrakīrti's Prasannapadā. As a matter of fact, Tathāgata is characterised as "*Sarvakalpa vikalpa jāla vāsanā prapañca vigata*" and there is neither *Śūnyatā* or *aśūnyatā* in the literal, absolute, sense in *nirvāṇa*.

It has to be admitted, however, that Wayman himself emphasized this "going beyond" while speaking of *nirvāṇa* in his thesis. He approvingly refers to Stcherbatsky's translation of the verse-3 of the Chapter XXV of Nāgārjuna's *Madhyamaka Kārikā*, as follows:— "What neither is released, nor is it ever reached, What neither is annihilation, nor is it eternality, What never disappears, nor has it been created, This is *nirvāṇa*". "The Mahāyāna *nirvāṇa*", says Wayman very rightly, "is described by the limitations avoided", while "the Hīnayāna *nirvāṇa* is described by what has been eliminated". But so far as the practical implications are concerned, Wayman had the rare insight of seeing that there is little practical difference in spite of difference on the theoretical level. Wayman raises this relevant question in respect of Yogācāra and Mādhyamika and answers as follows: "Does that theoretical difference between the two schools effect the practical treading of the path in the form of the Eightfold noble path of early Buddhism ? "The answer appears to be that there is no necessary practical difference"[4] Nāgārjuna says, "Every thing is valid for the one for whom voidness is valid" – "*Sarvaṃ ca yujyate tasya śūnyatā yasya yujyate*"[5] Such clarity in understanding certainly speaks volumes about the depth of insight into Buddhist thought on the part of Professor Wayman, although one may not agree with him always in all its subtle nuances, of course, as has been pointed out earlier in this paper.

References

1. Alex Wayman, 'The Buddhist "Not this, Not this", Philosophy East and West, Vol. XI, Number 3, Oct. 1961.
2. Cf. H.H. The Dalai Lama, *The Four Noble Truths,* Harper Collins Publishers India, Fourth Impression, 2000, p. 105.
3. Cf. Wayman, *Op. cit.,* Philosophy East and West, p. 102.
4. Cf. *ibid.*, p. 103.
5. Cf. *Madhyamaka Kārikā*, p. 24.